GERMAN TODAY

The Advanced Learner's
Guide

GERMAN TODAY

The Advanced Learner's Guide

W. B. LOCKWOOD

CLARENDON PRESS · OXFORD

1987

Oxford University Press, Walton Street, Oxford OX2 6DP

Oxford New York Toronto
Delhi Bombay Calcutta Madras Karachi
Petaling Jaya Singapore Hong Kong Tokyo
Nairobi Dar es Salaam Cape Town
Melbourne Auckland
and associated companies in
Beirut Berlin Ibadan Nicosia

Oxford is a trade mark of Oxford University Press

Published in the United States
by Oxford University Press, New York

British Library Cataloguing in Publication Data
Lockwood, W.B.
German today: the advanced learner's guide.
1. German language—Grammar—1950–
I. Title
438.2'421   PF3112
ISBN 0–19–815804–1
ISBN 0–19–815850–5 Pbk

Library of Congress Cataloging-in-Publication Data
Lockwood, W. B. (William Burley)
German today.
1. German language—Grammar—1950–
2. German language—Text-books for
foreign speakers—English. I. Title.
PF3112.L55 1987   438.2'421   86-28428
ISBN 0–19–815804–1
ISBN 0–19–815850–5 (pbk.)

Set by Hope Services, Abingdon, Oxon
Printed in Great Britain
at the University Printing House, Oxford
by David Stanford
Printer to the University

PREFACE

At the back of this publication lie my own endeavours as a learner; in its finished form it reflects teaching experience at university level. Its subject is the average language of today, spoken as well as written, i.e. that sort of German the student will wish to acquire actively.

A book of this kind admittedly owes much to the labours of predecessors in various fields. But, as I trust will be evident, my indebtedness to these is of a more general nature, not calling for individual mention. The present guide is rather the outcome of personal observation of the language and practical occupation with it. One particular acknowledgement, however, I must not fail to make: to my wife Erika, who, in this as in my other work on German, has throughout selflessly supported me with advice and constructive criticism.

W. B. Lockwood

Department of German
Reading University

CONTENTS

1. PRONUNCIATION

2. ORTHOGRAPHICAL MATTERS

ACCIDENCE

3. NOUNS

4. ADJECTIVES

5. ADVERBS

6. PRONOUNS

7. NUMERALS

8. VERBS

VOCABULARY

9. MODAL PARTICLES

10. ASPECTS OF WORD FORMATION

11. THE PROBLEM OF MEANING

12. REGIONAL DIVERSITY

SYNTAX

13. NOUNS

14. ADJECTIVES

15. ADVERBS

16. ARTICLES

17. PRONOUNS

19. PREPOSITIONS

20. NEGATION

21. AGREEMENT

22. CLAUSE COMBINATION

23. WORD ORDER

1. Pronunciation

CHILDREN can pronounce a foreign tongue simply by hearing it spoken. But older persons, as a rule, no longer retain this facility. Native speech habits have become so deeply engrained that the foreign pronunciation must be expressly taught. Not surprisingly, learning ability in this, as in other aspects, varies from student to student. Let it be said, however, that all, even those who may have felt discouraged, can expect to improve their performance very appreciably by a patient study of the basic phonetics of the language concerned.

German is spoken in many different ways; local accents are much in evidence and alternative pronunciations the order of the day. The Germans themselves are, of course, used to this and accordingly tolerant of forms not their own, a circumstance which tends to make matters a little easier for the foreigner.

ALPHABET

The names of the letters are as follows; for the values of the phonetic symbols, see pp. 2 ff.

A a [aa]	*H h* [haa]	*O o* [oo]	*V v* [fa·ǫ]
B b [bee]	*I i* [ii]	*P p* [pee]	*W w* [vee]
C c [tsee]	*J j* [jɔt]	*Q q* [kuu]	*X x* [ɪks]
D d [dee]	*K k* [kaa]	*R r* [ɛr, ɛɐ]	*Y y* ['ʏpsɪlɔn]
E e [ee]	*L l* [ɛl]	*S s* [ɛs]	*Z z* [tsɛt]
F f [ɛf]	*M m* [ɛm]	*T t* [tee]	
G g [gee]	*N n* [ɛn]	*U u* [uu]	

In addition: the modified vowels *Ä ä* [ɛɛ] or '*a*-Umlaut', *Ö ö* [øø] or '*o*-Umlaut', *Ü ü* [yy] or '*u*-Umlaut', and the sign ß 'scharfes *s*' occasionally replaced by *ss*, capitalized *SS*, or less usually, *sz*, *SZ*, whence the (common!) alternative name [ɛs-'tsɛt].

For special purposes, as computer print-outs, the modified vowels are spelt *ae*, *AE*, etc.

The letters *ss* are only used in intervocalic position after a short vowel: *wir müssen* 'we must'; otherwise double *s* is represented by *β*, thus after a long vowel or diphthong: *stoßen* 'to push', *beißen* 'to bite', or before a consonant: *ihr müßt* 'you must', and at the end of a word: *er muß* 'he must'. Contrast *Maße* 'measurements' with *Masse* 'mass' (having long and short *a* respectively).

To form the plural, the letters may add *'s* or they may be used
without change: *Aal schreibt sich mit zwei a's* or *zwei a* (also *Doppel-
a*) *'Aal* is written with two a's (double a)'. The letters are neuter: *das
A und das O* 'the beginning and the end', *ein großes B* 'a capital B',
ein kleines b 'a small b'. Exceptionally, the pronunciation may be spelt
out, e.g. *das Abece* [aabee'tsee] 'the ABC' and in the expression
etwas aus dem Eff-eff [ɛf'ɛf] *verstehen* 'to know something inside
out', alternative to *das Abc, aus dem ff.*

PHONETIC SYMBOLS AND THEIR VALUES

' denotes main stress on the syllable following, ˌ denotes subsidiary
stress.

Vowels

[a]   as most commonly in English *cat* [kat] ('front *a*')
[a·]   the half-long form of [a]
[aa]   the long form of [a] (heard in the northern pronunciation of *arm*
        [aam])
[ɑ]   the short form of [ɑɑ] ['back *a*']
[ɑɑ]   as in *arm* [ɑɑm]
[æ]   a variety of front *a* approaching [ɛ] (heard from some southern
        speakers, e.g. [kæt] instead of the usual [kat], often felt to be an
        affectation; not found in German)
[e]   the short form of [ee]
[ẹ]   a very short, non-syllabic form of [e]
[ee]   as in northern *pay* [pee]
[ɛ]   as in *yes* [jɛs]
[ɛɛ]   the long form of [ɛ]
[ə]   the sound represented by *-er* in *matter* [matə]
[əə]   as in *girl* [gəəl], not found in German
[ɐ]   a sound resembling [ə], but tending towards [a]
[i]   the short form of [ii]
[ị]   a very short, non-syllabic form of [i]
[ii]   as in northern *heel* [hiil]
[ɪ]   as in *hill* [hɪl]
[ɪɪ]   the long form of [ɪ]
[o]   the short form of [oo]
[ọ]   a very short, non-syllabic form of [o]
[oo]   as in northern *boat* [boot]
[ɔ]   as in *not* [nɔt]
[ɔ·]   the half-long form of [ɔ]
[ɔɔ]   the long form of [ɔ]
[œ]   the sound of [ɛ] with lips pouted

[œœ] the long form of [œ]
[ø] the short form of [øø]
[øø] the sound of [ee] with lips pouted
[u] the short form of [uu]
[u̯] a very short, non-syllabic form of [u]
[uu] as in northern *cool* [kuul]
[ʊ] as in *put* [pʊt]
[ʊʊ] the long form of [ʊ]
[y] the short form of [yy]
[yy] the sound of [ii] with lips pouted
[ʏ] the sound of [ı] with lips pouted
[ʏ̯] a very short, non-syllabic form of [ʏ]
[ʏʏ] the long form of [ʏ]
[ʌ] as in *puzzle* [pʌzl̩], not found in German

Nasalized vowels

[ã, ɛ̃, õ, œ̃] are nasalized (a, ɛ, o, œ); they generally occur in stressed syllables, when they are long [ãã], etc.

Diphthongs

These are [a·e̯, a·o̯, ɔ·ʏ̯]. They are falling diphthongs, i.e. the first segment is stressed, and also noticeably lengthened (half-long); the second segment is quite short and difficult to determine, hence alternative transcriptions, e.g. [ai, au, ɔi] or [aı, aʊ, ɔø], more exactly [a·i̯], etc. Further ['ʊi] and numerous other combinations of vowels arising from the vocalization of *r*, pp. 9 f.

Consonants

The glottal stop [ʔ], p. 8.
The aspirate [h] as in *hot* [hɔt]
The occlusives (plosives, stops) consisting of the tenues [p, t, k] (voiceless) and the mediae [b, d, g] (voiced) and [b̥, d̥, g̊] (unvoiced):

[p] as in *pot* [pɔt] ⎫
[t] as in *top* [tɔp] ⎬ (in German with more aspiration)
[k] as in *cot* [kɔt] ⎭

[b] as in *dab* [dab] [b̥] ⎫ We make these sounds in
[d] as in *bad* [bad] [d̥] ⎬ English if we pronounce *bad*,
[g] as in *nag* [nag] [g̊] ⎭ etc., in a whisper.

The nasals:

[m] as in *tom* [tɔm]
[m̩] syllabic [m]

[n] as in *don* [dɔn]
[n̩] syllabic [n]
[ŋ] as in *long* [lɔŋ]
[ŋ̩] syllabic [ŋ]

The liquids:

[l] as in *lot* [lɔt]
[l̩] syllabic [l]
[r] see p. 9.

The fricatives comprising voiceless [f, s, ʃ, ç, χ] and voiced [v, z, ʒ, j, ɣ]:

[f]   as in *foot* [fʊt]
[s]   as in *sea* [sii]
[ʃ]   as in *ship* [ʃɪp] (in German with the blade of the tongue pressed against the teeth ridge, giving a sharper sound)
[ç]   as in *hue* [çjuu] (the voiceless form of [j]) ·
[χ]   as in Scottish *loch* [lɔχ] (in German less rasping)

[v]   as in *vase* [vaaz]
[z]   as in *zoo* [zuu]
[ʒ]   as in *vision* [vɪʒn̩]
[j]   as in *you* [juu]
[ɣ]   the voiced form of [χ]

The affricates are voiceless [pf, ts, tʃ] and voiced [dʒ]:

[pf]   an intimate combination of [p] and [f], not found in English
[ts]   as in *its* [ɪts]
[tʃ]   as in *chill* [tʃɪl]
[dʒ]   as in *lodge* [lɔdʒ]

The Sounds of German

As we have implied above (p. 1), the pronunciation of German is not standardized in any absolute sense, and regional differences are, within limits, entirely acceptable in educated speech, more so than in English. Accordingly, in the examples below, some reference is made to variant pronunciations.

VOWEL SOUNDS

[a] *Mann* [man] 'man', *Nachbar* ['naχbaɑ] 'neighbour', *Rheuma* ('rɔ·ɣma] 'rheumatism'.
[aa] *Vater* ['faatɐ] 'father', *Staat* [ʃtaat] 'state', *Ahne* ['aanə] 'ancestor'. In the south, [a,aa] are commonly replaced by

[ɑ,ɑɑ], i.e. (man, 'fɑɑtɐ], etc. Notice the contrast with Standard English, which uses the front variety when short, the back when long: *man* with [a], *father* with [ɑɑ]. A similar contrast may occur locally in German, too.

In North German, a number of monosyllables are pronounced short, e.g. *Gras* [grɑs] 'grass', *Rad* [rɑt] 'wheel', further *Tag* [taχ] 'day', South German [grɑɑs, rɑɑt, tɑɑk].

[ɛ] *denn* [dɛn] 'for, because', *Äste* ['ɛstə] 'branches'.

[ɛɛ] may occur locally, in general corresponding to etymological *ä* (*äh*); it is heard before *r*, as explained on p. 6. Otherwise it is a spelling pronunciation of *ä* (*äh*) (normally [ee]), especially used to mark an orthographic contrast with *e, eh*, so distinguishing, for instance, *nähme* as ['nɛɛmə] from *nehme* ['neemə], 3rd sg. subj. pret. and pres. respectively of *nehmen* 'to take'.

[e] *Zement* [tse'mɛnt] 'cement'.

[ee] *Hefe* ['heefə] 'yeast', *Tee* [tee] 'tea', *Weh* [vee] 'pain, grief'; *schräg* [ʃreek] 'slanting', *nähme* ['neemə], see further under [ɛɛ].

[ə] *Befehl* [bə'feel] 'command', *Backe* ['bakə] 'cheek', *Mantel* ['mantəl] 'coat, overcoat', *Atem* ['aatəm] 'breath', *baden* ['baadən] 'to bathe, take a bath', *lächeln* ['lɛçəln] 'to smile', *wütend* ['vyytɛnt] 'furious', *Mäuschen* ['mɔ·ʏsçən] 'little mouse', *hauen* [ha·ʊən] 'to strike'. See also pp. 10, 14.

[ɐ] *besser* ['bɛsɐ] 'better', see further under [r]. May become [a] locally, e.g. Berlinese *Vata* for *Vater*.

[i] *Alibi* ['aalibi] 'alibi'.

[i̯] *Linie* ['liini̯ə] 'line', *Studium* ['ʃtuudi̯ʊm] 'study', *Allianz* [ali̯'ants] 'alliance', *seriös* [zeri̯'øøs] 'serious', see p. 7. See also under 'Diphthongs'.

[ii] 1 *wider*, 2 *wieder* ['viidɐ] 1 'against', 2 'again', *Industrie* [ɪndʊs'trii] 'industry', *Vieh* [fii] 'livestock', *ihn* [iin] 'him'.

[ɪ] *bin* [bɪn] 'am', *Dickicht* ['dɪkɪçt] 'thicket'. Upper German may substitute [i].

[o] *Chronist* [kro'nɪst] 'chronicler', *Motto* ['mɔto] 'motto'.

[o̯] *Memoiren* [me'mo̯aarən] 'memoirs'. See also under 'Diphthongs'.

[oo] *hoch* [hooχ] 'high', *Boot* [boot] 'boat', *Sohn* [zoon] 'son'.

[ɔ] *Holz* [hɔlts] 'wood', *Hochzeit* ['hɔχtsa·et] 'wedding'.

[œ] *können* ['kœnən] 'to be able'. Notice that *können* is distinguished from *kennen* 'to know' only by lip-rounding. Be careful not to substitute [ə], the nearest English sound.

[ø] *Zölibat* [tsøli'baat] 'celibacy'.

[øø] *töten* ['tøøtən] 'to kill', *höchst* [høøkst] 'most highly', *Söhne* ['zøønə] 'sons', *Goethe* ['gøøtə]. Notice that *töten* is distinguished only by lip rounding from *täten* ['teetən] pret. subj. pl. of *tun* 'to do'. Be careful not to substitute [əə], the nearest English sound.

[u]   *Lupine* [lu'piinə] 'lupin', *Vakuum* ['vaakuʊm] 'vacuum'.

[u̯]   *Statue* ['ʃtaatu̯ə] 'statue', *Situation* [ˌzitu̯atsi̯'oon] 'situation', *eventuell* [evɛ̃ntu̯'ɛl] 'possible, eventual', *Etui* [etu̯'ii] 'case', see p. 7.

[uu] *Mut* [muut] 'courage', *Kuh* [kuu] 'cow'.

[ʊ]   *dumm* [dʊm] 'foolish', *Konsul* ['kɔnzʊl] 'consul'. Upper German may substitute [u].

[y]   *Zypresse* [tsy'prɛsə] 'cypress'.

[yy] *süß* [zyys] 'sweet', *fühlen* ['fyylən] 'to feel', *lyrisch* ['lyyrɪʃ] 'lyrical'. Notice that *fühlen* is distinguished only by lip-rounding from *fielen* ['fiilən] pret. pl. of *fallen* 'to fall'.

[ʏ]   *füllen* [fʏlən] 'to fill', *Rhythmus* ['rʏtmʊs] 'rhythm'. It will be observed that *füllen* and *fühlen* (above) stand in the same phonetic relationship to one another as do 'fill' and 'feel'.

Alternative long vowels before *r*

Depending on the region, certain long vowels occur before *r* either in a closed or open form; both are widespread.

[ee,ɛɛ]   *Schere* ['ʃeerə, 'ʃɛɛrə] 'scissors', thus *Ähre* 'ear (of corn)' and *Ehre* 'honour' are indifferently ['eerə, 'ɛɛrə], see further p. 5.

[øø,œœ]   *Möhre* ['møørə, 'mœœrə] 'carrot'.

[oo,ɔɔ]   *Tor* (tooɐ, tɔɔɐ] '(large) door, fool'.

[ii,ɪɪ]   *hier* [hiiɐ, hɪɪɐ] 'here'.

[yy,ʏʏ]   *Schwüre* ['ʃvyyrə, 'ʃvʏʏrə] 'vows'.

[uu,ʊʊ]   *Schwur* [ʃvuuɐ, ʃvʊʊɐ] 'vow'.

Nasalized vowels

These may be present in words of French origin, but are very often Germanized, [ãã] becoming [aŋ], etc.

[ãã, aŋ]   *Chance* ['ʃããsə, 'ʃaŋsə] 'chance'.

[ɛ̃ɛ̃, ɛŋ]   *Teint* [tɛ̃ɛ̃, tɛŋ] 'complexion'.

[õõ, oŋ]   *Bon* [bõõ, bɔŋ] 'sales slip'.

[œ̃œ̃,œŋ]   *Parfum* [paa'fœ̃œ̃, -'fœŋ] 'perfume'.

The nasal vowel is short in unstressed position: [ã, aŋ] *engagieren* [ãga'ʒiirən, aŋga'ʒiirən] 'to engage'.

Vowel interchange in foreign words

The vowels [e, i, o, u, y, ø] occur characteristically in unstressed, open syllables and may be regarded as spelling pronunciations given to foreign words. Except when final (and in the combination [iə]), they are very often replaced by their lowered counterparts [ɛ, ı, ɔ. ʊ, ɣ, œ], so adapting to the phonetic pattern of the native elements in the vocabulary, hence alternatively *Zement* [tsɛ'mɛnt], *Alibi* ['aalıbi], etc. (above).

Another indication of vowel instability in words of this sort is seen in the interchange of long and (lowered) short, particularly frequent in the case of [ii] and [ı]. Thus *Politik* 'politics' may be heard not only as [poli'tiik], but just as often as [pɔlı'tık], similarly *politisch* 'political' may be [po'liitıʃ] or [pɔ'lıtıʃ]. By the same token *Island* ['iislant, 'ıslant] 'Iceland', *Israel* ['iisrael, 'ısraɛl], *Japan* ['jaapan, 'japan], *Roboter* ['roobɔtɐ, 'rɔbɔtɐ] 'robot', *Supermann* ['zuupɐman, 'zʊpɐ-] 'superman'.

As pronunciations of the letter *y*, the values [y,ɣ] are often replaced by i,ı]: *Zypresse*, *Rhythmus* (above) also [tsi'prɛsə, 'rıtmʊs].

Foreign words accented on a final syllable beginning with a vowel and preceded by *i* or *u* have a twofold pronunciation. In more formal speaking, or when emphasizing the word, the stress tends to remain on the syllable as described: *Allianz* [ali̯'ants] 'alliance', *seriös* [zeri̯'øøs] 'serious', *Nation* [natsi̯'oon] 'nation', *eventuell* [evɛntu̯'ɛl] 'eventual, possible', *Etui* [etu̯'ii] 'case'. In casual usage, however, the syllabic boundary tends to be moved back to include the consonant preceding the semi-vowel, when [i̯],but not [u̯], becomes consonantal: [a'ljants, ze'rjøøs, na'tsjoon, evɛn'tu̯ɛl, e'tu̯ii]. But [i̯] is preserved before a like vowel: *Alliierte* always [ali̯'ii̯ɐtə] 'allies'.

Let us, lastly, not forget to give exotic names their German spelling pronunciation: *Goliath* ['gooli̯at], *Sinai* ['ziina·e̯], *Zeus* [tsɔ·ɣs], *Achilles* [a'χılɛs].

Diphthongs

[a·e̯] *mein* [ma·e̯n] 'my, mine', *Waise* ['va·e̯zə] 'orphan'.
[a·o̯] *Haus* [ha·o̯s] 'house'.
[ɔ·ɣ̯] *Beule* ['bɔ·ɣ̯lə] 'boil, swelling', *Häuser* ['hɔ·ɣ̯zɐ] 'houses'.

It will be noticed that these diphthongs are appreciably different from those heard in the English words *mine* [main], *house* [haus], *boil* [boil].

Here may be mentioned the rare combination [ʊı] in *pfui!* [pfʊı] 'ugh! disgusting!' also *hui!* 'whoosh!', *ui!* (an exclamation of astonishment and wonder).

CONSONANT SOUNDS

Glottal stop

Usually defined as a consonant, the glottal stop or catch [ʔ] is a faint, cough-like sound produced by a sudden opening of the glottis, as may happen before an initial vowel. It can occur in English whenever a word beginning with a vowel is emphatically stressed: it's just 'ʔawful!

In German this sound commonly occurs with initial vowels, notably when these are fully stressed or pronounced in isolation: *Achtung* ['ʔaχtʊŋ] 'attention', *offen* ['ʔɔfən] 'open', also after un-stressed prefixes: *Beachtung* [bə'ʔaχtʊŋ] 'consideration', *eröffnen* [(ʔ)ɛɐ̯'ʔœfnən] 'to open', and occasionally elsewhere within a word: *Theater* [te'ʔaatɐ] 'theatre'. The glottal stop produces a staccato effect and is therefore avoided in singing. It prevents the liaison usual in English: contrast the hiatus in *ein und aus* ['ʔa·ɛn (ʔ)ʊnt 'ʔa·ọs] with the running on heard in 'in‿and‿out'. It does not occur, however, in various compound adverbs, as *darauf* [da'ra·ọf] 'on it', *herein* [hɛ'ra·ɛn] 'in', *hinaus* [hɪ'na·ọs] 'out', also *überall* ['yybəral] 'everywhere'. Exceptions are otherwise rare: we note *Handarbeit* ['handaaba·ẹt] 'needlework' as distinct from ['hant‚ʔaaba·ẹt] 'work done by hand'. The glottal stop is normally absent from the language as spoken in the far south. As a non-essential sound, we otherwise ignore it in our transcriptions.

Aspirate

The aspirate [h] is found at the beginning of a word, also when compounded, and in a couple of suffixes: *Hochhaus* ['hooχha·ọs] 'multi-storey building', *Hoheit* ['hooha·ẹt] 'Highness'. It is sounded medially in *Uhu* ['uuhuu] 'eagle owl' and in such foreign words as *subtrahieren* [zʊptra'hiirən] 'to subtract', but in this position the letter *h* normally functions as a mark of vowel length: *Zahn* [tsaan] 'tooth'. Intervocalic *h* may sometimes be pronounced for a special purpose, as for example in dictation: *gehen* ['gee-hən] for ordinary [geeən, geen].

Aitches are not dropped in German.

Voiceless occlusives [p, t, k]

[p] *piepsen* ['piipsən] 'to chirp', *Lippe* ['lɪpə] 'lip', *Hieb* [hiip] 'blow'.

[t] *tot* [toot] 'dead', *Dotter* ['dɔtɐ] 'yolk', *Tod* [toot] 'death', *Thron* [troon] 'throne', *Mädchen* ['meetçən] 'girl'.

[k] *Küche* ['kyyçə] 'kitchen', *backen* ['bakən] 'to bake', *Krug* [kruuk] 'jug', *Quelle* ['kvɛlə] 'source', *Achse* ['aksə] 'axle', *fliegt* [fliikt] 'flies'. In Upper German [k] rather than [ç] occurs in the ending -*ig*, e.g. *lustig* ['lʊstɪk] or ['lustik] 'cheerful'.

Voiced occlusives [b, d, g]

[b] *Bach* [baχ] 'brook', *Liebe* ['liibə] 'love', *schrubben* ['ʃrʊbən] 'to scrub'.

[d] *Ding* [dɪŋ] 'thing', *Ader* ['aadɐ] 'vein', *addieren* [a'diirən] 'to add'.

[g] *Geld* [gɛlt] 'money', *Wagen* ['vaagən] 'car', *Egge* ['ɛgə] 'harrow'.

These occlusives are most typical of the north, being sometimes replaced in Central, and especially in South German by their voiceless counterparts [b̥, d̥, g̊], thus *Bach* [b̥aχ], *Ader* ['aad̥ɐ], *Egge* [ɛg̊ə], etc.

Liquids [m, n, ŋ, l, r]

[m] *Mond* [moont] 'moon', *Heimat* ['ha·ɛmaat] 'home', *stumm* [ʃtʊm] 'dumb'.

[n] *neu* [nɔ·y̑] 'new', *drinnen* ['drɪnən] 'inside'.

[ŋ] *lang* [laŋ] 'long', *Menge* ['mɛŋə] 'crowd', *stinken* ['ʃtɪŋkən] 'to stink', *konkret* [kɔŋ'kreet] 'concrete'. In the north and south-east, final -*ng* may be pronounced [ŋk]: *lang* [laŋk].

[l] *Laus* [la·ȏs] 'louse', *Bild* [bɪlt] 'picture', *Wolle* ['vɔlə] 'wool'.

[r] is usually rolled and uvular, but is trilled in some southern districts. It occurs initially, after a consonant, and medially between vowels: *rot* [root] 'red', *Sprache* ['ʃpraaχə] 'language', *Ware* ['vaarə] 'merchandise'.

In certain areas, notably in the Rhineland, [r] may survive medially before a consonant when the preceding vowel is short: *Wort* [vɔrt] 'word'. In such cases, however, it commonly has a scraping sound, not infrequently turning into [χ], hence alternatively [vɔχt]. The pronunciation with [r] is often affected for some special purpose, as for particular clarity when dictating or making a formal speech, in theatrical declamation, or just for emphasis.

Otherwise *r* is regularly vocalized, becoming [ɐ].

Examples of final *r*: (after a short vowel) *Doktor* ['dɔktoɐ], popularly ['dɔktɐ] 'doctor', also in the prefix *er-* [ɛɐ-], reducible to [ɐ-]: *erlauben* [ɛɐ-, ɐ'la·ȏbən] 'to allow', similarly *her-, ver-, zer-*, (after a long vowel) *sehr* [zeeɐ] 'very', *wir* [viiɐ] 'we', *Ohr* [ooɐ] 'ear', *Uhr* [uuɐ] 'clock', *Gör* [gøøɐ] 'brat', *Tür* [tyyɐ] 'door'. On [aa] + *r*, see below.

Unstressed *er* in final syllables is realized as [ɐ]: *Wunder* ['vʊndɐ] 'miracle', *bewundert* [bə'vʊndɐt] 'admired', *Seher* [zeeɐ] 'seer', *höher* [høøɐ] 'higher', *Feier* [fa·e̯ɐ] 'celebration', *teuer* [tɔ·ɣɐ] 'dear', *Schauer* [ʃa·o̯ɐ] 'shower'.

Even where vocalization is the rule, occasional restoration of the consonantal pronunciation may be heard in the special circumstances referred to above.

Vocalization of medial *r* before consonant also occurs. It is universal when the preceding vowel is long: *Wert* [veeɐt] 'value', *regiert* [re'giiɐt] 'rules', *bohrt* [booɐt] 'bores', *hört* [høøɐt] 'hears'. In most areas this development also takes place when the preceding vowel is short: *Kerl* [kɛɐl] 'fellow', *Birne* ['bɪɐnə] 'pear', *Wort* [vɔɐt] 'word', *durch* [dʊɐç] 'through', *Wörter* ['vœɐtɐ] 'words', *mürbe* ['mʏɐbə] 'overripe'; [a] or [aa] + *r* are realized as [aa]: *scharf* [ʃaaf] 'sharp', *wahr* [vaa] 'true'. On the alternative, consonantal pronunciation, see above.

Orthographical *rr* having the same phonetic value as *r* is treated in the same way: *wirr* [vɪɐ] 'confused', *Wirrwarr* [vɪɐvaa] 'confusion', *zerrt* [tsɛrt, tsɛɐt] 'drags, tugs'.

It will be seen from the above that [ɐ] combines with vowels to form diphthongs and with diphthongs to form triphthongs; it is always a lightly pronounced, unstressed element.

See also 'Alternative long vowels before *r*', p. 6.

Syllabic [l̩, m̩, n̩, ŋ̍]

In informal style, the vowel [ə] is lost in the unstressed endings *-el*, *-em*, *-en*, which become syllabic [l̩, m̩, n̩]: *Mantel* [mantl̩] 'coat, overcoat' (as in English 'mantle'), *Atem* [aatm̩] 'breath', *baden* [baadn̩] 'to bathe, take a bath', likewise *lächeln* [lɛçl̩n] 'to smile', *wütend* [vyytn̩t] 'furious'.

In the case of [n̩], assimilation to a preceding labial or velar consonant leads to [m̩] or [ŋ̍] respectively: *schrubben* [ʃrʊbm̩] 'to scrub', *backen* [bakŋ̍] 'to bake', *Wagen* [vaagŋ̍] 'car'. The diminutive suffix *-chen*, however, is normally [-çən], p. 5.

Voiceless fricatives [f, s, ʃ, ç, χ]

[f]　*Faust* [fa·ọst] 'fist', *Affe* ['afə] 'monkey'; final *v* (only in foreign words) has this value: *Motiv* [mo'tiif] 'motive', also exceptionally *Vers* [fɛrs] 'verse' (see under [v]).

[s]　*dies* [diis] 'this', *Maß* [maas] 'measure', *essen* ['ɛsən] 'to eat', *mäßig* ['meesɪç] 'moderate', *Wespe* ['vɛspə] 'wasp', *hastig* ['hastɪç] 'hasty', *Prospekt* [pro'spɛkt] 'prospectus', *konstant*

[kɔn'stant] 'constant', *Skandal* [skan'daal] 'scandal'. Locally in the north: *spitz* [spɪts], *Stein* [sta·e̩n], see under [ʃ]. See also under [z] and p. 13.

[ʃ] *Schiff* [ʃɪf] 'ship', *Fisch* [fɪʃ] 'fish', also represented by *s* in initial *sp-*, *st-*: *spitz* [ʃpɪts] 'pointed', *Stein* [ʃta·e̩n] 'stone', this pronunciation also common in medial position in the case of foreign words: *Prospekt* [pro'ʃpɛkt], *konstant* [kɔn'ʃtant]; *sk* may be involved: *Skandal* [ʃkan'daal]; see under [s]. This sound is noticeably different from our *sh*, p. 4. See also under [ʒ].

[ç] can be described as the palatal form of [χ]. It occurs after front vowels: *echt* [ɛçt] 'genuine', *Echo* ['eeço] 'echo', *mich* [mɪç] 'me', *Dächer* ['dɛçɐ] 'roofs', *Löcher* ['lœçɐ] holes', *Bücher* ['byyçɐ] 'books', also in the suffix *-ig*: *lustig* ['lʊstɪç] 'cheerful', likewise *Lustigkeit* ['lʊstɪçka·e̩t] 'cheerfulness', in the diminutive-forming *-chen*: *Tischchen* ['tɪʃçən] 'little table', also after consonants: *Milch* [mɪlç] 'milk', *Kirche* ['kɪrçə, 'kɪɐçə] 'church', further *Adjektiv* ['atçɛktiif] 'adjective'. It can be heard initially: *China* ['çiina] 'China' (less usually ['kiina]).

In North and Central German, [ç] rather than [k] may be the value of *g* after a front vowel (*a*) before a voiceless consonant: *fliegt* [fliiçt] 'flies', or (*b*) when final: *flieg!* [fliiç] 'fly!', similarly *möglich* ['møøçlɪç] 'possible' (root *mög-*), also when final after a consonant: *Erfolg* [ɛɐ'fɔlç] 'success'.

[χ] can be described as the velar form of [ç]. It occurs after back vowels: *Dach* [daχ] 'roof', *Loch* [lɔχ] 'hole', *Buch* [buuχ] 'book'.

In North and Central German, [χ] rather than [k] may be the value of *g* after a back vowel (*a*) before a voiceless consonant: *sagt* [zaaχt] 'says', or (*b*) when final: *Zug* [tsuuχ] 'train', similarly *tauglich* ['ta·ɔχlɪç] 'fit, suitable' (root *taug-*).

Voiced fricatives [v, z, ʒ, j, ɣ]

[v] *weit* [va·e̩t] 'wide', *ewig* ['eevɪç] 'eternal'; except when final (see under [f], *v* in foreign words usually has this value: *Visum* ['viizʊm] 'visa', *evident* [evi'dɛnt] 'evident'.

[z] *so* [zoo] 'so', *lesen* ['leezən] 'to read'. In many southern districts replaced by [s], hence [soo, 'leesən]. See also pp. 13 f.

[ʒ] occurs in words of French origin: *Genie* [ʒe'nii] '(person of) genius', *Loge* ['looʒe] 'box (theatre), lodge', *Jackett* [ʒa'kɛt] 'jacket'. In ordinary speech often replaced by [ʃ], hence [ʃe'nii], etc.

[j] *Joch* [jɔχ] 'yoke'. In some northern areas, [j] rather than [g]

may be heard in intervocalic position: *fliegen* ['fliijən] 'to fly'. Locally in the north in a well-known substandard use, [j] replaces [g] at the beginning of a word, as in Berlinese *janz jut*.

[ɣ] is heard in some northern areas, occurring after a back vowel instead of [g] in intervocalic position: *Wagen* ['vaaɣən] 'car'.

Affricates [pf, ts, tʃ, dʒ]

[pf] *Pflaume* ['pfla·o̯mə] 'plum', *Apfel* ['apfəl] 'apple', *Tropf* [trɔpf] 'simpleton'.

[ts] *Zaun* [tsa·o̯n] 'fence', *schätzen* ['ʃɛtsən] 'to estimate', *Schatz* [ʃats] 'treasure', *Patient* [patsi̯'ɛnt] 'patient'; notice *jetzt* [jɛtst] 'now', colloquially often [jɛts].

[tʃ] *klatschen* ['klatʃən] 'to clap', *deutsch* [dɔ·y̯tʃ] 'German'. See also under [dʒ].

[dʒ] occurs only in foreign words: *Dschungel* ['dʒʊŋəl] 'jungle', in ordinary speech often replaced by [tʃ], hence ['tʃʊŋəl].

Also:

[ps] *Psalm* [psalm] 'psalm'.

[ks] *Xantippe* [ksan'tɪpə] 'quarrelsome female, shrew'.

Long consonants

These may arise in compounds: *wahllos* ['vaal,loos] 'indiscriminate', *ummodeln* ['ʊmmoodəln] 'to remodel', *unnatürlich* ['ʊnna,tyyɐlɪç] 'unnatural', *Schiffahrt* (divided *Schiff-fahrt*) ['ʃif,faat] 'shipping'. They also occur in colloquial style as the result of vowel loss, often accompanied by assimilation: *nennen* ['nɛnən>nɛnn] 'to call', *zusammen* [tsuu'zamən>-'zamn̩>-'zamm] 'together'.

Devoicing of [b, d, g] and [z] in compounds and connected speech

When preceded by a voiceless consonant, [b, d, g] are themselves devoiced. Compare *Bergbau* ['bɛrkb̥a·o̯] 'mining', *Hochdruck* ['hooχd̥rʊk] 'high pressure', *Aufgang* ['a·o̯fg̊aŋ] 'stairway' with *Bau* [ba·o̯] 'structure', *Druck* [drʊk] 'pressure', *Gang* [gaŋ] 'passage'; and in closely connected speech: *das Band* [das'b̥ant] 'the ribbon', *ich denke* [ɪç'd̥ɛŋkə] 'I think', even *sie spricht gut deutsch* [ziʃprɪç(t)'g̊uutd̥ɔy̯tʃ] 'she speaks German well'.

[z] is also devoiced in this environment. Compare *nachsenden* ['naχsɛndən] 'to send after', *Absicht* ['apsɪçt] 'intention', *Blödsinn* ['bløøtsɪn] 'nonsense', with *senden* ['zɛndən] 'to send', *Sicht* [zɪçt] 'sight', *Sinn* [zɪn] 'sense'. In connected speech: *ich sage* [ɪç'saagə] 'I say', *ob sie kommt?* [ɔpsi'kɔmt] '(I wonder) if she's coming?' When the preceding consonant is [s], the resulting long [ss] is reduced in casual speech, since long consonants are not an

average feature of the language: *Aussicht* ['a·o̧ssiçt] 'view' becoming ['a·o̧sıçt], similarly *das Seil* [das 'sa·ȩl] 'the rope', in quick speaking for practical purposes one word [da'sa·ȩl].

Assimilation of [s] to [ʃ]

In natural speech [s] is assimilated to following [ʃ], the resulting long [ʃʃ] being reduced in casual style: *Ausschnitt* ['a·o̧ʃʃnıt] 'cutting' becoming ['a·o̧ʃnıt], similarly *es scheint* [ɛʃ'ʃa·ent] 'it seems', practically [ɛ'ʃa·ent], or *Holzschuh* normally ['hɔltʃuu] 'clog'. By the same token, [s] may be assimilated to a preceding [ʃ], as commonly in the 2nd sg. present of verbs: *wünschst* [vʏnʃt] '(you) wish', *plauschst* [pla·o̧ʃt] '(you) chatter', beside more ponderous [vʏnʃst], etc.

ENGLISH AND FRENCH LOANS

In the pronunciation of borrowings from English, two different principles obtain. The word may be given either a German spelling pronunciation: *London* ['lɔndɔn], or else its native English pronunciation, when it will nevertheless be modified, more or less, to accord with German speech-habits: *Puzzle* [puzl̩] with German [ʊ] for English [ʌ], *Quiz* [kvıs], German lacking [w] and not using [z] at the end of a word. It is noticeable that German [ɛ] regularly reproduces English [a], e.g. *Camping* ['kɛmpıŋ], it being generally believed that such is, in fact, native practice. The source of the misconception lies in the employment of [æ] to represent the sound of *a*, i.e. ['kæmpıŋ], traditionally given in manuals of English, the phonetic symbol being equated with German *ä* (once written *ae*). In *Pullover* the stress falls on the second syllable, as also in *Pullunder* 'sleeveless pullover'—a sample of English made in Germany.

Occasionally, both the above principles compete: *Jazz* is either [jats] or [dʒɛs], the latter indeed often more thoroughly Germanized as [tʃɛs]—our 'chess'! *Gag* is normally indistinguishable from the native *Geck* 'dandy'.

By and large the same principles apply to the French loans. A common characteristic is the accent on the last syllable. Examples range from spelling pronunciations like *Per'son* 'person' or *Sol'dat* 'soldier' to successful reproduction of the foreign sounds, witness the nasal vowels (p. 6) and the consonant [ʒ] (p. 11). Compare further *Budget* [by'dʒee] 'budget', *Eleve* [e'leev] 'pupil (theatre)', *Jalousie* [ʒalu'zii] 'Venetian blind', *leger* [le'ʒeeɐ, -'ʒɛɛɐ) 'free and easy', *Niveau* [ni'voo] 'level', *Portemonnaie* [pɔrtmɔ'nɛɛ, -'nee] 'purse'. The spelling has sometimes been adpated, more or less, to the German pattern: *Bü'ro* 'bureau, office', *Fri'sör*, but also *Fri'seur* 'hairdresser', *Porträt* [pɔr'trɛɛ, -'tree] 'portrait', also *Portrait*. The word *Leutnant* [lɔ·y̆tnant] 'lieutenant' has been entirely Germanized. Under the influence of the spelling, final *-e* is generally pronounced in careful speech: *Bronze* ['brõõsə, 'brɔŋsə] 'bronze', *Bor'düre* 'border, trimming', and several words ending in *-age*, as *Garage* [ga'raaʒə] 'garage', including the pseudo-French *Blamage* [bla'maaʒə] 'disgrace, humiliation'.

Notice *das Service* [seɐ'viis] '(tea, coffee) service' and *der Service* ['søøɐvɪs, 'sœœɐ-] 'maintenance service', the same word borrowed from French and English respectively.

MODIFICATIONS IN CASUAL SPEECH

Various modifications are commonplace in conversational style.

The language does not take well to clusters of homorganic consonants; in such cases one or more may be lost: *weißt du?* ['va·e̥sd̥u] 'do you know?', *Kunststück* ['kʊnʃtʏk] 'work of art'.

Final *-e* is dropped in many districts, regularly so in the south, in examples like the following: *Aug'* 'eye', *Käs'* 'cheese', *müd'* 'tired', *träg'* 'indolent', *ich geh', red'* 'I go, talk', very commonly also in the 2nd person sing. ending after a dental consonant (p. 89): *du red'st, reit'st* 'you talk, ride'. In any part of the German-speaking world, *e* is ordinarily lost when it occurs after a vowel sound: *hauen* [ha·ọn] 'to strike', *stehen* [ʃteen] 'to stand'.

As explained on p. 10, the ending *-en* is most usually pronounced [n̩] when following a consonant: *spielen* [ʃpiiln̩] 'to play'. In such verbs as *hören* 'to hear' or *irren* 'to go astray', vocalization of *r* results: [høøɐn, ɪɐn] (pp. 9 f.). The phonetic consequences for *haben* 'to have' are drastic as change follows upon change: [haabm̩>haam> ham], all of which can be heard anywhere, any day. No less significant are the changes arising from *haben wir* 'have we': [haabm̩ viiɐ> haabm̩ miiɐ>haam miiɐ], finally shortened to [hamɐ]. By the same process of assimilation *bleiben wir* [bla·ẹbm̩ viiɐ] 'stay we' passes by comparable steps via [bla·ẹbm̩ miiɐ] to finally reach [bla·ẹmɐ]. Other verbs follow suit. It will be seen that, at one point in the changes, *wir* [viiɐ] becomes [miiɐ], i.e. *mir*. From such use, *mir* can, in substandard as in dialect, replace *wir* entirely, hence the well-known *mir haben* 'we have', etc., witness:

Der Scheich sagt zum Emir,
'Erst Zahl'm mir, dann gehmir'.
Der Emir sagt zum Scheich,
'Gehmir lieber gleich'.

Contracted forms of the definite article after a preposition belong, in certain cases, to standard style, e.g. *übern, überm* 'over the', in full *über den, über dem* (p. 188). One observes, however, that in some cases the contraction is normally ignored in the orthography, thus *auf den, auf dem* 'on the', even though often spoken *aufn, aufm*; only exceptionally is this everyday pronunciation reproduced in writing, generally as *auf'n, auf'm*. But even these spellings represent only half the truth as examples demonstrate. The phrases *untern Baum* and *unterm Baum* 'under the tree' are both usually heard as [ʊntɐm‿-'bɔ·ʏm], *untern, unterm Deckel* 'lid' as [ʊntɐn‿'dɛkl̩], and *untern, unterm Gang* 'passage' as [ʊntɐŋ‿'gaŋ], the actual pronunciation of *-n, -m* being in fact determined by the nature of the initial consonant of the word following.

Not only [ə], other unstressed vowels are also liable to be lost in ordinary conversation, as often as not with consequent assimilation of consonants, e.g. *ich-habe-ihn in-den Garten geschickt* [ɪçaabm̩‿nn̩‿'gaatn̩‿gəʃɪkt] 'I've sent him into the garden'. It goes without saying that, as in any language, commonly recurring sentences may be considerably clipped: *was ist denn los?* 'what's the matter?' can be heard as *was is'n los?* or further drastically reduced to *was'n los?*

It is often contended that colloquial pronunciations may be all well and good for native speakers, but that others should eschew them. To which we would reply: *Wenn du in Rom bist, tu wie die Römer tun.*

STRESS

One distinguishes between simple and compound words, in the former further differentiating between native (including thoroughly Germanized) words and those taken up more recently from other languages ('foreign words').

Simple words (simplexes) of native origin

In simplexes of native origin the stress, or accent, falls characteristically on the root: *'fahren* 'to go (in a vehicle)', *ge'fahren* 'gone', *be'fahren* 'to travel over', *ent'fahren* 'to escape', *er'fahren* 'to get to know', *'fahrig* 'erratic', *'Fahrer* 'driver' m., *'Fahrerin* 'do.' f., pl. *'Fahrerinnen*— *'hoffen* 'to hope', *'hoffentlich* 'hopefully', *'Hoffnung* 'hope'—*'Monat* 'month', pl. *'Monate* NB!

Exceptions to the above are few: *Fo'relle* 'trout', *Ho'lunder* 'elder', *Hor'nisse* 'hornet', *Wa'cholder* 'juniper', further *le'bendig* 'living' contrasting with its near-synonym *'lebend*.

Prefixes or suffixes (including inflexions) forming part of a simplex are unstressed, except as follows. Two prefixes: *ant-*, only in *'Antwort* 'answer' and its derivatives, and *ur-* as in *'Urkunde* 'document', are

fully accented, words of this type standing midway between the
simplexes and the compounds proper. The suffixes *-bar*, *-haft*, *-heit*,
-keit, *-kunft*, *-ling*, *-sal* [-zaal], *-sam* [-zaam], *-schaft*, *-tum* [-tuum] carry
a subsidiary stress: *'fahr,bar* 'passable, mobile', *'ernst,haft* 'serious',
'Minder,heit 'minority', *'Schwierig,keit* 'difficulty', *'An,kunft* 'arrival',
'Feig,ling 'coward', *'Scheu,sal* 'beast, horror', *ge'nüg,sam* 'frugal',
'Feind,schaft 'enmity', *'Reich,tum* 'wealth, riches'. This subsidiary
stress is not particularly prominent; in connected speech, it may be
barely perceptible, if at all. It is therefore not otherwise marked in our
transcriptions.

For special effect, a normally unstressed syllable can take a full
stress: *nicht g e gründet* ['geeˈgrʏndət], *b e gründet* ['beeˈgrʏndət]
wollte ich sagen 'I meant to say *g e gründet*, not *b e gründet*'.

Foreign words

The stress patterns of foreign words are more diversified than those of
native words, though in the majority of cases the accent falls on the
last syllable or on the one before it. The following examples, grouped
according to characteristic endings, illustrate a cross-section of the
more significant types with final stress, and give some indication of the
irregularities commonly encountered.

We begin with the termination *-ion*, e.g. *Nati'on*, *Missi'on* (details
of pronunciation, p. 7). When two syllables occur before the main
stress, the first one carries a light subsidiary accent: *,Inflati'on*. This
accent becomes more prominent if three or more syllables precede the
main stress: *,Assoziati'on*; in such cases, it is marked in the
transcriptions elsewhere.

Final stress is also regular with the common suffixes *-ist*, *-ität*, *-ur*,
hence *Poli'zist* 'policeman', *Pari'tät* 'parity', *Na'tur* 'nature'. These
formations often take additional (unstressed) native suffixes: *Poli'zistin*
'policewoman', *pari'tätisch* 'having parity', *na'türlich* 'natural', *Na'tür-
lichkeit* 'naturalness'.

Most words ending in *-ent*, adjectives as well as nouns, have final
stress: *kompe'tent* 'responsible, authoritative', *Do'zent* '(university)
lecturer', *Abituri'ent* 'candidate for the *Abi'tur* (secondary-school
leaving examination)', but notice *'Orient*, *'Okzident*, and negatives, as
'indolent (see further below). Final stressing as a rule with the parallel
suffix *-enz*, thus *Kompe'tenz*, but *'Indolenz*, and with the comparable
suffixes *-ant*, *-anz*, e.g. *arro'gant*, *Arro'ganz*.

Further, nouns ending in *-ei*, as *Par'tei* '(political) party', also taking
unstressed suffixes: *par'teiisch*, *par'teilich* 'partial'. This ending is
commonly attached to native words: *Auskunf'tei* 'information (*Auskunft*) office', especially in the extended form *-erei*, as *Gieße'rei*
'foundry', *Schweine'rei* 'mess'. Here may be included the countless

verbs with the infinitive in *-ieren*, as *fil'trieren* 'to filter', *stu'dieren* 'to study', and the odd one in *-eien*, e.g. *ka'steien* 'to chastize'.

Nouns ending in *-ell* are accented on this syllable: *Fla'nell* 'flannel', as are the many adjectives with this ending: *kultu'rell* 'cultural', *spezi'ell* 'special'. Also nouns and adjectives in *-al*, as *Re'gal* '(set of) shelves', *spezi'al*, a near-synonym of *spezi'ell* (details of pronunciation, p. 7). Some adjectives appear with the suffix *-isch*, as *physi'kalisch* 'relating to physics'. Typically final stress, too, with nouns and adjectives in *-ar* or *-är*, e.g. *Exem'plar* 'specimen, copy' (but not *'Kaviar* 'caviar'), *ato'mar* 'atomic', *Sekre'tär* 'secretary', *pre'kär* 'precarious'. Some adjectives appear with added *-isch*, as *exem'plarisch* 'exemplary', *mili'tärisch* 'military'.

Many nouns in *-ik* accent this syllable: *Mu'sik* 'music', *Poli'tik* 'politics, policy', but other stressings are also common, cf. *'Optik* 'optics, aspect', *'Technik* 'technique, engineering', further *Bo'tanik* 'botany', *Gram'matik* 'grammar(-book)', *Infor'matik* 'data-processing', *Germa'nistik* 'study of German language and culture', and the oceans *'Indik, At'lantik*, etc.

Adjectives in *-iv* have, for the most part, the main stress on this syllable: *mas'siv* 'massive', *,ostenta'tiv* 'ostentatious', but there are exceptions, as *'negativ, 'positiv*. Some of these may be used as nouns: *Mas'siv* 'massif', *'Negativ, 'Positiv*. Certain nouns with no formal adjectival correspondences have initial stress: *'Nominativ, 'Akkusativ*, etc.

Nouns ending in *-ie* may have the accent on this syllable: *Ma'rie* (slang) 'money, brass', *Gale'rie* 'gallery', but others have penultimate stress: *'Studie* 'study, sketch' (details of pronunciation, p. 5).

Varying accentuation in related words

Varying accentuation as between different members of the same word family is often met with:

'Alkohol 'alcohol', *Alko'holiker* 'alcoholic', *alko'holisch* (adj.)

Katholi'zismus 'catholicism', *Katho'lik* 'catholic', *ka'tholisch* (adj.)

Che'mie [ç-], less usually [k-] 'chemistry', *'Chemiker* 'chemist', *'chemisch* 'chemical'

Fotogra'fie 'photograph, -graphy', *Foto'graf* 'photographer', *foto-'grafisch* 'photographic' (also spelt *Photogra'phie*, etc.)

'Autor (pl. *Au'toren*) 'author', *Au'torin* 'authoress'

Dik'tator (pl. *Dikta'toren*) 'dictator', *dikta'torisch* 'dictatorial'

Compounds

In compounds, the first word normally takes the prominent, main stress, the second (or further words) having a lighter, subsidiary stress: *'Schlaf,zimmer* 'bedroom', *'Deckenbe,leuchtung* 'ceiling light(s)'. Taken together, giving *Schlafzimmerdeckenbeleuchtung*, the subsidiary stress is most marked on -*,decken-* in accordance with the meaning. Slight subsidiary stresses, often imperceptible in connected speech, are disregarded in the transcriptions below.

When the component parts of the compound are nouns, exceptions to the above rule are few. We notice *Jahr'zehnt*, -*'hundert*, -*'tausend* 'decade, century, millennium' and the religious term *Mutter'gottes* 'Madonna', also *Palm'sonntag* 'Palm Sunday'. Irregular shifts of accent are not unknown, thus *Nibe'lungenlied* 'Lay of the Nibelungs' beside the more professional-sounding *'Nibelungenlied*.

Compounds often contain adjectives, when the same general rule applies: *'feindselig* 'hostile', *'mühevoll* 'laborious', *'schwerverständlich* 'hard to understand', *'graufarben* 'grey-coloured', *'rothaarig* 'red-haired', *'altklug* 'precocious'. Nevertheless there are numerous exceptions, as follows.

'Vollmacht 'authority, power of attorney', *'Volltreffer* 'direct hit' exemplify the rule, but *Voll'endung* 'completion' from the verb *voll'enden* 'to complete', cf. its close synonym *voll'bringen*, also *voll'kommen* 'perfect'. Other exceptions include *Alt'weibersommer* 'Indian summer, gossamer', *Kar'freitag* 'Good Friday', and not a few proper names, as *Hohen'zollern*, *Schön'brunn*. Notice *'Allmacht* 'omnipotence', but with shift of accent *all'mächtig* 'omnipotent, almighty'. This pattern is occasionally found in nouns and adjectives formed with prepositions, e.g. *'Vorzug* 'merit', but *vor'züglich* 'meritorious, excellent'—the stressing not without relevance in the slogan quoted on p. 131—and recurring in synonymous *vor'trefflich*, further *'Abscheu* 'disgust', *ab'scheulich* 'disgusting'.

The negative prefix *un-* carries the main stress when qualifying a noun: *'Unglück* 'misfortune', whence also *'unglücklich* 'unfortunate'. Foreign words containing a comparable prefix may follow suit, as *'intolerant*, *'illegal* contrasting with *tole'rant*, *le'gal*, further *'desinteressiert* (*'uninteressiert*) 'disinterested (uninterested)', but *interes'siert* [ɪntrɛ-] 'interested'. Negative adjectives, however, not infrequently have non-initial stress, especially when derived from verbs: *un'denkbar* 'unthinkable', *unab'änderlich* 'unalterable' (positive *'abänderlich*); some examples have no positive, e.g. *un'nahbar* 'unapproachable', *uner'bittlich* 'implacable', *unaus'stehlich* 'insufferable'.

Variant stressings may be heard: *'Neujahr* or *Neu'jahr* 'New Year', *'unmöglich* or *un'möglich* 'impossible', cf. *'Arbeitgeber* 'employer', *'Arbeitnehmer* 'employee', but when used contrastively often *Arbeit-'geber*, -*'nehmer*.

When the first element of a compound has a purely intensifying function, the second element (which then contains the essential sense) may also take a main stress, thus *'hundsgemein* or *'hundsge'mein* 'very mean, low down'. It does not seem possible to formulate precise rules as to which stressing will be used, and since these are all affective words, a degree of personal choice is not excluded. Sentence rhythm, too, may be involved: we should expect *ein 'hundsgemeiner 'Kerl* 'a very mean fellow', but *er ist 'hundsge'mein*. Other examples: *saudumm* 'very silly', *splitternackt* 'stark naked', *steinreich* 'immensely rich', *stocktaub* 'stone-deaf'. When the intensifying component consists of two elements, the second carries an appreciable subsidiary accent, e.g. *'funkel,nagel'neu* 'brand new', *'mucks,mäuschen'still* 'quite still', *'mutter,seelenal'lein* 'utterly alone', *'sperr,angel'weit* 'wide open' (as a door). Notice also *in aller 'Herrgotts'früh* 'at the crack of dawn'. Change of stress can occasionally involve change of meaning: *'blutarm* 'anaemic', but with affective stressing *'blut'arm* 'poor as a church mouse'.

With separable verbs the chief accent falls on the preposition: *'aufgegangen*, *'untergegangen* 'risen, set', with inseparable verbs on the root (p. 104): *über'fordern* 'overtax', *unter'werfen* 'subdue', but exceptionally on the preposition, as follows. The verb *'einholen* means 'to catch up with', the verb *über'holen* 'to overtake', but in juxtaposition: *ich will ihn 'einholen und 'überholen* 'I want to catch up with him and overtake him'.

Alphabetical names are accented, in general, on the last letter: *EK* [ee'kaa] 'Iron Cross, *Eisernes Kreuz*', similarly *UB* 'university library, *Universitätsbibliothek*', *SPD* 'Social Democratic Party of Germany, *Sozialdemokratische Partei Deutschlands*', *USA* (pl.) 'USA' (otherwise *Vereinigte Staaten von Amerika*), *UdSSR* (*d* read as *dee*) 'USSR, *Union der Sozialistischen Sowjetrepubliken*'. *PKW*, more often *Pkw* 'car, *Personenkraftwagen*' and *LKW*, *Lkw* 'lorry, *Lastkraftwagen*' commonly have initial stress, as also the slangy *j.w.d.* for *janz* (=*ganz*, p. 12) *weit draußen*, e.g. *er wohnt j.w.d.* 'he lives a good way out of town'.

INTONATION

It is often remarked that German appears to be spoken with more energy and vigour, more abruptly, and rather louder than is usual in English. Conversely, to the German ear, English may sound mumbled and indistinct. These impressions are due, in the main, to differences in the intonation systems, as we now attempt to demonstrate.

If we pronounce the words *North Sea*, especially if we do so slowly and deliberately, we notice that both are spoken with a falling pitch; it may be described as a downward glide in the voice. The first word is the more prominent and the intonation of the two words can be represented graphically as ⌐ ⌐ . If now a German pronounces *Nordsee*, the pattern is quite different. The gentle glides are absent, the pitch falls sharply when *Nord-* is pronounced and does not rise for *-see*, i.e. graphically \ — . Similarly, we say *Christmas time* ⌐ — ⌐ (*-mas* being unstressed and without the glides of the stressed syllables), but German *Weihnachtszeit* \ — — . These matters are arrestingly illustrated when a German pronounces, e.g. *'Mickeymaus* or *'Teddybär*.

The same abrupt intonation is found in short statements containing one main stress: *es \regnet* 'it's raining', *sie \spielen* 'they're playing', *\Oma kommt* 'Granny's coming', *du \kennst sie ja* 'you know her of course', *Sie hören \Nachrichten (\Kurznachrichten)* 'you're listening to the news (news summary)'.

Turning next to longer sentences, it is important to observe that the intonation pattern depends, in the first place, on the significant stresses within the sentence. These naturally fall on the most essential words: *die 'Nachbarn kommen 'morgen aus den 'Ferien zu'rück* 'the neighbours are coming back from their holidays tomorrow'. The pitch of the voice rises at the first stress, and again on the following two stresses, to fall decisively on the fourth and final stress. All words without significant stress are passed over lightly and quickly, making the stressed elements all the more prominent. We may now re-mark the sample sentence to show the rise and fall of the voice: *die /Nachbarn kommen /morgen aus den /Ferien zu\rück*. An important word can be given extra emphasis, if the sense demands it, but the overall pattern of rise and falls remains unchanged. This is the typical intonation of a simple statement.

A statement may contain one or more subordinate clauses: *er /kannte eine alte ·/Frau, die in den ·/Wald ging, um \Holz zu holen* 'he knew an old woman who went into the forest to fetch wood'. Here the intonation pattern may be altered to the extent that the pitch on the significant stresses directly preceding the subordinate clauses (*Frau, Wald*) is somewhat higher than it would otherwise have been. The higher pitch thus signals the coming of a further clause. In the above sentence, the adjective *alte* is not particularly significant and plays no vital part in shaping the intonation pattern. But that could change: *es war keine ·/alte Frau, die in den /Wald ging, sondern eine \junge* 'it wasn't an old woman who went into the forest, but a young one'. Here *alte* takes the overriding stress in the clause concerned.

The stresses are not always so automatically recognizable as in the examples above; some patterns have to be learnt, as in the idiom *es*

/war einmal 'once upon a time' or in the first phrase of the following:
so /müde wir auch ·/sind (or ·/sein mögen), wir müssen /trotzdem
\weitermachen 'however tired we are (may be), we must carry on all
the same'. Notice: sie macht \zu 'she shuts' (e.g. the door,
understood), sie macht sie \zu 'she shuts it (the door), but sie macht
die \Tür zu 'she shuts the door', further \Tür zu! 'shut the door!',
but insistent /Tür \zu! also contrastive Tür /zu, nicht \auf! 'shut the
door, don't open it!' Notice the changing position of the stress in the
following: er springt hin\aus 'he jumps out' as opposed to e.g. er
springt zum \Fenster hinaus 'he jumps out of the window'.

The stresses of the German statement with their characteristic rising
pitch acquire a particular prominence, and something of a lilt, when
that statement is a list of items: im /Zoo waren ·/viele /Tiere zu sehen, /
Löwen und ·/Tiger, dazu /Bären, Ele/fanten, Ka·/mele, und die /
/drolligen \Affen 'there were lots of animals to be seen in the zoo,
lions and tigers, also bears, elephants, camels, and the comical
monkeys'.

Different patterns of intonation may emerge in questions. It is
convenient to distinguish two types according to whether the question
contains an interrogative word or not. In the former the question may
be asked with a falling intonation, as in an ordinary statement: was
\machst du da? 'what are you doing there?' This is then a very
matter-of-fact enquiry. However, the same question can be asked
with a rising intonation: was /machst du da? which implies a feeling of
special interest or concern on the part of the speaker; it sounds
friendly, or polite. Where there is no interrogative word, rising
intonation is usual: bist du /fertig? 'are you finished?', haben Sie noch
/Zeit für uns? 'have you still time for us?' In double questions,
however, the foregoing applies only to the first of the two questions,
in the second the significant stress has falling pitch: trinken Sie gern
/ Tee, oder ziehen Sie \Kaffee vor? 'do you like tea, or do you prefer
coffee?' /willst du, oder willst du \nicht? 'do you want to, or don't
you?'

In conclusion, a reading piece:

Der \Froschkönig

In alten /Zeiten, wo das /Wünschen noch ge·/holfen hat, /lebte ein
/König, dessen /Töchter waren /alle /schön, aber die /jüngste war ·/so
/schön, daß die /Sonne ·/selber, die doch /vieles ge/sehen hat, sich
ver/wunderte, so /oft sie ihr ins Ge\sicht schien. Nahe bei dem /Schloß
des /Königs lag ein /großer /dunkler \Wald, und in dem /Wald unter
einer alten /Linde war ein \Brunnen.

Wenn nun der /Tag sehr ·/heiß war, ging das /Königskind hi/naus in
den /Wald und /setzte sich an den /Rand des kühlen \Brunnens. Und

wenn die /Kleine ·/Langeweile hatte, nahm sie eine /goldene ·/Kugel, /warf sie in die /Höhe und fing sie wieder \auf; und /das war ihr /liebstes \Spielwerk.

Nun trug es sich einmal ·/zu, daß die goldene /Kugel der / Königstochter /nicht in ihr /Händchen fiel, das sie in die /Höhe gehalten hatte, sondern vor/bei auf die /Erde schlug und geradezu ins /Wasser hi\neinrollte. Die /Königstochter folgte ihr mit den /Augen ·/nach, aber die /Kugel ver\schwand, und der /Brunnen war /tief, ·/so /tief, daß man keinen \Grund sah.

Da fing sie an zu /weinen und /weinte immer ·/lauter und konnte sich /gar nicht \trösten. Und wie sie so ·/klagte, /rief ihr /jemand \zu: 'Was /hast du, /Königstochter? Du /schreist ja, daß sich ein /Stein er\barmen möchte.' Sie sah sich /um, woher die /Stimme /käme, da er/blickte sie einen /Frosch, der seinen /dicken, /häßlichen /Kopf aus dem \Wasser streckte.

(/Jakob und /Wilhelm \Grimm)

2. Orthographical Matters

WE refer to significant divergencies from English usage; they concern division of words and punctuation.

DIVISION OF WORDS

Simple words

Division is basically by syllables which, where possible, begin with a consonant. Hence one divides *ge-hört* 'heard' (perf. part.), *hö-ren* 'to hear', *hör-te* 'heard' (pret. sg.), *lär-mend* 'noisy'; examples where there is no consonant: *bau-en* 'to build' *Feu-er* 'fire', *Stau-ung* 'congestion', *Oze-an* 'ocean', *na-iv* 'naive'. But purely orthographical conventions may determine how the separated syllables are to be written, as follows.

Two consonants are split up: *Men-ge* 'crowd', *Hit-ze* 'heat', *fal-len* 'to fall', *ck* becoming *k-k*, e.g. *dek-ken* (*decken*) 'to cover'; *ß* is not divided: *schlie-ßen* 'to shut'. Certain combinations are understandably not divisible, as *ch, sch*, thus *Sa-che* 'thing', *mi-schen* 'to mix', but neither is *st*, thus *Ki-ste* 'box'. Three or more consonants are divided before the last one: *kämp-fen* 'to fight', *kämpf-te* 'fought' (pret. sg.), but *ch, sch, st* count as one consonant: *Ler-che* 'lark', *klat-schen* 'to clap', *sech-ste* 'sixth'.

When *l* or *r* follow *p, t, k*, or *b, d, g*, in foreign words, no division is made: *Diszi-plin* 'discipline', *Fa-brik* 'factory', and the same applies to *gn*, e.g. *Si-gnal* 'signal'; *ph, th* count as one consonant: *Diph-thong* 'diphthong'.

A division should never produce a single vowel, thus *April* 'April' is indivisible, but a diphthong may stand alone, as *Ei-che* 'oak'.

Compound words

The primary division is into component parts: *dar-auf* 'on it', *war-um* 'why', *Donners-tag* 'Thursday', *Wochen-ende* 'week-end', *ver-antworten* 'to be responsible for', *beweis-kräftig* 'conclusive'.

Foreign nouns are to be similarly separated, thus *Manu-skript* 'manuscript', though only good Latin scholars will appreciate why, for example, *Inter-esse* 'interest' is so divided.

PUNCTUATION

Punctuation is more regulated than it is in English, the most important differences concerning the use of the comma.

According to the general rule, a comma must stand before a new clause: *er erzählte von dem Ereignis, das sein Leben veränderte* 'he told of the event which changed his life', *ein Mensch, der weiß, was er will* 'a person who knows what he wants', *sie träumen davon, einmal in ein Land zu kommen, wo die Freiheit heimisch ist* 'they dream of one day coming to a country where liberty is indigenous', *ich verstehe nicht, warum er nicht kommt* 'I don't understand why he isn't coming', *schade, daß Sie nicht mitmachen!* 'a pity you're not taking part!', *die Krähen sind nicht nur Aasfresser, sondern auch eifrige Mäusejäger* 'crows are not only carrion-feeders but also keen mouse-hunters', *ich kann mich noch immer an den Tag erinnern, als ich zum erstenmal zur Schule ging* 'I can still remember the day when I first went to school'.

To the overall rule we notice certain exceptions. There is usually no comma before a single infinitive not further qualified: *sie hat vor einzukaufen* 'she intends to go shopping', contrasting with *sie hat vor, ein Haus zu kaufen* 'she intends to buy a house'; on the other hand: *ihr Vorhaben, zu kaufen, schien mir abwegig* 'her intention to buy seemed to me mistaken'. Further: *ich habe das Gefühl beobachtet zu werden*, but *ich habe das Gefühl, von der Polizei beobachtet zu werden* 'I feel I'm being watched by the police', also *er kam zu schauen*, but before two infinitives: *er kam, zu schauen und zu staunen* 'he came to gaze and wonder'.

A comma is not used before *und* when it precedes the last item on a list: *Erbsen, Bohnen, Kartoffeln und Zwiebeln* 'peas, beans, potatoes, and onions'. There is similarly no comma when *und* links two clauses having the same subject: *er begleitete sie bis zur Tür ihrer Wohnung und kehrte dann nach Hause zurück* 'he accompanied her to the door of her flat, and then returned home', but with different subjects: *der Schuß ging daneben, und der Hase kam mit dem Leben davon* 'the shot missed, and the hare got safely away'.

In conclusion, another, small difference regarding the colon. A word following a colon is often written with a capital, cf. *Karneval in Köln: Vier Nächte, die ich nie vergesse!* 'Carnival in Cologne: four nights I'll never forget!'

ACCIDENCE

3. Nouns

Gender and Declension

THE traditional division of nouns into strong and weak is of historic interest, but has little practical relevance for the language of today and cannot therefore be the basis of our exposition. We prefer three primary divisions according to the three genders, each with its own sections according to the formation of the plural. We distinguish in part between common and proper nouns.

Although the number of different terminations is quite small, and (if the gender be known) to a fair degree predictable, their overall distribution is nevertheless tantalizingly complex, giving rise to many types of declension. These, in turn, may be further complicated by the presence or otherwise of umlaut, not to mention that certain nouns do not change in the plural at all.

Variation in gender

Given the complex circumstances just mentioned, a degree of instability is, in the nature of things, only to be expected. There may be hesitation as to gender. This is evident in the case of certain foreign words, with fluctuation notably between masculine and neuter, e.g. *der* or *das Kata'pult* 'catapult', *der* or *das Radar* 'radar'; the feminine is less involved, but cf. *die* or *das Soda* 'soda'. It is difficult to say which of these alternatives is commoner. In other examples, however, one form may have wider currency than its rival. Both *der Dschungel* and *das Dschungel* 'jungle' are acceptable, but the former—its gender corresponds to that of the native synonym *der Urwald*—is more commonly found and could, one day, become the sole standard. At any rate, there is evolution in these matters, and it is not without interest to note that *die Dschungel* was once a third alternative.

Variation in gender also occurs among native words. *Dotter* 'yolk' may be used as a neuter (after the gender of synonymous *Eigelb*, the ordinary expression in North Germany) though the traditional masculine is also often found. But it is at local, non-literary level, that differences are most frequent; indeed, in such use, *Dotter* can be heard as a feminine. Other examples: standard *der Teller* 'plate', *die Butter* 'butter', *das Tuch* 'cloth', but locally (southern) *das Teller*, *der Butter*, (northern) *der Tuch*. Diversity means competition, which in turn engenders change. *Das Rückgrat* 'backbone' was, until this century, often *der Rückgrat* in standard language, too, masculine being its original gender, as still in *der Grat* 'ridge', the second element in the word. Only a few decades ago, the present standard *die Geisel* 'hostage' was normally *der Geisel*.

Gender differences may be functionally significant, as when stylistic registers are implied. In formal use, *Virus* 'virus' is treated as a neuter, as it is in Latin. But meanwhile this medical term has become a well-known word and, in casual style, has acquired the masculine gender, so matching most other nouns ending in *-us*. Compare further *der Filter* in homely use, hence *der Kaffeefilter* 'coffee-filter', *das Filter* in more technical contexts, hence *das Ölfilter* 'oil-filter'. The same difference plays at least some part in the as yet unresolved competition between *der/das Liter* 'litre' and *der/das Meter* 'metre'.

Some nouns have two genders corresponding to different meanings, e.g. *der Band* 'volume', *das Band* 'bond, ribbon' (see further below), *der Bund* 'federation, league', *das Bund* 'bundle, bunch (of keys)', *der Erbe* 'heir', *das Erbe* 'heritage', *der Gehalt* 'content', *das Gehalt* 'salary', *der Mo'ment* 'moment (of time)', *das Mo'ment* 'motive, factor', *der Schild* 'shield', *das Schild* 'sign-board, name-plate', *der See* 'lake', *die See* 'sea', *der Verdienst* 'earnings', *das Verdienst* 'merit'. Notice *der Balg* 'hide, skin, bellows, brat', but in the last (figurative) sense commonly *das Balg*, further *der Wurm* 'worm', but figuratively *das Wurm* '(little) mite', the shift of gender prompted by *d a s Kind* 'child'. Distinguish between the very frequently occurring *der Teil* 'part, section' and the less usual *das Teil* 'part, object, *Stück*', hence *Ersatzteil* (i.e. *Ersatzstück*) 'spare part', properly neuter, but since the semantic nuance is, in this case, not important, the compound tends to be treated as a masculine after the gender of the commoner simplex. On the other hand, *das Gegenteil* (i.e. *Gegenstück*) 'opposite (of)' is not so affected and its neuter gender unchallenged. The following, etymologically unrelated, words have, by a quirk of evolution, fallen together as homophonous pairs: *der Kiefer* 'jaw', *die Kiefer* 'pine-tree', *der Leiter* 'leader, conductor', *die Leiter* 'ladder', *der Tor* 'fool', *das Tor* 'large door, goal', likewise *der Hut* 'hat', beside *die Hut* 'care, keeping', a word confined to high style except in the everyday phrase *auf der Hut sein* 'be on one's guard'. On the other hand, in spite of their equally disparate meanings, *der Kunde* 'customer', *die Kunde* 'tidings' and *die Steuer* 'tax, rate', *das Steuer* 'steering-wheel, rudder' are etymologically akin, as are also *der Heide* 'heathen', *die Heide* 'heath'.

Variation in form

A degree of instability is, on occasion, apparent in the case endings. It may be that the new has not quite replaced the old. Nowadays, *Geck* 'dandy' ordinarily has sg. gen. *Gecks*, dat. *Geck* (p. 36). Previously, this word inflected like *Bär* (p. 35), hence sg. obl. *Gecken*, a form which still appears, now and then, in print. The fashionable, everyday word *Typ* 'type' (shortened from *Typus*, p. 36) regularly goes like *Geck*, but may, by analogy, turn up in the sg. obl. as *Typen*.

Variation is most prominent, however, in the formation of the plural, and here the reasons are generally transparent, too. For examples, *Mast* 'mast' traditionally belongs to the small group of masculine nouns having *-en* as the plural suffix, hence pl. *Masten* (p. 36). But meanwhile an alternative pl. *Maste* has come into being under the influence of the much more numerous group with plural suffix *-e* (p. 32). By the same token, *Muskeln* 'muscles' and others like it, also *Vettern* 'cousins' (p. 38), may be given as *Muskel, Vetter*, following the very much stronger group exemplified by *Bengel*, etc. (p. 40). *Kran* 'crane' and *Schalk* 'scamp, joker' have as their plurals indifferently *Krane, Schalke*, or *Kräne, Schälke*. They belong to a group of nouns, some of which have the plural with, but others without, umlaut (p. 32). The present words originally belonged to the latter, but have in the meantime been (so to speak) half assimilated to the former. It is to be expected that some day one of the variants will become dominant, but which is still in the stars. The same goes for *Gene'ral* 'general'; the plural can as easily be *Gene'rale* as *Gene'räle*, both patterns being commonplace (p. 33). The neuter word *Mal* 'mark' has pl. *Male* (p. 46), likewise such compounds as *Merkmal* 'mark, characteristic', *Muttermal* 'birth-mark', but *Denkmal* 'monument' has now *Denkmäler*, and similarly *Wicht* 'fellow', pl. *Wichte* (p. 31), but *Bösewicht* 'villain', pl. *Bösewichter*, secondary developments following a different declension (p. 34). Regional variations are by no means rare, and may appear in print; we refer (p. 41) to southern *Krägen* 'collars', *Wägen* 'cars', *Bögen* 'bows, arches', innovating forms with distinctive umlaut, beside northern and central German *Kragen, Wagen, Bogen*.

A number of nouns have two plurals according to meaning; the more common are: *die Bank*, pl. *Bänke* 'benches', *Banken* '(money-) banks'; *das Band*, pl. *Bande* 'bonds', *Bänder* 'ribbons'; *der Bau*, pl. *Baue* 'burrows', *Bauten* 'buildings'; *der Block*, pl. *Blöcke* 'blocks (of wood, stone)', *Blocks* 'blocks (of houses), (writing) pads'; *das Ding*, pl. *Dinge* 'things', *Dinger* 'trivial things'; *das Gesicht*, pl. *Gesichte* 'visions', *Gesichter* 'faces'; *der Laden*, pl. *Laden* 'shutters', *Läden* 'shops'; *die Mutter*, pl. *Mütter* 'mothers', *Muttern* 'nuts (for bolts)'. *Das Wort* 'word, saying' has pl. *Worte* in colloquial style, but the (not infrequently ignored) literary prescription is *Wörter* if the sense is 'single words', cf. *Wörterbuch* 'dictionary', *Worte* only when the meaning is 'connected words, sayings'—the plural of *Sprichwort*

'proverb' is nevertheless always *Sprichwörter*. Two originally independent words have fallen together in *der Strauß*, hence the totally
unrelated meanings 'ostrich, bunch (of flowers)', but they are
differentiated in the plural as *Strauße* and *Sträuße* respectively.

In one example the two plurals reflect stylistic differences: *das
Land*, pl. *Lande* (poetic), *Länder* (prosaic) 'lands, countries, provinces'.
In another case simplex and compound vary: *das Wasser* 'water'
occasionally forms a plural, as in the idiomatic *er ist mit allen Wassern
gewaschen* 'he's a sly customer'; on the other hand, the compound
Abwasser 'waste water (domestic, industrial)' is frequently used in the
plural, which is then *Abwässer*. Notice *die Sau* lit. 'sow', commonly
synonymous with *das Schwein* 'pig', also figuratively 'filthy pig', pl.
Säue, but speaking of wild pigs pl. *Sauen* (= *Wildschweine*)—the wild
sow is called *die Bache*.

Variation in gender and form

Variation involving gender as well as form may also be encountered to
a small extent. Beside the ordinary term *die Ecke* 'corner' there exists
a, now chiefly southern, variant *das Eck*, as such not in general use,
but standard in certain compounds, cf. *Dreieck* 'triangle', *Rechteck*
'rectangle' (p. 47). In other cases semantic or stylistic differences may
appear. Thus *die Schnecke* 'snail' has an Upper German variant *der
Schneck* (p. 36), in its literal sense restricted to local use. But only this
latter can have the figurative meaning seen in the expression *ein süßer
Schneck* 'a sweet (little) girl', in which sense the form is widely known
outside its Upper German home. A regional difference is seen again
in the southern *der Karren* (p. 40), northern *die Karre* 'cart, (slang)
old car, banger'. Compare further *das Rohr* (p. 46), also *die Röhre*
'pipe, tube', in these basic meanings interchangeable, but in certain
specialized senses one or the other, as *Rohr* 'reed', *Röhre* 'valve
(radio)', or such compounds as *Fernrohr* 'telescope', *Leuchtröhre*
'neon tube'; regional differences, too, may appear: southern *Backrohr*,
northern *Backröhre* 'oven'.

Common nouns

MASCULINE

(The sections are: plural ending *-e*, *-er*, *-en*, *-n*, *-s*, plural without an
ending, special plurals; for adjectival declension, see pp. 52 f.)

Plural ending -e

This is the main class. One distinguishes two large groups: nouns of one, and nouns of more than one, syllable.

Nouns of one syllable

	Sg.		Pl.
nom.	*der Weg* 'way'		*die Wege*
acc.	*den Weg*		*die Wege*
gen.	*des Weges*		*der Wege*
dat.	*dem Weg(e)*		*den Wegen*

Sg. gen. *Wegs* is an occasional alternative, but only *-es* is possible if the word already ends in a sibilant, hence *Bus* 'bus', gen. *Busses*, *Riß* 'tear, fissure', *Sitz* 'seat', gen. *Risses*, *Sitzes*, likewise *Fisch* 'fish', gen. *Fisches*.

Sg. dat. *Wege* is commoner in written than spoken style. In most instances, the alternative forms are optional, when feeling for sentence rhythm or literary propriety will play a part. However, nouns ending in a vowel do not normally have the longer form, cf. *Schuh*, *Bau*, *Floh*, below. The longer form is never used in certain phrases, as *aus Stein gehauen* 'hewn out of stone', *von Ort zu Ort* 'from place to place'. But in other expressions it may be obligatory, as *jemanden zu Rate ziehen* 'to call upon someone for advice' (*Rat*).

Words of foreign origin usually go as follows: *Film* 'film', sg. gen. *Films*, dat. *Film*, but e.g. *Text* 'text', preferably gen. *Textes*, for euphonic reasons and cf. *Bus*, above.

Among the exceptionally large number of nouns so declined are *Berg* 'hill, mountain', *Fleck* (cf. *Flecken*, p. 40) 'patch, spot', *Herd* 'hearth, cooking-stove', *Kerl* 'chap, guy', *Kern* 'kernel, nucleus', *Rest* 'remainder', *Schelm* 'rascal', *Specht* 'woodpecker', *Steg* 'footbridge', *Stern* 'star', *Wert* 'value'; *Schreck* (especially colloquial) 'fright' has no plural, cf. *Schrecken*, p. 40.

Blick 'look', *Blitz* '(flash of) lightning', *Hirsch* 'stag', *Knirps* 'little fellow, collapsible umbrella', *Ring* 'ring', *Schild* 'shield', *Schlips* 'tie', *Schlitz* 'slot', *Schnitt* 'cut', *Schritt* 'step', *Sinn* 'sense', *Stich* 'sting', *Strick* 'thin rope, cord, line', *Tisch* 'table', *Wicht* 'fellow' (p. 29), *Wind* 'wind', *Wirt* '(mine) host'.

Brief 'letter', *Krieg* 'war', *Sieg* 'victory'.

Eid 'oath', *Feind* 'enemy', *Greis* 'old man', *Keim* 'germ', *Kreis* 'circle', *Pfeil* 'arrow', *Preis* 'price, prize', *Steig* 'path', *Stein* 'stone', *Teich* 'pond', *Teil* 'part' (p. 28), *Wein* 'wine'.

Freund 'friend'.

Further, certain nouns with stem vowels *a*, *o*, *u*, also *au*, including *Aal* 'eel', *Anker* 'anchor', *Arm* 'arm', *Dachs* 'badger', *Farn* 'fern', *Grad* 'degree', *Grat* 'ridge, crest (of a mountain range)', *Halm* 'blade (of grass), straw (for drinking)', *Kran* (pl. also *Kräne*) 'crane', *Klaps* 'slap', *Lachs* 'salmon', *Mast* (pl. also *Masten*) 'mast', *Pfad* 'path', *Schalk* (pl. also *Schälke*) 'scamp, joker', *Spalt* 'cleft, narrow opening', *Star* 'starling', *Tag* 'day'.

Dolch 'dagger', *Dorsch* 'cod (from the Baltic)', *Forst* (pl. also *Forsten*) '(managed) forest', *Horst* 'eyry', *Klops* 'meat-ball', *Molch* 'newt (or newt-like creature)', *Mond* [oo] 'moon', *Ort* 'place, village', *Schlot* 'chimney-stack, funnel, lout', *Stoff* 'material', *Strolch* 'vagabond, scoundrel', *Thron* 'throne'.

Druck 'print, impression', *Flur* 'vestibule', *Fund* 'find', *Gurt* '(cartridge, seat) belt', *Huf* 'hoof', *Hund* 'dog', *Kurs* 'course, track, rate of exchange', *Luchs* 'lynx', *Punkt* 'point, dot', *Ruf* 'call', *Schuft* 'scoundrel', *Schuh* (sg. gen. *Schuhs*, dat. *Schuh*) 'shoe'.

Bau (sg. gen. *Baus*, dat. *Bau*) 'burrow', *Laut* 'sound', *Strauß* 'ostrich'.

But the majority of nouns with modifiable vowels have umlaut in the plural, thus *Ast* 'branch', pl. *Äste*. Among other nouns forming their plural in this way are *Arzt* (sg. gen. *Arztes*) 'doctor', *Bach* 'stream', *Balg* 'skin, hide, bellows, brat' (p. 28), *Ball* 'ball', *Band* 'volume', *Bart* 'beard', *Brand* 'fire, conflagration', *Dampf* 'steam', *Fall* 'fall, case', *Gang* 'corridor, course (menu), gear (in a vehicle)', *Gast* 'guest', *Hahn* 'cock', *Hang* 'slope', *Kahn* '(small) boat, punt', *Kamm* 'comb', *Klang* 'sound', *Kran* (pl. also *Krane*) 'crane', *Kranz* 'garland, wreath', *Markt* 'market', *Marsch* 'march', *Napf* '(small) basin', *Pfahl* 'stake, post', *Plan* 'plan', *Platz* 'place, square', *Rang* 'rank', *Saal* (pl. *Säle*) 'large room', *Sarg* 'coffin', *Satz* 'sentence', *Schatz* 'treasure', *Schlag* 'blow', *Schrank* 'cupboard', *Schwan* 'swan', *Schwanz* 'tail', *Stab* 'staff', *Stall* 'stable', *Stamm* 'stem, tribe', *Strand* 'shore, beach', *Tanz* 'dance', *Wall* 'rampart', *Zahn* 'tooth', *Zwang* 'constraint'.

Block 'block (of wood, stone)', pl. *Blöcke*, similarly *Bock* 'buck, trestle', *Chor* [k] 'chorus, choir', *Floh* (sg. gen. *Flohs*, dat. *Floh*) 'flea', *Frosch* 'frog', *Hof* 'yard, farm, court', *Kloß* (pl. *Klöße*) 'dumpling, rissole', *Klotz* 'block (of wood), blockhead', *Knopf* 'button', *Kopf* 'head', *Rock* 'coat, jacket', *Sohn* 'son', *Stock* 'stick', *Storch* 'stork', *Strom* 'large river, torrent', *Topf* 'pot', *Ton* 'tone, sound', *Trog* 'trough', *Wolf* 'Wolf'.

Bund 'federation, league', pl. *Bünde*, similarly *Busch* 'bush', *Fluch* 'curse', *Flug* 'flight', *Fluß* (pl. *Flüsse*) 'river', *Fuchs* 'fox', *Fuß* (pl. *Füße*) 'foot', *Grund* 'bottom, reason', *Hut* 'hat', *Schuß* (pl. *Schüsse*) 'shot', *Schwur* 'vow', *Stuhl* 'chair', *Turm* 'tower', *Wurf* 'throw', *Zug* 'train, march, procession'.

Bauch 'belly, abdomen', pl. *Bäuche*, similarly *Baum* 'tree', *Brauch* 'custom', *Gaul* 'horse, nag', *Raum* 'room', *Saum* 'seam', *Schlauch* 'pipe, hose', *Strauß* 'bunch (of flowers)', *Traum* 'dream', *Zaun* 'fence'.

Nouns of more than one syllable

Sg. nom.	*der Pfirsich* 'peach'	Pl.	*die Pfirsiche*
acc.	*den Pfirsich*		*die Pfirsiche*
gen.	*des Pfirsichs*		*der Pfirsiche*
dat.	*dem Pfirsich*		*den Pfirsichen*

Nouns ending in a sibilant (see under *Weg*, p. 31) have sg. gen. in *-es*, thus *Kiebitz* 'lapwing', gen. *Kiebitzes*.

Among nouns declined as above are *Kranich* 'crane (bird)', *Teppich* 'carpet', *Habicht* 'goshawk', *Käfig* 'cage', *König* 'king', *Hering* 'herring', and the many nouns formed with the living suffix *-ling*, as *Flüchtling* 'refugee', *Keimling* 'seedling', *Neuling* 'novice', *Schmetterling* 'butterfly', further *Monat* 'month' (p. 15), *Mo'rast* 'marsh', *Iltis* (pl. *Iltisse*) 'polecat'.

Next, miscellaneous words of foreign origin, including *Appa'rat* 'apparatus, appliance', *As'pekt* 'aspect', *Atlas* (pl. *Atlasse*, also *At'lanten*, p. 41) 'atlas', *Cha'rakter* (pl. *Charak'tere*) 'character', *Dia'log* 'dialogue', *Diph'thong* 'diphthong', *Globus* (pl. *Globusse*, also *Globen*, p. 36), '(terrestrial) globe' *Im'puls* 'impulse' (often in pl. with sense 'ideas, suggestions'), *Kaktus* (pl. *Kaktusse*, more formally *Kak'teen*, p. 36) 'cactus', *Ko'loß* (pl. *Ko'losse*) 'colossus', *Kompaß* (pl. *Kompasse*) 'compass', *Kon'flikt* 'conflict', *Mo'ment* 'moment (of time)', *Pinguin* 'penguin', *Re'flex* 'reflex', *Spi'on* 'spy', *Tre'sor* 'safe', *Tri'umph* 'triumph', *Zirkus* (pl. *Zirkusse*) 'circus'.

Certain foreign endings are typically associated with this declension, e.g. *-al*: *Po'kal* 'goblet, (sports) cup', *Vo'kal* 'vowel', *-ar* or *-är*: *Kommen'tar* 'commentary', *Missio'nar*, South German also *Missio'när* 'missionary', *Aktio'när* 'shareholder (further examples below), *-ier* [-iɐ]: *Kava'lier* 'man polite towards women, beau', *Offi'zier* 'officer', *-an*: *Fa'san* (though pl. now also *Fa'sanen*, p. 35) 'pheasant', *Oze'an* 'ocean', *Ro'man* 'novel', and the half-foreign *Grobian* 'ruffian'.

A small number of nouns have umlaut in the plural, as *Ka'nal* 'canal, drain', *Kardi'nal* 'cardinal', *Al'tar* 'altar', *Pa'last* 'palace', *Bischof* 'bishop', *Te'nor* 'tenor', pl. *Ka'näle*, *Bischöfe*, etc. *Gene'ral* 'general' makes the plural indifferently *Gene'rale* or *Gene'räle*, with *Admi'ral* 'admiral' imitating.

As with native words (see below), certain foreign words may, for euphonic reasons, optionally have sg. gen. *-es*, cf. from items above

As'pekt, Kon'flikt, Mo'ment, Tri'umph 'triumph', *Pa'last*, gen. *As'pekts* or *As'pektes*, etc.

Many dissyllabic nouns formed with unaccented prefixes follow this declension, but through the close association of the stressed syllable with a corresponding monosyllabic simplex, alternative sg. gen. *-es*, dat. *-e*, are also found, thus *Entwurf* (pl. *Entwürfe*) 'design, draft, plan', gen. *Entwurf(e)s*, dat. *Entwurf(e)*, cf. *Wurf*, p. 32. Gen. *-es* may, in any case, sometimes be preferred for euphonic reasons, thus *Befund* (pl. *Befunde*) 'finding', gen. commonly *Befundes*. Nouns of comparable structure often have no corresponding simplex, but nevertheless follow suit, as *Bericht* 'report', *Beweis* 'proof', *Bezirk* 'area, district', *Erfolg* (pl. *Erfolge*) 'success', *Ertrag* (pl. *Erträge*) 'yield', *Gewinn* 'gain, profit', *Verlust* (pl. *Verluste*) 'loss', *Vermerk* 'note, observation, endorsement', *Versuch* (pl. *Versuche*) 'attempt'. Nouns formed with stressed prefixes, on the other hand, are not so liable to close association with the simplexes and are less likely to have the alternative endings, thus *Ausblick* 'view', gen. usually *Ausblicks*, dat. *Ausblick*, similarly *Umzug* (pl. *Umzüge*) 'procession', *Unfall* (pl. *Unfälle*) 'accident', *Vorhang* (pl. *Vorhänge*) 'curtain'. The same is in part true when simplexes are compounded with another word, e.g. *Bahnhof* (pl. *Bahnhöfe*) 'station', *Rotwein* 'claret', gen. *Bahnhofs*, *Rotweins*, dat. *Bahnhof, Rotwein*. But, at the same time, rhythmic considerations may be involved. One rather expects, e.g. *Hauptmann* 'captain', gen. *Hauptmanns*, but *Ehemann* 'husband', gen. *Ehemannes*.

Plural ending *-er*

A minor class, consisting of the nouns given below, with umlaut in the plural where applicable.

Sg.	nom.	*der Geist* 'mind, spirit'	Pl.	*die Geister*
	acc.	*den Geist*		*die Geister*
	gen.	*des Geistes*		*der Geister*
	dat.	*dem Geist(e)*		*den Geistern*

Singular variants as under *Weg*, p. 33.

Thus *Gott* (pl. *Götter*) 'god', *Leib* 'body', *Mann* (pl. *Männer*) 'man, husband', *Mund* (pl. *Münder*) 'mouth', *Rand* (pl. *Ränder*) 'edge, rim', *Ski* [ʃii] (sg. gen. *Skis*, dat. *Ski*) 'ski', *Strauch* (pl. *Sträucher*) 'bush', *Wald* (pl. *Wälder*) 'wood, forest', *Wurm* (pl. *Würmer*) 'worm'.

Irrtum 'error', *Reichtum* 'riches, wealth', sg. gen. *Irrtums*, pl. *Irrtümer*, etc., and the compound *Bösewicht* 'villain', see p. 29.

Plural ending *-en*

Two types are distinguished, the differences applying to the singular only. The first type, numerically by far the larger, declines as follows.

Sg. nom. *der Bär* 'bear'   Pl. *die Bären*
    acc. *den Bären*   *die Bären*
    gen. *des Bären*   *der Bären*
    dat. *dem Bären*   *den Bären*

Thus *Bub* (South German) 'lad', *Christ* 'Christian', *Fink* 'finch', *Fürst* 'prince', *Graf* 'count', *Held* 'hero', *Hirt* 'herdsman', *Lump* 'lout', *Mensch* 'person', *Narr* 'fool', *Oberst* 'colonel', *Ochs* 'ox' (also *Ochse*, p. 37), *Prinz* '(royal) prince', *Tor* (mainly literary) 'fool', *Vorfahr* 'ancestor'.

The most numerous constituents of this declension are nouns of foreign origin stressed on the final syllable, as *Ath'let* 'athlete', *Archi'tekt* 'architect', *Astro'nom* 'astronomer', *Ban'dit* 'bandit', *Demo'krat* 'democrat', *Geo'graph* 'geographer', *Kame'rad* 'comrade', *Kandi'dat* 'candidate', *Katho'lik* 'catholic', *Phan'tast* 'visionary', *Philo'soph* 'philosopher', *Pi'lot* 'pilot', *Re'krut* 'recruit', *Ty'rann* 'tyrant'; also *Fa'san* 'pheasant', pl. *Fa'sanen* now commoner than *Fa'sane*, p. 33. Three endings associated with this declension are particularly common; they are *-ant*: *Dia'mant* 'diamond', *Ele'fant* 'elephant', *Tra'bant* 'satellite', *-ent*: *Diri'gent* 'conductor (musical)', *Interes'sent* 'interested party', *Rezen'sent* 'reviewer (of books, etc.)', and above all the very productive *-ist*: *Germa'nist* 'student of German language and culture, *'Gros'sist* 'wholesaler', *Harfe'nist* 'harpist', *Proku'rist* 'chief clerk', *Spezia'list* 'specialist', *Sta'tist* 'extra (theatre, film)'.

One noun takes *-n* in the oblique singular: *Herr* 'gentleman, Lord, Mr', obl. sg. *Herrn*, pl. *Herren*.

In casual conversation, there is a tendency to ignore the redundant sg. acc. dat. inflexion—the genitive is not likely to occur at this level, p. 149—thus *ich seh' den Polizist* 'I see the policeman', *ich hab's dem Polizist gesagt* 'I've told the policeman'. Such use is partly a matter of education, and many feel it to be intolerably substandard, though the same speakers may well adopt such forms when talking to children. In certain cases, however, the uninflected forms are well established, e.g. acc. dat. *Oberst* 'colonel', common in speaking and not unknown in writing, but still *Obersten* in 'correct' style, according to the initiated, and the same may be claimed for other nouns from the above list, e.g. *Fasan, Diamant, Elefant*. A stylistic nuance may be discernible: one could conceivably hear (and read) *ich höre den Fink zwitschern* 'I hear the finch chirping', but the same in more literary style *ich höre den Finken schlagen*. In this connection we may note that the compounds *Buchfink* 'chaffinch', *Grünfink* 'greenfinch', etc.—not to mention *Dreckfink* 'filthy fellow'—never have the inflexion (but of course gen. sg. *Buchfinken*, etc.). It is not surprising that a term like *Teddybär*, so often in the mouths of children, also seldom takes the inflexion in naturally used language. There is thus some movement towards the second type of declension next mentioned below; see also p. 28 f.

In the case of the second type it is further necessary to distinguish between (A) nouns of one, and (B) and (C) nouns of more than one, syllable.

(A)   Sg. nom. *der Strahl* 'beam, ray'   Pl. *die Strahlen*
        acc. *den Strahl*   *die Strahlen*
        gen. *des Strahles*   *der Strahlen*
        dat. *dem Strahl(e)*   *den Strahlen*

Singular variants as under *Weg*, p. 31.

Thus *Dorn* 'thorn', *Geck* (sg. gen. *Gecks*, dat. *Geck*; see p. 29) 'dandy', *Latsch* (familiar) 'shoe, slipper', *Mast* (pl. also *Maste*, p. 32) 'mast', *Nerv* 'nerve', *Pfau* 'peacock', *Psalm* 'psalm', *Schmerz* 'pain', *Spatz* 'sparrow', *Staat* 'state', *Typ* (also *Typus*, below) 'type', *Zins* 'rent', pl. interest'. On *Schneck* 'girl' (going like *Geck*) see p. 30.

(B)   Sg. nom. *der Autor* 'author'   Pl. *die Au'toren*
        acc. *den Autor*   *die Au'toren*
        gen. *des Autors*   *der Au'toren*
        dat. *dem Autor*   *den Au'toren*

Thus *Di'rektor* 'director, headmaster', *Doktor* 'doctor', *Pro'fessor* 'professor', *Re'aktor* 'reactor', *Tumor* 'tumour', also *Dämon* (pl. *Dä'monen*) 'demon'. It will be noticed that only foreign words are involved in the foregoing, the syllable before the plural termination taking the accent and causing a shift of stress. But a native word exceptionally following this declension retains initial stress throughout: *Lorbeer* 'laurel', *Untertan* 'subject (of a state, etc.)'. The foreign word *Papa'gei* 'parrot' likewise retains its stress.

(C)   Sg. nom. *der Ritus* 'rite'   Pl. *die Riten*
        acc. *den Ritus*   *die Riten*
        gen. *des Ritus*   *der Riten*
        dat. *dem Ritus*   *den Riten*

Thus *Genius* 'genus (spirit)', *Globus* (formal style, otherwise pl. *Globusse*, p. 33) '(terrestrial) globe', *Kubus* 'cube', *Mythus* (also *Mythos*) 'myth', *Radius* 'radius', *Rhythmus* 'rhythm', *Typus* (also *Typ*, above) 'type', *Virus* (masc. in popular style, otherwise neut., p. 49) 'virus', *Zyklus* 'cycle (of years, etc.)'. Further, all nouns ending in *-ismus*, many of which can form plurals, as *Angli'zismus* 'Anglicism', *Orga'nismus* 'organism', pl. *Angli'zismen*, etc. *Kaktus* 'cactus' has pl. *Kak'teen* [-'teeən]; also a less formal declension, p. 33.

Plural ending -n

One distinguishes four groups. The most significant consists of those nouns which end in -e, excepting the few mentioned below under *Name* and, of course, those forming the quite distinct adjectival declension, pp. 52 f.

	Sg. nom.	*der Affe* 'monkey'	Pl.	*die Affen*
	acc.	*den Affen*		*die Affen*
	gen.	*des Affen*		*der Affen*
	dat.	*dem Affen*		*den Affen*

Thus *Bote* 'messenger', *Bube* 'knave', *Bursche* 'adolescent boy', *Drache* 'dragon', *Erbe* 'heir', *Falke* 'falcon, hawk', *Fatzke* '(conceited) fool', *Gatte* 'husband' (rather formal, pl. *die Gatten* 'the married couple'), *Gefärte* 'companion', *Genosse* 'comrade' (also political), *Geselle* 'journeyman, pal, chap', *Hase* 'hare', *Heide* 'heathen', *Insasse* 'inmate, occupant', *Knabe* 'boy' (mainly formal style), *Junge* 'boy', *Laie* 'layman', *Löwe* 'lion', *Neffe* 'nephew', *Ochse* (also *Ochs*, p. 35) 'ox', *Pate* 'godfather', *Pfaffe* 'priest' (derogatory), *Rabe* 'raven', *Riese* 'giant', *Schurke* 'scoundrel', *Schütze* 'marksman, rifleman', *Sklave* 'slave', *Zeuge* 'witness (person)'.

Many names of nationalities and the like follow this declension, including *Böhme* 'Bohemian', *Däne* 'Dane', *Friese* 'Frisian', *Fran'zose* 'Frenchman', *Hesse* 'Hessian', *Jude* 'Jew', *Portu'giese* 'Portuguese', *Sachse* 'Saxon'.

Also many foreign words (stressed on the penultimate), among them *Ex'perte* 'expert', *Ga'nove* 'crook, scoundrel', *Kol'lege* 'colleague', *Kom'plize* 'accomplice', *Polito'loge* 'political scientist', *Schim'panse* 'chimpanzee'.

The remaining three, all minor, groups (A), (B), and (C), are differentiated by varying declension in the singular.

(A)	Sg. nom.	*der Bauer* 'farmer'	Pl.	*die Bauern*
	acc.	*den Bauern*		*die Bauern*
	gen.	*des Bauern*		*der Bauern*
	dat.	*dem Bauern*		*den Bauern*

Thus *Nachbar* (alternatively according to B) 'neighbour', otherwise only proper names of peoples: *Bayer* 'Bavarian', *Pommer* 'Pomeranian', *Ungar* 'Hungarian'.

(B)	Sg. nom.	*der Konsul* 'consul'	Pl.	*die Konsuln*
	acc.	*den Konsul*		*die Konsuln*
	gen.	*des Konsuls*		*der Konsuln*
	dat.	*dem Konsul*		*den Konsuln*

Thus *Nachbar* (alternatively according to A) 'neighbour', also *See* (pl. *Seen* ['zeeən] 'lake', further *Muskel* 'muscle', *Pan'toffel* 'slipper', *Stachel* 'prickle, sting', but in ordinary speaking mostly pl. *Muskel*, etc., similarly *Vetter* 'cousin' (p. 29), and such forms sometimes get into print. On *Geisel* 'hostage', see p. 28.

(C)	Sg. nom.	*der Name* 'name'	Pl.	*die Namen*
	acc.	*den Namen*		*die Namen*
	gen.	*des Namens*		*der Namen*
	dat.	*dem Namen*		*den Namen*

Thus *Buchstabe* 'letter (of alphabet)', *Funke* 'spark', *Gedanke* 'thought', *Glaube* 'belief', *Wille* 'will'. Also *Friede* 'peace', notably in religious or poetic language, but otherwise *Frieden* (p. 40).

Plural ending -*s*

A class embracing nouns of various origins.

Sg. nom.	*der Test* 'test'	Pl.	*die Tests*
acc.	*den Test*		*die Tests*
gen.	*des Tests*		*der Tests*
dat.	*dem Test*		*den Tests*

Here belong, firstly, numerous foreign words, especially of English or French provenance, as *Bankier* [baŋ'kjee] 'banker', *Block* 'block (of houses), (writing) pad', *Bungalow* 'bungalow', *Chef* 'chief, boss, chef', *Cousin* 'cousin', *Job* '(especially casual) job', *Klub* 'club', *Mili'tär* 'military officer', *Park* 'park', *Por'tier* [-'tjee] 'porter, janitor', *Rowdy* (pl. also spelt *Rowdies*) 'rowdy', *Salon* 'drawing-room', *Scheck* 'cheque', *Schal* 'scarf, shawl', *Schock* 'shock', *Streik* 'strike (of workmen, etc.)', *Teenager* 'teenager', *Twen* 'person in the twenties' ('made in Germany' from Eng. 'twenty'), *Waggon* [va'gɔ̃ɔ̃, va'gɔŋ] 'railway carriage'. Also any other foreign words, particularly those ending in a vowel other than -*e*, like the following names of exotic creatures: *Go'rilla, Kiwi, Gecko, Emu*.

Secondly, a few native nouns mostly ending in a vowel or diphthong, as *Uhu* 'eagle-owl', *Stau* 'tailback', *Nackedei* (humorous) 'naked person, esp. child', several of them nursery words: *Opa*, or as some prefer, *Opi* 'granddad', *Vati* 'daddy', *Po* or *Po'po* (from *Podex*) 'bottom, backside', *Wau'wau* 'bow-wow'.

Many other examples are abbreviated words, for which this is in fact the regular declension: *Krimi* (*Krimi'nalroman*) '(crime) thriller', *Profi* (*Professio'nal*) 'professional', *Pulli* (*Pul'lover*) 'pullover', *Sozi* (*Sozia'list*) 'Labourite', *Trafo* (*Transfor'mator*) 'transformer', similarly *Lkws* 'lorries', *Pkws* '(private) cars', p. 19. The term *Azubi* 'trainee' may also be feminine (p. 45), the source being *Auszubilden-*

de(r). Further *Treff* 'rendezvous' (short form of *Treffen* n. 'meeting') and *Trupp* 'small group, squad' (*Truppe* f. 'troops').

Lastly, a few words have a colloquial alternative plural in *-s*, among them *Bengels* 'rascals', *Kumpels* 'miners', *Onkels* 'uncles', p. 40, *Kerls* 'chaps', p. 31, *Jungens* or (northern) *Jungs* 'lads', p. 37.

Plural without an ending

Apart from a few exotic terms (see Special Plurals below), the nouns concerned are those ending in *-er*, *-el*, *-en*. All are common types, but the first mentioned constitute by far the largest group, containing as they do the highly productive category of agent nouns. We therefore select an item from this group as our sample paradigm. Nouns with modifiable vowel may, or may not, take umlaut.

Sg. nom.	*der Denker* 'thinker'	Pl.	*die Denker*
acc.	*den Denker*		*die Denker*
gen.	*des Denkers*		*der Denker*
dat.	*dem Denker*		*den Denkern* .

Among the many nouns so declined are *Becher* 'beaker', *Drechsler* 'turner', *Fechter* 'fencer', *Hefter* 'folder', *Hehler* 'receiver (of stolen goods)', *Helfer* 'helper', *Lehrer* 'teacher', *Meter* (also neut., p. 28) 'metre', *Redner* 'speaker, person making a speech', *Sprecher* 'speaker, person speaking', *Teller* 'plate', *Treffer* 'hit, goal', *Wecker* 'alarm-clock'.

Filter (also neut., p. 28) 'filter', *Finder* 'finder', *Finger* 'finger', *Gewinner* 'winner', *Gewinnler* 'profiteer', *Liter* (also neut., p. 28) 'litre', *Richter* 'judge', *Ringer* 'wrestler', *Schwimmer* 'swimmer', *Winter* 'winter', *Winzer* 'wine-grower', *Zwinger* 'castle keep'.

Flieger 'aviator', *Genießer* 'epicure', *Kiefer* 'jaw', *Kriecher* 'toady', *Riecher* (familiar) 'nose', *Verlierer* 'loser'.

Eimer 'bucket', *Geier* 'vulture', *Leiter* 'leader, conductor', *Neider* 'envious person', *Reißer* 'bestseller', *Reiter* 'rider', *Schneider* 'tailor', *Zuschneider* 'cutter'.

Kreuzer 'cruiser', *Meuterer* 'mutineer', *Seufzer* 'sigh'.

Further, certain nouns with stem vowels *a*, *o*, *u*, also *au*, or their umlauted counterparts including:

Adler 'eagle', *Ameri'kaner* 'American', *Anlasser* 'starter (car)', *Dampfer* 'steamer', *Fahrer* 'driver', *Halter* 'holder', *Kater* 'tomcat, hangover', *Lacher* 'laugh', *Maler* 'painter', *Panzer* 'tank, (medieval) armour', *Partner* 'partner', *Schlager* '(musical) hit'; *Bäcker* 'baker', *Engländer* 'Englishman', *Gärtner* 'gardener', *Kläger* 'plaintiff', *Schläger* 'brawler, (tennis) racket, (golf) club', *Träger* 'porter'.

Boxer 'boxer', *Hocker* 'stool', *Jodler* 'yodeller', *Kocher* 'cooker',

Sommer 'summer', *Trommler* 'drummer'; *Höcker* 'hump', *Köcher* 'quiver', *Schmöker* 'useless old book'.

Drucker 'printer', *Hummer* 'lobster', *Nebenbuhler* 'rival', *Schmuggler* 'smuggler', *Schuldner* 'debtor', *Zuber* 'tub'; *Drücker* 'latch', *Führer* 'leader, guide', *Hüter* 'keeper', *Müller* 'miller', *Schüler* 'schoolboy, pupil'.

Gauner 'thief, scoundrel', *Hauer* '(boar's) tusk', *Maurer* 'bricklayer'; *Gläubiger* 'creditor', *Läufer* 'runner', *Säufer* 'tippler'.

A handful of nouns forms the plural with umlaut: *Acker* '(tilled) field', *Hammer* 'hammer', *Schwager* 'brother-in-law', *Vater* 'father'; *Bruder* 'brother'; pl. *Äcker*, etc., *Brüder*.

Examples of nouns ending in *-el* include:
Bengel 'rascal', *Deckel* 'lid', *Engel* 'angel', *Hebel* 'lever'; *Gipfel* 'summit', *Winkel* 'corner, recess', *Wipfel* (high style) 'tree-top'; *Giebel* 'gable', *Riegel* 'bar, bolt', *Spiegel* 'mirror', *Stiefel* 'boot', *Ziegel* 'tile, brick'; *Meißel* 'chisel'; *Löffel* 'spoon'; *Bügel* 'handle, (clothes) hanger, stirrup', *Flügel* 'wing', *Gürtel* 'belt, cordon', *Schlüssel* 'key', *Würfel* 'cube, die', *Zügel* 'rein'.

Also *Stapel* 'pile'; *Onkel* 'uncle'; *Buckel* 'hump, (familiar) back', *Kumpel* 'miner', *Pudel* 'poodle'.

But others with a modifiable vowel have umlaut, as *Apfel* 'apple', *Mangel* 'shortage, fault', *Mantel* 'overcoat', *Nagel* 'nail', *Sattel* 'saddle', *Schnabel* 'beak'; *Vogel* 'bird'; pl. *Äpfel*, etc., *Vögel*.

Examples of nouns ending in *-en* (which do not, of course, add a further *n* in the dative plural) include:
Besen 'broom', *Felsen* (with a literary alternative nom. sg. *Fels*, and see p. 54) 'rock, crag', *Fetzen* 'rag, scrap (of paper)', *Flecken* (cf. *Fleck*, p. 31) 'patch, spot, (small) market town', *Rechen* 'rake', *Schrecken* (cf. *Schreck*, p. 31) 'fright, terror', *Stecken* 'stick'; *Frieden* (also *Friede*, p. 38) 'peace', *Riemen* 'strap, thong'; *Leisten* 'last', *Reifen* 'tyre', *Reigen* 'round dance', *Streifen* 'strip'.

Also *Balken* 'beam, joist', *Ballen* 'bale', *Drachen* 'kite (toy), quarrelsome female', *Haken* 'hook', *Karren* 'cart' (p. 30), *Laden* 'shutter', *Lappen* 'cloth, duster', *Rahmen* 'frame', *Samen* 'seed', *Spaten* 'spade'; *Bolzen* 'peg, bolt', *Knoten* 'knot', *Posten* 'post', *Tropfen* 'drop'; *Brunnen* 'well', *Busen* 'bosom', *Kuchen* 'cake'; *Daumen* 'thumb', *Haufen* 'heap'.

But others with a modifiable vowel have umlaut, as *Faden* 'thread', *Garten* 'garden', *Graben* 'ditch', *Hafen* 'harbour', *Kasten* 'box, cupboard', *Laden* 'shop', *Magen* 'stomach', *Schaden* (often in pl.) 'damage'; *Boden* 'floor, loft', *Ofen* 'stove, (electric) fire, oven'; pl. *Fäden*, *Böden*, etc.

The following have umlaut locally in southern usage: *Kragen* 'collar', *Wagen* 'car', and *Bogen* 'bow, arch, sheet (of paper)'—but not *Ellbogen* 'elbow'.

Special plurals

Bau 'structure, building', gen. *Baus*, pl. *Bauten.*
Sporn 'spur', gen. *Sporns*, pl. *Sporen.*
Various terms of foreign origin ending in -*as*, -*os*, -*us*; they form the sg. gen. without change: *Atlas* 'atlas', pl. *At'lanten* (formal style, otherwise as on p. 33), *Heros* 'hero, demigod', pl. *He'roen, Kustos* 'custodian, curator', pl. *Kus'toden.* A few Latin loans retain the exotic plural: *Modus* 'method, (grammatical) mood', pl. *Modi*, similarly *Numerus* '(grammatical) number', *Terminus* '(technical) term'. Fourth-declension loans form the plural without change, thus becoming indeclinable in German: *Kasus* '(grammatical) case', *Lapsus* 'lapse', *Passus* 'passage (of text)'.
Pharao 'pharaoh', gen. *Pharaos*, pl. *Phara'onen.*

In compounds, where reference is to occupation, -*mann* 'man' changes to -*leute* 'people' in the plural, thus *Bergmann* 'miner', *Geschäftsmann* 'businessman', *Kaufmann* 'shopkeeper', *Seemann* 'seaman', pl. *Bergleute*, etc. Compare *Ehemann* 'married man', pl. *Eheleute* 'man and wife, married people', *Ehemänner* 'married men'. Similarly *Gewährsmänner*, -*leute* 'informants', the former emphasizing that all are men, the latter denoting informants as such, possibly including women. But only *Hampelmänner* 'jumping jacks', *Schneemänner* 'snowmen', *Staatsmänner* 'statesmen', and as a rule *Müllmänner* 'dustmen'.

FEMININE

(The sections are: plural ending -*e*, -*en*, -*n*, -*s*, plural without an ending; for adjectival declension, see pp. 52 f.)

Plural ending -*e*

There are two groups. The first, much the larger, comprises essentially nouns of one syllable having a modifiable vowel or diphthong subject to umlaut in the plural.

Sg.	nom.	*die Hand* 'hand'	Pl.	*die Hände*
	acc.	*die Hand*		*die Hände*
	gen.	*der Hand*		*der Hände*
	dat.	*der Hand*		*den Händen*

Thus *Angst* 'anxiety', *Axt* '(long-shafted) axe', *Bank* 'bench', *Gans* 'goose', *Kraft* 'strength, force', *Macht* 'power', *Magd* 'maid-servant', *Nacht* 'night', *Stadt* 'town', *Wand* 'wall' (p. 130).

Brust 'breast, chest', pl. *Brüste*, similarly *Frucht* 'fruit', *Gruft* 'vault', *Kluft* 'cleft', *Kuh* 'cow', *Kunst* 'art', *Luft* 'air, (poetic) breeze', *Lust* 'desire', *Nuß* (pl. *Nüsse*) 'nut', *Schnur* 'string, flex', *Wurst* 'sausage'.

Braut 'bride', pl. *Bräute*, similarly *Faust* 'fist', *Haut* 'skin', *Laus* 'louse', *Maus* 'mouse', *Sau* 'sow, (filthy) pig', also pl. *Sauen*, p. 30. Further: *Auskunft* 'information' (often in pl. *Auskünfte*), similarly *Über'einkunft* 'agreement', *Zusammenkunft* 'meeting', also *Geschwulst* 'swelling'.

The second, very small group consists of nouns ending in *-sal* or *-nis*.

Sg. nom.	*die Drangsal* 'suffering'	Pl.	*die Drangsale*
acc.	*die Drangsal* (literary)		*die Drangsale*
gen.	*der Drangsal*		*der Drangsale*
dat.	*der Drangsal*		*den Drangsalen*

Thus *Mühsal* (literary) 'hardship', also *Besorgnis* (pl. *Besorgnisse*) 'worry', *Kenntnis* knowledge', often used in the plural.

Plural ending *-en*

An extremely large class, embracing nouns of one, and more than one, syllable. It contains all words with the endings *-ei*, *-heit*, *-keit*, *-schaft*, *-ung*, further very many foreign words including all those ending in *-ik*, *-ion*, *-ität* and various others (below), and finally all feminines formed with the derivative suffix *-in*.

Sg. nom.	*die Art* 'kind, species'	Pl.	*die Arten*
acc.	*die Art*		*die Arten*
gen.	*der Art*		*der Arten*
dat.	*der Art*		*den Arten*

Thus, among nouns of one syllable: *Bahn* 'course, railway, orbit', *Bank* '(money) bank', *Bucht* 'bay', *Burg* '(medieval) castle', *Fahrt* 'journey', *Flur* '(cultivated) land, pasture', *Flut* 'tide, flood', *Form* 'form, shape', *Frau* 'woman, wife', *Furt* 'ford', *Glut* 'blaze, glow', *Jagd* 'hunt', *Last* 'load, weight', *Mark* (poetic) 'boundary, frontier', *Pflicht* 'duty', *Qual* 'torment', *Schar* 'company, troop', *Schlacht* 'battle', *Schrift* 'writing', *Schuld* 'debt', *Spur* 'trace', *Stirn* (also *Stirne*, p. 44) 'forehead', *Tat* 'deed', *Tour* 'tour, outing', *Tracht* '(traditional) costume', *Tür* (also *Türe*, p. 44) 'door', *Uhr* 'clock, watch', *Wahl* 'choice, election', *Welt* 'world', *Werft* 'shipyard', *Zahl* 'number', *Zeit* 'time'.

Among nouns of more than one syllable: *Arbeit* 'work, labour',

Gegend 'region, tract', *Ansicht* 'view, opinion', *Aussicht* 'view, prospect', *Nachricht* '(item of) news', and the group of *Gebühr* 'fee, charge', *Geburt* 'birth', *Gefahr* 'danger', *Gestalt* 'form, shape', *Gewalt* 'force'; further *Bäcke'rei* 'bakery', *Kanz'lei* 'chancery', *Par'tei* '(political) party'; *Freiheit* 'freedom', *Krankheit* 'illness', *Schönheit* 'beauty'; *Grausamkeit* 'cruelty', *Kleinigkeit* 'trifle', *Süßigkeit* 'sweetness', pl. 'sweets'; *Botschaft* 'message', *Freundschaft* 'friendship', *Mannschaft* 'crew, team'.

Examples of foreign words: *Fab'rik* 'factory', *Gram'matik* 'grammar(-book)', *Praktik* 'practice', pl. '(sharp) practices, dodges'; *Dimensi'on* 'dimension', *Kauti'on* 'surety, bail', *Positi'on* 'position'; *Formali'tät* 'formality', *Rari'tät* 'rarity, curio', *Universi'tät* 'university'; further *Biblio'thek* 'library', *Kul'tur* 'culture', *Ma'nier* [-'niɐ] 'manner', *No'tiz* 'notice, note', *Predigt* 'sermon', *Sub'stanz* 'substance', *Ten'denz* 'tendency'.

Nouns formed with the feminine suffix *-in* double the *n* before the plural ending: *Köchin* '(female) cook', *Näherin* 'seamstress', *Prin'zessin* 'princess', pl. *Köchinnen*, etc.

In foreign words, the exotic singular ending *-a* is lost before the plural *-en*, as *Firma* 'firm', *Razzia* '(police) raid', *Villa* [v-] 'villa', pl. *Firmen*, etc.; similarly *-is*, as *Basis* 'basis, base, grass roots', *Dosis* 'dose', *Praxis* 'surgery, consulting room', pl. *Basen*, etc.; *Ga'laxis* 'galaxy' makes pl. *Ga'laxien*.

Plural ending *-n*

Another particularly large class. It comprises, for the greater part, the multifarious nouns of native or foreign origin ending in *-e* (including *-ee* and *-ie*). The smaller part, relatively speaking, is made up of the not so few nouns ending in *-el* and (with two exceptions, p. 45) those in *-er*.

Sg. nom.	*die Beere* 'berry'	Pl. *die Beeren*
acc.	*die Beere*	*die Beeren*
gen.	*der Beere*	*der Beeren*
dat.	*der Beere*	*den Beeren*

Among the great number of words ending in *-e*, we further note *Biene* 'bee', *Birne* 'pear', *Blume* 'flower', *Brücke* 'bridge', *Ecke* 'corner', *Eiche* 'oak', *Ente* 'duck', *Erde* 'earth' (with ancient dative ending in the phrase *auf Erden* 'on earth'), *Fahne* 'flag', *Farbe* 'colour', *Flasche* 'bottle', *Folge* 'consequence', *Gabe* 'gift', *Geige* 'violin', *Gemeinde* 'congregation', *Geschichte* 'history', *Glosse* 'gloss, satirical remark', *Haube* 'bonnet', *Herberge* 'inn', *Höhe* 'height', *Karte* 'card', *Kasse* 'till, cash desk', *Katze* 'cat', *Kehle* 'throat', *Kette* 'chain', *Kirche* 'church', *Kirsche* 'cherry', *Küche* 'kitchen', *Lage* 'position', *Lampe* 'lamp', *Lüge* 'lie', *Miete* 'rent', *Münze* 'coin', *Narbe* 'scar', *Nase* 'nose', *Niere* 'kidney', *Piste* 'track, course', *Planke* 'plank', *Quote* 'quota', *Ratte* 'rat', *Rede* 'speech, address', *Reise* 'journey', *Sache* 'thing, matter', *Scheune* 'barn', *Schlange* 'snake', *Schule* 'school', *Seele* 'soul', *Skizze* 'sketch', *Spende* 'donation', *Sprache* 'speech, language', *Stimme* 'voice', *Stirne* (also *Stirn*, p. 42) 'forehead', *Straße* 'street, road', *Suppe* 'soup', *Szene* 'scene', *Tante* 'aunt', *Tasche* 'bag, pocket', *Tasse* 'cup', *Tiefe* 'depth', *Träne* 'tear', *Treppe* 'stairs', *Türe* (also *Tür*, p. 42) 'door', *Vase* [v-] 'vase', *Weise* 'way, manner', *Wiese* 'field, meadow', *Woche* 'week', *Zehe* 'toe', *Zeile* 'line (of writing)', *Zelle* 'cell', *Ziege* 'goat', *Zunge* 'tongue'. Foreign nouns of more than two syllables have penultimate stress, thus *Ba'racke* 'barrack', *Epi'sode* 'episode', *Gra'nate* 'shell (from a gun)', *Har'pune* 'harpoon', *Kra'watte* 'tie', *Le'gende* 'legend', *Man'schette* 'cuff (on a sleeve), paper wrapper (for flowers)', *O'ase* 'oasis', *Po'saune* 'trombone', *Re'torte* 'retort', *Syna'goge* 'synagogue'. Also *Re'vue* [re'vyy] 'revue, review', pl. *Re'vuen* [-'vyyən].

A number of nouns end in *-ee*; they have final stress, e.g. *Al'lee* 'tree-lined avenue', pl. *Al'leen* [-'leeən], similarly *Fee* 'fairy', *I'dee* 'idea', *Mo'schee* 'mosque', *Orchi'dee* 'orchid', *Tour'nee* 'tour (theatrical)', further the native German word *See* 'sea, breaker'.

Nouns in *-ie* have, for the major part, final stress, thus *Batte'rie* 'battery', pl. *Batte'rien* ['riiən], similarly *Jalou'sie* [ʒ-] 'Venetian blind', *Kalo'rie* 'calory', *Litur'gie* 'liturgy', *Par'tie* 'match, excursion', *Phanta'sie* 'imagination, fantasy', *Rhapso'die* 'rhapsody', *Sinfo'nie* 'symphony'. But a considerable minority places the accent on the syllable before the ending, as *Ko'mödie* [ko'møødiə] 'comedy', pl. *Ko'mödien* [-'møødiən], similarly *Peter'silie* 'parsley', *Tra'gödie* 'tragedy'; this type is more prevalent with dissyllabic nouns, e.g. *Furie* 'Fury, hellcat', *Mumie* 'mummy', *Orgie* 'orgy', *Prämie* 'prize, premium', *Serie* 'series'.

Nouns ending in *-el* include *Angel* 'hinge', pl. *Angeln*, similarly *Bibel* 'bible', *Dattel* 'date (fruit)', *Fabel* 'fable', *Fessel* 'fetter', *Fiedel* 'fiddle', *Formel* 'formula', *Gabel* 'fork', *Geisel* 'hostage' (p. 28), *Geißel* 'scourge', *Gurgel* 'throat, gullet', *Hummel* 'bumble-bee', *Insel* 'island', *Kachel* '(glazed) tile', *Kar'toffel* 'potato', *Muschel* 'mussel, shell', *Regel* 'rule', *Schachtel* 'box', *Schindel* 'shingle (for roofing)', *Schüssel* 'bowl', *Semmel* 'roll (bread)', *Tafel* 'laid table (high style), tablet, panel, blackboard', *Waffel* 'wafer', *Wurzel* 'root'.

Nouns ending in *-er* include *Ader* 'vein', pl. *Adern*, similarly *Feder* 'feather, pen', *Kiefer* 'pine-tree', *Leier* 'lyre', *Leiter* 'ladder', *Mauer* 'wall' (p. 130), *Mutter* 'nut (for a bolt)', *Nummer* 'number (of a telephone, house), size', *Scheuer* (South German) 'barn', *Schwester* 'sister', *Steuer* 'tax, rate', *Ziffer* '(written) number'.

Plural ending -s

A small class, but embracing nouns of various types.

Sg. nom.	*die Kamera* 'camera'	Pl.	*die Kameras*
acc.	*die Kamera*		*die Kameras*
gen.	*der Kamera*		*der Kameras*
dat.	*der Kamera*		*den Kameras*

A number of English loanwords figure here, including *Bar* 'bar (for drinks)', further *Lady* 'lady', *Lobby* '(political) lobby', *Party* 'party (social gathering)', *Story* 'story', pl. *Ladys*, occasionally *Ladies*, etc. There are some exotic borrowings, as *Kobra* 'cobra', *Maina* 'myna'. Nursery words belonging here are *Mutti* 'mummy', *Oma*, or as some prefer, *Omi* 'granny'. *Lok* 'loco' (*Lokomo'tive*) is a commonly used abbreviation, as are *Kripo* 'C.I.D.' (*Krimi'nalpolizei*) and *Schupo* a familiar form of *Schutzpolizei* 'constabulary', further *Uni* for *Universi'tät* 'university'. The term *Azubi* 'trainee' may also be masculine (p. 38), the source being *Auszubildende(r)*.

Plural without an ending

Two native nouns follow this declension.

Sg. nom.	*die Tochter* 'daughter'	Pl.	*die Töchter*
acc.	*die Tochter*		*die Töchter*
gen.	*der Tochter*		*der Töchter*
dat.	*der Tochter*		*den Töchtern*

Also *Mutter* 'mother', pl. *Mütter*; notice the form *Muttern* in the colloquial idiom *wie bei Muttern* 'just like being at home with mother'.
The foreign word *Spezies* 'species' forms the plural without change.

NEUTER

(The sections are: plural ending in *-e*, *-er*, *-en*, *-ien*, *-n*, *-s*, plural without an ending, special plurals; for adjectival declension, see pp. 52 f).

Plural ending -e

This is the main class. One distinguishes two groups: nouns of one, and nouns of more than one, syllable.

Nouns of one syllable

Sg. nom.	*das Jahr* 'year'	Pl.	*die Jahre*
acc.	*das Jahr*		*die Jahre*

gen. *des Jahres*   *der Jahre*
dat. *dem Jahr(e)*   *den Jahren*

Singular variants as under *Weg*, p. 31.

Thus *Band* 'bond', *Beil* 'axe', *Bein* 'leg', *Brot* 'bread', pl. 'loaves, slices', *Bund* 'bundle, bunch (of keys)', *Ding* (pl. also *Dinger*, p. 48) 'thing', *Fell* 'animal's coat, hide', *Gas* 'gas', *Gift* 'poison', *Gleis* 'track, rails', *Haar* 'hair', pl. common esp. in colloquial style, p. 310, *Heer* 'army', *Heft* 'exercise-book', *Joch* 'yoke', *Land* 'land' (poetic, p. 30), *Los* 'fate, lot, lottery ticket', *Mal* 'mark', *Maß* 'measure', *Meer* 'sea', *Netz* 'net', *Paar* 'pair', *Pferd* 'horse', *Pult* 'desk', *Recht* 'right', *Reich* 'kingdom, realm', *Rohr* 'pipe, tube' (p. 30), *Roß* (pl. *Rosse*) 'steed', *Salz* 'salt', *Schaf* 'sheep', *Schiff* 'ship', *Schwein* 'pig', *Seil* 'rope', *Sieb* 'sieve', *Spiel* 'game', *Stück* 'piece', *Tau* 'thick rope', *Teil* 'piece, object', *Tor* 'gate(way)', *Werk* 'work', *Wort* (pl. also *Wörter*, p. 29) 'word', *Ziel* 'aim', *Zeug* 'stuff, material', pl. in compounds, as *Fahrzeuge* 'vehicles', *Flugzeuge* 'aeroplanes', cf. further *Werkzeug* 'tool' or collectively 'tools', *Werkzeuge* 'separate tools'.

Exceptionally with umlaut *Floß* 'raft', pl. *Flöße*.

Nouns of more than one syllable

Sg. nom. *das Gebot* 'commandment'   Pl. *die Gebote*
acc. *das Gebot*   *die Gebote*
gen. *des Gebots*   *der Gebote*
dat. *dem Gebot*   *den Geboten*

On the occasional use of sg. gen. *-es*, dat. *-e* in dissyllabic nouns formed with unaccented prefixes, i.e. *Gebotes*, *Gebote*, see p. 34. Nouns ending in a sibilant (see under *Weg*, p. 31) have sg. gen. *-es*, thus *Gewächs* 'growth, plant', gen. *Gewächses*. Most neuters formed in this way decline as above, notably *Gebet* 'prayer', *Gebiet* 'area, territory', *Gedicht* 'poem', *Gefäß* 'vessel, receptacle, basin', *Gefühl* 'feeling', *Gelenk* 'joint (chiefly anatomical)', *Gemisch* 'mixture', *Gerät* 'implement, apparatus', *Geräusch* 'sound', *Gericht* 'course (meal), court (of law)', *Gerücht* 'rumour', *Geschäft* 'business, shop', *Geschenk* 'present', *Geschöpf* 'creature', *Geschoß* (pl. *Geschosse*) 'projectile (bullet, shell), storey', *Geschütz* 'gun, cannon', *Gesetz* 'law', *Gesicht* 'vision, apparition', *Gespräch* 'conversation', *Gesuch* 'application', *Getränk* 'drink', *Gewehr* 'gun, rifle', *Gewicht* 'weight', *Gewürz* 'spice, condiment'. Also *Verbot* 'prohibition', *Verhör* 'interrogation', *Verlies* 'dungeon'.

Further neuter nouns in *-nis* (gen. *-nisses*, pl. *-nisse*), among them *Bedürfnis* 'requirement', *Bekenntnis* 'confession, creed', *Bündnis* 'alliance', *Ereignis* 'event', *Erzeugnis* 'product', *Erlebnis* 'experience', *Gefängnis* 'prison', *Geheimnis* 'secret', *Geschehnis* 'happening', *Gleich-*

nis 'parable', *Hindernis* 'hindrance', *Geständnis* 'confession, admission', *Verzeichnis* 'list, inventory', *Vorkommnis* 'occurrence', *Zeugnis* 'testimony'.

Otherwise, very few native words follow this declension. We note *Urteil* 'sentence, judgement' and the compounds *Jahr'hundert* 'century', *Jahr'tausend* 'millennium' comparing the plurals *Hunderte*, *Tausende* 'hundreds, thousands', further *Dreieck* 'triangle', *Rechteck* 'rectangle', also *Rückgrat* 'backbone'.

The majority of nouns in this declension are of foreign origin, typically stressed on the final syllable. Examples: *A'syl* 'refuge', *A'tom* 'atom', *Ban'kett* 'banquet', *Dupli'kat* 'duplicate', *Formu-'lar* 'form (for filling in)', *Insti'tut* 'institute', *Ka'mel* 'camel', *Kon'zert* 'concert', *Kompli'ment* 'compliment', *Kroko'dil* 'crocodile', *Manu'skript* 'manuscript', *Me'tall* 'metal', *Mikro'phon* 'microphone', *Mo'dell* 'model', *Mole'kül* 'molecule', *Mo'ment* 'motive, factor', *Pa'pier* 'paper', *Pro'dukt* 'product', *Re'gal* 'set of shelves', *Re'zept* 'recipe', *Semi'nar* 'seminar(y)', *Sta'tiv* 'tripod (for camera)', *Tele'skop* 'telescope', *Zi'tat* 'quotation. The grammatical terms *Adjektiv* ['at-] 'adjective' and *Substantiv* 'noun' have initial stress. Certain words may, for euphonic reasons, optionally have sg. gen. *-es*, cf. from items above *Kon'zert*, gen. *Kon'zerts* or *Kon'zertes*, similarly *Kompli'ment*, *Manu'skript*, *Mo'ment*, *Pro'dukt*, *Re'zept*.

Plural ending -er

A large class, always with umlaut where applicable. There are two groups: nouns of one, and nouns of more than one, syllable.

Nouns of one syllable

Sg. nom.	*das Dach* 'roof'	Pl.	*die Dächer*
acc.	*das Dach*		*die Dächer*
gen.	*des Daches*		*der Dächer*
dat.	*dem Dach(e)*		*den Dächern*

Singular variants as under *Weg*, p. 31.

Thus *Amt* 'office', *Bad* 'bath, spa', *Balg* 'brat' (p. 28), *Blatt* 'leaf, sheet (of paper)', *Faß* (pl. *Fässer*) 'barrel', *Glas* 'glass', *Grab* 'grave', *Kalb* 'calf', *Lamm* 'lamb', *Land* (pl. also *Lande*, p. 46) 'land, country, province', *Rad* 'wheel', *Tal* 'valley'.

Dorf 'village', pl. *Dörfer*, similarly *Holz* 'wood, timber', *Horn* 'horn', *Korn* '(grain of) corn', *Loch* 'hole', *Schloß* (pl. *Schlösser*) 'castle', *Volk* 'people', *Wort* (pl. also *Worte*, p. 46) 'word'.

Buch 'book', pl. *Bücher*, similarly *Gut* 'treasure, estate, farm', pl.

also 'goods', *Huhn* '(general term for) chicken, hen', *Tuch* 'cloth, sheet', *Wurm* '(little) mite'.

Haupt 'head (high style), chief', pl. *Häupter*, similarly *Haus* 'house', *Kraut* 'herb, cabbage'.

Further *Biest* (familiar) 'beast, unpleasant person', *Bild* 'picture', *Brett* 'board, plank, tray', *Ding* (familiar) 'trivial thing', *Ei* 'egg', *Feld* 'field', *Geld* 'money', *Glied* 'limb', *Kind* 'child', *Kleid* 'dress', *Licht* 'light', *Lied* 'song', *Nest* 'nest', *Reis* 'twig', *Rind* 'ox, cow', pl. 'cattle', *Schwert* 'sword', *Viech* (familiar) 'animal, creature', *Vieh* (no pl.) 'livestock', *Weib* 'woman' (in colloquial style pejorative).

Nouns of more than one syllable

Sg. nom.	*das Gehalt* 'salary'	Pl.	*die Gehälter*
acc.	*das Gehalt*		*die Gehälter*
gen.	*des Gehalts*		*der Gehälter*
dat.	*dem Gehalt*		*den Gehältern*

On the occasional use of sg. gen. -*es*, dat. -*e* in nouns of more than one syllable, i.e. *Gehaltes, Gehalte*, see under *Pfirsich*, p. 33.

This is the minor group, but contains words of various types. Firstly, half a dozen nouns of comparable formation to the above: *Gemach* 'chamber', *Gewand* 'garment, raiment', further *Gemüt* 'mind, heart, feeling', *Geschlecht* 'sex, race, lineage', *Gesicht* 'face', *Gespenst* (gen. *Gespenstes*) 'ghost'.

Secondly, neuter nouns ending in -*tum*, a few of which often form plurals: *Altertum* 'antiquity', pl. *Altertümer*, similarly *Besitztum* 'property, estate', *Heiligtum* 'holy place or object'.

Thirdly, miscellaneous items, including *Scheusal* 'beast, horror', pl. *Scheusäler*, similarly *Spi'tal* 'infirmary', also *Regi'ment* 'regiment', and the compound *Denkmal* 'monument' (p. 29).

Plural ending -*en*

A relatively small class falling into two groups: nouns of one, and nouns of more than one, syllable.

Nouns of one syllable

Sg. nom.	*das Bett* 'bed'	Pl.	*die Betten*
acc.	*das Bett*		*die Betten*
gen.	*des Bettes*		*der Betten*
dat.	*dem Bett(e)*		*den Betten*

Singular variants as under *Weg*, p. 31.

Thus *Hemd* 'shirt', *Ohr* (gen. *Ohrs*) 'ear' and a few items of foreign origin: *Fakt* (mainly in the pl.) 'fact', *Skript* 'script, notes', *Verb*

'verb'. Also *Herz* 'heart', with exceptional forms in the sg. gen. *Herzens*, dat. *Herzen*, but also dat. *Herz*, as commonly in the literal sense and in the idiom *mit Herz*, e.g. *eine Frau mit Herz* 'a warm-hearted woman', (sticker on a car window) *fahre mit Herz* 'drive with consideration'.

Nouns of more than one syllable

These are of foreign origin, sometimes having non-initial stress.

Sg. nom.	*das Ju'wel* 'jewel'	Pl.	*die Ju'welen*
acc.	*das Ju'wel*		*die Ju'welen*
gen.	*des Ju'wels*		*der Ju'welen*
dat.	*dem Ju'wel*		*den Ju'welen*

Thus *In'sekt* 'insect', *Sta'tut* 'statute'.

Most nouns of classical origin ending in *-a* change this to *-en* in the plural, e.g. *Dogma* 'dogma', pl. *Dogmen*, similarly *Drama* 'drama', *Para'digma* 'paradigm', *Prisma* 'prism', *Thema* 'theme, subject'.

Nouns of classical origin ending in *-um* also change to *-en*, e.g. *Album* 'album', pl. *Alben*, similarly *A'quarium* 'aquarium', *Datum* 'date', pl. also 'data', *Evan'gelium* 'gospel', *Gremium* '(authoritative) body', *Indi'viduum* 'individual', *Kol'legium* 'corporate body' (e.g. of teachers), *Medium* 'medium', *Monstrum* 'monster', *Mu'seum* 'museum', *Podium* 'platform, stage', *Spektrum* 'spectrum', *Studium* 'study', *Zentrum* 'centre'. Similarly *Lexikon* 'lexicon, dictionary', pl. *Lexiken* (see also p. 52).

Also *Konto* 'account (at a bank)', *Risiko* 'risk', pl. *Konten*, etc.

Epos 'epic poem', pl. *Epen*, has no inflexion in the sg. gen., likewise *Virus* 'virus' (p. 36), pl. *Viren*.

Plural ending *-ien*

Only a handful of foreign nouns follow this declension; they have final stress.

Sg. nom.	*das Fos'sil* 'fossil'	Pl.	*die Fos'silien*
acc.	*das Fos'sil*		*die Fos'silien*
gen.	*des Fos'sils*		*der Fos'silien*
dat.	*dem Fos'sil*		*den Fos'silien*

Thus *Ad'verb* [at-] 'adverb', *In'diz* 'indication (as evidence)', *Materi'al* 'material', *Mine'ral* 'mineral', *Parti'zip* 'participle', *Prin'zip* 'principle', *Privi'leg* 'privilege', *Rea'genz* 'reagent'.

Plural ending -*n*

Three words only constitute this class.

Sg. nom.	*das Auge* 'eye'	Pl.	*die Augen*
acc.	*das Auge*		*die Augen*
gen.	*des Auges*		*der Augen*
dat.	*dem Auge*		*den Augen*

Thus *Ende* 'end', *Interesse* [ɪn'trɛsə] 'interest, concern'.

Plural ending -*s*

A class embracing nouns of various types.

Sg. nom.	*das Echo* 'echo'	Pl.	*die Echos*
acc.	*das Echo*		*die Echos*
gen.	*des Echos*		*der Echos*
dat.	*dem Echo*		*den Echos*

Here we have, first and foremost, numerous nouns of foreign origin ending in a vowel, notably those in -*o*, other examples being *Bü'ro* 'office, bureau', *G(h)etto* 'ghetto', *Ka'sino* 'casino', *Kom'mando* 'command(o)', *Lotto* 'numbers pool, lotto', *Motto* 'motto', some of them abbreviated words, as *Auto* 'car' (*Automo'bil*), *Foto* or *Photo* 'photograph', the usual term today—without the colloquial connotations of our 'photo' (with change of gender from *Photogra'phie* f.), *Kino* 'cinema' (with change of gender from *Kinemato'graph* m.). A few terms in -*a* follow suit, as *Komma* 'comma' (see p. 52), *Lama* 'llama', *Sofa* 'sofa', *Zebra* ['tseebra] 'zebra', further *Ge'nie* [ʒ-] 'person of) genius', *Komi'tee* 'committee', *Ta'bu* (alternatively with initial stress) and the English loans *Baby*, *Hobby*, *Pony* ['pɔni] with plurals regularly *Babys*, etc.; abbreviated words include *Dia* '(lantern) slide' (*Diaposi'tiv*) and *Taxi* 'taxi' (based on *Taxa'meter* m. 'taximeter').

Next, sundry other nouns of foreign provenance, as *Deck* 'deck', *Dock* 'dock', *Ho'tel* 'hotel', *Karu'sell* 'merry-go-round', *Ku'vert* 'envelope', also (originally Low German) *Wrack* 'wreck'. There are some abbreviated words, as *La'bor* 'lab.' (*Labora'torium*) and *Kol'leg* 'lecture, course of lectures' (now the standard term, formerly *Kol'legium*).

Further, a few adjectives substantivized without the usual endings (p. 52), as *Leck* 'leak' and the meteorological *Hoch* 'high', *Tief* 'low'.

Lastly, a few items have a colloquial alternative plural in -*s*. They may be diminutives adding this ending, as *Mädchens* or *Mädels* 'lasses', *Fräuleins* 'young ladies', or they may be foreign words substituting for a less usual or bookish plural, as *Albums* 'albums', *Kontos* 'accounts', otherwise *Alben*, *Konten*, p. 49.

Plural without an ending

The nouns concerned are those ending in *-er*, *-el* and *-en* (together with the diminutives in *-chen* and *-lein*), further a group ending in *-e*.

Sg. nom.	*das Fenster* 'window'	Pl.	*die Fenster*
acc.	*das Fenster*		*die Fenster*
gen.	*des Fensters*		*der Fenster*
dat.	*dem Fenster*		*den Fenstern*

Thus *Feuer* 'fire', *Filter* (also masc., p. 28) 'filter', *Geländer* 'railing', *Gewitter* 'thunder-storm', *Liter* (also masc., p. 28) 'litre', *Man'över* 'manœuvre', *Messer* 'knife', *Meter* (also masc., p. 28) 'metre', *Muster* 'pattern, sample', *Opfer* 'sacrifice', *Ruder* 'oar, rudder', *Se'mester* 'term (of six months)', *Steuer* 'steering-wheel, rudder', *The'ater* 'theatre', *Ungeheuer* 'monster', *Wunder* 'wonder, miracle', *Zimmer* 'room'.

Exceptionally with umlaut *Kloster* 'monastery, convent', pl. *Klöster*, and *Lager* 'camp, warehouse', pl. also *Läger*, especially in the second sense.

Examples of nouns ending in *-el*: *Drittel* 'third', *Ferkel* 'piglet', *Kabel* 'cable', *Ka'pitel* 'chapter', *Kar'nickel* 'bunny rabbit', *Mädel* 'girl, lass', *Mitbringsel* 'small present brought for somebody', *Mittel* 'device, means', *Schnitzel* 'scrap, slice, veal cutlet', *Segel* 'sail', *Spek'takel* 'uproar, racket, fuss', *Viertel* 'quarter'.

Examples of nouns ending in *-en* (which do not add a further *n* in the dative plural): *Becken* '(wash)basin, sink', *Kissen* 'cushion', *Wappen* 'coat of arms', *Zeichen* 'sign', and a few foreign words: *Nomen*, a term embracing nouns and adjectives, also *Pro'nomen* 'pronoun', and *Omen* 'omen' (see also p. 52).

The majority of words belonging to this group are substantivized infinitives, though the verbal connection may be weak or even broken altogether (p. 256), e.g. *Andenken* 'souvenir', *Bedenken* 'objection, reservation', *Gebrechen* 'physical defect', *Leiden* 'suffering, ailment', *Rennen* 'race', *Schreiben* (rather formal) 'letter', *Treffen* 'gathering, rally', *Verbrechen* 'crime', *Vergehen* 'offence', *Versprechen* 'promise'.

Here belong also nouns with the diminutive suffixes *-chen* or *-lein*, e.g. *Mädchen* 'girl, lass', *Türchen* 'little door', *Fräulein* 'Miss, young lady', *Küchlein* 'chicken'. In ordinary style, a noun forming its plural in *-er*, exceptionally retains the termination, hence *Kindchen* 'little child', pl. *Kinderchen*, similarly *Dingerchen* 'little trivial things', *Würmerchen* 'little worms, little mites' (*Ding*, *Wurm*, pp. 48, 34). But this practice does not apply when the diminutive is an independent lexical item, e.g. *Weibchen* 'female (of a species)' does not change in the plural, contrasting with *Weiberchen* 'little women, hussies' (*Weib*, p. 48).

Examples of nouns ending in *-e* are notably *Gebäude* 'building', *Gebilde* 'formation, structure', *Gebirge* 'mountain-range', *Gehäuse* 'case, casing', *Gehege* 'enclosure, pen', *Gelübde* 'solemn vow', *Gemälde* [gə'meeldə] 'painting', *Gemenge* '(loose) mixture', *Gewölbe* 'vault'. Also *Knie* 'knee', pl. *Knie* ['kniiə], dat. *Knien* ['kniiən].

Special plurals

The substantivized infinitives *Bemühen* 'effort, trouble', *Bestreben* 'endeavour', *Vergnügen* 'pleasure' have as their plurals *Bemühungen*, *Bestrebungen*, *Vergnügungen*.

A few terms taken from Latin may retain an exotic plural: *Kom'positum* 'compound' (as a term of grammar), sg. gen. *Kom'positums*, pl. *Kom'posita*, similarly *Neutrum* 'neuter', also *Fixum* 'fixed salary', *Praktikum* 'practical course'; the Greek loan *Lexikon* 'lexicon, dictionary' has likewise pl. *Lexika*, but a naturalized alternative *Lexiken* (p. 49) is also quite common. The two words *Genus* 'gender' and *Tempus* 'tense' are unchanged in the sg. gen., the plurals being *Genera*, *Tempora*.

Some usages sound rather pedantic, e.g. *Kommata* 'commas', *Omina* 'omens', now generally *Kommas*, *Omen*, see pp. 50 f.

SUBSTANTIVIZED ADJECTIVES

Adjectives may be substantivized; they retain their adjectival inflexions (pp. 57 f.), thus from *blau* 'blue':

Weak declension

Sg. nom.	*der Blaue* 'the blue one'		*die Blaue* 'the blue one'	
acc.	*den Blauen*	masc.	*die Blaue*	fem.
gen.	*des Blauen*		*der Blauen*	
dat.	*dem Blauen*		*der Blauen*	
Sg. nom.	*das Blaue* 'the blue one'	Pl.	*die Blauen* 'the blue ones'	
acc.	*das Blaue*	neut.	*die Blauen*	
gen.	*des Blauen*		*der Blauen*	
dat.	*dem Blauen*		*den Blauen*	

Strong declension

Sg. nom. *Blaues* 'something blue' Pl. *Blaue* 'blue ones'
    acc. *Blaues*   *Blaue*
    gen. —   *Blauer*
    dat. *Blauem*   *Blauen*

Correspondingly Sg. nom. *Blauer* masc., *Blaue* fem., as vocatives.

Mixed declension

Sg. nom. *ein Blauer* 'a blue one'   *eine Blaue* 'a blue one'
    acc. *einen Blauen* masc.   *eine Blaue* fem.
    gen. *eines Blauen*   *einer Blauen*
    dat. *einem Blauen*   *einer Blauen*

Sg. nom. *ein Blaues* 'a blue one' Pl. *keine Blauen* 'no blue ones'
    acc. *ein Blaues* neut.   *keine Blauen*
    gen. *eines Blauen*   *keiner Blauen*
    dat. *einem Blauen*   *keinen Blauen*

APPENDIX

Nouns found only in the singular or only in the plural

Understandably, a large number of nouns, both abstract and concrete, occur in the singular only. Among the former are (masc.) *Eifer* 'zeal', *Fleiß* 'diligence, hard work', *Gefallen* 'favour', *Mut* 'courage', (fem.) *Demut* 'humility', *Liebe* 'love', *Ruhe* 'rest', *Trauer* 'grief, mourning', (neut.) *Gewissen* 'conscience', *Künstlertum* 'artistry', *Verständnis* 'understanding', and many substantivized infinitives (p. 255), as *Denken* '(mode of) thought', *Lachen* 'laughing', *Warten* 'waiting'. Among concrete nouns: (masc.) *Hafer* 'oats', *Käse* (gen. *Käses*) 'cheese', *Rauch* 'smoke', *Regen* 'rain', (fem.) *Asche* 'ashes', *Butter* 'butter', *Milch* 'milk', *Wolle* 'wool', (neut.) *Blei* 'lead', *Eis* 'ice', *Obst* [oopst] 'fruit', *Wild* 'game, venison'.

In certain cases, plurals may be called for. These are then formed periphrastically, e.g. *Regenfälle* 'rains' from *Regenfall* 'fall of rain', or *Obstsorten* 'fruits' from *Obstsorte* 'sort, or kind, of fruit'. A synonym may also do service, as *Früchte*, pl. of *Frucht* 'fruit'.

A much smaller number of nouns occur in the plural only; these include *An'nalen* 'annals', *Au'spizien* 'auspices', *Einkünfte* 'income', *Eltern* 'parents', *Faxen* 'tomfoolery', *Ferien* 'holidays', *Flausen* 'silly talk', *Flitterwochen* 'honeymoon', *Geschwister* 'brother(s) and sister(s)', *Habseligkeiten* 'belongings, traps', *Honorati'oren* 'local dignitaries', *Hosenträger* '(pair of) braces', *Kal'daunen* 'tripe, guts', *Kinkerlitzchen* 'knicknacks', *Kosten* 'costs', *Lebensmittel* 'groceries', *Leute* 'people', *Machenschaften* 'machinations', *Masern* 'measles', *Möbel* 'furniture', *Mo'neten* (familiar) 'money, cash', *Perso'nalien* 'personal particulars', *Preti'osen* 'jewellery', *Repres'salien* 'reprisals', *Röteln* 'German measles', *Schwuli'täten* (familiar) 'difficulties', *Spesen* 'expenses, charges', *Spiritu'osen* '(alcoholic) spirits', *Tropen* 'tropics', *Trümmer* 'ruins, debris', *Umtriebe* 'subversive activities', *Unbilden der Witterung* 'inclemency of the weather', *Wirren* 'disorders, unrest'.

The plurals *Ostern* 'Easter', *Pfingsten* 'Whitsuntide', and *Weihnachten* 'Christmas' take a singular verb, p. 311.

Should a singular form be required, a compound with some other word will be appropriate, thus *Möbelstück* 'piece of furniture', *(der) Elternteil* (officialese) 'parent', *Feiertag* '(day which is a) holiday'.

The word *Hose* may be used in the plural without change of number: *er kaufte sich neue Hosen*, or *eine neue Hose* 'he bought himself new trousers'. In a few expressions, however, only the plural form is possible, e.g. *ein Paar Hosen, ein Paar kurze Hosen* 'a pair of trousers, a pair of shorts', *sie hat die Hosen an* 'she wears the trousers'.

As far as inflexions are concerned, these nouns naturally follow the appropriate declensions. *Fels* 'rock (the substance)' is uninflected, having no genitive; cf. *Felsen*, p. 40.

The names of languages, as *Deutsch* 'German', *Englisch* 'English', *Französisch* 'French', do not inflect (see p. 163), nor do the more exotic names, as *(das) Hindi, (das) Urdu.*

Proper Nouns

Names of persons

The names of persons have gen. -*s* regardless of gender: *Heinrich* 'Henry', *Petra* ['peetra] 'Petra', gen. *Heinrichs, Petras*; likewise surnames: *Herrn/Frau Holms Haus* 'Mr/Mrs Holm's house'. In more formal style, gen. -*(e)ns* occurs occasionally: *Irene, Faust*, gen. *Irenens, Faustens*, but ordinarily *Irenes, Fausts*. Names ending in [s], e.g. *Hans* 'John' and such surnames as *Heß* and those ending in -*us* like *Li'borius*, also *Dietz, Marx*, cannot take -*s*. By a bookish convention, the missing ending may be represented by an apostrophe: *Marx' Werke* 'the works of M.', but the living language prefers *die Werke von Marx*. Equally artificial is the use of -*s* after names ending in -*sch*, as *Bratfisch, Hirsch*, gen. *Bratfischs, Hirschs*, forms not found with the common nouns *Bratfisch* 'fried fish', *Hirsch* 'stag', [-ʃs] forming no part of the phonetic system. The common nouns *Mutter* 'mother' and *Schwester* 'sister' may, in familiar style, be treated as personal names, when they form the genitives *Mutters*, *Schwesters*; in the same way *Tante* 'aunt' can form *Tantes*, while the pet words *Mutti* 'mummy', *Oma* or *Omi* 'granny' are regularly so treated. If preceded by an article or other inflected word, the genitive loses its ending, p. 187.

Christus 'Christ' has gen. *Christi*, common in *vor Christi* (*Geburt* 'birth' understood) 'BC', *nach Christi* 'AD' (also *vor, nach Christus*, the pedestrian alternatives); *Jesus* has gen. *Jesu*, hence *Jesu Christi*.

Surnames are often used in the plural, either unchanged or with the ending *-s* according to a nuance of sense: *die Baier* 'the Baiers, people like Baier', cf. *die Baier dieser Welt* 'the Baiers of this world', but *(die) Baiers* '(the) Baiers, members of the Baier family'. Should the name end in a sibilant, the ending is *-ens*, as *(die) Vossens, Schwarzens* (*Voß, Schwarz*). The ending *-s* is also used to form the plural of Christian names: *Heinrichs, Petras* 'Henrys, Petras', unless they end in a sibilant when no change occurs: *beide Hans* 'both Johns'. In formal style, *-n* may occur: *die beiden Isolden* 'the two Isoldes'.

Names of vehicles, etc.

Motor cars are masculine: *der Mer'cedes, Opel, Wartburg*, among foreigners *der Fiat, Ford, Wolga*. Aeroplanes are feminine: *die Heinkel, Messerschmidt*, similarly *die Boeing* ['bøøıŋ], *IL 18* [ii εl 'axtsεn]; ships, too, are feminine: *die Bismarck, Otto Hahn*.

Names of towns and countries

The names of towns are neuter: *das altehrwürdige Fulda* 'time-honoured Fulda', *das mo'derne Ingolstadt* 'modern Ingolstadt'. Where possible, they form the genitive with *-s*, thus *Brüssel* 'Brussels', *Wien* 'Vienna', gen. *Brüssels, Wiens*. Nouns ending in a sibilant, e.g. *Cottbus, Müritz, Pa'ris*, cannot form a distinctive genitive, hence e.g. *die Straßen von Paris* or *die Pariser Straßen*, see p. 59.

The names of countries are for the most part neuter, as *Deutschland* 'Germany', *Frankreich* 'France', *Polen* 'Poland', gen. *Deutschlands*, etc., similarly provinces and the like: *Bayern* 'Bavaria', *Lothringen* 'Lorraine', *Sachsen* 'Saxony', also continents: *Eu'ropa* 'Europe', *Asien* 'Asia', gen. *Bayerns, Eu'ropas*, etc. If preceded by an article or other inflected word, the genitive loses its ending, p. 187.

In a few instances, names of countries are masculine or feminine. In the case of the former they may be used with the article, as optionally (*der*) *I'rak* 'Iraq', or usually *der Su'dan* 'the Soudan'. Feminines always take the article: *die Schweiz* 'Switzerland', *die Tschechoslowa-'kei* 'Czechoslovakia', *die Tür'kei* 'Turkey', further the provinces *die Lausitz* 'Lusatia', *die Pfalz* 'the Palatinate'; one neuter follows this pattern: *das Elsaß* 'Alsace'. A few names occur as plurals: *die Niederlande* 'the Netherlands', *die Vereinigten Staaten, die US'A* 'the United States, the USA'.

Names of mountains

The names of mountains are chiefly masculine: *der Brocken*, similarly mountain ranges: *der Harz, Jura, Spessart, Taunus*, but there are a few feminines: *die Eifel, Rhön*. Some occur as plurals: *die Alpen* 'the Alps', *die (Hohen, Niederen) Tauern* 'the (High, Low) Tauern'. Among foreign examples: *der O'lymp* 'Olympus', *U'ral* 'Urals', *Ve'suv* 'Vesuvius'; *die Sierra Nevada*.

Names of rivers

The majority of river names in Germany are feminine: *die Donau* 'Danube', *Elbe, Fulda, Mosel* 'Moselle', *Oder, Spree, Weser*, but a minority of names, including some important ones, are masculine: *der Inn, Main, Neckar, Rhein* 'Rhine'. With foreign names, however, the masculine is the more prevalent gender: *der Ama'zonas* 'Amazon', *Ganges* ['gaŋgɛs], *Nil* 'Nile', *Tiber, Trent*. Typically feminine, however, are names ending in *-a*: *die Wolga* 'Volga' and *-e*: *die Seine, Themse* 'Thames'.

4. Adjectives

THE predicative adjective is uninflected: *der Brief ist lang* 'the letter is long', *die Häuser sind alt* 'the houses are old'.

The attributive adjective forms three declensions: weak, strong, and mixed.

WEAK DECLENSION

The adjective is qualified by the definite article, a demonstrative or certain interrogative and indefinite adjectives, also by *all* 'all', etc.; further details, p. 166.

Masculine

Sg. nom.	*der lange Brief* 'the long letter'	Pl. *die langen Briefe*
acc.	*den langen Brief*	*die langen Briefe*
gen.	*des langen Briefes*	*der langen Briefe*
dat.	*dem langen Brief(e)*	*den langen Briefen*

Feminine

Sg. nom.	*die dumme Gans* 'the silly goose'	Pl. *die dummen Gänse*
acc.	*die dumme Gans*	*die dummen Gänse*
gen.	*der dummen Gans*	*der dummen Gänse*
dat.	*der dummen Gans*	*den dummen Gänsen*

Neuter:

Sg. nom.	*das alte Haus* 'the old house'	Pl. *die alten Häuser*
acc.	*das alte Haus*	*die alten Häuser*
gen.	*des alten Hauses*	*der alten Häuser*
dat.	*dem alten Haus(e)*	*den alten Häusern*

STRONG DECLENSION

The adjective is either (1) unqualified or else (2) qualified by an uninflected word, excepting proper names and other nouns in the genitive and certain indefinite adjectives; details of these and minor exceptions on pp. 166 f.

Masculine:

Sg. nom.	*guter Stoff* 'good material'	Pl. *gute Stoffe*
acc.	*guten Stoff*	*gute Stoffe*
gen.	*guten Stoffes*	*guter Stoffe*
dat.	*gutem Stoff(e)*	*guten Stoffen*

Feminine:

Sg. nom.	*warme Suppe* 'hot soup'	Pl.	*warme Suppen*
acc.	*warme Suppe*		*warme Suppen*
gen.	*warmer Suppe*		*warmer Suppen*
dat.	*warmer Suppe*		*warmen Suppen*

Neuter:

Sg. nom.	*schönes Haar* 'beautiful hair'	Pl.	*schöne Haare* 'do.'
			(collectively)
acc.	*schönes Haar*		*schöne Haare*
gen.	*schönen Haares*		*schöner Haare*
dat.	*schönem Haar(e)*		*schönen Haaren*

MIXED DECLENSION

The adjective is qualified by the indefinite article or similarly inflecting word (*kein, mein, unser*, etc., p. 60). The present declension differs from the weak only to the extent that strong forms occur after uninflected *ein, kein, mein*, etc.

Masculine:

Sg. nom.	*ein langer Brief*	Pl.	*keine langen Briefe*
	'a long letter'		'no long letters'
acc.	*einen langen Brief*		*keine langen Briefe*
gen.	*eines langen Briefes*		*keiner langen Briefe*
dat.	*einem langen Brief(e)*		*keinen langen Briefen*

Feminine:

Sg. nom.	*eine dumme Gans*	Pl.	*meine dummen Gänse*
	'a silly goose'		'my silly geese'
acc.	*eine dumme Gans*		*meine dummen Gänse*
gen.	*einer dummen Gans*		*meiner dummen Gänse*
dat.	*einer dummen Gans*		*meinen dummen Gänsen*

Neuter:

Sg. nom.	*ein altes Haus*	Pl.	*unsere alten Häuser*
	'an old house'		'our old houses'
acc.	*ein altes Haus*		*unsere alten Häuser*
gen.	*eines alten Hauses*		*unserer alten Häuser*
dat.	*einem alten Haus(e)*		*unseren alten Häusern*

Stem changes due to inflexion

Adjectives in *-el* contract in the inflected forms, as *eitel*: *ein eitler Mensch* 'a conceited person', *dunkel*: *im dunklen* (less usually *dunkeln*) *Wald* 'in the dark wood'. Adjectives in *-en* often contract in the spoken form, but the contraction is not normally shown in writing, e.g. *trocken*: *die trockene* (commonly spoken *trockne*) *Luft* 'the dry air'. Adjectives in -er may likewise drop e in the spoken language, thus *finster*: *im finstren* (also *finstern*) *Wald* 'in the dark wood', but generally written *im finsteren Wald*. When the ending -er is preceded by a diphthong, however, contraction is the rule in the written language too, as *teuer*: *teure Mieten* 'expensive rents' or *sauer*: *ein saurer Apfel* 'a sour apple'. Contraction also in the case of adjectives of foreign origin stressed on the penultimate, as *in'teger*, *ma'kaber*: *ein integrer Cha'rakter* 'an upright man', *ein makabres Schauspiel* 'a macabre spectacle', but *ein 'cleverer Kunde* 'a slick customer'. Adjectives ending in a vowel lose this before the inflexional endings, as *müde*: *die müden Beine* 'the tired legs'. The slangy *me'schugge*, however, inserts *n*: *ein meschuggener Kerl* 'a crazy chap', a device sometimes heard in colloquial style with a handful of other exotic adjectives, notably *lila* and *rosa*: *das lilane Kleid* 'the mauve dress', *eine rosane Bluse* 'a pink blouse', otherwise *lila Kleid*, etc. below.

The adjective *hoch* changes to *hoh-* in the inflected forms: *der hohe Berg*, *die hohen Berge* 'the high mountain(s)'. In two examples, inflecting forms are orthographically joined to the noun qualified: *der Hohepriester* 'the high priest', *ein Hoherpriester* 'a high priest', *Hohepriester* 'high priests', etc., and *das Hohelied* 'the Song of Songs', gen. *des Hohenlied(e)s*.

INDECLINABLE ADJECTIVES

A few adjectives of foreign provenance are treated as indeclinables, e.g. *orange* [o'rãã3(e), o'raŋ3(ə)], *lila*, *rosa*: *ein orange Vorhang* 'an orange curtain', *das lila Kleid* 'the mauve dress', *rosa Bänder* 'pink ribbons'—alternatively one could use *orangefarben* 'orange-coloured', etc., with the normal declensional endings: *ein orangefarbener Vorhang*, etc. On colloquial inflexions, see above.

The everyday colloquialisms *klasse* and *prima*, both meaning something like 'first rate, top notch', much favoured by juvenile speakers, are not inflected: *ein klasse* (or *prima*) *Film*.

Indeclinable adjectives in -er are formed from the names of towns and villages: *der Berliner Bär* 'the Berlin Bear' (city emblem), *die Hahndorfer Straße* 'Hahndorf Street', *das Gothaer Programm* 'the Gotha Programme', *Wiener Walzer* 'Vienna waltzes', *im Kölner Dom* 'in Cologne cathedral', *auf der Lüneburger Heide* 'on Lüneburg Heath', similarly *eine Schweizer Bank* 'a Swiss bank'. Names ending in *e* only require *r*, hence *der Travemünder Hafen* 'Travemünde harbour'. Those in -en usually drop *e*, cf. *Pils(e)ner Bier* 'Pilsen beer', or else lose the ending altogether: *die Göttinger Sieben* 'the Göttingen

Seven'. There are other occasional contractions, e.g. *Basler* from *Basel* 'Basle', *Zürcher* from *Zürich* 'Zurich'. Nouns already ending in *er* cannot avail themselves of the present termination, but they can achieve the same effect—more or less—by standing in apposition: *die Han'nover-Messe* 'the Hanover Trade Fair'.

A number of adjectives cannot be used attributively and therefore exist only in the uninflected form, p. 170.

Alternative formations

In addition to the formation in *-er* above, the names of certain towns also form adjectives by adding *-isch*, e.g. idiomatically *Kölnisch Wasser* 'eau de Cologne'. The ending may be added to already existing *-er*, as *wienerischer Charme* 'Viennese charm'. Names ending in *-er* or *-ar* often take the ending *sch*, as *Han'noverscher Schweißhund* 'Hanover Bloodhound', *Die Goslarsche Zeitung* 'The Goslar Gazette'. This ending has become productive in connection with surnames regardless of termination: *die Hegelsche Philosophie* 'Hegelian philosophy', also in informal contexts in the usage of the educated: *der Barkesche Aufsatz* 'Barke's essay'.

POSSESSIVE ADJECTIVES

	masc.	fem.	neut.	all genders
Sg. nom.	*mein* 'my'	*meine*	*mein*	Pl. *meine*
acc.	*meinen*	*meine*	*mein*	*meine*
gen.	*meines*	*meiner*	*meines*	*meiner*
dat.	*meinem*	*meiner*	*meinem*	*meinen*

Thus *dein* 'your (familiar sg.), thy', *sein* 'his, its', *ihr* 'her, their' and *Ihr* 'your' (polite sg. and pl.).

Also *unser* 'our', but in the spoken language often contracting in the inflected forms: *unsre*, *unsrer*, likewise *unsren*, *unsrem*, *unsres*, also *unsern*, *unserm*, *unsers*, but all normally written without contraction, i.e. *unsere*, *unserer*, etc. On the other hand, *euer* 'your' (familiar pl.) regularly contracts in the written language, too:

	euer			euer
Sg. nom.	*euer*	*eure*	*euer*	Pl. *eure*
acc.	*euren*	*eure*	*euer*	*eure*
gen.	*eures*	*eurer*	*eures*	*eurer*
dat.	*eurem*	*eurer*	*eurem*	*euren*

(On the contractions, cf. *finster*, *teuer*, p. 59).

In letters, 2nd person adjectives are spelt with a capital: *Dein*, *Euer*.

DEMONSTRATIVE ADJECTIVES

	masc.	fem.	neut.	all genders
Sg. nom.	*dieser* 'this'	*diese*	*dieses*	Pl. *diese*
acc.	*diesen*	*diese*	*dieses*	*diese*
gen.	*dieses*, *-en*	*dieser*	*dieses*, *-en*	*dieser*
dat.	*diesem*	*dieser*	*diesem*	*diesen*

Gen. sg. *-en*, less common, but coming into use after the analogy of the strong declension above, especially before a noun not further qualified: *ein Kongreß diesen Zuschnitts* 'a congress of this format'. Also occasionally sg. nom. acc. neut. *dies* (abbreviation peculiar to this word); in pronominal use, however, it is by far the commoner form, p. 71.

Thus *jener* 'that'.

Further *solcher*, *-e*, *-es* 'such a' declining like the strong adjective, also *ein solcher* or *ein 'derartiger* (mixed decl.) and uninflected *solch*, in addition *so ein*, or simply *so*, pp. 207 f., then *der'selbe* 'the same' consisting of the definite article and *-selbe* declining weak, i.e. sg. acc. masc. *denselben*, etc., cf. its bookish synonym *der nämliche*, also *der gleiche* properly 'the identical', but so often passing as the equal of *derselbe*, and lastly *'derjenige* . . . , (*der*) 'that . . . (who, which)'. When stressed, *der*, *die*, *das* have demonstrative force 'this, that', p. 201.

INTERROGATIVE ADJECTIVES

These are *welcher*, *-e*, *-es* 'which? what?' declining like the strong adjective, also uninflected *welch*, and *was für* (*ein*, *eine*, *ein*) 'what kind of (a)?', p. 212.

RELATIVE ADJECTIVE

This is again *welcher*, *-e*, *-es* 'which' declining like the strong adjective, also uninflected *welch*, p. 324.

INDEFINITE ADJECTIVES

Included here are *aller*, *-e*, *-es* (also uninflected *all*, p. 219) 'all', *jeder*, *-e*, *-es* 'each, every', *mancher*, *-e*, *-es* (also uninflected *manch*, p. 228) 'many (a)', *einiger*, *-e*, *-es* and its (more typically Upper German) synonym *etlicher*, *-e*, *-es* 'some (not a lot, not many)', all declining like the strong adjective, but with an alternative (historically older) gen.

sg. masc. neut. -es. Other items: *der andere* 'the other' (weak declension), *ein anderer* 'another' (mixed declension), pl. *andere* 'other', often contracting in the spoken, but not usually in the written language, e.g. *andre, andren* or *andern*, etc., cf. *unser* (p. 60), neut. *andres*—but *anders* 'otherwise' (adverbial genitive)—further *kein, keine, kein* 'no, not a, not any' inflecting like *mein* (p. 60), and *viel* 'much' with *wenig* 'little' mostly invariable in the singular unless preceded by the definite article (p. 225), but pl. *viele* 'many', *wenige* 'few' regularly decline though uninflected forms are, except in the genitive, common alternatives in writing as well as speaking. In the plural only: *beide* (also *die beiden*) 'both' and *mehrere* 'several'.

In the singular, *jeder* (above) may have a variant *ein jeder* (mixed declension); *jeglicher, ein jeglicher* (strong and mixed declensions respectively) are occasional literary synonyms.

COMPOUND ADJECTIVES

Compound adjectives, typically consisting of two elements, are a common and productive feature of the language. The first element is, in the main, another adjective, a noun, or a verb, the mode of composition being closely comparable to that of compound nouns, pp. 120 ff. The term adjective naturally includes participles.

Adjective (or adverb) plus adjective

Formation is by juxtaposition: *bittersüß* 'bitter–sweet', *feuchtfröhlich* 'boozy', *hellwach* 'wide awake', *naßkalt* 'cold and wet', *schwarzweiß* 'black and white', *taubstumm* 'deaf and dumb'. Examples with participles are illustrated on p. 64.

Noun plus adjective

The noun appears in a variety of forms. It may be juxtaposed: *himmelhoch* 'sky-high', *stockfinster* 'pitch-dark', *zeitraubend* 'time-consuming', *gottvergessen* or *-verlassen* 'god-forsaken', or it may occur in some inflected form: *kriegsmüde* 'war-weary', *arbeitsreich* 'busy', *riesengroß* 'gigantic', *geistesgestört* 'mentally deranged', *jahrelang* 'lasting for years', *kinderleicht* 'dead easy'. The inflected forms need not be consistent: *richtung-* or *richtungsweisend* 'pointing the way, trend-setting', *herzkrank* 'suffering from heart trouble', *herzensfroh* 'overjoyed', *liebevoll* 'affectionate', *liebeskrank* 'love-sick'.

Verb plus adjective

The stem of the verb provides the first element: *gehfähig* 'able to walk', *schreibfaul* 'lazy about writing letters', *treffsicher* 'unerring'; an inflexional -e may occur: *leseblind* 'word-blind'.

Compounds with more than two elements

These are relatively few in number, but some are very familiar: *sternhagelvoll* 'blind drunk', *kohlrabenschwarz* 'deep black', *mucksmäuschenstill*, an emphatic form of *mäuschenstill* 'as quiet as a mouse', *sperrangelweit offen* 'wide open'.

COMPARISON

Positive	Comparative	Superlative
tief 'deep'	*tiefer* 'deeper'	*der (die, das) tiefste* 'the deepest'; predicative only, p. 174: *am tiefsten*

Intensifying gen. pl. *aller-* may be added to the superlative: *der allertiefste* 'the deepest of all, the very deepest'.

Comparative and superlative inflect like the positive: *der tiefere, tiefste Brunnen, ein tieferer, unser tiefster Brunnen* ('well'), *tieferes, tiefstes Rot* ('red').

For stems ending in a sibilant [s, ʃ], the affricate [ts], a dental [t, d], further after a long vowel or after a diphthong, the superlative suffix is *-est-*: *süß* 'sweet', *frisch* 'fresh', *stolz* 'proud', *fest* 'tight', *wild* 'wild': *der süßeste, frischeste, stolzeste, festeste, wildeste*, further *früh* 'early', *schlau* 'sly, smart': *der früheste, schlaueste*; in the spoken language *e* is often dropped after the vowel sound, hence *frühste, schlauste*, alternatives which may equally well be written. There are certain exceptions: *groß* 'big' (below), also words of more than one syllable ending in *-isch*: *praktisch* 'practical', e.g. *die praktischste Methode*, and participial formations not stressed on the final syllable: *bedeutend* 'important', *ausgezeichnet* 'excellent', e.g. *der bedeutendste, ausgezeichnetste Mann*, but with stressed final syllable: *berühmt* 'famous' regularly *der berühmteste Mann*.

A certain number of adjectives of one syllable containing *a, o, u*, modify in the comparative and superlative:

> *alt* 'old', *älter, der älteste*
> *groß* 'big', *größer, der größte*
> *jung* 'young', *jünger, der jüngste*

Thus *arg* (mainly a southern word) 'bad', *arm* 'poor', *hart* 'hard', *kalt* 'cold', *lang* 'long', *scharf* 'sharp', *stark* 'strong, stout', *warm* 'warm'; *grob* 'rough, coarse'; *dumm* 'silly', *klug* 'clever', *kurz* 'short'.

Notice *hoch* 'high', *höher, höchste* ['høøkstə], and *nah(e)* 'nearby', *näher, nächste* ['neekstə] 'nearest, next'.

But more examples do not modify: *blank* 'bare, bright', thus *blanker, blankeste*, similarly *falsch* 'false, wrong', *kahl*, 'bare, bald', *klar* 'clear', *knapp* 'close', *lahm* 'lame, feeble', *matt* 'languid', *rasch* 'quick', *sanft* 'soft', *schlank* 'slim', *zahm* 'tame', *zart* 'gentle, delicate'; *doof* 'daft', *froh* 'glad', *hohl* 'hollow', *roh* 'raw, rough', *toll* 'mad', *voll* 'full'; *bunt* 'motley, gaudy', *stumpf* 'blunt'.

Not surprisingly, usage may sometimes fluctuate, e.g. *blaß* 'pale', *glatt* 'smooth', *krank* 'sick, ill', *naß* 'wet', *schmal* 'slender, narrow', comparative *blasser* or *blässer*, etc., the variation being at least partly regional. The unmodified forms seem to be more widespread, many speakers regarding the modified forms as substandard—or humorous.

Adjectives of more than one syllable never modify with the sole exception of *gesund* 'healthy', *gesünder*, *gesündeste*.

Suppletive comparison: *gut* 'good', *besser* 'better', *beste* 'best'; *viel* 'much', *mehr* (uninflected) 'more', *meiste* 'most'; *wenig* 'little', *weniger* (uninflected) or in some contexts *minder* 'less(er)', *wenigste* or *mindeste* 'least'.

Contraction in the comparative

Adjectives in *-el* contract in the comparative: *dunkel* 'dark', *dunkler*. Those in *-en* may do so in the spoken style: *trocken* 'dry', *trockner*, but normally written *trockener*. Adjectives in *-er* may also lose *e* in the spoken language: *finster* 'dark', *finstrer*, in writing mostly *finsterer*. But in the inflected forms of these last two, contraction is the rule in writing as well as speaking: *trocknere Luft* 'drier air', *ein finstrerer Wald* 'a darker wood'. Where the ending *-er* is preceded by a diphthong, the *e* is elided in all inflected forms in the written language, too: *teuer* 'dear, expensive', *teurer*, etc. Cf. p. 59.

Compounds

Of interest here are compounds of the type adjective (or adverb) plus participle. Two types are distinguished: those taking inflexions at the end in the usual way and those inflecting the first component. The former are adjectives which have developed a new, figurative sense: *hochtrabend* 'high-falutin', *hochtrabender*, *der hochtrabendste*, likewise *wohltuend* 'comforting, pleasant', *zartfühlend* 'sensitive, tactful'. In the second type, each component retains its literal meaning: *hochgelegen* 'high-lying', *höhergelegen*, *der höchstgelegene*, similarly *guteingerichtet* 'well-appointed', *bessereingerichtet*, *der besteingerichtete*. But there are various exceptions. The common term *vielversprechend* 'promising' has always final inflexions; conversely, the equally common *naheliegend* 'reasonable, fairly obvious (as of an assumption)' makes *näherliegend*, *der nächstliegende*. Fluctuation between the two types is not unknown either, an everyday example being *weitgehend* 'far-reaching', *weitgehender* or *weitergehend*, *der weitgehendste* or *weitestgehende*. Especially in speaking, a superlative may combine both types, for instance logically correct *die meistgelesene Zeitung* 'the most read newspaper' becoming *die meistgelesenste Zeitung*.

Less frequently, the main element is an ordinary adjective, as *leichtfaßlich* 'easily comprehended', *leichter faßlich*, (predicative form only) *am leichtesten faßlich*, similarly *schwerverständlich* 'hard to understand'. Isolated superlative forms in daily use are *der best-* and *größtmögliche* 'the best, greatest possible'.

Adjectives with no positive

Certain comparatives and superlatives, formed from adverbs or prepositions, have no positive.

Comp. *der*, etc.,	Superl.
äußere 'outer, exterior'	*äußerste* 'outermost, utmost'
innere 'inner, interior'	*innerste* 'innermost'
obere 'upper, superior'	*oberste* 'uppermost'
untere 'lower, inferior'	*unterste* 'lowest'
vordere 'front, fore-'	*vorderste* 'front, foremost'
hintere 'back, rear'	*hinterste* '(very) back'

Notice the common comparative *mittlere* 'middle, medium'.

Defective comparison also with:

erstere 'former'	*erste* 'first'
letztere 'latter'	*letzte* 'last'

Periphrastic comparison

To a limited extent and in special circumstances, comparison is expressed by *mehr* 'more', *am meisten* 'most'. This is notably the case with a participle retaining its verbal character, when the superlative may also be *meist-*, e.g. *das mehr geschätzte Buch* 'the more valued book', *das am meisten geschätzte* or *das meistgeschätzte Buch* 'the most valued book', thus contrasting with the regular synthetic comparison when the participle is purely adjectival: *das angesehenere, angesehenste Mitglied* 'the more esteemed, most esteemed member'.

Indeclinable adjectives naturally require periphrastic forms: *die mehr, am meisten rosa Vorhänge* 'the pinker, pinkest curtains'. The comparative *mehr* is required in such phrases as *mehr tot als lebendig* 'more dead than alive'. It is a common alternative in association with *immer* when speaking of a gradual increase: *er wird immer mehr unsicher* beside *immer unsicherer* 'he is becoming more and more uncertain'.

Finally, it seems convenient to mention here a widespread colloquialism. The operative factor has been the ambiguity of the word *mehr*, which is both adjective and adverb. From a sentence like *mein Vetter verliert mehr Geld* 'my cousin is losing more money' the language has re-evaluated the adjective as an adverb and by analogy created an adverbial superlative: *mein Vetter verliert am meisten Geld* 'the most money' instead of the regular *das meiste Geld*. The construction is sometimes seen in print: (preface to a grammar) *am meisten Neues findet man in der Laut- und Formenlehre* 'most innovations will be found in the phonology and morphology', alternatively *das meiste Neue*.

5. Adverbs

THE uninflected adjective can, with relatively few exceptions, function as an adverb: *tief* 'deep, deeply', see further p. 175. The exceptions can generally be inferred from the sense, e.g. *regnerisch* 'rainy', *schwanger* 'pregnant', *verderblich* 'perishable', the opposites *krank* 'sick, ill' and *gesund* 'healthy', also the colours: *grün* 'green', *rot* 'red', etc., but *schwarz* 'black' occurs adverbially in a figurative sense, cf. *er fährt schwarz* 'he travels without a ticket, drives without a licence'. But there are cases when this approach fails. Whereas *eng* 'narrow' can be used adverbially, its close synonym *schmal* cannot, nor can *breit* 'broad', so that a sentence like 'Cologne people often speak broad' must be rephrased in translation, say, *die Kölner haben oft eine breite Aussprache*. The adjectives *spitz* 'pointed' and *stumpf* 'blunt(ed)' cannot be used as adverbs either; our 'pointedly' could be rendered *gezielt*, while *frei heraus* or comparable idiom is required for 'bluntly'. One will beware of interference from English in these, partly lexical matters, e.g. *bewußtlos* 'unconscious' = 'having lost consciousness' cannot in the nature of the case function as an adverb; our 'unconsciously', close in sense to 'involuntarily, instinctively', expresses a different concept for which German requires a different word, namely *unbewußt*.

Notice adj. *lang* 'long', adv. *lange*, and the adverbs *rechts*, *links* 'right, left'.

Occasionally, the suffix *-lich* is purely adverbial: *getreulich* 'faithfully', *wahrlich* 'truly' (adj. *getreu*, *wahr*), further *bekanntlich* 'as is (well) known' (adj. *bekannt*), analogically *versehentlich* 'inadvertently' (no corresponding adj.); *grob* 'gross' and *sicher* 'certain' can be both adj. and adv., *gröblich* 'grossly', *sicherlich* 'certainly' only adv., and the same applies to *frei* 'free' and *schwer* 'heavy', but with the difference that the purely adverbial forms have become lexically independent: *freilich* 'admittedly, to be sure', *schwerlich* 'hardly'.

In a single instance, the suffix *-lings* is added to the adjective: *blind* 'blind', *blindlings* 'blindly', beside *blind* in a few contexts, e.g. *sie schreibt blind* 'she touch-types'.

An adverbial genitive based on *Weise* 'manner' is of not uncommon occurrence, and is moderately productive. It may, exceptionally, be the sole adverbial form, cf. *möglich* 'possible', *möglicherweise* 'possibly' (though not in the negative: *das kann er unmöglich gemacht haben* 'he cannot possibly have done that'), but it is more often an

alternative, as *unerwartet* or *unerwarteterweise* 'unexpectedly'. On the
other hand, the forms are not necessarily interchangeable: contrast
die Kinder entwickeln sich normal 'the children are developing
normally' with *die Kinder entwickeln sich normalerweise gut* 'the
children normally develop well'. This is the commonest function of
the form in question, cf. further *er ging glücklich ins Büro* 'he went
happily, i.e. in a happy mood, to the office', with *er ging glücklicher-
weise ins Büro* 'he went, fortunately, to the office'. English sometimes
draws attention to this nuance by adding 'enough': *komisch* 'funnily,
in a funny way', *komischerweise* 'funnily enough'. Among idiomatic
uses we notice the obligatory cliché *unbekannterweise* found in
phrases like *grüßen Sie Ihren Herrn Vater unbekannterweise von mir*
'give your father my kind regards even though we are not acquainted'.

Less frequent is a parallel formation seen in such examples as
bekanntermaßen 'as is (well) known' (= *bekanntlich* above); among
everyday words are *einigermaßen* 'to some (limited) extent' and
gewissermaßen 'so to speak, as it were', also more literally 'to a certain
degree', differentiated in meaning from the simple adverb *gewiß*
'certainly'.

COMPARISON

Comparison closely follows that of the adjective: *tief* 'deep, deeply',
tiefer 'deeper, more deeply', *am tiefsten* 'deepest, most deeply', also
aufs (occasionally *auf das*) *tiefste* with the nuance 'in the deepest way
imaginable', e.g. *wir waren aufs tiefste betroffen* 'we were most deeply
shocked'. Notice:

  lange 'long', *länger, am längsten*
  hoch 'high', *höher, am höchsten* [am 'høøkstən]
  nah(e) 'near', *näher, am nächsten* [am 'neekstən]
  gut, also *wohl* 'well', *besser* 'better, rather', *am besten* 'best'
  wohl 'comfortably, pleasantly', *wohler, am wohlsten*
  bald 'soon', *eher* 'sooner, more likely', *am ehesten* 'soonest, most
  likely'
  gern(e) 'gladly, willingly', *lieber* 'better, rather', *am liebsten* 'best',
  e.g. *das habe ich am liebsten* 'that I like best', locally also *gerner, am
  gernsten*
  oft 'often', *öfter, am öftesten*, but usually *am häufigsten*
  viel 'much', *mehr* 'more', *am meisten*, also *meist* 'most(ly)'
  wenig 'little', *weniger* or *minder* 'less', *am wenigsten* 'least', *zum*
  (NB!) *mindesten* 'at least'.

Certain superlatives are used adverbially without inflexion, including
äußerst 'extremely', *ergebenst* 'most humbly' (old-world concluding

formula in letters), *freundlichst* 'most kindly', *höflichst* 'most politely', *schleunigst* 'with all speed'. Formations of this sort are to all intents and purposes independent lexical items, and some show a degree of semantic change. Thus the superlative sense is often somewhat toned down in *höchst* 'highly, exceedingly', it has acquired an idiomatic function in *gefälligst* 'kindly, if you please' commonly used as an expression of annoyance, and in *längst*, cf. *ich habe es längst vergessen* 'I've long since forgotten it' or *längst nicht so viel Geld* 'not so much money by far'. The adverbs *möglichst* 'as much as ever possible' and *tunlichst* 'whenever feasible' have no corresponding adjective.

A small number of adverbs prefix (unstressed) *zu-* to the uninflected superlative, as *zutiefst* (= *aufs tiefste*) 'most deeply', further *zuerst* 'firstly', *zunächst* 'firstly, for the time being', *zuletzt* 'lastly', *zumeist* (beside *meist*) 'mostly', cf. *erstens*, etc. below, also *zuoberst*, *zuunterst* 'right at the top, bottom'.

A few adverbs form a superlative in *-ens*, including *bestens* (= *aufs beste*), e.g. *wir wurden bestens bedient* 'we were excellently served', similarly *schönstens* lit. 'in the nicest way imaginable', e.g. *ich lasse sie schönstens grüßen* 'I give her my very kindest regards'. Other examples: *erstens* 'firstly' (p. 80), *nächstens* 'soon, shortly', *letztens* 'lastly', *meistens* 'mostly, usually', *höchstens* 'at (the) most', *wenigstens* or *mindestens* 'at least', *frühestens*, *spätestens* 'at the earliest, latest'.

6. Pronouns

PERSONAL PRONOUNS

Sg. nom.	*ich* 'I'			Pl.	*wir* 'we'		
acc.	*mich* .				*uns*		
gen.	*meiner*				*unser*		
dat.	*mir*				*uns*		

Sg. nom.	*du* 'you (familiar), thou'			Pl.	*ihr* 'you (familiar), ye'		
acc.	*dich*				*euch*		
gen.	*deiner*				*euer*		
dat.	*dir*				*euch*		

Sg. nom.	*er* 'he'	*sie* 'she'	*es* 'it'	Pl.	*sie* 'they'	=	*Sie* 'you (polite sg. and pl.)
acc.	*ihn*	*sie*	*es*		*sie*	=	*Sie*
gen.	*seiner*	*ihrer*	*dessen*		*ihrer*	=	*Ihrer*
dat.	*ihm*	*ihr*	*ihm*		*ihnen*	=	*Ihnen*

Reflexive (sg. and pl.) acc. dat. *sich* 'himself, herself, itself, themselves, yourself or yourselves (polite)'.

In letter writing, 2nd person pronouns are spelt with a capital: *Du*, *Ihr*, etc.

   es may be elided to *'s* representing a common pronunciation which can appear in writing, particularly in familiar style, and in poetry.

   Notice that *Sie* 'you' is literally 'They', p. 191.

   The above genitives are in somewhat restricted use, pp. 192 f.

POSSESSIVE PRONOUNS

	masc.	fem.	neut.		all genders
Sg. nom.	*meiner* 'mine'	*meine*	*mein(e)s*	Pl.	*meine*
acc.	*meinen*	*meine*	*mein(e)s*		*meine*
gen.	*meines*	*meiner*	*meiner*		*meiner*
dat.	*meinem*	*meiner*	*meinem*		*meinen*

Neut. *meins* is the commoner form and dominant in the spoken language.

Similarly *deiner* 'yours (familiar sg.), thine', *seiner* 'his, its', *ihrer* 'hers, theirs' and *Ihrer* 'yours (polite)', *unserer* (colloquial contractions as for the corresponding adjective, p. 60) 'ours', *eurer* 'yours (familiar pl.)'. In letters *Deiner*, *Eurer*.

Less usual formations are *der meine, die meine, das meine* and the extended variants *der meinige*, etc. 'mine', etc., and occasional survivals of an uninflected type *mein*, etc., pp. 200 f.

DEMONSTRATIVE PRONOUNS

These are *dieser, -e, -es* 'this (one)' and *jener, -e, -es* 'that (one)', then *ein solcher, eine solche, (ein) solches*, pl. *solche*, or *ein derartiger* 'such (a one)', *der'selbe* with *der nämliche, der gleiche* 'the same (one)', *derjenige, der* 'that one who', all declining like the corresponding adjectives, p. 61; further *so einer* 'such (a one)', declining like *meiner* 'mine' above. The pronoun *der* 'this (one), that (one)' has a somewhat different declension from its adjectival counterpart:

	masc.	fem.	neut.		all genders
Sg. nom.	*der*	*die*	*das*	Pl.	*die*
acc.	*den*	*die*	*das*		*die*
gen.	*dessen*	*deren*	*dessen*		*deren*, also
	or *des*	or *der*	or *des*		*derer, der*

(Short alternatives rare; on the use of the forms, pp. 201 f.)

	masc.	fem.	neut.		all genders
dat.	*dem*	*der*	*dem*		*denen*

INTERROGATIVE PRONOUNS

Sg. nom.	*wer* 'who?'	*was* 'what?'
acc.	*wen*	*was*
gen.	*wessen*	*wessen*
dat.	*wem*	*was*

Archaic gen. *wes* survives in a few expressions, see pp. 202, 213

Further *welcher, -e, -es* 'which (one)?' and sg. *was für einer, eine, ein(e)s* or (as commonly in North Germany) *was für welcher, -e, -es* 'what sort (of one)?'. Here *welcher* declines like the corresponding adjective (p. 61), *einer* goes like *meiner* 'mine', p. 70.

RELATIVE PRONOUNS

The relative ordinarily used today declines as follows:

	masc.	fem.	neut.		all genders
Sg. nom.	*der* 'who, which, that'	*die*	*das*	Pl.	*die*
acc.	*den*	*die*	*das*		*die*
gen.	*dessen*	*deren*	*dessen*		*deren*
dat.	*dem*	*der*	*dem*		*denen*

In much less common use, p. 323:

Sg. nom.	*welcher* 'who, etc.'	*welche*	*welches*	Pl. *welche*
acc.	*welchen*	*welche*	*welches*	*welche*
gen.	—	—	—	—
dat.	*welchem*	*welcher*	*welchem*	*welchen*

Invariable *was* may function as a relative, p. 324.

INDEFINITE PRONOUNS

The following inflect like the corresponding adjectives: *jeder, -e, -es*, variant *ein jeder*, in literary style also (*ein*) *jeglicher* 'each one, everyone', similarly *mancher*, also *manch einer, eine, ein(e)s* 'many a one', pl. *manche* 'many', *der andere* 'the other (one)', *ein anderer* 'another (one)', pl. *andere* 'others'; *keiner* 'no one, none', pl. *keine* 'none' inflects like *meiner* 'mine' p. 70.

These occur in the plural: *alle* 'all', *einige* or *etliche* 'some (not many)', but also (with essentially the same value) as sg. nom. acc. neut. *alles, einiges* or *etliches*, likewise *beide* or *die beiden* 'both', *mehrere* 'several', further *welche* 'some', more indefinitely *irgendwelche*, sg. *beides, mehreres, welches, irgendwelches.*

Unchanged in the singular: *viel* 'much', (*ein*) *wenig* '(a) little', but declining in the plural: *viele* 'many', *wenige* 'few'.

The pronoun *jedermann* 'everyman', also (= *jeder*) 'everyone, everybody' forms gen. *jedermanns.*

The pronouns *jemand* 'someone, somebody, anyone, anybody' and *niemand* 'no one, nobody' make gen. *jemands, niemands*, more bookishly *jemandes, niemandes*; acc. *jemanden, niemanden*, dat. *jemandem, niemandem* are current especially in literary style, but uninflected forms are also regularly met with and are very common in the spoken language. These words are treated in the same way in the Upper German idioms *jemand anderer, niemand anderer* 'someone else, no one else', acc. *jemand(en) anderen*, etc., but in more general use *jemand anders, niemand anders*, usually invariable. In colloquial style *jemand* may be replaced by *wer*, acc. *wen*, dat. *wem*, but there is no genitive; both may be qualified by *irgend* to emphasize the notion of indefiniteness: *irgend jemand, irgendwer* 'someone or other, anyone at all'. Also *einer* = *man* 'one', acc. *einen*, dat. *einem*; the missing genitive is expressed by the possessive adjective *sein*, p. 221. Distinct from the foregoing and declining like *meiner* (p. 70) is sg. *einer, eine, ein(e)s* 'one', also 'someone' = *jemand*, more vaguely *irgendeiner* 'someone or other' = *irgend jemand*, further *der eine . . . der andere* 'the one . . . the other', pl. *die einen . . . die anderen* 'some . . . others'.

The following are invariable: *ein'ander* 'each other, one another', *etwas* or *was* 'something, anything', more vaguely *irgend etwas*, *irgendwas* 'do.', *nichts* 'nothing, not . . . anything', *gar nichts* 'nothing at all'. Also *selbst* with the more colloquial variant *selber* 'self'; *ich*, *wir selbst* or *selber* 'I myself, we ourselves', etc., further *sich selbst* or *selber* (acc. dat.) 'oneself'. The indefinite *man* 'one' does not itself inflect, acc. and dat. being supplied from *einer* (above).

COMPOUND PRONOUNS

Compounded with -*wegen*, *um*. . . *willen*

Personal: *meinetwegen* 'on my account', similarly *deinet-*, *seinet-*, *ihret-* (*Ihret-*), *unseret-*, *euret-* 'on your account, etc.'; *um* . . . *meinetwillen* 'for my sake, etc.'

Demonstrative: masc. neut. sg. *dessentwegen*, *um* . . . *dessentwillen*, fem. sg., all genders pl. *derentwegen*, *um* . . . *derentwillen* 'on account of this/that, for the sake of this/that', as a relative 'on account of which, for the sake of which'. These are literary forms only, pp. 202, 323; the everyday *deswegen* is now purely a conjunction 'therefore'.

In obsolescent use also comparable forms compounded with -*halben*, e.g. *meinethalben* synonymous with *meinetwegen*.

Compounded with -*gleichen*

Invariable -*gleichen* combines with a form of the personal pronoun giving rise to an indefinite pronoun; it is treated as a singular, p. 200: *meinesgleichen* 'one like me', idiomatically often 'my equal(s), the like(s) of me', similarly *deines-*, *seines-*, *ihres-* (*Ihres-*), *unseres-*, *eures-* 'one like you, etc.'. Further the demonstrative *der'gleichen* 'something like this/that, suchlike', also used adjectivally, pp. 208 f.; it is thus distinct from *des'gleichen* 'ditto, likewise'.

7. Numerals

CARDINAL NUMBERS

0 *null*, 1 *eins*, 2 *zwei*, also *zwo*, 3 *drei*, 4 *vier*, 5 *fünf* (locally [fʏmf], 6 *sechs* [zɛks], 7 *sieben*, 8 *acht*, 9 *neun*, 10 *zehn*. The form *zwo* is a creation of the telephone age to avoid confusion with *drei*; it is now often heard in ordinary conversation.

11 *elf*, 12 *zwölf*, 13 *dreizehn*, 14 *vierzehn* (*vier-* often shortened to [fɪr-], etc., pp. 9 f.), 15 *fünfzehn* (casually often [fʊf-]), 16 *sechzehn* ['zɛçtseen], 17 *siebzehn* (*sieb-* often shortened to ['zɪp-], 18 *achtzehn* ['aχtseen], 19 *neunzehn*, 20 *zwanzig*. Unless emphasized, *-zehn* in 13 to 19 is usually pronounced [-tsɛn].

21 *einundzwanzig*, 22 *zweiundzwanzig*, 30 *dreißig*, 40 *vierzig* (*-vier* as in 14), 50 *fünfzig* (*fünf-* as in 15), 60 *sechzig* ['zɛçtsɪç], 70 *siebzig* (*sieb-* as in 17), 80 *achtzig* ['aχtsɪç], 90 *neunzig*, 100 *hundert* 'a hundred', *ein hundert* 'one hundred'.

101 *hunderteins*, 102 *hundertzwei*, 120 *hundertzwanzig*, 121 *hunderteinundzwanzig*, 200 *zweihundert*, 201 *zweihunderteins*, 300 *dreihundert*, 1,000 *tausend* 'a thousand', *ein tausend* 'one thousand'. Also 101 *(ein)hundertundeins*, etc., especially when counting.

1,001 *tausendeins*, 1,066 *tausendsechsundsechzig*, 1,100 *tausendeinhundert*, in quoting dates also *elfhundert*, 2,000 *zweitausend*, 100,000 *hunderttausend*, 1,000,000 *eine Milli'on*, 2,000,000 *zwei Millionen*, 1,000,000,000 *eine Milli'arde* (= *tausend Millionen*), 2,000,000,000 *zwei Milliarden*, 1,000,000,000,000 *eine Billi'on* (= *eine Million Millionen*). Also 1,001 *(ein)tausendundeins*, etc., including dates: 1986 often *neunzehnhundertundsechsundachtzig*.

Widespread in the centre and south is the colloquial addition of a plural *-e* to the numbers 'two' to 'twelve', commonly heard in telling the time: *es ist sechse* 'it's six o'clock', *es schlägt siebene* 'it's striking seven'. The idiom *alle viere*, on the other hand, is universal and standard: *er streckte alle viere von sich* 'he gave up the ghost'; it is also commonly heard in the dative: *auf allen vieren* 'on all fours'.

There is a tendency to read out longer numbers in pairs, e.g. the street number *Glockengasse 4711* is *siebenundvierzig elf*; the telephone number 2 65 23 (so printed) will commonly be so spoken, i.e. *zwei fünfundsechzig dreiundzwanzig*.

Observations on the forms—Number 'one'

The (neuter) form *eins* is used in counting: *eins und eins ist zwei* 'one and one are two', and in comparable contexts: *eins Komma zwei (1, 2)* 'one point two (1·2)', *er fährt mit dem 1A (eins A) Bus* 'he goes on the 1A bus'. Otherwise, except as mentioned below, the numeral inflects for number and case, the forms being as for the indefinite article, p. 58: *ein Löffel* 'one spoon', *eine Gabel* 'one fork', *ein Messer* 'one knife'. If, in the written word, the numerical sense would not be clear from the context, this will be indicated by spaced type or by italics, rarely by an accent: *éin*. In speaking, of course, *ein* 'one' carries a stress, while *ein* 'a' has none. The numeral preceded by the definite article or a demonstrative regularly follows the weak declension: *der (dieser) eine Löffel* 'the (this) one spoon'. Should the numeral stand alone, the masc. nom. is *einer* (also in other pronominal use, pp. 221 f.), the neut. nom. acc. *eines* or *eins*. The alternative neuters are both common, reflecting the pronunciation as the case may be. Generally speaking, *eins* will be expected if unstressed, but in stressed position either may occur. The following may then illustrate average practice: *hast du ein Messer? — ja, ich habe eins* (unstressed) 'have you a knife?—yes, I have one', but *brauchst du Messer? — ja, aber nur eines* or *eins* (stressed) 'do you need any knives?—yes, but only one'.

The numeral is uninflected in the expressions *ein für allemal* 'once and for all', *ein und alles* in phrases of the type *sie war sein ein und alles* 'she was his one and all' and *ein bis zwei*, e.g. *das reicht für ein bis zwei Tage* 'it will last for one to two days', also in such contexts as *zwischen ein und zwei (drei*, etc.) *Grad* 'between one and two (three, etc.) degrees', p. 310. Our 'one or two' may be invariable *ein oder zwei*, e.g. *in jeder Klasse gibt es ein oder zwei Hochbegabte* 'in every class there are one or two highly gifted ones', but one may also use (similarly invariable) *ein, zwei*, and likewise *zwei, drei*, etc.: *ich bleibe ein, zwei (zwei, drei) Wochen* 'I'm staying for a week or two (two or three weeks)'. The numeral further commonly remains unchanged in *ein und derselbe* 'one and the same, the very same': *in ein und demselben Augenblick* 'at the very same moment', but for special emphasis inflected forms may be used: *in einem und demselben Augenblick*. Notice *ein Uhr* 'one o'clock' distinct from *eine Uhr* 'one (or a) clock'. Like all cardinals it is unchanged in composition: *die Eintagsfliege* 'day-fly'.

In conclusion, 'one' in *hundert-*, *tausend(und)eins* 101, 1001. These numbers are but rarely encountered in a syntactical context—our 'I had a hundred and one things to do' is represented in German by *ich hatte tausenderlei zu tun*—and are even more rarely seen written out in words. When they do occur attributively there are two possibilities: either invariable *hunderteins*, e.g. *hunderteins Fässer* '101 barrels', or else *hundertundein* inflecting: *hundertundein Faß, in hundertundeinem*

Faß '(in) 101 barrels'. The latter construction will be heard in connection with money: *hundertundeine Mark* '101 marks—we recall that *Mark* is in any case invariable—and this is the literary solution, as illustrated by the celebrated book title *Tausendundeine Nacht* 'Arabian Nights'. But, in the nature of the case, occurrences are minimal and not necessarily consistent. A sentence from the introduction in our copy of the book just mentioned reads: *mein Herr und Gebieter, ich habe Euch in tausendundeiner Nacht* (sg. after the title) *tausendundeine Geschichten* (pl. in keeping with a feeling of plurality) *erzählt, sagte Scheherasade* 'my lord and master, I have told you in one thousand and one nights one thousand and one tales, said Sheherazade'.

Numbers 'two' and 'three'

These make the genitive *zweier, dreier* in high style; a following adjective may be strong or weak, p. 168: *der Vater zweier* (*großer*, or *großen*) *Söhne* 'the father of two (big) sons', but ordinarily *der Vater von zwei* (*großen*) *Söhnen*. These numbers may add dat. *-en*, see next section.

In a few compounds *Zwie-* occurs instead of the usual *Zwei-*, e.g. *Zweikampf* m. 'duel', but *Zwiegespräch* n. 'dialogue', *Zwiespalt* m. 'inner conflict', *Zwietracht* f. *discord*, also *Zwielicht* n. 'twilight'.

Numbers 'two' to 'twelve'

These may add dat. *-en*, except *sieben* 'seven' which already ends in *-en*. Such forms are felt to be more colloquial than the uninflected alternatives: *einem hat er ins Bein, zweien* (or *zwei*) *in den Rücken geschossen* 'one he shot in the leg, two in the back', *einer von dreien* (or *drei*) 'one in (out of) three', *mit unseren vieren* (or *vier*) 'with our four (e.g. children)'. Further *die Tiere gingen zu zweien* (but usually *zu zweit*, p. 80) *in die Arche* 'the animals went into the ark in twos'—other possible formulations: *je zwei* or *zwei und zwei* 'two by two'. Cf. *auf allen vieren*, p. 74.

Numbers 'hundred' and 'thousand'

As in English, these may be qualified by indefinite pronouns: *mehrere hundert Pfund wurden gezahlt* 'several hundred pounds were paid', *der Nachthimmel leuchtet mit vielen tausend Sternen* 'the night sky shines with many thousand stars'. They are regularly substantivized: *ich gebe noch sechs dazu, damit das Hundert voll ist* 'I am adding another six to make up the hundred'; they often occur in the plural: *der Betrag geht in die Hunderte* 'the amount runs into the hundreds', *Tausende und Abertausende hatten sich zu den Festlichkeiten eingefunden* 'thousands upon thousands had gathered for the festivities', *die Heuschrecken erschienen zu Hunderttausenden* 'the locusts appeared

in hundreds of thousands'; see further under 'Substantivization',
below. Notice the varying genitive morphology: *die Anstrengungen
weniger Hunderte Wissenschaftler* 'the efforts of a few hundred
scientists', but *die Anstrengungen Hunderter Wissenschaftler*—less
stiffly *die Anstrengungen von Hunderten (von) Wissenschaftlern*. It
will be seen that *Wissenschaftler* can be used in apposition, in which
connection the numeral may be found written with a small initial: *die
Anstrengungen von hunderten Wissenschaftlern*, similarly *eine Bibliothek
mit tausenden Büchern* 'a library with thousands of books'. On 'a
hundred and one', etc., see pp. 75 f.

'Dozen'

German *das Dutzend* is treated in principle like *hundert, tausend*, see
previous section: *zwei Dutzend Eier* 'two dozen eggs', *Dutzende von
Kisten* 'dozens of chests', or in apposition *Dutzende Kisten*, both
stylistically neutral.

'Umpteen'

German has two roughly comparable, slangy expressions, *x* [ɪks] and
zig, the latter abstracted from *zwanzig*, etc.—'umpteen' is based on
'thirteen', etc.: *er rast auf seinem Motorrad mit x Sachen* (or *zig
Sachen*) *durch die Botanik* 'he races through the countryside on his
motorbike at umpteen kilometres an hour'; needless to add, both
Sachen and *Botanik* in these senses are at least equally slangy.

Substantivization

The numbers, i.e. the figures, can be treated as nouns when they are
feminine: *die Null, Eins, Zwei*, pl. *die Nullen, Einsen, Zweien*,
similarly *die Hundert, die Tausend* contrasting with *das Hundert, das
Tausend*, which denote the quantity rather than the actual figure,
p. 76. In South German a masculine derivative is more usual from
'one' onwards: *der Einser, Zweier*, pl. *die Einser, Zweier*. Thus *ich
habe in Deutsch eine Eins* (southern *einen Einser*) *bekommen* 'I've got
a "one" (the top grade) in German', but all say *Eins zu Null für mich*
'one up to me' lit. 'one–nil for me', from sporting parlance; in the
same way *sie gewannen Zwei zu Eins* 'they won two–one'. Where the
meaning is the number as such, as opposed to the figure, the plural is
formed without change: *das ist genug Proviant für die drei* 'that is
enough food for the three of them', the numeral being written with a
small initial unless it has the character of a proper noun: *die Großen
Drei* 'the Big Three', *der Rat der Zwölf* 'the Council of Twelve'.

Masculine derivatives in *-er* have various applications. We notice
first the sequence (commonly in the plural): *die Einer* 'the units', *die
Zehner* 'the tens', *die Hunderter* 'the hundreds', *die Tausender* 'the

thousands'. Such forms are constantly employed in connection with money; for instance, any coin or note worth five of anything in any currency could be called *der Fünfer* lit. 'fiver'. In ordinary use *der Fünfer* is primarily *das Fünfpfennigstück* 'the 5-pf. piece', similarly *der Zehner* 'the 10-pf. piece' (though usually called *der Groschen*) and *der Fünfziger* 'the 50-pf. piece' (with the expression *ein falscher Fuffziger* lit. 'a bad 50-pf. piece' i.e. 'a slippery customer, a bad lot' reproducing a casual pronunciation, p. 74). On the other hand, in the nature of things, *der Hunderter* is the *Hundertmarkschein* 'the 100-mark note', *der Tausender* 'the 1,000-mark note'.

Other daily usage may be illustrated by the following: *er ist ein Dreißiger* or *er ist in den Dreißigern* 'he is in his thirties', with feminine equivalents: *eine fesche Mittvierzigerin* 'a stylish woman in her mid-forties'. These forms may be used attributively: *die zwanziger (20er) Jahre dieses Jahrhunderts* 'the twenties of this century', *wir fahren mit der achtundzwanziger (28er) Straßenbahn* 'we go on the 28 tram', also commonly heard in dealing with stamps: *eine achtziger Marke = eine Marke zu achtzig Pfennig* 'an 80-pf. stamp', *zwei achtziger Marken* 'two 80-pf. stamps', alternatively *eine Achtziger* (feminine!), *zwei Achtziger*. Attributive and noun are otherwise generally written as one word: *das Dreiertreffen* 'the meeting of the Three', *die Viererbande* 'the Gang of Four', *die Sechserpackung* 'the packet of six'—in other cases similar concepts may be expressed by a different construction, as *der Rat der Zwölf* p. 77.

Compound cardinals

These include *einerlei* 'one kind (of)', *zweierlei* 'two kinds (of)', *dreierlei* 'three kinds (of)', etc., consisting of the numeral with the genitive inflexion *-er* plus now extinct *Lei* f. 'kind, sort', the terms thus being originally adverbial genitives meaning 'of one kind', etc. They are invariable and treated as neuter singulars *das ewige Einerlei* (cliché) 'the never-ending monotony, always the same thing', *daraus geht zweierlei hervor* 'two distinct matters arise from that'. These numerals are commonly used as attributives, in which function they are closest to their origin; the number of the noun following is that which it would have had were it not qualified: *auf dreierlei Art und Weise* 'in three different ways', *hunderterlei (tausenderlei) Sachen waren noch zu erledigen* 'a hundred (thousand) odds and ends were still to be settled'. We may add that indefinites are similarly formed, e.g. very commonly *allerlei* 'all kinds (of)', *beiderlei* 'both kinds of' with the following noun in the singular, *keinerlei* 'no kind, or kinds, of', *vielerlei* 'many kinds (of)': *Leipziger Allerlei* lit. 'Leipzig All-sorts' (a mixed vegetable dish), *Schüler beiderlei Geschlechts* (the standard expression) *besuchen diese Schule* 'pupils of both sexes attend this school', *er hat keinerlei Chancen* 'he had no chances at all', *viel und vielerlei*, for which see p. 224.

Multiplicatives are formed by adding *-mal* to the cardinal: *einmal* 'once', *zweimal* 'twice', *dreimal* 'thrice, three times', *viermal* 'four times', etc., also *x-mal* or *zigmal* 'umpteen times', *duzendmal* 'a dozen times', further *eineinhalbmal* or *anderthalbmal* 'one and a half times', etc. Examples: *sie hat fünfmal versucht* 'she has tried five times', *einmal eins ist eins* 'once one is one', *zweimal eins ist zwei* 'twice one are two', etc.; iterative use is equally common: *einmal am Tag* 'once a day', *zweimal in der Woche* (*im Monat, im Jahr*) 'twice a week (a month, a year)'. The suffix *-ig* is required for adjectival forms: *einmalig* 'unique', *zweimalig* 'occurring twice', etc. The first is an everyday word: *ein einmaliges Angebot* 'a unique offer', also in a derivative sense: *das war einmalig* 'it was unprecedented, quite out of the ordinary', the others belong to more formal style and can only be used attributively: *nach einem dreimaligen* (more ordinarily *dritten*) *Versuch wurde der Plan aufgegeben* 'after a third attempt the plan was abandoned'. Indefinites, also literary words, are *oft-, mehr-, vielmalig* 'frequent, repeated'; they are associated with the corresponding adverbs *oftmals*, etc.

Other multiplicatives are formed by adding *-fach* to the cardinal: *einfach* 'simple, single', *zweifach* 'double, twofold', *dreifach* 'treble, threefold', *vierfach* 'quadruple, fourfold', etc., *milli'onenfach* 'a million times', also *x-fach* or *zigfach* 'umpteen times', *dutzendfach* 'a dozen times', further *eineinhalbfach* or *anderthalbfach* 'one and a half times', etc. Examples: *eine einfache Fahrkarte* 'a single ticket' (as opposed to a return), *der Antrag muß in zweifacher Ausfertigung ausgestellt werden* 'the application must be made out in duplicate'. These numerals are often substantivized: *er verlangt das Dreifache* 'he is asking three times the amount', and adverbial use is also common: *die Methode hat sich hundertfach bewährt* 'the method has proved itself a hundredfold' when it overlaps with *hundertmal* 'a hundred times' above. We may notice the indefinites *mehrfach, vielfach* 'manifold, repeated', often adverbial: *man hat mich mehrfach* (or *vielfach*) *danach gefragt* 'I've frequently been asked about it'. These multiplicatives have given rise to a verbal series: *vereinfachen* 'to simplify', *verzweifachen* 'to increase twofold', etc., further *vervielfachen* 'to increase by many times'.

The variant formations *-faltig* or as generally *-fältig* '-fold' in the numerical sense are obsolete or obsolescent: (Menge) *denn wenn Kain siebenfältig gerächt werden soll, so Lamech siebenundsiebzigfach* 'if Cain shall be avenged sevenfold, truly Lamech seventy and sevenfold'. The following, however, remain in everyday use: *einfältig*, but meaning 'simple-minded', and the indefinites *mannigfaltig* (NB!) and *vielfältig* 'manifold', whence the verb *vervielfältigen* 'to duplicate, make copies of'.

ORDINAL NUMBERS

These are formed from the cardinals by the addition of *t* from 2 to 19, of *st* from 20 upwards, to which are further added the necessary adjectival endings. The 'first' and 'third' are irregular, 'seventh' may contract, 'eighth' drops one *t* as in English: 1st *der*, *die*, *das erste*, (*ein*) *erster*, (*eine*) *erste*, (*ein*) *erstes*, 2nd *zweite*, widely also, mainly in speaking *zwote*, 3rd *dritte*, 4th *vierte*, 5th *fünfte*, 6th *sechste*, 7th *siebente* or quite commonly *siebte*, 8th *achte*, 9th *neunte*, 10th *zehnte*, 11th *elfte*, 12th *zwölfte*, 13th *dreizehnte*, 14th *vierzehnte*, 15th *fünfzehnte*, 16th *sechzehnte*, 17th *siebzehnte*, 18th *achtzehnte*, 19th *neunzehnte*. Corresponding to '1st, 2nd, 3rd, 4th', etc., German puts *1., 2., 3., 4.*

20th *zwanzigste*, 21st *einundzwanzigste*, 30th *dreißigste*, 40th *vierzigste*, 50th *fünfzigste*, 60th *sechzigste*, 70th *siebzigste*, 80th *achtzigste*, 90th *neunzigste*, 100th *hundertste*, 101st *hundertunderste*, in speaking sometimes *hundertundeinste*, 102nd *hundertundzweite*, *-zwote*, 120th *hundertundzwanzigste*, 121st *hunderteinundzwanzigste*, 200th *zweihundertste*, 1,000th *tausendste*, 1,000,000th *millionste*; 'umpteenth' *x-te* (cf. our 'nth').

Ordinals take the regular adjectival endings: *König Heinrich der Achte* 'King Henry the Eighth', *die Ehefrauen König Heinrichs des Achten* 'the wives of King Henry the Eighth'. They are like superlatives in that they have an inflexion in non-attributive positions: *Gerhard ist Klassenerster* (*Klassenbester*) 'G. is top of the class', *sie kam als erste durchs Ziel* 'she was the first to cross the finishing line'. But stem forms are found in composition: *die Erstaufführung* 'the première', *das Zweitauto* 'the second car' (as opposed to *das Erstauto*, e.g. of a two-car family), *der dritthöchste Berg* 'the third highest mountain', *die viertletzte Stelle* 'the fourth place from the end'. Substantivization is seen in *das Zehnt* 'the tithe', compare also the common expressions *zu zweit*, *zu dritt*, *zu viert*, e.g. *sie kamen zu viert* 'they came in fours, or in a group of four'. Adverbs add *-ens* to the stem: *erstens* 'firstly', *zweitens* 'secondly', *drittens* 'thirdly', *viertens* 'fourthly', etc.

FRACTIONS

'(The) half' is *die Hälfte*, e.g. *die eine Hälfte* 'the one half', (*die*) *zwei Hälften* '(the) two halves', *die Hälfte mußte weggeworfen werden* 'half had to be thrown away'.

The adjective 'half' is *halb*, e.g. *ein halbes Kilo* 'half a kilo', *zum halben Preis* 'at half price', sometimes with the meaning 'small' as *ein halbes Zimmer* 'a small-sized room' as opposed to *ein Zimmer* 'a (full-sized) room', without an article: *halb Lübeck war dabei* 'half L. was present' (figuratively speaking). It is occasionally made into a noun: *das ist nichts Halbes und nichts Ganzes* 'it is neither one thing nor the other', and is also used adverbially: *frisch gewagt ist halb gewonnen* 'a good start is half the battle'; it easily forms compounds as *halbamtlich* 'semi-official', *halbwüchsig* 'adolescent', *Halbinsel* 'peninsula', *Halbzeit* 'half-time'.

In the singular, *die Hälfte* with its dependent genitive is optionally replaceable by *halb*, which then qualifies the noun in question: *die Hälfte der Mannschaft* 'half of the team', *die halbe Mannschaft* 'half the team'. Replacement extends to the plural: *die Hälfte der Spieler* 'half of the players', *die halben Spieler* 'half the players', but such use in the plural is stigmatized as somewhat substandard if only because it is often ambiguous, cf. *die halben Kartoffeln* understandable both as 'the half-potatoes' and as 'half the potatoes'. Nevertheless the construction is prevalent in the ordinary colloquial, which does not take too kindly to the genitive.

After numerals 'half' is *einhalb*: 1½ *eineinhalb* or *anderthalb*, 2½ *zweieinhalb*, 3½ *dreieinhalb*, etc. These are invariable: *eineinhalb Stunden* 'one and a half hours', but *eine und eine halbe Stunde* 'one hour and a half'.

The other fractions have the ending *-tel* (originally *Teil* 'part' added to the ordinal) and are neuter: ⅓ *Drittel*, ¼ *Viertel*, ⅕ *Fünftel*, ⅙ *Sechstel*, ⅐ *Siebentel*, also *Siebtel*, ⅛ *Achtel*, ⅑ *Neuntel*, ⅒ *Zehntel*, 1/20 *Zwanzigstel*, 1/100 *Hundertstel*, 1/1,000 *Tausendstel*, 1/1,000,000 *Millionstel*; ⅔ *zwei Drittel*, ¾ *drei Viertel*, etc. When 'three-quarters' is felt to be a single concept, as when telling the time, it is written as one word, e.g. *dreiviertel zwei* 'a quarter to two', p. 82. The fraction *Viertel* often forms compounds, thus *eine Viertelstunde* 'a quarter of an hour', hence also *eine Dreiviertelstunde* '(a period of) three-quarters of an hour', also written with a small initial: *eine viertel Stunde, eine dreiviertel Stunde*, common also in *fünfviertel Stunden* 'in an hour and a quarter'.

DISTRIBUTIVES

These consist of the distributive particle *je* 'each' and a following cardinal: *er zahlte je zehn Mark für die Bilder* 'he paid ten marks each for the pictures', *man verkauft jetzt Kleinkindermahlzeiten in appetitlichen Einmachgläschen, je eins für zwei Mahlzeiten ausreichend* 'now they're selling meals for toddlers in nice little bottling jars, each one sufficient for two meals'.

TELLING THE TIME

Sample sentences: *wieviel Uhr ist es?* or *wie spät ist es?* 'what time is it?', further *wieviel Uhr haben Sie?* 'what time do you make it?', *es ist eins* or *ein Uhr* 'it is one o'clock', *es ist fünf (Minuten) nach eins* 'it is five (minutes) past one', *zehn nach eins* 'ten past one', *es ist* (especially North German) *Viertel nach eins*, otherwise generally *Viertel zwei* for original (and occasionally still heard) *Viertel auf* ('towards') *zwei* 'a quarter past one', *zwanzig nach eins* 'twenty past one', *fünf vor halb zwei* 'twenty-five past one', *halb zwei* 'half past one', *fünf nach halb zwei* 'twenty-five to two', *zwanzig vor zwei* 'twenty to two', (esp. northern) *Viertel vor zwei*, otherwise generally *dreiviertel zwei* for (occasional) *dreiviertel auf zwei* 'a quarter to two', *zehn vor zwei* 'ten to two', *fünf vor zwei* 'five to two', *es ist genau zwei* (also colloquially *zweie*, p. 74) or *zwei Uhr* 'it is exactly two o'clock'.

The twenty-four hour clock is usual in official announcements: *Programmbeginn 9.15* (*neun Uhr fünfzehn*) 'programme starts at 9.15 a.m.', *Abflug 0.25* (*null Uhr fünfundzwanzig*) 'take off 0.25 hours', *der Überlandbus kommt um 21.45* (*einundzwanzig Uhr fünfundvierzig*) *an* 'the country bus arrives at 9.45 p.m.', and these forms are also freely used when talking about such matters, much more so than in English. But for the rest the ordinary clock is the rule, with *vormittags* (abbreviated *vorm.*) and *nachmittags* (*nachm.*) corresponding to 'a.m.' and 'p.m.' respectively. The above items from the twenty-four hour clock may also be written *9 Uhr 15, 0 Uhr 25, 21 Uhr 45*, i.e. as they are spoken.

GIVING THE DATE

Sample sentences: *der wievielte ist heute?* or *heute ist der wievielte?*, alternatively *welches Datum haben wir heute?* 'what is the date today?'—*heute ist der 1. (erste) Mai* 'today is the first of May'. The same question may take the form *den wievielten haben wir heute?*, alternatively *welches Datum haben wir heute?*, and the answer *heute haben wir den 1. (ersten) Mai*. Further: *es ist der 1. Mai* 'it is the 1st of May', *der Erste des Monats* 'the first of the month', *es ist der 2. (zweite, often zwote, p. 80) Mai* 'it is the 2nd of May'.

Other examples: *am wievielten hat sie Geburtstag?* 'on what date does her birthday fall?—*am 16. (sechzehnten) Februar* 'on the 16th of February', *zum wievielten wurde er angestellt?* 'as from what date was he appointed?'—*zum 1. (ersten) dieses Monats* 'as from the 1st of this month', *wann läuft die Kündigungsfrist ab?* 'when does the period of notice expire?'—*am 30. (dreißigsten) März nächstes Jahr* 'on the 30th of March next year'. Further: *an welchem Tag wollen Sie abreisen?* 'on which (or, what) day do you wish to leave?'—*am Montag* 'on Monday', *an einem Montag* 'on a Monday'. Notice *Händel starb 1759 (siebzehnhundertneunundfünfzig* or *siebzehnhundertundneunundfünfzig)* or *im Jahre 1759* 'Handel died in (the year) 1759'; in recent German *in 1759* (in imitation of English practice) is a third, and quite common, variation.

In formal style, time at which may be expressed by the accusative, pp. 147 f.: *die Versteigerung findet Freitag, den 3. (dritten) Juni, statt* 'the auction will take place on Friday, the 3rd of June', similarly at the head of a letter: *Emden, den 9. Juli 1986,* also *am 9. Juli* and this (otherwise everyday colloquial form) is the more dignified written style; it is usual, for instance, on legal documents.

Days of the week, all masc.: *Sonntag* (abbrev. *So.*) 'Sunday', *Montag* usually ['moon-] (*Mo.*) 'Monday', *Dienstag* (*Di.*) 'Tuesday', *Mittwoch* (*Mi.*) 'Wednesday', *Donnerstag* (*Do.*) 'Thursday', *Freitag* (*Fr.*) 'Friday', *Sonnabend* or *Samstag* (*Sa.*) 'Saturday', the latter alternative essentially a word of the south and west, but becoming common elsewhere and necessary when an abbreviation is required, since the former would be confused with *Sonntag*. The plural is formed with -*e*, but the singular tends to remain uninflected: *in den frühen Stunden des Mittwoch*, less usually *Mittwochs* 'in the early hours of Wednesday'. As illustrated by the examples above, these names are often used with an article, but in certain cases such use is optional: *er macht (einen) blauen Montag* 'he's taking Monday off (unofficially)', *wir haben (den) Dienstag frei* 'we have Tuesday off'. At the same time articles may be absent, as in English: *er kommt Sonnabend (nachmittag)* 'he's coming on Saturday (afternoon)'.

Months, all masc.: *Januar*, Upper German *Jänner* (abbrev. *Jan.*, *Jän.*), *Februar* (*Febr.*), *März*, *A'pril*, *Mai*, *Juni*, *Juli* (the last two sometimes *Juno*, *Julei*, artificial forms arising for clarity, as when telephoning; they are not normally written), *Au'gust* (*Aug.*), *Sep'tember* (*Sept.*), *Ok'tober* (*Okt.*), *No'vember* [-'vɛm-] (*Nov.*), *De'zember* (*Dez.*). They tend not to decline: *in den ersten Tagen des Januar* 'in the first days of January', and are commonly used with the definite article (p. 187).

8. Verbs

THE German verb, like its English counterpart, has two synthetic tenses in the active voice, i.e. present and preterite. The remaining tenses, and the whole of the passive voice, are formed analytically using *sein* 'to be', *werden* 'to become', *haben* 'to have' as auxiliaries. The conjugation of these is as follows.

The auxiliary *sein*

Infinitives: present *(zu) sein* 'to be', perfect *gewesen (zu) sein* 'to have been'

Participles: present *seiend* 'being', perfect *gewesen* 'been'

Indicative

	Present	Preterite	Future
Sg. 1	*ich bin* 'I am'	*war* 'was'	*werde sein* 'shall be'
2	*du bist*	*warst*	*wirst* ⎫
3	*er ist*	*war*	*wird* ⎪
Pl. 1	*wir sind*	*waren*	*werden* ⎬ *sein*
2	*ihr seid*	*wart*	*werdet* ⎪
3	*sie sind*	*waren*	*werden* ⎭

Perfect *ich bin gewesen* 'I have been', etc.
Pluperfect *ich war gewesen* 'I had been', etc.
Future perfect *ich werde gewesen sein* 'I shall have been', etc.

Subjunctive

Present *ich sei, du seist, er sei, wir seien, ihr seit, sie seien*—the only verb today with a complete present subjunctive paradigm, all others preserving no more than the 3rd singular.

Preterite *ich wäre, due wärest, er wäre, wir wären, ihr wäret, sie wären*, alternatively *du wärst, ihr wärt* corresponding to the naturally spoken forms.

Future *er werde sein*
Perfect *ich sei gewesen*, etc.
Pluperfect *ich wäre gewesen*, etc.
Future perfect *er werde gewesen sein*

(Conditional)

The present conditional is expressed either by the preterite *ich wäre* 'I would be', etc., or else analytically:

$$\left.\begin{array}{l} \textit{ich würde} \\ \textit{du würdest} \\ \textit{er würde} \end{array}\right\} \textit{sein} \qquad \left.\begin{array}{l} \textit{wir würden} \\ \textit{ihr würdet} \\ \textit{sie würden} \end{array}\right\} \textit{sein}$$

The perfect conditional is expressed either by the pluperfect *ich wäre gewesen* 'I would have been', etc., or else analytically: *ich würde gewesen sein*, etc.

Imperative: (familiar) sg. *sei!* pl. *seid!* (polite) *seien Sie!* 'be!'

The auxiliary *werden*

The infinitives: present *(zu) werden* 'to become', perfect *worden* or *geworden (zu) sein* 'to have become'

Participles: present *werdend* 'becoming', perfect *worden*, when not used as an auxiliary *geworden* 'become'

Indicative

	Present	Preterite	Future	
Sg. 1	*ich werde* 'I become'	*wurde* 'became'	*werde werden* 'shall be-	
2	*du wirst*	*wurdest*	*wirst* ⎫	come'
3	*er wird*	*wurde*	*wird* ⎪	
Pl. 1	*wir werden*	*wurden*	*werden* ⎬ *werden*	
2	*ihr werdet*	*wurdet*	*werdet* ⎪	
3	*sie werden*	*wurden*	*werden* ⎭	

Perfect *ich bin geworden* 'I have become', etc.
Pluperfect *ich war geworden* 'I had become', etc.
Future perfect *ich werde geworden sein* 'I shall have become', etc.

Subjunctive

Present *er werde*
Preterite *ich würde, du würdest, er würde, wir würden, ihr würdet, sie würden*
Future *er werde werden*
Perfect *ich sei geworden*, etc.
Pluperfect *ich wäre geworden*, etc.
Future perfect *er werde geworden sein*

(Conditional)

The present conditional is expressed either by the preterite *ich würde* 'I would become', etc., or else analytically (and tautologically, p. 262) *ich würde werden*, etc.

The perfect conditional is expressed either by the pluperfect *ich wäre geworden* 'I would have become', or else analytically: *ich würde geworden sein*, etc.

Imperative: (familiar) sg. *werde!* pl. *werdet!* (polite) *werden Sie!* 'become!'

The auxiliary *haben*

Infinitives: present *(zu) haben* 'to have', perfect *gehabt (zu) haben* 'to have had'

Participles: present *habend* 'having', perfect *gehabt* 'had'

Indicative

	Present	Preterite	Future	
Sg. 1	*ich habe* 'I have'	*hatte* 'had'	*werde haben* 'shall have'	
2	*du hast*	*hattest*	*wirst*	⎤
3	*er hat*	*hatte*	*wird*	⎥
Pl. 1	*wir haben*	*hatten*	*werden*	⎬ *haben*
2	*ihr habt*	*hattet*	*werdet*	⎥
3	*sie haben*	*hatten*	*werden*	⎦

Perfect *ich habe gehabt* 'I have had', etc.
Pluperfect *ich hatte gehabt* 'I had had', etc.
Future perfect *ich werde gehabt haben* 'I shall have had', etc.

Subjunctive

Present *er habe*
Preterite *ich hätte, du hättest, er hätte, wir hätten, ihr hättet, sie hätten*
Future *er werde haben*
Perfect *er habe gehabt*
Pluperfect *ich hätte gehabt*, etc.
Future perfect *er werde gehabt haben*

(Conditional)

The present conditional is expressed either by the preterite *ich hätte* 'I would have', etc., or else analytically: *ich würde haben*, etc. The perfect conditional is expressed either by the pluperfect *ich hätte gehabt* 'I would have had', etc., or else analytically: *ich würde gehabt haben*, etc.

Imperative: (familiar) sg. *hab(e)!*, pl. *habt!* (polite) *haben Sie!* 'have!' Both forms of the familiar singular are found in print, but the short form prevails in the spoken language.

Main verbs

WEAK CONJUGATION

Most verbs follow the weak conjugation; they make the preterite and
perfect participle by means of a *t*-suffix.

ACTIVE VOICE

Infinitives: present *(zu) loben* 'to praise', perfect *gelobt (zu) haben* 'to
have praised'
Participles: present *lobend* 'praising', with perfect system *gelobt*
'praised

Indicative

	Present	Preterite
Sg. 1	*ich lobe* 'I praise'	*lobte* 'praised'
2	*du lobst*	*lobtest*
3	*er lobt*	*lobte*
Pl. 1	*wir loben*	*lobten*
2	*ihr lobt*	*lobtet*
3	*sie loben*	*lobten*

Future *ich werde loben* 'I shall praise', etc.
Perfect *ich habe gelobt* 'I have praised', etc.
Pluperfect *ich hatte gelobt* 'I had praised', etc.
Future perfect *ich werde gelobt haben* 'I shall have praised', etc.

Subjunctive

Present *er lobe*
Preterite (wanting)
Future *er werde loben*
Perfect *er habe gelobt*
Pluperfect *ich hätte gelobt*, etc.
Future perfect *er werde gelobt haben*

(Conditional)

Present *ich würde loben* 'I would praise', etc.
Perfect *ich hätte gelobt* or *ich würde gelobt haben* 'I would have
praised, etc.

Imperative: (familiar) sg. *lobe(e)!* pl. *lobt!* (polite) *loben Sie!* 'praise!'
Both forms of the familiar singular are found in print, but the short
form is more usual in speaking.

PASSIVE VOICE

Infinitives: present *gelobt (zu) werden* 'to be praised', perfect *gelobt worden (zu) sein* 'to have been praised'
Participle: perfect *gelobt* 'praised'

Indicative

Present *ich werde gelobt* 'I am praised', etc.
Preterite *ich wurde gelobt* 'I was praised', etc.
Future *ich werde gelobt werden* 'I shall be praised', etc.
Perfect *ich bin gelobt worden* 'I have been praised', etc.
Pluperfect *ich war gelobt worden* 'I had been praised', etc.
Future perfect *ich werde gelobt worden sein* 'I shall have been praised', etc.

Subjunctive

Present *er werde gelobt*
Preterite *ich würde gelobt*, etc.
Future *er werde gelobt werden*
Perfect *ich sei gelobt worden*, etc.
Pluperfect *ich wäre gelobt worden*, etc.
Future perfect *er werde gelobt worden sein*

(Conditional)

Present *ich würde gelobt* or (tautologically) *ich würde gelobt werden* 'I would be praised', etc.
Perfect *ich wäre gelobt worden* or *ich würde gelobt worden sein* 'I would have been praised', etc.

Imperative: (familiar) sg. *werde (sei) gelobt!* pl. *werdet (seid) gelobt!* (polite) *werden (seien) Sie gelobt!* 'be praised!'. In the nature of the case, this imperative is for most verbs more theoretical than real. In the present instance, the alternative forms with *sein* (expressing state rather than action, pp. 249 f.) are usual: *sei gelobt, o Herr!* 'be praised, O Lord!'

Among the many verbs so conjugated are *bellen* 'bark', *brüllen* 'bellow, roar', *danken* (+ dat.) 'thank', *dienen* (+ dat.) 'serve', *fassen* 'grasp', *fischen* 'fish', *holen* 'fetch', *hören* 'hear', *kämmen* 'comb', *kochen* 'cook, boil', *lachen* 'laugh', *machen* 'make, do', *nähen* 'sew', *packen* 'pack', *pflücken* 'pick, pluck', *reifen* 'ripen', *sagen* 'say', *spielen* 'play', *stellen* 'place', *strafen* 'punish', *täuschen* 'deceive', *teilen* 'divide', *wählen* 'choose', *wünschen* 'wish', *zahlen* 'pay', *zeigen* 'show'.

Observe *fragen* 'ask', normally regular, but also (through attraction to the strong conjugation) locally pres. sg. 2 *frägst*, 3 *frägt*, in high style occasionally pret. sg. 1 *frug*, etc., and corresponding subjunctive, especially the idiom *es früge sich, ob* virtually the same as *es fragt sich, ob* 'the question is whether' or 'it is doubtful whether', see further under 'Preterite Subjunctive', p. 261.

The verb *brauchen* 'need' commonly forms a pret. subj. *bräuchte* (inflecting like the pret. indic. *brauchte*); on its use, see p. 291. Two other weak verbs, *bringen* 'bring' and *denken* 'think', also form a pret. subj., see below.

Notice that a small number of verbs such as *beantragen* 'apply for', *ratschlagen* 'deliberate', *veranlassen* 'cause' are weak, being formed from nouns, e.g. *Antrag* 'application', not from the strong verbs *tragen, schlagen, lassen*, similarly *handhaben* 'handle.'

Since weak verbs are far and away the predominant class, they set the pattern for neologisms, as *nerven* (slang) 'pester, strain', *röntgen* ['rœntǧən, 'rœn(t)ʃən] 'X-ray' (from *Carl Röntgen*), *saugen* 'vacuum', including loanwords, e.g. from English: *flirten* ['flœɐtən, 'flɪɐtən] 'flirt', *grillen* 'grill', *kicken* 'kick' (especially a football), *kidnappen* ['kɪdnɛpən] 'kidnap', *managen* ['mɛnɛdʒən] 'manage', *parken* 'park', *stoppen* 'stop, time (with a stop watch)', further *jobben* ['dʒɔbən] 'take a (temporary) job', *stressen* 'exhaust', *tanken* 'fill up with petrol', *tippen* 'tip, guess, have a flutter', independent developments from *Job, Streß, Tank, Tip*.

Verbs conjugated with *sein*

The auxiliary *haben* (as above) is replaced by *sein* in the case of intransitive verbs of motion (and certain others, see pp. 243 ff.):

Infinitive: *reisen* 'travel'

Indicative: perfect *ich bin gereist* 'I have travelled', pluperfect *ich war gereist* 'I had travelled', future perfect *ich werde gereist sein* 'I shall have travelled', etc.

Subjunctive: perfect *ich sei gereist*, pluperfect *ich wäre gereist*, etc., future perfect *er werde gereist sein*, (Conditional) perfect *ich wäre gereist* or *ich würde gereist sein* 'I would have travelled', etc.

Among verbs so conjugated are *eilen* 'hasten', *folgen* 'follow', *landen* 'land'.

Dental stems, etc.

Verbs with stems ending in *d* or *t* have *e* before the terminations *-st, -t, -te*, etc.

Infinitive: *reden* 'speak'
Participles: present *redend*, perfect *geredet*
Present sg. 1 *rede*, 2 *redest*, 3 *redet*, pl. 1 *reden*, 2 *redet*, 3 *reden*
Preterite sg. 1 *redete*, 2 *redetest*, 3 *redete*, pl. 1 *redeten*, 2 *redetet*, 3 *redeten*
Imperative: (familiar) sg. *red(e)!* pl. *redet!* (polite) *reden Sie!*

Thus *baden* 'bathe, take a bath', *schaden* (+ dat.) 'harm', *arbeiten* 'work', *beten* 'pray', *mieten* 'hire, rent', *retten* 'save', *antworten* (+ dat.) 'answer', *fürchten* 'fear', *warten* 'wait'.

Likewise stems in *m* or *n* preceded by an occlusive or fricative, as *atmen* 'breathe', *widmen* 'dedicate', *begegnen* 'meet, encounter', *öffnen* 'open', *zeichnen* 'draw, sketch', hence *atmet* 'breathes', etc.

Sibilant stems

Verbs with stems ending in *s*, *ss/ß*, or *z*, *tz*, drop the *s* of the 2nd sg. present termination, thus falling together with the 3rd sg., e.g. *reisen* 'travel', *hassen* 'hate', *weißen* 'whitewash', *tanzen* 'dance', *setzen* 'put, set':

Present sg. 1	*reise*	*hasse*	*weiße*	*tanze*	*setze*
2	*reist*	*haßt*	*weißt*	*tanzt*	*setzt*
3	*reist*	*haßt*	*weißt*	*tanzt*	*setzt*

Similarly *hopsen* 'hop', *boxen* 'punch, box', sg. 2, 3 *hopst*, *boxt*.

Verbs in *-eln*, *-ern*

These verbs inflect as follows:

Infinitive: *handeln* 'act', *flüstern* 'whisper'
Participles: present *handelnd*, *flüsternd*, perfect *gehandelt*, *geflüstert*
Present sg. 1 *handle*, 2 *handelst*, 3 *handelt*, pl. 1 *handeln*, 2 *handelt*, 3 *handeln*, sg. 1 *flüstere*, 2 *flüsterst*, 3 *flüstert*, pl. 1 *flüstern*, 2 *flüstert*, 3 *flüstern*
Preterite sg. 1 *handelte*, *flüsterte*, etc.
Subjunctive: present sg. 3 *handle*, *flüstere*
Imperative: (familiar) sg. *handle! flüstere!* pl. *handelt! flüstert!* (polite) *handeln Sie! flüstern Sie!*

An alternative spelling *flüstre* for *flüstere* may be found; it reflects a common pronunciation.

Thus *lächeln* 'smile', *schütteln* 'shake', *tadeln* 'blame', *klettern* 'climb', *wandern* 'wander, ramble', *zittern* 'tremble'.

Stem-vowel change, etc.

The following verbs change their stem vowel *e* to *a* in the preterite and perfect participle: *brennen* 'burn', *kennen* 'know', *nennen* 'name', *rennen* 'run', thus pret. *brannte*, perf. part. *gebrannt*, etc.

The verbs *senden* 'send, broadcast' and *wenden* 'turn' are conjugated either as above: *sandte*, *wandte*, *gesandt*, *gewandt*, or else without vowel change: *sendete*, *wendete*, *gesendet*, *gewendet*. As for *senden* 'send', both types are common, but there is never vowel change when the meaning is 'broadcast'. Used in a literal sense, *wenden* commonly occurs without vowel change, in spoken style exclusively so, but in figurative senses the alternative forms may be required: *er wandte sich ans Gericht* 'he applied to the court'. When intransitive, however, only *wendete, gewendet* are permissible.

Two verbs show other irregularities in the preterite and perfect participle; exceptionally among weak verbs, they form a preterite subjunctive, the endings of which are as for the indicative. They are: *bringen* 'bring', pret. *brachte* (subj. *brächte*), perf. part. *gebracht*, and *denken* 'think', pret. *dachte* (subj. *dächte*), perf. part. *gedacht*.

STRONG CONJUGATION

Strong verbs make the preterite and perfect participle by change of stem vowel, the participle having an *n*-suffix. The inflexions are as follows.

Infinitive: *tragen* 'carry'
Participles: present *tragend* 'carrying', perfect *getragen* 'carried'

Indicative

	Present	Preterite
Sg. 1	*ich trage* 'I carry'	*trug* 'carried'
2	*du trägst*	*trugst*
3	*er trägt*	*trug*
Pl. 1	*wir tragen*	*trugen*
2	*ihr tragt*	*trugt*
3	*sie tragen*	*trugen*

Subjunctive

Present *er trage*
Preterite *ich trüge, du trüg(e)st, er trüge, wir trügen, ihr trüg(e)t, sie trügen*. The 2nd person forms are free variants, except when phonetic considerations require the retention of *e*, as *stündest, stündet*, from *stehen* 'stand'.
Imperative: (familiar) sg. *trag(e)!* pl. *tragt!* (polite) *tragen Sie!* 'carry!'
Both forms of the familiar singular are common in print, but the short form is usual in speaking.

The compound tenses are formed as in the weak conjugation, above: future *ich werde tragen* 'I shall carry', perfect *ich habe getragen* 'I have carried', etc., etc. Similarly the passive: present *ich werde getragen* 'I am carried', etc., etc.

Additional remarks

Certain imperatives are irregular and most of these never take *-e*, e.g. *befiehl!* 'command!', details in the Alphabetical List below.

Verbs with stems ending in *d* or *t* have *e* before the termination *-t* of the 2nd pl. present and imperative, thus *bindet, fechtet* from *binden* 'tie', *fechten* 'fence'; often also before the terminations *-st* and *-t* of the 2nd and 3rd sg. present: *bindest, bindet*; on the other hand *fichst, ficht*, since many verbs have special forms for these persons, see Alphabetical List.

Verbs with stems ending in *s* or *ß* have *e* before the termination *-st* of the 2nd sg. preterite, thus *bliesest, bissest*, from *blasen* 'blow', *beißen* 'bite'.

The stem vowels *a* and *o*, as well as *u* (cf. *trug*, above), are modified in the preterite subjunctive, thus *barg, bärge, bog, böge*, from *bergen* 'conceal', *biegen* 'bend'. A few subjunctives, however, take a different vowel, cf. *befahl, beföhle*, from *befehlen* 'command', see Alphabetical List.

Perfect participle without *ge-*

Reference has already been made to *worden* beside *geworden*, p. 85. We now notice the types regularly forming the participle without the prefix *ge-*, as follows.

Firstly, all simple verbs not stressed on the stem syllable, principally the very numerous type, mainly of foreign origin, ending in *-ieren* as *analy'sieren* 'analyse', *dezi'mieren* 'decimate', *gratu'lieren* 'congratulate', *korri'gieren* 'correct', *re'gieren* 'rule', *skiz'zieren* 'sketch', *telefo'nieren* 'telephone', perf. part. *analy'siert*, etc., further the few verbs in *-eien: prophe'zeien* 'prophesy', perf. part. *prophe'zeit* (but not the religious *bene'deien* 'bless': *gebene'deit*), and a handful of others, as *kra'keelen* 'brawl', *po'saunen* or *trom'peten* 'trumpet', perf. part. *kra'keelt*, etc.

Secondly, verbs already formed with the prefix, e.g. *gestatten* 'permit', perf. part. *gestattet*, as well as all other unstressed prefixes, see under 'Verbs with prefixes', pp. 104 ff. It will be noticed that such pairs as *denken* 'think', *gedenken* 'commemorate' and *hören* 'hear', *gehören* 'belong to', share the same perf. part. *gedacht, gehört*.

From strong to weak conjugation

Given that the weak conjugation is dominant (p. 89), it is understandable that strong verbs should sometimes come under its influence and themselves develop weak forms. At first, these will occur side by side with the traditional strong forms, but may eventually replace them. Several instances are common talking points today, for example *backen* 'bake'. Is the preterite to be *backte* or the 'correct', i.e. traditional, but oddly sounding *buk*? There is no doubt that the weak form is gaining ground. Furthermore, the living language shows a clear preference for *a* as the stem vowel throughout, as confirmed by a marked tendency in recent years to make present sg. 2 *backst*, 3 *backt*, instead of the 'correct', *bäckst*, *bäckt*, the weak conjugation then supplanting the strong except for the perfect participle. Several verbs in the 'Alphabetical List' below are today in a comparable stage of transition. We may note, too, that in a special, North German application of the verb *backen* in the sense of 'cake', used of compressed snow sticking to the soles of boots, etc., conjugation is already weak throughout. In such matters, the spoken language tends to be a step or two ahead of the written style.

The process illustrated above has been continuing all through the recorded history of the language, with weak forms creeping in and the number of strong verbs gradually decreasing. The most durable forms in this process tend to be the perfect participles, seeing that they are so often used as adjectives and may in this way acquire a life of their own. So it has come about that there are participles still in use today, even though the verbs with which they were originally associated are now extinct. Examples are *gedunsen* or *aufgedunsen* 'swollen' (especially the face), *erkoren* or *auserkoren* 'elect', *verschollen* 'lost, missing (presumed dead)', *versonnen* 'lost in thought, pensive', *zerschlissen* 'torn to shreds' (as clothing).

Alphabetical list of strong (and partially strong) verbs with principal parts, etc.

The parts appear in the following order: infinitive, imperative sg. if irregular, 2nd and 3rd present sg. (pres. 2, 3), 1st (or 3rd) preterite sg. (pret.) with subjunctive (subj.) if irregular, perfect participle (pp.) with *ist* if parts of *sein* are used as auxiliary, also with *hat* if parts of *haben* instead of *sein* are used in some application of the verb in question. In cases of ambiguity, verbs are marked transitive (tr.) or intransitive (intr.). On the use of *sein* to express state, see pp. 249 f.

backen 'bake', pres. 2 *bäckst* or *backst*, 3 *bäckt* or *backt*, pret. *backte*, obsolescent *buk*, pp. *gebacken*. Commentary above
befehlen 'command', *befiehl!* pres. 2 *befiehlst*, 3 *befiehlt*, pret. *befahl* (subj. *beföhle*), pp. *befohlen*. Thus *empfehlen* 'recommend'.
beginnen 'commence', pres. 2 *beginnst*, 3 *beginnt*, pret. *begann* (subj. *begönne*, also *begänne*), pp. *begonnen*.
beißen 'bite', pres. 2, 3 *beißt*, pret. *biß*, pp. *gebissen*.
bergen 'conceal', *birg!*, pres. 2 *birgst*, 3 *birgt*, pret. *barg*, pp. *geborgen*.

bersten 'burst, crack' intr., pres. 2, 3 *birst*, pret. *barst*, pp. *(ist) geborsten*.

bewegen 'induce', pres. 2 *bewegst*, 3 *bewegt*, pret. *bewog*, pp. *bewogen*. Conjugated weak, the meaning is 'move (physically or emotionally)'.

biegen 'bend', pres. 2 *biegst*, 3 *biegt*, pret. *bog*, pp. *gebogen*; pp. with *sein* when the meaning is 'turn (a corner, into a street)', e.g. *er ist um die Ecke gebogen* 'he has turned the corner', *das Auto war in die Neue Straße gebogen* 'the car had turned into New Street'.

bieten 'offer', pres. 2 *bietest*, 3 *bietet*, pret. *bot*, pp. *geboten*.

binden 'tie, bind', pres. 2 *bindest*, 3 *bindet*, pret. *band*, pp. *gebunden*.

bitten 'request', pres. 2 *bittest*, 3 *bittet*, pret. *bat*, pp. *gebeten*.

blasen 'blow', pres. 2, 3 *bläst*, pret. *blies*, pp. *geblasen*.

bleiben 'remain', pres. 2 *bleibst*, 3 *bleibt*, pret. *blieb*, pp. *(ist) geblieben*.

braten 'roast', pres. 2 *brätst*, 3 *brät*, pret. *briet*, pp. *gebraten*.

brechen 'break', *brich!*, pres. 2 *brichst*, 3 *bricht*, pret. *brach*, pp. *gebrochen*.

dreschen 'thresh, thrash', *drisch!*, pres. 2 *drischst*, 3 *drischt*, pret. *drosch*, pp. *gedroschen*.

dringen 'penetrate, press' intr., pres. 2 *dringst*, 3 *dringt*, pret. *drang*, pp. *(ist) gedrungen*, e.g. *Regenwasser ist durch das Dach gedrungen* 'rain water has penetrated the roof', however: *der Gläubiger hat auf Zahlung gedrungen* 'the creditor has pressed for payment'.

empfehlen, see *befehlen*.

erlöschen 'be extinguished', *erlisch!*, pres. 2 *erlischst*, 3 *erlischt*, pret. *erlosch*, pp. *(ist) erloschen*. The simplex *löschen* 'extinguish' is weak.

erschallen 'sound, resound', pres. 2 *erschallst*, 3 *erschallt*, pret. *erscholl* or *erschallte*, pp. *erschollen* or *erschallt*. The simplex *schallen* with comparable meanings is now weak throughout.

erschrecken 'be frightened', *erschrick!*, pres. 2 *erschrickst*, 3 *erschrickt*, pret. *erschrak*, pp. *(ist) erschrocken*. Intr. *-schrecken* occurs in other combinations, notably *zurückschrecken* 'shrink back', but here the prevailing conjugation is now weak. Tr. *erschrecken* 'frighten', like its synonymous simplex *schrecken*, has always followed the weak conjugation.

essen 'eat', *iß!*, pres. 2, 3 *ißt*, pret. *aß*, pp. *gegessen*.

fahren 'go (in a vehicle, ship)', pres. 2 *fährst*, 3 *fährt*, pret. *fuhr*, pp. *(ist) gefahren*; in the sense 'drive (a vehicle)', pp. *(hat) gefahren*. There is hesitancy with the expression *Ski fahren* 'ski', used indifferently with *sein* or *haben*.

fallen 'fall', pres. sg. 2 *fällst*, 3 *fällt*, pret. *fiel*, pp. *(ist) gefallen*.

fangen 'catch', pres. 2 *fängst*, 3 *fängt*, pret. *fing*, pp. *gefangen*.

fechten 'fence', *ficht!*, pres. 2 *fichst*, 3 *ficht*, pret. *focht*, pp. *gefochten*.

finden 'find', pres. 2 *findest*, 3 *findet*, pret. *fand*, pp. *gefunden*.

flechten 'plait', *flicht!*, pres. 2 *flichst*, 3 *flicht*, pret. *flocht*, pp. *geflochten*.

fliegen 'fly', pres. 2 *fliegst*, 3 *fliegt*, pret. *flog*, pp. intr. (*ist*), tr. (*hat*) *geflogen*.

fliehen 'flee', pres. 2 *fliehst*, 3 *flieht*, pret. *floh*, pp. intr. (*ist*), tr. (*hat*) *geflohen*.

fließen 'flow', pres. 2, 3 *fließt*, pret. *floß*, pp. (*ist*) *geflossen*.

fressen 'eat (of animals, otherwise vulgar)', *friß!*, pres. 2, 3 *frißt* (substandard *freßt*), pret. *fraß*, pp. *gefressen*.

frieren 'freeze, feel cold', pres. 2 *frierst*, 3 *friert*, pret. *fror*, pp. *gefroren*.

gären 'ferment', pres. 2 *gärst*, 3 *gärt*, pret. *gor*, also *gärte*, pp. *gegoren*, also *gegärt*. Always weak in figurative use, when commonly impersonal: *es gärte im Land* 'there was unrest in the country'.

gebären 'bear, give birth', pres. 2 *gebierst*, 3 *gebiert* high style, obsolescent, ordinarily *gebärst*, *gebärt* (e.g. *sie gebärt gerade* 'she's just giving birth'), pret. *gebar*, pp. *geboren* high style, obsolescent, today paraphrases usual, as *sie brachte (hat . . . gebracht) ein Kind zur Welt* 'she brought (has brought) a child into the world'. Cf. *sie ist am 10. November geboren* 'she was born on the 10th of November' (ordinary way of referring to a person now living), *sie wurde . . . geboren* 'she was born . . . ' (person deceased; in formal style also of a person still living), *sie war in Wien geboren, verbrachte jedoch den Großteil ihres Lebens in Berlin* 'she had been born in Vienna, but spent most of her life in Berlin'. The present participle is common in the expression *Erstgebärende* 'woman (or, women) having her (their) first child'.

geben 'give', *gib!*, pres. 2 *gibst*, 3 *gibt*, pret. *gab*, pp. *gegeben*.

gedeihen 'thrive', pres. 2 *gedeihst*, 3 *gedeiht*, pret. *gedieh*, pp. (*ist*) *gediehen*.

gehen 'go', pres. 2 *gehst*, 3 *geht*, pret. *ging*, pp. (*ist*) *gegangen*.

gelingen 'succeed' impersonal, pres. *gelingt*, pret. *gelang*, pp. (*ist*) *gelungen*. Thus *mißlingen* 'fail'.

gelten 'be valid, carry weight', *gilt!*, pres. 2 *giltst*, 3 *gilt*, pret. *galt* (subj. *gölte*), pp. *gegolten*.

genesen 'recover (from illness), convalesce': only in literary or formal style, and barely viable except in the infinitive: *wie mag die Welt genesen?* 'how can the world recover (from its ills)?' and in the perfect system, e.g. *er ist (war) genesen* 'he has (had) recovered', further substantivized pres. part., cf. *Genesungsheim* definable as *Erholungsheim für Genesende* 'convalescents'. The everyday term is *sich erholen*.

genießen 'enjoy', pres. 2, 3 *genießt*, pret. *genoß*, pp. *genossen*.

geschehen 'happen' 3rd person only, pres. *geschieht*, pret. *geschah*, pp. *(ist) geschehen*.

gewinnen 'win', pres. 2 *gewinnst*, 3 *gewinnt*, pret. *gewann* (subj. *gewönne*, also *gewänne*), pp. *gewonnen*.

gießen 'pour', pres. 2, 3 *gießt*, pret. *goß*, pp. *gegossen*.

gleichen 'resemble', pres. 2 *gleichst*, 3 *gleicht*, pret. *glich*, pp. *geglichen*.

gleiten 'glide', pres. 2 *gleitest*, 3 *gleitet*, pret. *glitt*, pp. *(ist) geglitten*.

glimmen 'glimmer', pres. 2 *glimmst*, 3 *glimmt*, pret. *glomm*, pp. *geglommen*. Now also occasionally weak.

graben 'dig', pres. 2 *gräbst*, 3 *gräbt*, pret. *grub*, pp. *gegraben*.

greifen 'seize', pres. 2 *greifst*, 3 *greift*, pret. *griff*, pp. *gegriffen*.

halten 'hold', pres. 2 *hältst*, 3 *hält*, pret. *hielt*, pp. *gehalten*.

hängen 'hang' intr., pres. 2 *hängst*, 3 *hängt*, pret. *hing*, pp. *gehangen*. Tr. *hängen* is weak.

hauen 'strike, hew, clobber, thrash', pres. 2 *haust*, 3 *haut*, pret. *hieb* (only in the sense 'struck') or *haute* (all senses), pp. *gehauen*.

heben 'lift', pres. 2, *hebst*, 3 *hebt*, pret. *hob*, pp. *gehoben*.

heißen 'be called', pres. 2, 3 *heißt*, pret. *hieß*, pp. *geheißen*.

helfen 'help' (+ dat.), *hilf!*, pres. 2 *hilfst*, 3 *hilft*, pret. *half* (subj. *hülfe*), pp. *geholfen*.

klimmen 'climb' intr., pres. 2 *klimmst*, 3 *klimmt*, pret. *klomm*, also *klimmte*, pp. *(ist) geklommen*, also *geklimmt*. Normally occurs as *emporklimmen* 'climb (up)', also *erklimmen* 'climb' tr., pp. *(hat) erklommen, erklimmt*, all essentially literary words, the ordinary terms being *klettern* intr., *besteigen* tr.

klingen 'sound, resound', pres. 2 *klingst*, 3 *klingt*, pret. *klang*, pp. *geklungen*.

kneifen 'pinch', pres. 2 *kneifst*, 3 *kneift*, pret. *kniff*, pp. *gekniffen*.

kommen 'come', pres. 2 *kommst*, 3 *kommt*, pret. *kam*, pp. *(ist) gekommen*.

kriechen 'creep', pres. 2 *kriechst*, 3 *kriecht*, pret. *kroch*, pp. *(ist) gekrochen*.

laden 'load, invite', pres. 2 *lädst*, 3 *lädt*, also 2 *ladest*, 3 *ladet*, pret. *lud*, pp. *geladen*.

lassen 'let, allow', pres. 2, 3 *läßt*, pret. *ließ*, pp. *gelassen*.

laufen 'run, walk', pres. 2 *läufst*, 3 *läuft*, pret. *lief*, pp. intr. *(ist)*, tr. *(hat) gelaufen*. Examples of transitive use: *er hat einen neuen Re'kord gelaufen* 'he has run a new record', *er hat sich eine Blase gelaufen*: 'he has got a blister from running (or, walking)', *er hat einen Weg für uns gelaufen* 'he has run an errand for us'. There is hesitancy with expressions like *Schlittschuh laufen* 'skate', used indifferently with *sein* or *haben*.

leiden 'suffer', pres. 2 *leidest*, 3 *leidet*, pret. *litt*, pp. *gelitten*.
leihen 'lend', pres. 2 *leihst*, 3 *leiht*, pret. *lieh*, pp. *geliehen*.
lesen 'read', *lies!*, pres. 2, 3 *liest*, pret. *las*, pp. *gelesen*.
liegen 'lie', pres. 2 *liegst*, 3 *liegt*, pret. *lag*, pp. (South German *ist*) *gelegen*.
lügen 'tell a lie', pres. 2 *lügst*, 3 *lügt*, pret. *log*, pp. *gelogen*.
mahlen 'grind', pres. 2 , *mahlst*, 3 *mahlt*, pret. *mahlte*, pp. *gemahlen*.
meiden 'avoid, shun', pres. 2 *meidest*, 3 *meidet*, pret. *mied*, pp. *gemieden*. The concept 'avoid' generally rendered by *vermeiden*.
melken 'milk', pres. 2 *melkst*, 3 *melkt*, pret. *melkte*, obsolescent *molk*, pp. *gemolken*, also *gemelkt*.
messen 'measure', *miß!*, pres. 2, 3 *mißt*, pret. *maß*, pp. *gemessen*.
mißlingen, see *gelingen*.
nehmen 'take', *nimm!*, pres. 2 *nimmst*, 3 *nimmt*, pret. *nahm*, pp. *genommen*.
pfeifen 'whistle', pres. 2 *pfeifst*, 3 *pfeift*, pret. *pfiff*, pp. *gepfiffen*.
preisen 'praise', pres. 2, 3 *preist*, pret. *pries*, pp. *gepriesen*.
quellen 'gush forth, swell (by being placed in water)', *quill!*, pres. 2 *quillst*, 3 *quillt*, pret. *quoll*, pp. *gequollen*. Tr. *quellen* 'cause to swell' is weak.
raten 'advise', pres. 2 *rätst*, 3 *rät*, pret. *riet*, pp. *geraten*.
reiben 'rub', pres. 2 *reibst*, 3 *reibt*, pret. *rieb*, pp. *gerieben*.
reißen 'tear', pres. 2, 3 *reißt*, pret. *riß*, pp. *gerissen*.
reiten 'ride (an animal)', pres. 2 *reitest*, 3 *reitet*, pret. *ritt*, pp. intr. (*ist*), tr. (*hat*) *geritten*.
riechen 'smell', pres. 2 *riechst*, 3 *riecht*, pret. *roch*, pp. *gerochen*.
ringen 'wrestle', pres. 2 *ringst*, 3 *ringt*, pret. *rang*, pp. *gerungen*.
rinnen 'run, flow', pres. 2 *rinnst*, 3 *rinnt*, pret. *rann*, pp. *(ist) geronnen*.
rufen 'call', pres. 2 *rufst*, 3 *ruft*, pret. *rief*, pp. *gerufen*.
salzen 'salt', pres. 2, 3 *salzt*, pret. *salzte*, pp. *gesalzen*.
saufen 'drink (of animals, otherwise vulgar)', pres. 2 *säufst*, 3 *säuft*, pret. *soff*, pp. *gesoffen*.
saugen 'suck', pres. 2 *saugst*, 3 *saugt*, pret. *sog* or *saugte*, pp. *gesogen* or *gesaugt*—the weak pret. and pp. used in technical contexts, e.g. *sie hat (mit dem Staubsauger Staub) gesaugt* 'she's been using the vacuum-cleaner', p. 89.
schaffen 'create', pres. 2 *schaffst*, 3 *schafft*, pret. *schuf* (also *schaffte* as the commoner alternative in certain idioms, e.g. *schaffte Platz* 'made room', *schaffte Ordnung* 'put things straight'), pp. *geschaffen*. In its other meanings 'do' and (West German) 'work', this verb is weak, also in compounds as *abschaffen* 'do away with, abolish', then *anschaffen*, *beschaffen*, *verschaffen*, all with meanings in the range of 'get, obtain, procure'. But notice adjectival *beschaffen* 'having a certain nature', whence *Beschaffenheit* 'state, condition'.

scheiden 'part', pres. 2 *scheidest*, 3 *scheidet*, pret. *schied*, pp. intr. (*ist*), tr. (*hat*) *geschieden*.

scheinen 'shine, seem', pres. 2 *scheinst*, 3 *scheint*, pret. *schien*, pp. *geschienen*.

scheißen 'shit', pres. 2, 3 *schießt*, pret. *schiß*, pp. *geschissen*.

schelten 'scold', *schilt!*, pres. 2 *schilst*, 3 *schilt*, pret. *schalt*, pp. *gescholten*.

scheren 'cut, shear', pres. 2 *scherst*, 3 *schert*, pret. *schor*, pp. *geschoren*. A quite different word is *sich scheren* 'bother (about), etc.', conjugated weak.

schieben 'push, shove', pres. 2 *schiebst*, 3 *schiebt*, pret. *schob*, pp. *geschoben*.

schießen 'shoot', pres. 2, 3 *schießt*, pret. *schoß*, pp. intr. (*ist*), tr. (*hat*) *geschossen*.

schinden 'flay, torture', pres. 2 *schindest*, 3 *schindet*, pret. *schindete*, pp. *geschunden*.

schlafen 'sleep', pres. 2 *schläfst*, 3 *schläft*, pret. *schlief*, pp. *geschlafen*.

schlagen 'beat, strike', pres. 2 *schlägst*, 3 *schlägt*, pret. *schlug*, pp. *geschlagen*.

schleichen 'creep, sneak', pres. 2 *schleichst*, 3 *schleicht*, pret. *schlich*, pp. (*ist*) *geschlichen*.

schleifen, 'sharpen', pres. 2 *schleifst*, 3 *schleift*, pret. *schliff*, pp. *geschliffen*. The ultimately related *schleifen* 'trail, drag; raze to the ground' follows the weak conjugation.

schließen 'close', pres. 2, 3 *schließt*, pret. *schloß*, pp. *geschlossen*.

schlingen 'wind, sling, twist', pres. 2 *schlingst*, 3 *schlingt*, pret. *schlang*, pp. *geschlungen*.

Also *hinunterschlingen* 'gulp down', *verschlingen* 'devour'.

schmeißen 'fling, throw', pres. 2, 3 *schmeißt*, pret. *schmiß*, pp. *geschmissen*.

schmelzen 'melt', *schmilz!*, pres. 2, 3 *schmilzt*, pret. *schmolz*, pp. intr. (*ist*), tr. (*hat*) *geschmolzen*.

schneiden 'cut', pres. 2 *schneidest*, 3 *schneidet*, pret. *schnitt*, pp. *geschnitten*.

schreiben 'write', pres. 2 *schreibst*, 3 *schreibt*, pret. *schrieb*, pp. *geschrieben*.

schreien 'shout', pres. 2 *schreist*, 3 *schreit*, pret. *schrie*, pp. *geschrien* [-'ʃriiən].

schreiten 'step, stride', pres. 2 *schreitest*, 3 *schreitet*, pret. *schritt*, pp. (*ist*) *geschritten*. A literary word.

schweigen 'be silent', pres. 2 *schweigst*, 3 *schweigt*, pret. *schwieg*, pp. *geschwiegen*.

schwellen 'swell' intr., pres. 2 *schwillst*, 3 *schwillt*, pret. *schwoll*, pp. (*ist*) *geschwollen*. When transitive weak.

schwimmen 'swim, float' intr., pres. 2 *schwimmst*, 3 *schwimmt*, pret. *schwamm* (subj. *schwömme*), pp. (*hat* or *ist*) *geschwommen*. The auxiliary *sein* is used if direction is stated: *er ist über den Fluß, zum anderen Ufer geschwommen* 'he has swum across the river, to the other bank'. In other cases, *haben* is preferred in the North: *ich habe* (South *bin*) *heute viel geschwommen* 'I've been swimming a lot today'.

schwinden 'dwindle, disappear', pres. 2 *schwindest*, 3 *schwindet*, pret. *schwand*, pp. (*ist*) *geschwunden*. In the sense 'disappear' most commonly *verschwinden*.

schwören 'swear (an oath)', pres. 2 *schwörst*, 3 *schwört*, pret. *schwor* (subj. *schwüre*), pp. *geschworen*.

sehen 'see', *sieh!* or (in the sense '*vide*' always) *siehe!*, pres. 2 *siehst*, 3 *sieht*, pret. *sah*, pp. *gesehen*.

sieden 'boil', pres. *siedest*, 3 *siedet*, pret. *sott* or *siedete*, pp. *gesotten* or *gesiedet*. A dying word, ordinarily replaced by *kochen*, only the participles retaining much currency, as *gesotten*, also *hartgesotten* 'hard-boiled' (especially in the figurative sense) and the literary *siedend heiß* 'boiling hot'. Also the technical term *Siedepunkt* 'boiling point'.

singen 'sing', pres. 2 *singst*, 3 *singt*, pret. *sang*, pp. *gesungen*.

sinken 'sink', pres. 2 *sinkst*, 3 *sinkt*, pret. *sank*, pp. (*ist*) *gesunken*.

sinnen 'muse, reflect', pres. 2 *sinnst*, 3 *sinnt*, pret. *sann*, pp. *gesonnen*. A literary word, in limited use, a commoner term being *sich besinnen* with comparable meanings. The expressions *gesinnt* 'minded' and the (literary) *gesonnen sein* 'to intend' are not parts of the above verb.

sitzen 'sit', pres. 2, 3 *sitzt*, pret. *saß*, pp. (South German *ist*) *gesessen*.

spalten 'split', pres. 2 *spaltest*, 3 *spaltet*, pret. *spaltete*, pp. tr. (*hat*), intr. (*ist*) *gespalten*, also *gespaltet*.

speien 'vomit, spew', pres. 2 *speist*, 3 *speit*, pret. *spie*, pp. *gespien* [-'ʃpiiən].

spinnen 'spin', pres. 2 *spinnst*, 3 *spinnt*, pret. *spann*, pp. *gesponnen*.

sprechen 'speak' *sprich!*, pres. 2 *sprichst*, 3 *spricht*, pret. *sprach*, pp. *gesprochen*.

sprießen 'sprout', pres. 2, 3 *sprießt*, pret. *sproß*, pp. (*ist*) *gesprossen*.

springen 'jump', pres. 2 *springst*, 3 *springt*, pret. *sprang*, pp. (*ist*) *gesprungen*.

stechen 'sting, stab', *stich!*, pres. 2 *stichst*, 3 *sticht*, pret. *stach*, pp. *gestochen*.

stehen 'stand', pres. 2 *stehst*, 3 *steht*, pret. *stand* (subj. *stünde*, also *stände*), pp. (South German *ist*) *gestanden*.

stehlen 'steal', *stiehl!*, pres. 2 *stiehlst*, 3 *stiehlt*, pret. *stahl*, pp. *gestohlen*.

steigen 'climb, rise' intr., pres. 2 *steigst*, 3 *steigt*, pret. *stieg*, pp. *(ist) gestiegen*.

sterben 'die', *stirb!*, pres. 2 *stirbst*, 3 *stirbt*, pret. *starb* (subj. *stürbe*), pp. *(ist) gestorben*, also pret. 3 *verstarb(en)*, pp. *verstorben*.

stieben 'fly off (dust, sparks)', pres. 2 *stiebst*, 3 *stiebt*, pret. *stob*, also *stiebte*, pp. *gestoben*, also *gestiebt*.

stinken 'stink', pres. 2 *stinkst*, 3 *stinkt*, pret. *stank*, pp. *gestunken*.

stoßen 'push', pres. 2, 3 *stößt*, pret. *stieß*, pp. *gestoßen*; also intr., e.g. *zu jemandem stoßen* 'meet up with someone', *auf Widerstand stoßen* 'meet with resistance', pp. *(ist) gestoßen*.

streichen 'stroke, spread, cross out', pres. 2 *streichst*, 3 *streicht*, pret. *strich*, pp. *gestrichen*; also intr. in the sense 'wander', pp. *(ist) gestrichen*.

streiten 'quarrel', pres. 2 *streitest*, 3 *streitet*, pret. *stritt*, pp. *gestritten*.

tragen 'carry', pres. 2 *trägst*, 3 *trägt*, pret. *trug*, pp. *getragen*.

treffen 'meet, hit', *triff!*, pres. 2 *triffst*, 3 *trifft*, pret. *traf*, pp. *getroffen*.

treiben 'drive, put forth (buds, etc.)', pres. 2 *treibst*, 3 *treibt*, pret. *trieb*, pp. *getrieben*; also intr. in the senses 'drift, sprout', pp. *(ist) getrieben*.

treten 'kick', *tritt!*, pres. 2 *trittst*, 3 *tritt*, pret. *trat*, pp. *getreten*; also intr. in the senses 'step, tread', pp. *(ist) getreten*.

trinken 'drink', pres. 2 *trinkst*, 3 *trinkt*, pret. *trank*, pp. *getrunken*.

trügen 'deceive (by nature)', pres. 2 *trügst*, 3 *trügt*, pret. *trog*, pp. *getrogen*; 'deceive (with intent)' is *betrügen*.

verbleichen 'fade', pres. 2 *verbleichst*, 3 *verbleicht*, pret. *verblich*, pp. *(ist) verblichen*. The simplex *bleichen* 'fade, bleach' is weak.

verderben 'spoil, ruin', *verdirb!*, pres. 2 *verdirbst*, 3 *verdirbt*, pret. *verdarb* (subj. *verdürbe*), pp. *verdorben* (also *verderbt*, but only as an adjective 'corrupt'); intr. 'become spoiled, deteriorate', pp. *(ist) verdorben*.

verdrießen 'vex, gall', pres. 3 *verdrießt*, pret. *verdroß*, pp. *verdrossen*. The infinitive is often found: *ich lasse mir den Tag nicht verdrießen* 'I won't have the day spoilt', otherwise only used in the 3rd sg.: *sein Verhalten verdrießt einen* 'his attitude galls one'; the perf. part. is common as an adjective meaning 'peevish' and in the negative *unverdrossen* 'unwearied, patient'.

vergessen 'forget', *vergiß!*, pres. 2, 3 *vergißt*, pret. *vergaß*, pp. *vergessen*.

verlieren 'lose', pres. 2 *verlierst*, 3 *verliert*, pret. *verlor*, pp. *verloren*.

verschleißen 'wear out', pres. 2, 3 *verschleißt*, pret. *verschliß*, pp. *verschlissen*.

weben 'weave' in the literal sense now weak, but when used figuratively pret. *wob*, pp. *gewoben*.

wachsen 'grow', pres. 2, 3 *wächst*, pret. *wuchs*, pp. *(ist) gewachsen*.

wägen 'weigh (one's words)', pres. 2 *wägst*, 3 *wägt*, pret. *wog*, pp. *gewogen*. Cf. *wiegen*. The synonym *abwägen* and *erwägen* 'consider' are commoner than the simplex.

waschen 'wash', pres. 2 *wäschst* (ordinarily [vɛʃt], p. 13), 3 *wäscht*, pret. *wusch*, pp. *gewaschen*.

weichen 'give way, yield', pres. 2 *weichst*, 3 *weicht*, pret. *wich*, pp. (*ist*) *gewichen*.

weisen 'direct, point', pres. 2, 3 *weist*, pret. *wies*, pp. *gewiesen*.

werben 'enlist, canvass', *wirb!*, pres. 2 *wirbst*, 3 *wirbt*, pret. *warb* (subj. *würbe*), pp. *geworben*.

werfen 'throw', *wirf!*, pres. 2 *wirfst*, 3 *wirft*, pret. *warf* (subj. *würfe*), pp. *geworfen*.

wiegen 'weigh', pres. 2 *wiegst*, 3 *wiegt*, pret. *wog*, pp. *gewogen*. This verb and *wägen* (above) are doublets; the weak verb *wiegen* 'rock' is quite a different word, being derived from *Wiege* 'cradle'.

winden 'wind, twist', pres. 2 *windest*, 3 *windet*, pret. *wand*, pp. *gewunden*.

zeihen 'accuse', pres. 2 *zeihst*, 3 *zeiht*, pret. *zieh*, pp. *geziehen*. Obsolescent, more usual words for 'accuse' being the weak verbs *beschuldigen*, *bezichtigen*. Also *verzeihen* 'excuse', an everyday word like its synonym *entschuldigen*.

ziehen 'pull, move', also intr., pres. 2 *ziehst*, 3 *zieht*, pret. *zog*, pp. (intr. *ist*) *gezogen*.

zwingen 'compel', pres. 2 *zwingst*, 3 *zwingt*, pret. *zwang*, pp. *gezwungen*.

IRREGULAR INFLEXION

Two verbs have irregular inflexion.

The verb *tun* 'do'

Participles: present *tuend* 'doing', perfect *getan* 'done'

Present sg. 1 *tue* '(I) do', 2 *tust*, 3 *tut*, pl. 1 *tun*, 2 *tut*, 3 *tun*; subj. sg. 3 *tue*

Preterite sg. 1 *tat* '(I) did', 2 *tatst*, 3 *tat*, pl. 1 *taten*, 2 *tatet*, 3 *taten*; subj. sg. 1 *täte*, etc.

Imperative (familiar) sg. *tu(e)!* pl. *tut!* (polite) *tun Sie!* 'do!'

The verb *wissen* 'know'

Participles: present *wissend* 'knowing', perfect *gewußt* 'known'

Present sg. 1 *weiß* '(I) know', 2 *weißt*, 3 *weiß*, pl. 1 *wissen*, 2 *wißt*, 3 *wissen*; subj. sg. 3 *wisse*.

Preterite sg. 1 *wußte* '(I) knew', 2 *wußtest*, 3 *wußte*, pl. 1 *wußten*, 2 *wußtet*, 3 *wußten*; subj. sg. 1 *wüßte*, etc.

Imperative (familiar) sg. *wisse!* pl. *wißt* (polite) *wissen Sie!* 'know!'
It will be noticed that the conjugation of *wissen* is, in principle,
comparable to that of the Modal Auxiliaries below.

MODAL AUXILIARIES

Infinitive *dürfen* 'be allowed'   Perf. part. *gedurft*
Present sg. 1 *darf* '(I) am allowed', 2 *darfst*, 3 *darf*, pl. 1 *dürfen*, 2
dürft, 3 *dürfen*; subj. sg. 3 *dürfe*.
Preterite sg. 1 *durfte* '(I) was allowed', 2 *durftest*, 3 *durfte*, pl. 1
durften, 2 *durftet*, 3 *durften*; subj. sg. 1 *dürfte*, etc.

Infinitive *können* 'be able'   Perf. part. *gekonnt*
Present sg. 1 *kann* '(I) am able, can', 2 *kannst*, 3 *kann*, pl. 1 *können*, 2
könnt, 3 *können*; subj. sg. 3 *könne*.
Preterite sg. 1 *konnte* '(I) was able, could', 2 *konntest*, 3 *konnte*, pl. 1
konnten, 2 *konntet*, 3 *konnten*; subj. sg. 1 *könnte*, etc.

Infinitive *mögen* 'like'   Perf. part. *gemocht*
Present sg. 1 *mag* '(I) like, may', 2 *magst*, 3 *mag*, pl. 1 *mögen*, 2 *mögt*,
3 *mögen*; subj. sg. 3 *möge*.
Preterite sg. 1 *mochte* '(I) liked, might', 2 *mochtest*, 3 *mochte*, pl. 1
mochten, 2 *mochtet*, 3 *mochten*; subj. sg. 1 *möchte*, etc.

Similarly *vermögen* 'be able' (mainly literary, more formal than
können)—on the participial form *vermögend*, see p. 172.

Infinitive *müssen* 'have to'   Perf. part. *gemußt*
Present sg. 1 *muß* '(I) have to, must', 2 *mußt*, 3 *muß*, pl. 1 *müssen*, 2
müßt, 3 *müssen*; subj. sg. 3 *müsse*.
Preterite sg. 1 *mußte* '(I) had to', 2 *mußtest*, 3 *mußte*, pl. 1 *mußten*, 2
mußtet, 3 *mußten*; subj. sg. 1 *müßte*, etc.

Infinitive *sollen* 'be obliged to, be said to'   Perf. part. *gesollt*
Present sg. 1 *soll* '(I) am obliged to, am said to', 2 *sollst*, 3 *soll*, pl. 1
sollen, 2 *sollt*, 3 *sollen*; subj. sg. 3 *solle*
Preterite sg. 1 *sollte* '(I) was obliged to, was said to, should, ought to',
2 *solltest*, 3 *sollte*, pl. 1 *sollten*, 2 *solltet*, 3 *sollten*.
On the participial form *sollend*, see pp. 288 f.

Infinitive *wollen* 'want, wish'   Perf. part. *gewollt*
Present sg. 1 *will* '(I) want, wish', 2 *willst*, 3 *will*, pl. 1 *wollen*, 2 *wollt*, 3
wollen; subj. sg. 3 *wolle*
Preterite sg. 1 *wollte* '(I) wanted, wished', 2 *wolltest*, 3 *wollte*, pl. 1
wollten, 2 *wolltet*, 3 *wollten*
On the participial form *wollend*, see p. 290.

REFLEXIVE CONJUGATION

A number of verbs exist solely in the reflexive form; the object pronoun is commonly in the accusative, much less so in the dative. The tenses of the perfect system are conjugated with *haben*.

(Accusative pronoun)

Infinitives: present *sich* etc. *(zu) beeilen* '(to) hurry', perfect *sich* etc. *beeilt (zu) haben* '(to) have hurried'
Participle: *sich* etc. *beeilend* 'hurrying'

Indicative

Present *ich beeile mich* 'I hurry', *du beeilst dich, er beeilt sich, wir beeilen uns, ihr beeilt euch, sie beeilen sich*
Future *ich werde mich beeilen* 'I shall hurry'
Preterite *ich beeilte mich* 'I hurried'
Perfect *ich habe mich beeilt* 'I have hurried'
etc., etc.

Subjunctive

Present *er beeile sich*
etc., etc.

(Conditional)

Present *ich würde mich beeilen* 'I would hurry'
etc., etc.

Imperative: (familiar) *beeil(e) dich! beeilt euch!* (polite) *beeilen Sie sich!*

Other purely reflexive verbs conjugated as above include *sich behelfen* 'make shift', *sich bemächtigen* (+ gen.) 'seize, take possession of', *sich besinnen* 'reflect', *sich bewerben (um)* 'apply (for)', *sich entschließen* 'resolve', *sich erholen* 'recover (from an effort, illness)', *sich erkundigen* (*nach*) 'enquire (about)', *sich gedulden* 'have patience', *sich schämen* 'be ashamed', *sich sehnen* (*nach*) 'long (for)', *sich verirren* 'get lost', *sich verlieben* 'fall in love', *sich verspäten* 'be late', *sich weigern* 'refuse', *sich widersetzen* (+ dat.) 'oppose'. The verbs *sich belaufen* (*auf* + acc.) 'amount (to), add up (to)' and *sich ereignen* 'happen' are used in the 3rd person only.

(Dative pronoun)

Infinitives: present *sich* etc. *ein(zu)bilden* '(to) imagine', perfect *sich* etc. *eingebildet (zu) haben* '(to) have imagined'

Participle: *sich* etc. *einbildend* 'imagining'

Indicative

Present *ich bilde mir ein* 'I imagine', *du bildest dir ein, er bildet sich ein, wir bilden uns ein, ihr bildet euch ein, sie bilden sich ein*
Future *ich werde mir einbilden* 'I shall imagine'
Preterite *ich bildete mir ein* 'I imagined'
Perfect *ich habe mir eingebildet* 'I have imagined'
etc., etc.

Subjunctive

Present *er bilde sich ein*
etc., etc.

(Conditional)

Present *ich würde mir einbilden* 'I would imagine'
etc., etc.

Imperative: (familiar) *bild(e) dir ein! bildet euch ein!* (polite) *bilden Sie sich ein!*

Transitive verbs can normally make reflexive forms at will, e.g. *sich* (acc.) *schneiden* 'cut oneself', *sich* (dat.) *schaden* 'damage oneself'; see further pp. 277 f.

VERBS WITH PREFIXES

Verbs with prefixes fall into two classes according to whether the prefix is unstressed and inseparable, or stressed and separable. Some prefixes may be either inseparable or separable.

Inseparable prefixes

The following prefixes are always inseparable: *be-, emp-, ent-, ver-, zer-*, e.g. *bestellen* 'order', *empfangen* 'receive', *entehren* 'dishonour', *erfinden* 'invent', *verkaufen* 'sell', *zerreißen* 'tear'. In point of morphology such verbs are no different from the ordinary run of simple verbs except that they form the perfect participle without *ge-*, hence *bestellet, empfangen, entehrt, erfunden, verkauft, zerrissen*.

Separable prefixes

The separable prefix is commonly also a preposition, of which the following are always separable: *an-, auf-, bei-, mit-, nach-* (but see *nachvollziehen*, p. 107), *vor-, zu-*, further *ab-*, e.g. *anklagen* 'accuse', *aufgeben* 'give up', *beifügen* 'enclose', *mitarbeiten* 'collaborate', *nachtun* 'imitate' *vorschlagen* 'propose', *zubereiten* 'prepare (e.g. a meal)', and *abweichen* 'deviate'.

Conjugation is as follows:
Infinitives: *an(zu)klagen* '(to) accuse', *angeklagt (zu) haben* '(to) have accused'
Participles: *anklagend* 'accusing', *angeklagt* 'accused'
Imperatives: (familiar) sg. *klag(e) an!* pl. *klagt an!* (polite) *klagen Sie an!* 'accuse!'
Sample tenses: present *ich klage an* 'I accuse', future *ich werde anklagen* 'I shall accuse', preterite *ich klagte an* 'I accused', perfect *ich habe angeklagt* 'I have accused', present passive *ich werde angeklagt* 'I am accused'.

On the position of the separated prefix in the sentence, see under 'Verbs with separable Prefix', pp. 337 f.

Separable prefixes are formed by other parts of speech, notably by adverbs as *fort-*, *nieder-*, *weg-*, e.g. *fortschicken* 'send off', *niederlegen* 'lay down', *wegwerfen* 'throw away', also *ein-*, e.g. *einrichten* 'arrange', common too *her-*, *hin-*, e.g. *hergeben* 'give away', *hinsetzen* 'set down'. Further, a great number of compound adverbs as *entgegen-*, *zurück-*, *zusammen-*, e.g. *entgegensehen* 'expect, await', *zurücktreiben* 'drive back', *zusammenflicken* 'patch up', also combinations with *da-*, e.g. *davonlaufen* 'run off', and especially with *her-*, *hin-*, e.g. *herbeischaffen* 'procure', *hinausgehen* 'go out'.

Numerous adjectives form separable prefixes, cf. *fernsehen* 'watch television', *stillegen* (*still-legen*) 'shut down (as a factory)', *totschießen* 'shoot dead', *wettmachen* 'make up for'; they are sometimes used adverbially, cf. *blindschreiben* 'touch-type', *festnageln* 'nail down', *irreführen* or *-leiten* 'lead astray'. In a handful of examples a participle or an infinitive occurs as a prefix: *verlorengehen* 'get lost', *liegenbleiben* 'be left (untouched, unsold, etc.)'. A few nouns are also involved: *stattfinden* 'take place', *teilnehmen* 'take part'. Finally, the prefix may be a word with no independent existence, as *dar-*, e.g. *darstellen* 'represent', in more limited use *inne-*, e.g. *innehalten* 'stop, pause', and the compound forms *hin'tan-*, *ein'her-*, e.g. *hintanlassen* 'disregard', *einherschreiten* 'stride along in a stately manner'.

Prefixes used with *sein* and *werden* are not joined to the finite parts of the verb: *ob sie dabei sind?* '(I wonder) if they are there', but *ich werde dabeisein* 'I'll be there', *ich hoffe dabeizusein* 'I hope to be there', similarly *als es bekannt wurde* 'when it became known', but in the perfect: *als es bekanntgeworden ist*. Exceptionally, prefix and verb are written separately in the idiom *hinzu* (or *dazu*) *kommt* 'in addition, what is more'; it comes first in its sentence or clause.

Prefixes inseparable and separable

The prefixes chiefly concerned are *durch-*, *über-*, *um-*, *unter-*, *wider-*; for other cases, see below. When separable, prefix and verb most commonly retain their literal meanings, though not necessarily so, and may have developed a figurative meaning or meanings as well. When inseparable, the literal meaning is frequently modified, the word taking on a specialized or figurative sense. Verbs with inseparable prefixes are always transitive, even when the corresponding simple verb is intransitive, and this may be the only difference between a separable and an inseparable formation. In many cases, separable and inseparable alternatives exist side by side, but in not a few instances only the one or the other occurs. These matters may now be illustrated.

Separable, prefix stressed	Inseparable, prefix unstressed
durchlaufen 'run through' intransitive	*durchlaufen* 'run through, traverse
durchreisen 'travel through' intransitive	*durchreisen* 'travel through, tour'
durchschauen 'see or look through' in the literal sense	*durchschauen* 'see through' in the figurative sense
durchsehen 'see or look through, examine, revise'	——
durchboxen 'force through' casual style	——
——	*durchnässen* 'drench'
überlaufen 'run or flow over'	*überlaufen* 'overrun'
übersetzen 'cross' (as a river), also transitive 'ferry over'	*übersetzen* 'translate'

The majority of verbs prefixed with *über-* are inseparable only, e.g. *überbringen* 'deliver', *übertreiben* 'exaggerate', *überwinden* 'overcome', *überzeugen* 'convince'.

umgehen 'go round, make a detour, haunt, deal (*mit* 'with')'	*umgehen* 'by-pass, circumvent'
umrahmen 'put into a different frame'	*umrahmen* 'frame'
umfallen 'fall over or down'	——
umkehren 'turn back'	——
umkommen 'lose one's life'	——
——	*umarmen* 'embrace'
——	*umgarnen* 'ensnare'
——	*umgrenzen* 'circumscribe, limit'

Separable, prefix stressed	Inseparable, prefix unstressed
unterstehen 'take shelter'	*unterstehen* 'be subordinate to', *sich unterstehen* 'dare', *untersteh dich!* 'don't you dare!'
unterhalten 'hold under' (as one's head under water)	*unterhalten* 'entertain'
untergehen 'go down, sink, perish'	——
——	*unterwerfen* 'conquer'
widerhallen 'echo, resound'	——
widerspiegeln 'reflect'	——
——	*widerlegen* 'refute'
——	*widerrufen* 'revoke'
——	*widersprechen* 'contradict'
——	*widerstehen* 'resist'
wiederaufbauen 'rebuild'	*wiederholen* 'repeat' (the sole example)
wiedereröffnen 're-open' etc. etc.	

Other prefixes involved include *hinter-*. As a separable prefix it survives to a certain extent in regional use, e.g. *hinterschlucken* 'swallow', perf. part. *hintergeschluckt*, more standard language having *herunter-* or *hinunterschlucken*, p. 178. But this prefix is most familiar in inseparable use, e.g. *hintergehen* 'deceive', *hinterlassen* 'bequeath', *hinterlegen* 'deposit, give in trust', *hinterziehen* 'evade (taxes)', perf. part. *hintergangen*, etc. The prefix *voll-* may occur unstressed, e.g. *vollführen* 'perform', *vollstrecken* or *-ziehen* 'carry out' (a sentence), perf. part. *vollführt*, etc.; it is likewise inseparable in *nach(zu)vollziehen* '(to) re-live', perf. part. *nachvollzogen*. But when the literal sense 'full' is dominant, the prefix takes the stress: *vollpacken* 'pack full', perf. part. *vollgepackt*. Verbs prefixing *'not-*, e.g. *notlanden*, are treated as inseparable, at least in their finite parts: *das Flugzeug notlandete* 'the plane made a forced landing', but generally perf. part. *notgelandet* rather than *genotlandet* and infinitive with *zu* usually *notzulanden* in preference to *zu notlanden*.

As a verbal prefix *miß-* is unstressed: *mißbrauchen* 'misuse, abuse', *mißhandeln* 'ill-treat', perf. part. *mißbraucht, mißhandelt*; a stressed form as in *mißgebildet* 'misshapen' is purely adjectival, there being no other verbal parts.

Double prefixes

Some verbs have double prefixes: (inseparable, all weak, p. 89) *beantragen* 'apply for', *verabscheuen* 'detest', hence e.g. *ich beantrage, verabscheue, ich habe beantragt, verabscheut,* (separable) *anerkennen* 'recognize, acknowledge', *beibehalten* 'keep, maintain', hence e.g. *ich erkenne an, behalte bei, ich habe anerkannt, beibehalten*, cf. also *nachvollziehen* in previous section.

Inseparable *sich über'anstrengen* 'over-exert oneself' forms the more popular-sounding perf. part. *über'angestrengt* in addition to the regular *über'anstrengt*. The verb *'uraufführen* 'perform (a play), show (a film) for the first time in public' has perf. part. *'uraufgeführt*, but no synthetic conjugation.

Compound verbs

There are in German a fair number of compound verbs. A few are derived from compound nouns, e.g. *frühstücken* 'breakfast' from *das Frühstück* or *wetteifern* 'emulate' from *der Wetteifer*. Others are variously formed, as *mutmaßen* 'presume', *nacht-* or *schlafwandeln* 'walk in one's sleep', *rechtfertigen* 'justify', *weissagen* 'prophesy'. All such verbs follow the weak conjugation, hence perf. part. *gefrühstückt, gewetteifert* (contrasting with *wettgemacht* from *wettmachen*, differently formed, p. 105), etc.

A small number of compound verbs use only two forms: infinitive and perfect participle; they have thus no synthetic conjugation, as *kunststopfen* 'mend invisibly', perf. part. *kunstgestopft*. In other cases only an infinitive exists: *kannst du kopfrechnen?* 'can you do mental arithmetic?'

VOCABULARY

9. Modal Particles

WHILE in other respects retaining their proper meanings, a number of adverbs have also come to be used in such a way that they express the attitude of the speaker, and in this function are appropriately termed modal particles. As such, they have no clearly definable meanings and consequently often no regular English equivalents, all the more so since their use tends to be highly idiomatic. It is not uncommon to find two such particles used together for mutual reinforcement or qualification. These words are present at all stylistic levels, but proliferate above all in everyday speech. Analogous particles are, of course, not unknown in English and usage in the two languages occasionally corresponds entirely, e.g. *einfach* 'simply': *ich habe einfach keine 'Zeit* 'I simply have no time'. Such examples require no further mention here.

The modal particles illustrated below include the most typical and commonly used. As we are dealing in the first place with spoken language, the significant stresses have been marked, though it must be added that alternative stressings are possible in certain cases. It will be seen that the particles themselves are, for the most part, unstressed.

aber——traditionally meaning 'but, however', as a modal particle it frequently lends emphasis: *du kommst doch 'gern, nicht wahr? — aber 'ja!* 'you do want to come, don't you?—of course I do!', or it may convey surprise: *ihr seid* (or *seid ihr*, p. 328) *aber ge'wachsen!* 'I say, how you've grown!' In other examples either, or both, of these nuances may be present, depending on the circumstances: *dieser Rum hat's aber 'in sich!* 'my word, this rum does have a kick!' Emphasis may amount to approval or disapproval: *das Essen war aber 'gut* 'the food really was good', *die Bedienung war aber 'lahm* 'the service really was poor'—needless to say, these are different from *das Essen aber war 'gut* 'the food, however, was good', etc.

The present particle combines with *auch* to give particular emphasis: *er hat 'alles, aber auch 'alles verloren* 'he has lost everything, absolutely everything'.

auch——modifies the sense in a number of ways. It is, however, often difficult to decide whether the word is to be taken as a modal particle or whether its function is still that of an adverb 'also, too, even'. Intonation may play a part, but some sentences lend themselves to more than one interpretation. Consider: *bist du 'auch zufrieden?*

'are you, too, satisfied?' beside *bist du auch zu'frieden?* which, however, can mean either 'are you also satisfied?' or 'are you really satisfied?', the original adverbial 'also' easily being felt as a modal element 'really', if the occasion warrants it. Another example: depending on the wider context, the question *haben Sie auch die 'Pakete geliefert?* can be understood either as 'did you also deliver the parcels?' or 'did you manage to deliver the parcels?'

Modal use occurs unequivocally as follows. Firstly, in rhetorical questions in optional association with *denn*, cf. *Herr Weiß arbeitet nicht mehr — warum 'sollte er (denn) auch?* or simply *wa'rum (denn) auch? — er ist jetzt Rentner* 'Mr White isn't working any more—why should he?—he's a pensioner now'. Secondly, as a comment on a previous clause: *weil sie müde waren von ihrem langen Weg, schliefen sie auch 'bald ein* 'since they were tired from their long journey, they (therefore) soon fell asleep'. Similarly as a comment on a sentence, spoken or implied; strengthening *ja* is optionally used as well: *dieser Anzug war sehr preisgünstig — er sieht (ja) auch so 'aus* 'this suit was very cheap—and it looks like it', *du warst (ja) auch 'krank* 'you were ill on top of it', *unser Vorrat reicht (ja) auch nicht 'aus* 'our supplies aren't sufficient either', *man kann es (ja) auch 'lassen* 'one can leave it for that matter'. Modality, too, in the often used phrase *oder auch nicht*, e.g. *Sie können die Ware mitnehmen oder auch 'nicht* 'you can take the goods with you or not (as you like)', where *auch* mollifies the negative, the phrase sounding less abrupt than the stark *oder 'nicht*.

The present particle is regularly used with *nur*, e.g. *ohne auch nur zu 'lächen* 'without so much as a smile'. It is a standard constituent of concessive clauses, pp. 264 ff.

bloß——as an adverb it means 'only', as a modal particle it occurs in wishes, again corresponding to 'only': *wenn er bloß 'bleiben würde!* 'if he would only stay!'. It also occurs in warnings when it carries a stress: *'bloß aufpassen!* '(mind you) watch your step!' or '(mind you) take care!', *laß dich 'bloß nicht drauf ein!* 'don't you have anything to do with it!' In other commands, the particle may have emphatic force without being stressed: *treten Sie bloß 'ein!* 'just step inside!', *'geh bloß* 'go, by all means'. It is found in questions: *wo 'ist bloß das Haus?* 'where can the house be?', *wo 'ist denn bloß wieder diese Straßenkarte?* '(so) just where is that road map again?', and in negative replies when it is stressed: *'bloß jetzt nicht* or *'bloß nicht jetzt* 'not now, of all times'.

The present particle is more or less the equivalent of the stylistically superior *nur* (p. 117) which could replace it in the above examples, though sounding slightly weaker, *bloß* being the more vigorous particle. In positive commands the two particles convey different shades of meaning: *seid bloß ver'nünftig* 'do be sensible' = 'stop being silly,' *seid nur ver'nünftig* 'try to be sensible'. Often intechangeable with '*ja* below.

denn——otherwise a conjunction meaning 'for, because' (but originally an adverb 'then'), this word exercises its modal functions chiefly in questions. It is commonly added to these lest they should sound too abrupt, and also to convey a note of friendliness or interest. Instead of *warum?* 'why?', *wo?* 'where?', *was wollen Sie?* 'what do you want?', *wer hat hier Vorfahrt?* 'who has right of way here?', one very often finds *wa'rum denn?*, '*wo denn?*, *was 'wollen Sie denn?*, *wer hat denn hier 'Vorfahrt?* Similarly in indirect questions and other subordinate clauses: *ich fragte, wer denn noch 'kommen sollte* 'I asked who else would be coming', *wir wollten nur sehen, was denn da 'wächst* 'we just wanted to see what was growing there'. The particle is stressed in questions asked after one has noticed that something is not what one had believed it to be: *wenn sie nicht Renate heißt, wie heißt sie 'denn?* 'if she's not called R., then what is she called?'

In given contexts special nuances may appear, in particular an element of surprise: *spricht er denn ja'panisch?* 'can he actually speak Japanese?', *haben sie denn 'kein Verständnis für unsere schwierige Lage?* 'have they really no appreciation of our difficult situation?' The question *hast du denn nicht 'aufgepaßt?* 'weren't you paying attention?' carries an implicit reproach, in the often heard *was 'sollen wir denn machen?* 'what a r e we to do?' the particle highlights the dilemma.

The present particle often strengthens the adverb *so*, e.g. *und so gebot denn 'Joseph über das ganze Land Ägypten* 'and so (= as a result) J. ruled over all the land of Egypt'.

doch——commonly occurs both stressed and unstressed. We first note that, when stressed, this word is used as a strong affirmation: *ist sie ganz zufrieden?* — '*doch* 'is she quite satisfied?—certainly'. It is always so used in reply to a negative question: *ist sie nicht glücklich?* — *doch* 'isn't she happy?—oh yes, she is'. It similarly contradicts a negative statement: *es kommt nicht zu einem Streik* — '*doch, es kommt dazu* 'it won't come to a strike—oh yes, it will come to that'. From such usage *doch* developed into a stressed modal particle: *es ist 'doch zu einem Streik gekommen* 'so it came to a strike after all', and compare Galileo's alleged aside *und sie bewegt sich 'doch* 'and yet it (the earth) does move'.

The unstressed particle performs other duties. It can underline a statement, with a hint of contradiction: *du has doch Zeit ge'nug* 'you've plenty of time though', thus rather different from *du hast ja Zeit ge'nug*, p. 116. Other examples: *man wird doch nicht 'glauben, daß er es gemacht hat* 'people just won't believe that he did it', *das wollen Sie doch 'sicher nicht, oder?* 'but you surely don't want it, do you?'. In wishes *doch* corresponds to 'only': *wenn er doch* (= *nur, bloß*) *'bleiben würde!* 'if he would only stay!'

The present particle emphasizes an imperative: *steh doch 'auf!* 'get up, I say!', *seien Sie doch nicht 'böse!* 'oh, don't be so angry!' It has the same function in exclamations: *wie 'klein ist doch die Welt!,* or less elegantly *wie 'klein die Welt doch ist!* 'how small the world is!' Similarly in the construction with the finite verb first (p. 329) *hatte ich doch 'Glück!* 'how lucky I was!' The particle further occurs in sentences in which one is trying to recall something, when it is usually followed by *gleich*, e.g. *ich meine die Stadt zwischen Weimar und Gotha, wie 'heißt sie doch gleich?* 'I mean the town between W. and G., what is it called again?' It is also found in statements put in the form of a question: *wir werden uns doch 'wiedersehen?* 'we will be seeing each other again, won't we?', more or less the same as *wir werden uns 'wiedersehen, nicht wahr?*, or with the best of both worlds *wir werden uns doch 'wiedersehen, nicht wahr?*—but of course quite distinct from the stressed particle (above): *wir werden uns 'doch wiedersehen* 'we shall see each other again whatever happens'.

The particle is often followed by *mal* (below): *wir sehen uns doch mal 'wieder, nicht wahr?* 'we'll be seeing each other again sometime or other, won't we?', *mach doch mal die 'Tür zu!* 'shut the door, if you don't mind!', *gib ihm doch mal sein 'Geld* 'give him his money while you're at it', (advertising slogan for telephone) *ruf doch mal 'an* 'just pick up a phone'. Thus by adding *mal* sentences sound more casual or considerate. Contrast *'schreib doch mal!* 'just drop a line sometime!' with *'schreib doch!* 'do write!' or 'start writing, I say!' or similar energetic English wording depending on the circumstances.

eben——as an adverb it means 'very recently, just', as modal particle it often implies that the speaker accepts the situation: *das Reisen in fremden Ländern ist eben 'teuer* 'travel in foreign countries happens to be expensive', *das 'ist eben so* 'it just is so'. It may confirm a reason: *er war eben ein 'tüchtiger Tischler* 'you see, he was a good carpenter', or underline a proposal: *dann gib es eben 'auf!* 'then simply give it up!' In the above usages *eben* is widely replaced in the south by *halt* (in medieval times an adverb meaning 'rather'), hence alternatively *das Reisen in fremden Ländern ist halt 'teuer*. This regionalism may occur in print, though not in high style.

The particle *eben* can be further used as an answer agreeing with what has been said; *ja* or *nein* may be understood: *das Problem wird dadurch einfacher* — (*'ja,*) *'eben* 'the problem thereby becomes simpler—(yes), it does'*, *das Problem wird dadurch nicht einfacher* — (*'nein*), *eben 'nicht* 'the problem does not thereby become simpler—(no,) it doesn't'.

eigentlich——in its literal sense chiefly an attributive adjective 'real, actual', the modal particle developing from an adverbial use 'really, actually'. One of these words may be the idiomatic equivalent, e.g. *sie ist eigentlich sehr 'nett* 'she is actually very nice'. However, other shades of modality may appear, according to the wider context: the same sentence could also be a casual remark 'by the way, she's very nice', or imply a mild contradiction 'but I find her very nice'—this particle as much as any must be studied *in situ*.

The present word is equally common in questions, when it may be added to avoid an impression of abruptness: *was 'wollen Sie eigentlich?* 'what was it you were wanting?', in this function interchangeable with *denn*. In fact, both particles are often used together to the same effect: *was 'wollen Sie denn eigentlich?* As in statements, other nuances may be present in questions, too, e.g. *sind sie eigentlich ver'wandt?* 'are they actually related?'

This particle is often given in answers: *hast du dir das Haus auch so vorgestellt? — eigentlich 'nicht* 'did you think the house would look like that?—not really'. It may, optionally, stand first in the sentence: *eigentlich wollten wir* (= *wir wollten eigentlich*) *in den Urlaub nach 'Italien fahren, haben es uns dann doch anders überlegt* 'we originally wanted to go to Italy for our holidays, but then we changed our minds', and hence alternatively *eigentlich ist sie sehr 'nett* (above).

The present word can be stressed when, however, it fully retains its literal meaning: *wie heißt sie 'eigentlich?* 'what is her real name?', thus distinct from *wie 'heißt sie eigentlich?* being simply 'what is her name?', and also different from *wie heißt sie 'denn?*, p. 113.

einmal, see *mal*

erst——occurs typically in a brief assertion capping another: *Rudolf soll sehr klug sein* 'R. is said to be very clever', and the reply: *und erst 'Norbert!* or *und 'Norbert erst!* 'but nothing compared with N.!' If the first assertion is in the negative, the modal phrase *erst 'recht nicht* is used: *im Londoner Straßenverkehr ist man seines Lebens nicht sicher, und in Paris erst 'recht nicht!* 'your life's not your own in the traffic in L., not to speak of P.!' See also under *mal*.

In non-modal use *erst* is a temporal adverb, cf. *ich fahre erst um 'sechs Uhr* 'I'm not going until six o'clock'.

etwa——basically an adverb meaning 'approximately', as a modal particle it is commonly found in questions to which the answer will hopefully be a contradiction: *hast du etwa 'Angst* 'are you afraid?' but with the force of our 'you're not afraid, are you?', cf. (with tongue in cheek) *heißt du etwa 'Rumpelstilzchen?* 'can your name be R.?' The particle also occurs in negative statements: *'denk nicht etwa* (or *etwa nicht*), *daß ich hier bleibe* 'don't think for a moment that I'm staying here'.

gleich——literally meaning 'immediately', in modal use acting as an emotive reinforcement: *wirst du gleich 'ruhig sein!* '(for heaven's sake), will you be quiet!', *ihr braucht euch nicht gleich 'aufzuregen* 'there's really no need for you to get worked up'. See also under *doch*.

halt, see *eben*.

ja——an adaptation of the affirmative adverb, it commonly occurs both stressed and unstressed. In the former use it is found with an imperative as a vigorous intensifier: *sei 'ja ein artiges Kind!* 'do be a good child!', *komm 'ja nicht zu spät!* 'don't you be too late!', and similarly in a statement with *sollen*, e.g. *du sollst 'ja nicht hingehen* 'you are not to go there on any account'. The particle is also used in negative replies: *soll ich den Witz noch mal erzählen?* — *'ja nicht* 'shall I tell the joke again?—no, for heaven's sake'. It is often interchangeable with *'bloß*, especially when followed by *nicht*, as in the examples just quoted, hence *komm 'bloß nicht zu spät!*, etc., also more weakly *komm 'nur nicht zu spät*, p. 112. It may also be strengthened by either of these: (stern warning) *daß bloß* (or *nur*) *'ja niemand vom Nachbarn abschreibt!* amounting to 'don't let me catch anyone copying from his neighbour!'

When unstressed the particle has other functions. It can underline a statement, the tone being neutral or friendly: *du hast ja Zeit ge'nug* 'you've plenty of time, for sure', thus rather different from *du hast doch Zeit ge'nug*, pp. 113 f. Other examples: *Sie 'wissen ja, daß sie eine neue Enkelin bekommen haben* 'you know, of course, that they've got a new granddaughter', *man 'wollte ihm ja helfen, aber er hat's nicht zugelassen* 'people did want to help him, but he wouldn't allow it', *das 'eilt ja nicht* 'there's no hurry at all!'. Often explanatory, as in answers to questions: *kann der Junge gut Klavier spielen?* — *ja, er übt ja 'jeden Tag* — *nein, er übt ja 'nie* 'can the boy play the piano well?—yes, you see he practises every day—no, you see he never practises'. In exclamations the particle may express surprise: *ihr habt ja eine 'neue Wohnung!* 'oh, so you've got a new flat!'; in other examples it is simply emphatic: *das ist ja 'unerhört!* 'I say, it is outrageous!'

mal——in origin the abbreviated form of *einmal* 'once', with which it may be interchangeable: *ich hab ihn 'mal* (or *'einmal*) *getroffen* 'I once met him'. When unstressed, *mal* is a modal particle. It is commonly heard in requests: *hol mal den 'Korb!* 'just fetch the basket!' with the implication that it won't be difficult to do so, it's just lying over there, for instance. Other examples: *stellt euch das mal 'vor!* 'just imagine it!', *kommen Sie mal 'mit!* 'just come with me (or, us)!' Elliptical use is not uncommon in association with on infinitive: *mal 'sehen!* for, say, *wir wollen mal 'sehen* 'let's just see!' The present particle is often supported by *erst* but without any tangible change in feeling: *(wir wollen) erst mal 'sehen!* Use is common in other types of sentence, too, and with the same implications: *kannst du mal 'nachsehen, ob es noch dort ist?* 'can you just look if it's still there?', *wenn du erst mal so 'alt bist wie ich, dann wirst du's anders sehen* 'when you're as old as me (but sounding rather like 'just wait till . . . '), then you'll see it in a different light'.

Although often corresponding to 'just', *mal* occurs more frequently, i.e. it occurs in contexts where we may find 'just' expendable, as *'sagt mir mal* '(just) tell me!', or when 'just' would be ambiguous or have a different meaning: *können Sie mir mal die 'Karten zeigen?* 'can you show me the tickets?', *ich habe es mir mal 'angesehen* 'I've had a look at it'.

The close association between *mal* and *einmal* in their original meaning has been noted above. As a consequence, (unstressed) *einmal* is often found as an alternative to *mal* in its modal functions also. Indeed, it is the usual form in the far south, where it is colloquially pronounced [amal], hence e.g. *hol einmal den 'Korb*, etc. Sometimes *einmal* will be preferred elsewhere, too, especially in writing, as *man nehme nun einmal 'an* 'let us now just assume', where the (rather more dignified) full form goes better with the (elevated) subjunctive.

nur——literally 'only', has a range comparable to *bloß*. It is often used emphatically: *binden Sie den Knoten so 'fest wie nur möglich* 'tie the knot as tightly as you possibly can', *nur 'nicht vergessen!* 'don't forget, whatever you do!' It is a familiar word in exclamations: *nur 'Mut!* 'never say die!', *nur 'weiter* 'carry on!', (stylistically rather elevated) *nur 'zu!* go on! come along!'

On the regional synonym *man*, see p. 141. See further under *bloß*.

ruhig——developing from the adverbial sense 'quietly', it has come to express assurance: *das darf man ruhig be'haupten* 'one may safely say that', *er kann ruhig bei uns über'nachten* 'it will be all right for him to stay overnight at our place'.

schon——the ultimate starting-point for its various modal uses being

the sense 'already': *bist du 'schon fertig?* 'are you finished already?';
when the adverb is unstressed, 'already' may be dispensed with, so
slight is the meaning: *bist du schon 'fertig?* 'are you finished?'
Indeed, the present particle can become an empty word: *wissen Sie,
daß er hier ist?* — *ja, ich 'weiß schon* 'do you know that he is
here?—yes, I know'. Yet at the same time an emphatic function has
developed, merging into modal use: *schon dieser 'kleine Garten ist
ihm zu viel* 'even this little garden is too much for him', *das 'kostet
schon einiges* 'that costs quite a bit', *solche Infos können dabei helfen,
im Toto schon eher mal die 'Richtigen zu tippen* 'such pieces of
information can be of help, giving (you) a better chance of filling in
the pools correctly'. In other examples, the particle may be stressed:
hat's weh getan? — *och, ein bißchen 'schon* 'did it hurt?—oh, it did a
bit'.

As a modal particle *schon* expresses, further, a fairly confident
supposition: *er 'wird schon nach Haus finden* 'he'll find his way
home, I should think'. It therefore often adds a note of reassurance:
wird er kommen? — *ich 'glaube schon* 'will he be coming?—oh, I
think so', *es ist schon 'gut* 'it's quite all right', *'so schlimm wird's
schon nicht sein* 'it won't be so bad, you know'.

Next, by a further shift, the particle comes to reinforce abrupt,
petulant commands in familiar style: *sei schon 'ruhig! wirst du schon
'ruhig!* both meaning 'be quiet, I say!' In other commands it
commonly expresses impatience: *'gib es ihm schon!* 'well, give him
it!', *be'eil dich schon!* 'hurry up then!', (substandard) *'mach schon!*
'get a move on!', *nun haut schon 'ab !* 'now clear off!' where *nun* is
as much an empty word as 'now'. The particle is used in threats and
warnings: *ich werde ihm schon 'zeigen* 'I'll show him, that I will!'
Modal use is also found in rhetorical questions: *was soll man schon
'sagen?* 'what is one supposed to say?' The particle can also convey a
limiting sense: *er hat sich schon 'Zeit genommen für die Arbeit, aber
das Ergebnis läßt viel zu wünschen übrig* 'he has, it is true, taken time
over the job, but the result leaves much to be desired'.

When stressed, the word has modal force in two set phrases. In the
first, *das 'schon*, it indicates assent combined with a reservation, e.g.
someone says *London ist eine Reise wert* 'L. is worth a visit', and another
comments *das 'schon* 'yes, it is', implying, however, that there are
negative aspects, which will then generally be mentioned, say, *aber die
Luftverschmutzung durch die vielen Autos ist nicht direkt gesundheits-
fördernd* 'but the air pollution caused by all the motorcars isn't exactly
conducive to health'. In the second set phrase, *eigentlich 'schon*, the
emphasized particle expresses unqualified assent: *hast du dir das Zimmer
auch so vorgestellt?* — *eigentlich 'schon* 'and did you imagine the room
would be like that?—yes, I really did' (= *eigentlich 'ja*).

In some functions this particle may be replaced in the north by *wohl* (q.v.).

überhaupt——basically an intensifying adverb and as such carrying a stress: *es geht Sie über'haupt nichts an* 'it doesn't concern you in the least', though English idiom may disregard the emphasis: *das einzige Stück dieser Art, das über'haupt je gefunden wurde* 'the only piece of this kind which was ever found'. In modal use it commonly corresponds to 'altogether': *er ist über'haupt ein unverläßlicher Typ* 'he is altogether an unreliable type'. Although regularly accented *über'haupt*, the alternative *'überhaupt* may be heard in emotional speech.

Otherwise the particle occurs in questions; it is then, however, unstressed. English 'at all' can express the nuance involved, though idiomatically often ignored: *ist sie überhaupt ver'heiratet?* 'is she married (at all)?', *hast du ihn überhaupt ge'sehen?* 'have you seen him at all?', *wann 'kommen sie überhaupt?* 'well, when will they be coming?'

vielleicht——occurs in exclamations: *'du hast* (or *'hast du*, p. 329) *vielleicht Glück!* 'how lucky you are!', *das 'war* (or *'war das*) *vielleicht ein Durcheinander!* 'what a muddle that was!' Modal use has, of course, arisen from the basic sense 'perhaps'.

wohl——expresses, firstly, a fairly confident supposition: *das wird wohl das 'beste sein* 'that will be best, I should think'. It can therefore convey reassurance: *der liebe 'Gott wird wohl helfen* '(don't worry!) the good Lord will provide'. A quite different use is seen when the particle reinforces abrupt, petulant commands in familiar style: *sei wohl ver'nünftig!* 'be sensible, I say!', *bringt wohl die Sachen wieder 'her!* 'see that you bring the things back here!', *wirst du wohl für fünf Minuten den 'Mund halten!* '(for heaven's sake) keep your mouth shut for five minutes!' Different again is the use in rhetorical questions: *wer ist gekommen? — (na,) 'wer wohl?* 'who's come?—(well,) who do you suppose?'

In its literal meaning 'well' the present word often bears a stress: *er fühlt sich 'wohl* 'he feels well (commonly also, comfortable)'. So stressed, the word occurs in modal use in the set phrase *das 'wohl* which indicates assent combined with a reservation: *könnten Sie jetzt eine Anzahlung machen?* 'could you now make a deposit?', and the answer *das 'wohl* 'yes, certainly', but implying that the rest of the money, or some of it, is not yet available, and thus different from *ja 'wohl*, the (emphatic) assent pure and simple.

The present particle, often found in literature, is current particularly in the north, *schon* largely taking its place in the centre and south.

10. Aspects of Word Formation

COMPOUND NOUNS

A STRIKING property of the German language is the enormous number of compound nouns to be found in everyday use and the ease with which new examples can be created. Compounds are of various types. At its simplest, a compound consists of two elements, the first of which may be another noun, an adjective, an adverb or preposition, or a verb; a numeral may also be involved, see pp. 78, 80 f. A mixture of types is commonplace in compounds consisting of more than two elements, p. 123. The compound takes its gender from the last element, except in a few instances (p. 124).

Noun plus noun

In this, the only complex type morphologically, the first noun appears in a variety of forms. It may be juxtaposed: *der Apfelmus* 'apple sauce', *die Gartenschau* 'horticultural show', *das Lastauto* 'lorry', *die Mondnacht* 'moonlight night'. A few feminines in *-e* are so used when they either retain their full form, as *der Reiseleiter* 'tour leader', *die Speisekammer* 'pantry', *die Wäscheklammer* 'clothes peg', or else drop *-e* as in *der Grenzfall* 'borderline case', *der Kirschbaum* 'cherry tree', *das Sprachlabor* 'language laboratory', as does also the neuter *Ende*, e.g. *der Endspurt* 'final spurt'.

In a second variety, the first element appears in the genitive singular—the genitive traditionally stood before its noun, p. 153: *die Tageszeitung* 'daily newspaper', *der Kriegsberichterstatter* 'war correspondent', *das Volksmärchen* 'folktale'; it occasionally represents a plural: *der Freundeskreis* 'circle of friends'. This distinctive termination has spread to a large number of feminine nouns: *die Liebesheirat* 'love match', *der Geburtstag* 'birthday', *das Hilfszeitwort* 'auxiliary verb', including words with the suffixes *-heit*, *-keit*, *-schaft*, *-ung*, and (the originally foreign) *-ion* and *-ität*, e.g. *der Seltenheitswert* 'scarcity value', *die Gültigkeitsdauer* 'period of validity', *das Freundschaftsspiel* 'friendly match', *der Regierungswechsel* 'change of government', *die Situationskomik* 'situational comedy', *die Neutralitätserklärung* 'declaration of neutrality', but e.g. *die Raritätensammlung* 'collection of curios'.

Comparable formations occur when the genitive singular ends in *-n*, cf. *die Hasenscharte* 'hare-lip', *das Bauernhaus* 'farm-house', or in *-en*, cf. *das Bärenfell* 'bearskin', *die Heldenbrust* (humorous) 'manly chest'. The first element here is often a feminine word, thus from *Küche, Sonne,* e.g. *der Küchentisch* 'kitchen table', *der Sonnenschein* 'sunshine', and just occasionally a neuter, thus from *Auge,* e.g. *die Augenbraue* 'eyebrow'; in such examples *-n* is the archaic gen. sg. ending. In other cases the inflexion represents the gen. pl., as *der Blumenstrauß* 'bunch of flowers', *der Frauenchor* 'women's choir'. The massive occurrence of *-en* in the formation of compounds has led, in a few instances, to its use when there is no compatible genitive: *der Schwanengesang* 'swan-song', *das Sternenbanner* 'Stars and Stripes' (gen. sg. *Schwan(e)s, Stern(e)s,* pl. *Schwäne, Sterne*). With nouns having the feminine suffix *-in* the compositional link is *-innen,* e.g. *der Sekretärinnenposten* 'post of secretary'. Plural formations are seen again in examples of the type *Kindergarten,* often also singular in sense, cf. *das Hühnerei* 'hen's egg' beside *Hühnerstall* 'hencoop'. There are some plurals in *-e,* as *das Pferderennen* 'horse race or racing', with singular reference *der Pferdeschwanz* 'horse's tail'. But only very occasionally can a meaningful distinction be made between singular and plural, as *das Gotteshaus* 'the house of God' beside *die Götterdämmerung* 'twilight of the gods'. In general, number is irrelevant and has ceased to be felt.

With so much variation it is not surprising that, in certain cases, a word in composition appears in different forms, while the working of analogy has, on occasion, led to forms which (like *Schwanen-* above) have no independent existence. We instance: *die Buchhandlung* 'book-shop', *der Bücherschrank* 'book-case', *der Kirchhof* 'church-yard', *die Kirchenmaus* 'church mouse', *das Schweinsleder* 'pigskin', *das Schweinefleisch* 'pork'. The term *Wortregister* is synonymous with *das Wörterverzeichnis* 'index of words', 'estate agent' is either *der Haus-* or *Häusermakler,* one finds indifferently *die Namens-* or *Namenänderung* 'change of name'. Notice *das Gasthaus* '(modest) hotel', *das Gästehaus* 'guest-house', *der Landmann* 'farmer, country-man', *der Landsmann* 'fellow-countryman'. In a few cases there may be more than two possibilities: *das Maus-, Mause-,* or *Mäuseloch* 'mouse hole', *die Herzkrankheit* 'heart disease', *das Herzeleid* 'heart-ache', *der Herzenswunsch* 'dearest wish', *das Mannweib* 'hermaphro-dite', *das Mannsbild* (pejorative) 'man, male', *der Mannesstolz* 'manly pride', *die Männerstimme* 'male voice'. Finally, regional differences sometimes appear, the (far) south often preferring the compositional link *-s,* e.g. *der Fabriksarbeiter* 'factory-hand', *der Rindsbraten* 'roast beef' as opposed to more widely used *Fabrikarbeiter, Rinderbraten,* but notice *der Hemdsärmel* 'sleeve', southern unexpectedly also *Hemdärmel.* Compare *der Lausejunge* 'young rascal', southern *Lausbub.*

Adjective plus noun

The adjective forming the first element is uninflected: *die Blausäure* 'prussic acid', *der Fernsprecher* (officialese) 'telephone', *die Großmutter* 'grandmother', *das Hochland* 'highlands', *die Kaltmiete* 'basic rent (without heating)', *die Mager-*, *Vollmilch* 'skimmed, unskimmed milk'.

Occasionally the free-standing adjective and the adjective in composition remain very close and may be in part interchangeable, as *das neue Jahr*, *das Neujahr* 'new year, New Year', but in general the compound so formed is a totally independent lexical item: *die alte Stadt* means 'the town which is old', whereas *die Altstadt* means 'the old part of the town'. The examples in the paragraph above are thus, semantically, fully representative of these formations.

Adverb or preposition plus noun

This is another large contingent: (with an adverb) *die Außenwand* 'outside wall', *der Eingang* 'entrance', *die Herkunft* 'origin', *die Herablassung* 'condescension', *die Hinreise* 'outward journey', *der Innenminister* 'Minister of the Interior', *die Niederlage* 'defeat', *der Oberlauf* 'upper reaches (of a river)', *der Zusammenschluß* 'amalgamation', (with a preposition) *die Anklage* 'accusation', *der Aufstieg* 'ascent', *das Ausland* 'foreign countries', *das Beiboot* 'dinghy', *die Durchreiche* 'service hatch', *das Fürwort* 'preposition', *der Gegenwind* 'head wind', *der Hinterkopf* 'back of the head', *die Inzucht* 'inbreeding', *der Mittäter* 'accomplice', *der Nachruf* 'obituary', *der Nebenmann* 'neighbour' (at table etc.), *das Obdach* 'shelter', *der Übermensch* 'superman', *die Umgegend* 'surrounding area', *die Untergruppe* 'subgroup', *der Vorabend* 'evening before', *der Widerspruch* 'contradiction', *der Zutritt* 'admittance', *die Zwischenlandung* 'stop-over'.

Verb plus noun

In these compounds the stem of the verb forms the first element: *der Denkzettel* '(unpleasant) reminder', *der Fahrstuhl* 'lift', *das Gehwerk* '(clock) movement', *die Gießkanne* 'watering can', *der Lachkrampf* 'fit of laughing', *die Sparbüchse* 'money-box', *der Streichkäse* 'cheese spread', *das Treibholz* 'driftwood', *das Wohnzimmer* 'living room'.

A few stems use an inflexional -e, e.g. *der Ladebaum* 'derrick', *das Lösegeld* 'ransom', *das Säugetier* 'mammal', *die Schiebetür* 'sliding door'; notice *der Bindestrich* 'hyphen', *die Lesebrille* 'reading glasses', but *der Bindfaden* 'string', *die Lesart* 'version, reading', and *das Sterbebett* 'death-bed' beside the irregular formation *die Sterbensangst* 'mortal fear'.

Compounds of more than two elements

It will be apparent from the examples in the preceding sections that the two-element compound easily comes to be felt as expressing a single concept. That being the case, it is not difficult to add a second concept. This may be expressed by a simplex: *die Erdbeerpflanze* 'strawberry plant', *das Hochzeitskleid* 'wedding dress', *das Süßwasserfisch* 'freshwater fish', or by another two-element compound: *das Eisenbahnzeitalter* 'railway age', *das Fußballänderspiel* 'international football match', *der Sonntagsausflug* 'Sunday excursion'. Five-element compounds are not unusual either: from *der Umweltschutz* 'protection of the environment' one effortlessly forms *Umweltschutzmaßnahmen* 'measures for the protection of the environment', but here the line is generally drawn; 'special measures for the protection of the environment' would be best translated *Sondermaßnahmen zum Umweltschutz*. Nevertheless it is occasionally possible to go further: from *die Fahrkarte* 'ticket' one can progress via *Rückfahrkarte* 'return ticket' to *Sonderrückfahrkarte* 'special return ticket' or, moving in another direction, one can form *die Fahrkartenausgabe* 'issue of tickets'. This last word can, in railway parlance at least, readily combine with the others as *(Sonder)rückfahrkartenausgabe* 'issue of (special) return tickets'. In this way as many as six elements have been involved. But this will be the limit. In fact, compounds consisting of so many elements are usually just made up for fun, like the perennial *der Donaudampfschiffahrtsgesellschaftskapitän* 'Danube Steamship Company's captain'.

Mention may be made, in conclusion, of a small, but increasing number of compounds, met with in the written language, which are derived from a phrase comprising an adverb or preposition, a noun and a verb. Thus from *(eine Maschine) in Betrieb setzen* 'start up (a machine)' has been formed *die Inbetriebsetzung* 'starting up'. Other examples, all likewise feminine: *Instandhaltung* 'maintenance, upkeep', *Inangriffnahme* 'tackling (of a job)', *Außerkraftsetzung* 'invalidation', *Einbezugnahme* 'involvement', *Zurschaustellung* 'display' (of talent, etc.). In spite of some similarity the above are naturally distinct from examples in which the verbal element is a substantivized infinitive, p. 255: *das Inkrafttreten* 'taking effect', *das Zustandekommen* 'coming about'.

Compounds and equivalent modes of expression

German predilection for compound nouns, going far beyond English practice, means that the compound is often standard in German in cases where English has no corresponding formation: *ein Augenpaar* 'a pair of eyes', *ein Beweisstück* 'a piece of evidence', *der Erdmittel-*

punkt 'the centre of the earth', *die Hauskatze* 'the domestic cat' or 'the pet cat', *das Herzas* 'the ace of hearts', *der Schierlingsbecher* 'the cup of hemlock', *das Sonnensystem* 'the solar system', *eine Zeitperiode* 'a period of time', *eine Frauen-, Männergeschichte* 'an affair with a woman, with a man', and other examples *passim* elsewhere in this book. Some compounds occur only in fixed expressions: *aus Leibeskräften* 'for all one's worth', *in Sekundenschnelle* 'in a matter of seconds'.

Nevertheless not a few compounds have an analytical counterpart: *ein Liebeswort* or *ein Wort der Liebe* 'a word of love', *die Pressefreiheit* or *die Freiheit der Presse* 'the freedom of the press', similarly *das Direktorenamt* beside *das Amt eines Direktors* 'the office of director, or headmaster' and *die deutsche Gegenwartssprache* equivalent to *die deutsche Sprache der Gegenwart* 'the German language at the present day', or a circumlocution may be in use: *seine Schauspielertätigkeit* can be expressed as *seine Tätigkeit als Schauspieler* 'his activity as an actor'.

A note on gender

A compound nearly always takes the gender of its last component, there being no more than a handful of exceptions, as may be now explained.

In older German a noun in composition sometimes modified its form and gender. Later, such modifications were normally levelled out, but the old difference in gender has remained in *die Antwort* 'the answer' beside *das Wort* 'the word'. More recently formed compounds are not affected: *das Machtwort* 'word of authority', *das Schlußwort* 'closing words'. A relic of the ancient difference is seen again in *die Demut* 'the humility' beside the base word *der Mut* 'the courage'. In this instance, however, the more recent compounds may follow either the expected masculine or, quite exceptionally, the feminine. The choice seems largely arbitrary; some have actually been recorded with either gender. The present distribution is as follows: (fem.) *die Anmut* 'grace, charm', *die Großmut* 'magnanimity', *die Langmut* 'patience', *die Sanftmut* 'gentleness', *die Schwermut* 'melancholy', *die Wehmut* 'wistful longing for something lost or past', (masc.) *der Edelmut* 'noble-mindedness', *der Freimut* 'frankness', *der Gleichmut* 'equanimity', *der Hochmut* 'pride, arrogance', *der Kleinmut* 'faint-heartedness', *der Mißmut* 'sullen temper', *der Übermut* 'exuberance', *der Unmut* 'annoyance', *der Wankelmut* 'vacillation'. Let us briefly add that *die Armut* 'poverty' is unconnected, consisting of *arm* 'poor' and an otherwise discarded abstract suffix.

Notice further *die Scheu* 'shyness', but *der Abscheu* 'abhorrence'; on *das Rückgrat* 'backbone' beside *der Grat* 'ridge', see pp. 27 f.

Compounds based on *Teil* duly reflect the double gender of this word: the commoner masculines, including *der Anteil* 'share', *der Elternteil* 'parent', *der Nachteil* 'disadvantage', *der Vorteil* 'advantage', but also some neuters, as *das Abteil* 'compartment', *das Erbteil* 'share in an inheritance', *das Gegenteil* 'opposite', see further p. 28.

FORMATION OF THE FEMININE

As an almost universal rule, the feminine is formed from the masculine by the addition of the suffix *-in*, e.g. *Held* 'hero', *Heldin* 'heroine', *Kellner* 'waiter', *Kellnerin* 'waitress'. Final *-e* of the masculine is lost before the suffix: *Erbe* 'heir', *Erbin* 'heiress'. The feminine form is usually obligatory where in English no distinction is made: *Gefährte, Gefährtin* 'companion', *Läufer, Läuferin* 'runner', *Schriftsteller, -stellerin* 'writer', but see under 'General Use of the Masculine', pp. 308 f.

Umlaut before the suffix is not uncommon: *Fuchs*, 'fox', *Füchsin* 'vixen', *Gott* 'god', *Göttin* 'goddess', *Landsmann, -männin* 'compatriot', *Schwager* 'brother-in-law', *Schwägerin* 'sister-in-law', *Wolf* 'wolf', *Wölfin* 'she-wolf'. But feminines without umlaut are more numerous: *Gatte* 'husband', *Gattin* 'wife' (rather formal, polite) and synonymous *Herr Gemahl, Frau Gemahlin* (more formal still), *Genosse, Genossin* 'comrade', *Nachbar, Nachbarin* 'neighbour', *Pate* 'godfather', *Patin* 'godmother', *Sklave, Sklavin* 'slave'. Such forms are regular in the case of feminines derived from agent nouns ending in *-er*, as *Fahrer, Fahrerin* 'driver', *Bildhauer, -hauerin* 'sculptor, sculptress'. Notice *Beamtin* from *Beamte(r)* 'official' (p. 161) and the exceptional *Prin'zessin* 'princess' beside *Prinz* 'prince', *Dia'kon* 'deacon; male nurse', *Diako'nissin* '(Lutheran) nursing sister'; *Oberin* means '(hospital) matron', *Ober* (short for *Oberkellner* 'head waiter') is mostly used in the vocative: *Herr Ober!* 'waiter!'.

The ending regularly occurs in names denoting nationality and the like: *Ire, Irin* 'Irishman, -woman', *Grieche, Griechin* 'Greek', *Preuße, Preußin* 'Prussian'. Umlaut may occur: *Schwabe, Schwäbin* 'Swabian', further *Jude* 'Jew', *Jüdin* 'Jewess', also *Fran'zose, Fran'zösin* 'Frenchman, -woman', but not in other foreign names, hence *Jugo'slawe, -'slawin* 'Yugoslav', *Russe, Russin* 'Russian', *Schotte, Schottin* 'Scotsman, -woman'; *Isra'eli* makes feminine *Isra'elin* 'Israeli'. (We observe that the adjectives follow suit as far as umlaut is concerned: *schwäbisch* 'Swabian', *jugo'slawisch* 'Yugoslavian', *fran'zösich* 'French', *schottisch* 'Scottish', *jüdisch* 'Jewish', *russisch* 'Russian'.)

In certain cases an agent noun exists in the feminine only: *Frauenrechtlerin* 'suffragette', *Kindergärtnerin* 'kindergarten teacher', *Ser'viererin* 'waitress'—a fairly recent word competing with *Kellnerin* above, *Wöchnerin* 'maternity case'. In other examples the feminine is the form usually met with—as *Platzanweiserin* 'usherette', *Stenoty'pistin* 'short-hand typist', *Wäscherin* 'washerwoman'.

In the colloquial of the more southern parts the suffix may be added to the woman's surname: *die Müllerin* 'Mrs Miller'; in north-western districts a suffix *-sche* is used instead: *die Müllersche.*

DIMINUTIVES

Diminutive nouns play an important part in the language, written as well as spoken, and call for our close attention, the more so since English has very little that is comparable.

Formation

Diminutives are chiefly formed with the neuter suffixes *-chen* and *-lein*; the declension on pp. 51 f. Examples: *Fensterchen, -lein* 'small window': *Fenster* 'window', *Tischchen, -lein: Tisch* 'table'; umlaut of *a, o, u* is usual: *Schätzchen, -lein: Schatz* 'treasure', *Söhnchen, -lein: Sohn* 'son', *Mütterchen, -lein: Mutter* 'mother'. Nouns in *-e* or *en* lose these endings: *Entchen, -lein: Ente* 'duck', *Gärtchen, -lein: Garten* 'garden'. A word (or stem) ending in *ch* or *g* will normally use only the *lein*-suffix: *Büchlein: Buch* 'book', *Äuglein: Auge* 'eye', but the double diminutive forms *Büchelchen, Äugelchen* may occur in informal style; *Wägelchen* is the recognized diminutive of *Wagen* 'car'. Conversely, a noun ending in *l* normally takes only the *-chen* suffix, as *Spielchen: Spiel* 'game'.

In a few examples *-chen* is added, more or less ad hoc, without causing the expected umlaut: *Mamachen* 'mummy', *Tantchen* 'auntie', *Frauchen* 'wifey, dog's mistress', similarly the name *Paulchen* from *Paul*, comparable to various familiar formations current especially in the north, e.g. *Dummchen!* 'you little silly!', *Geduldchen!* 'be (a little) patient!', *sachtchen* 'quietly', also *guten Tagchen* 'good morning, etc.', *gute Nachtchen* 'good night'.

In the unaffected colloquial of the south, the place of *-chen* is commonly taken by regional variants such as *-el* (*-l*), *-le, -li*, also *-erl*, all neuter. One or two have been adopted in the standard language, notably *Mädel* 'girl, lass' beside *Mädchen*. These suffixes may appear in personal names, e.g. *Hänsel, Gretel*, parallel to *Hänschen, Gretchen*; with names, however, the natural gender usually asserts itself, p. 310. In Upper German a familiar *-i* diminutive often occurs, the gender of the source word being retained: *der Bub* 'the lad', *der Bubi* 'the laddie', whence *Bubikopf* 'bobbed hair'—an expression remembered by some; also in pet names: *Wolfi* 'Wolfgang', *Anni* 'Anna'.

Stylistic differences

If we ignore a handful of isolated examples (p. 128), the two main diminutive suffixes are seen to be stylistically quite distinct: *-chen* alone is the living and productive form, both in speech and writing, and hence very much commoner than *-lein*, which belongs to literary, especially poetic language; its attributes in this milieu may be so predominantly stylistic that nothing tangible remains of any diminutive function: (folk-song) *wenn ich ein Vöglein wär' / und auch zwei Flüglein hätt', / flög' ich zu dir* 'were I a bird and had I two wings, I'd fly to thee'. This form is often found in fairy tales: *das häßliche junge Entlein* 'the ugly duckling', though the other suffix is no less familiar: *Dornröschen* 'Sleeping Beauty'.

Semantics and uses

Diminutives occur in their literal meanings in various clichés: *er hat kein Fünkchen Verstand* 'he hasn't a (even a tiny) spark of intelligence', *der Himmel war klar ohne ein Wölkchen* 'the sky was clear without a (even a tiny) cloud'. They can, on occasion, be used effectively side by side with the basic word: *die Inseln und Inselchen der Südsee* 'the isles and islets of the South Seas', *die Leute stehen in Gruppen und Grüppchen herum* 'people are standing around in groups, large and small'.

A word basically indicating smallness easily acquires an affective nuance which may become dominant: *ein hübsches Sümmchen* 'a tidy little sum', and in fact most diminutives are used in this way. Thus the concept 'small house' will normally be expressed as *kleines Haus*, since *Häuschen* has unmistakable overtones, not to mention that it is also a euphemism for 'lavatory'. This last apart, *Häuschen* has a wide range of less concrete application expressing anything from pride and pleasure to sorrow or contempt, according to context. In other words, by the use of the diminutive a touch of emotion is added to the sentiments already inherently present in the subject-matter: *stolz zeigte sie uns ihr neues Häuschen* 'proudly she showed us her new house', *in diesem armseligen Häuschen sollte er sein Leben beschließen* 'in this miserably poor house he was to end his days', the actual size of the house being of no essential account in either case. This function is strikingly evident in an example which by its very nature cannot express diminution proper: *Wetter* makes *Wetterchen* in reference to exceptional conditions, hence one says: *ein Wetterchen ist das!* 'what (glorious, or wretched) weather it is!'

In some examples a fixed nuance attaches to the diminutive form: *Dämchen* is 'lady in inverted commas', *Freundchen* 'friend' strongly ironic, *Jüngelchen* means something like 'callow youth'. But in the majority of such cases the nuance is appreciative: *Häschen* 'nice (little) rabbit', *Mäuschen* 'nice (little) mouse', both also 'pet, darling' when speaking to small children: *Hündchen* 'doggy' is often preferred where we simply say 'dog' since the basic term *Hund* tends to have a somewhat pejorative overtone, pp. 134 f.

The diminutive has frequently achieved a greater or lesser degree of lexical independence: *Brot* 'bread', *Brötchen* 'roll'—one can of course speak of *große Brötchen* 'large rolls'—*Decke* 'blanket', *Deckchen* 'doily', *Kopf* 'head', *Köpfchen* 'brains', *Rippe* 'rib', *Rippchen* 'cutlet', *Stern* 'star', *Sternchen* 'asterisk', *Teil* 'part', *Teilchen* 'particle'—some retaining a literal sense too, as commonly *Köpfchen*, *Sternchen*. Contrast coarse *Maul* '(human) mouth' with endearing *Mäulchen*. Compare *Luft* 'air, (poetic) breeze' with *Lüftchen*, the ordinary term for 'gentle breeze'. Semantic change can actually break the connection with the source word: *Bauer* 'farmer', *Baüerchen* 'burp', *Frucht* 'fruit', *Früchtchen* 'young rascal', *Leib* 'body', *Leibchen* 'bodice'. Lexical independence is further illustrated by items now existing solely in the diminutive form, as *Mädchen* 'girl' reduced from obsolete *Mägdchen* (*Magd* 'maid'), *Ohrläppchen* 'earlobe', *Radieschen* 'radish', *Veilchen* 'violet', and the colloquial *Kittchen* 'gaol'. The diminutive is sometimes the only possible form in idiomatic expressions: *sie sind ganz aus dem Häuschen* 'they're over the moon', *alles geht wie am Schnürchen* 'everything's going like clockwork', *jetzt bist du wirklich ins Fettnäpfchen getreten* 'now you've really put your foot in it', (slangy) *bei dir ist wohl ein Rädchen locker?* 'are you all right in your head?', further *ins Röhrchen blasen* 'to take the breathalyser test'.

Very occasionally the diminutive functions as a singulative: *Staub* 'dust', *Stäubchen* 'speck of dust', locally *Gräschen* 'blade of grass', otherwise *Grashalm*. Other examples on p. 310.

As indicated above, the *lein*-suffix is largely confined to certain literary genres, only a few examples occurring in the everyday language. They are mainly independent lexical items which have lost any diminutive sense: *Fräulein* 'miss', then *Männlein*, *Weiblein* 'man, woman', often with a suggestive nuance absent from *Männchen*, *Weibchen*, which also do duty as standard terms for male and female: *Walfischmännchen* 'bull whale'. Some prefer *Küchlein* 'chicken' to (northern) *Kücken*, *Küken*. Another isolated word is *Scherflein* (*der Witwe*) '(widow's) mite', often in the cliché *ich habe mein Scherflein beigetragen* 'I've made my little contribution'. The form *Büchlein* '(small) book' is common in written style.

Although the diminutive is such a productive form among concrete nouns, not all such words can be so used. The term *Flagge* 'flag, esp. ensign', cannot form a diminutive, but basically synonymous *Fahne* regularly makes *Fähnchen* 'small flag, esp. paper flag, pennant'. Many nouns ending in -*en* are without a diminutive form in the standard language, as *Besen* 'broom', *Becken* 'wash-basin', *Boden* 'floor, loft', but diminutives may occur in local use, e.g. Central *Beselchen*, Upper German *Beserl*. The insect names *Biene* 'bee' and *Käfer* 'beetle'—both colloquially also 'nice young lady'—form hypocoristic *Bienchen*, *Käferchen*, but less pleasantly sounding *Fliege* 'fly', *Spinne* 'spider', *Wanze* 'bug' cannot in the nature of the case follow suit.

11. The Problem of Meaning

As one progresses in the study of a foreign tongue, one becomes aware that a given word in one language does not necessarily have its exact opposite number in the other. Sometimes the differences are rather obvious, but others are less evident and can easily be overlooked. The aim here is to illustrate in some sort the nature and scope of the problem of meaning.

To start with the more obvious: English distinguishes between 'watch' and 'clock', but German makes do with *Uhr* for both concepts; vice versa, English knows only 'rope' where German uses *Seil* as the generic term but nevertheless needs *Tau* when particularly thick rope is concerned, hence *Tauziehen* 'tug of war'. Similarly 'castle' is *Burg* in reference to a fortified medieval building, now often in ruins, but *Schloß* for a more recent, palatial building: *Burg Harlech*, *Schloß Windsor*. Other cases can be more involved.

English requires only 'wall' where German has *Wand* and *Mauer*; indeed, a third term *Wall* is often needed. The first, the broadest and most general term, is used for walls primarily envisaged as enclosing a space, in particular one lived in: *das Haus hat vier Wände* 'the house has four walls', hence *die Hauswand gegenüber* 'the wall of the house opposite', *Innen- und Außenwände* 'inside and outside walls', *Trennungswand* 'dividing wall (in a house, etc.)', also *Wandmalerei* 'wall-painting', *Wandzeitung* 'wall-newspaper'. It is used for any wall not made of brick or stone, e.g. *Holzwand* 'wooden wall'. It further denotes a natural wall, hence *Felswand* 'wall of rock', *die Eiger-Nordwand* 'the north face of the Eiger'. A wall is termed *Mauer* when it is built of brick or stone, generally bonded by mortar; using the word draws attention to these building materials, hence always *Ziegel-, Steinmauer* 'wall of brick, stone'. While *Seitenwand* 'side-wall' is the overall term, *Seitenmauer* envisages the brick or stone in it. The different concepts may appear side by side: *die Klagemauer, Westwand des einstigen Tempels* 'the Wailing Wall, west wall of the former temple', *die Rückwand der Vorhalle ist noch ein Teil der alten Kirchenmauer* 'the rear wall of the porch is a relic of the old church wall'. In certain terms only *-mauer* is possible, e.g. *Brandmauer* 'fire(proof) wall'; it is often free-standing: *Gartenmauer* 'garden wall', *Stadtmauer* 'city wall', *die Chinesische Mauer* 'the Great Wall of China'. Lastly, the term *Wall* denotes a wall built of stone, generally without bonding; *Steinwälle* is the correct way of naming those stone walls which in England often divide fields, but are little known in Germany. More typically, *Wall* denotes a large defensive wall, as *Hadrianswall*. In East German officialese the Berlin Wall—*diese Trennungsmauer quer durch Berlin* 'this dividing wall right across B.'—is called *der Antifaschistische Schutzwall* 'the Antifascist Rampart', otherwise universally known as *die (Berliner) Mauer*.

In figurative use the basic distinctions between *Wand* and *Mauer* are often clearly visible: *die Wände haben Ohren* 'the walls have ears', *es ist, um an den Wänden hochzugehen* 'it's enough to drive you up the wall', *der Nebel war wie eine Wand vor uns* 'the fog was like a wall in front of us', but *es war, wie wenn man gegen eine Mauer anrennen würde* 'it was like running up against a brick wall'; notice *Mauer des Schweigens* 'wall of silence', *Schallmauer* 'sound barrier', *Mauerblümchen* 'wall-flower'.

A number of nouns in the one language have multiple meanings not paralleled in the other. Consider *Bahn*. The most usual meaning will be 'railway' (in full *Eisenbahn*), followed perhaps by 'tramway' (*Straßenbahn*); the word may also be used to mean 'train' or 'tram': *Sie können mit jeder Bahn fahren* 'you can take any train (tram)'. But other senses are commonplace, too, as 'traffic lane' (*Fahrbahn*), 'track' (*Rennbahn*), 'orbit' (*Umlaufbahn*), 'length (of material, wallpaper)' (*Stoff-, Tapetenbahn*)—it cannot, however, substitute for *Autobahn* 'motorway'. Heard in isolation, the word *Zug* first calls to mind a train (*Eisenbahnzug*). But it also expresses such concepts as 'expedition, campaign, procession'; there are further meanings like 'traction, pull, move (as at chess)'. It often figures in compounds, among them *Ab-, Ein-, Gegenzug* 'departure, arrival, countermove or train coming in the opposite direction', also *Vorzug* 'merit' whence *vor'züglich* 'meritorious, excellent'. Words with so many meanings lend themselves to punning: (advertising slogan of the *Deutsche Bundesbahn* 'German Federal Railway') *die Seniorenkarte* ('Senior Citizen's Ticket')—*ein vorzüglicher Zug der Bahn*.

The principle just illustrated may be seen again in other parts of speech. We select an adjective, the ubiquitous *schön*, mostly thought of as meaning 'beautiful', which indeed often applies: *eine schöne Frau* 'a beautiful woman'; on the other hand *ein schöner Mann* is idiomatically 'a handsome man'. In many contexts this basic meaning is weakened or otherwise modified: *schönes Wetter* 'fine weather'—to express 'beautiful weather' something like *herrliches Wetter* is needed—*in schönster Ordnung* has the same sense as *in bester Ordnung* 'in apple-pie order', *schöne Literatur* translates 'belles-lettres'. Next, *schön* may correspond to 'nice': *das war schön* (= *nett*) *von ihr* 'it was nice of her', or to 'kind': *schöne Grüße* 'kind regards', and compare adverbial *danke schön* 'thank you very much' with older English 'thank you kindly'. It enters into fixed expressions, as *das ist alles schön und gut* 'that's all very well'; other idioms include *sich schön machen* 'make oneself look smart or attractive', *jemandem schön tun* 'play up to someone'. Used adverbially, the word may have an emphatic function, especially in colloquial style: *ich habe ganz schön geschwitzt* 'I didn't half sweat'.

The languages may, at first sight, appear to have matching words for the same objects, but which closer inspection shows to be not quite the case. A tree has 'branches' and 'twigs', *Äste* and *Zweige*, but the concepts covered are not necessarily the same. *Äste* denotes the main branches growing out of the trunk, *Zweige* not only the twigs, but the branches forking off from the *Äste* as well; if the former require to be distinguished, then *kleine Zweige* will be needed. Thinner *Äste* may be termed *Ästchen*. But German has no word stylistically comparable to 'bough'.

Our 'street' and 'road' denote rather different concepts, but for ordinary purposes German is adequately served by *Straße*; similarly *Hauptstraße* means indifferently 'main street' or 'main road'. Now one may come across a term *Landstraße* which the context will show to apply to a road between two or more places. The English learner may well hit on 'country road' as his native equivalent and, quite unconsciously, associate with the German term the connotations proper to the English. *Landstraße* will thus be understood, or rather misunderstood, as a relatively quiet, picturesque road. But for the native speaker a *Landstraße* is more like a *Hauptstraße*, busy and bustling, and neutral as to scenery. A German travelling along an English country road would most likely refer to it simply as *Straße*. The nuances are untranslatable.

One may next notice that German has in *Gasse* a second word for a street. This term, however, is more typically restricted to small, narrow streets, as may be observed from street names. It often occurs as the diminutive *Gäßchen*; it may have a quaint, old-fashioned flavour. But not everywhere, for regional differences appear: in Vienna *Gasse* is the usual word for 'street', *Straße* being used for the main thoroughfares, in fact rather like our 'road'. A street urchin is then a *Gassenbub* as well as a *Straßenjunge*.

A street in a town is often named *Weg*, comparable to our 'Way'. But the German word has a wider range in that it is often needed where English has 'path', as *Gartenweg* 'garden path', further *Fußweg* 'footpath', *Radweg* 'cycle path'. German *Pfad* corresponds more to 'trail, track', cf. the idiomatic expression *Ziegenpfad* lit. 'goat path' used of a track on a hill-side, one that is narrow and troublesome to negotiate. Consequently *Fußpfad* suggests a rough path over wild country, unlike *Fußweg* just mentioned, which refers to a path for pedestrians. German has a further approximate synonym in *Steig* 'path, way', often seen in street names and figuring in such terms as *Bahnsteig* '(railway) platform', *Bürger-* or *Gehsteig*, also *Gehweg* (p. 139) 'pavement'.

In conclusion the observation that German has no real equivalent of 'lane'—the unusual term *Heckenweg* lit. 'hedge way', given in some dictionaries, sounds more like a definition than a translation. The best one can do idiomatically is to call it *Weg*. Needless to add, phrases like 'leafy lane, lovers' lane' have no genuine correspondences in German, the nuances simply cannot be recaptured in translation.

Turning aside from the lanes to the fields, and looking closely, one may become aware of differences perhaps not fully appreciated before. If asked the German for 'field', our answer will naturally be *Feld*—and vice versa. Suppose we next enquire of native speakers what a field/*Feld* looks like, the English informant will almost surely start to describe a field of grass, as this is the concept which generally springs first to mind. The German, for his part, will without fail speak of a field growing corn or root crops, because for him *Feld* is first and foremost synonymous with *Acker*, the ploughed field; the grass field he calls *Wiese*. Dictionaries seem to prefer the equation *Wiese* = 'meadow', but in fact *Wiese* has a much wider sense and can designate any grass-covered space of reasonable size, including a small lawn. Notice the common combination *Feld- und Wiesenblumen*, the former being cornflowers, poppies, and so forth, the latter daisies, cowslips, and the like, an expression corresponding to our 'wild flowers' and contrasting with *Gartenblumen* 'garden flowers'. It now goes without saying that 'green fields' will normally be given as *grüne Wiesen*. One may have cause to say, e.g. *die Felder sind noch grün* 'the fields are still green', implying that the crop is not yet ripe, but *grüne Felder* is somewhat unusual, there being little call for it since *grün* is not a typical attribute of *Feld*.

We take two more examples involving etymologically cognate words. The first concerns the pair *Sturm* 'storm', an identification which is nevertheless somewhat misleading since the primary meaning of *Sturm* today is *Sturmwind* 'hard wind'—Shakespeare's 'The Tempest' is called *Der Sturm*—and cf. *es stürmt* 'it's blowing a gale'. The equation *Sturm* = 'storm' is only valid in the figurative senses and in some compounds: *Sturm im Wasserglas* 'storm in a teacup', *Schneesturm* 'snow storm', especially of the violent sort with high wind such as occurs in the mountains, in milder forms *Schneegestöber* or *Schneetreiben*. The second example is seen in *Morgen* 'morning'. A German au pair girl coming to this country was pleased to hear that all that would be required of her was 'a morning's work', only to be disappointed to find that she was occupied until lunch. She had equated 'morning' with *Morgen*—who wouldn't? The trouble is that *Morgen*, when used to mark a definite period of time, ends with the 'second breakfast' (*zweites Frühstück*) between ten and eleven. What was actually asked of her was *eine Vormittagsbeschäftigung*.

Unsuspected differences can be embarrassing in other ways. Take *Verdauung* 'digestion'. This correspondence is, in fact, only valid in the physiologist's sense, i.e. as a process involving the whole alimentary tract. In everyday use *Verdauung* is envisaged as taking place in the intestines, hence the doctor enquires *haben Sie heute schon Verdauung gehabt?* 'have your bowels been opened today?' If we must refer to our digestion in German company, then let us speak of our *Magen* 'stomach', and by the way call 'indigestion' *Magenverstimmung*, or if we mean 'heartburn' *Sodbrennen*. More or less in this connection, it is curious that we need three words 'abdomen, belly, tummy' belonging to such different registers, whereas the German synonym *Bauch* is stylistically neutral and can be freely employed.

Differences can depend on context. A simple example: *Hände hoch!* 'hands up!' may be useful on the battlefield, but would be hilarious in the classroom, where the call is *meldet euch!* Consider the following: the *Hausfrau* and the housewife say respectively *ich muß das Zimmer lüften* 'I'll have to air the room', whereupon they open the windows. They could also say *ich muß die Kleider lüften* 'I'll have to air the clothes', but what they do next is not the same—the *Hausfrau* hangs them out on a line or lays them on the grass to freshen in the breeze or sun, the practice of airing clothes in an airing-cupboard being apparently an Anglo-Saxon peculiarity. Properly speaking, *Kleider lüften* should be paraphrased, say 'put clothes out to sweeten in the air', our 'air clothes' being rendered by, say, *die Kleider fertig trocknen*.

The most commonly used words may be potential pitfalls. Such a case is *Mädchen* 'girl'. The English word can be familiarly applied to a woman of any age, but the most distinguishing fact about a *Mädchen* is that she is n o t married, hence *Mädchenname* 'maiden name'. The term may be freely used of unmarried women up to about thirty, after which one normally speaks of *ein älteres Mädchen*, the equivalent of 'spinster'. Girls of seventeen or eighteen are generally called *junge Mädchen* lit. 'young girls'. In English 'young girl' denotes rather a child of, say, between eight and fourteen, for which German has no characteristic epithet; a girl in this age group is simply *Mädchen*.

The nature of the feeling behind words poses a special problem. *Hund* and 'dog' denote the same creature, but the former has a built-in pejorative tone, hence in figurative use, e.g. *der ist ein Hund* 'he's a rotter', hence also a certain tendency in conversation to substitute a non-committal or pleasant diminutive: *Hündchen*, *Hundl*, *Hundi*. And what of *Hündin* 'bitch'? The English word is loaded enough, but the German is colourless, merely drawing attention to the anatomy, a bit like 'she dog'. Rats are pretty repulsive wherever found, but the word *Ratte* is not so unlovely as 'rat', witness *Landratte* 'landlubber', *Leseratte* 'bookworm'. A film 'The Soho Rat' was shown in Germany under the title *Die Ratte von Soho*, but this of itself can have meant little to the audiences who would not instinctively see in *Ratte* the villain of the piece; a paraphrase *der Gauner von Soho* would have been nearer the mark. Something of the same is seen in the recently introduced expression *die Falken und die Tauben* after the English 'the hawks and the doves'. The German is a formally correct translation, yet it falsifies an essential nuance, for *Falken* calls to mind the noblest of birds; there is nothing hawkish about them. Perhaps a less accurate translation *Habichte* 'goshawks' would have made it possible to salvage something of the rapacity implicit in the English word 'hawk'.

12. Regional Diversity

THERE has often been occasion elsewhere in this book to refer to regional as opposed to more general use. Such differences are particularly noticeable in the vocabulary, a very large number of words having regional rather than general validity. It should be emphasized that regional use is not to be taken as a synonym for dialect. The words concerned are acceptable in standard forms of the language and can appear in print. Dialect is quite a different proposition, as may now be seen.

Dialect and standard

In England pure dialect is a thing of the past, having finally died out in the early years of the present century; only in the forms of Lowland Scots can one hear anything approaching genuine dialect today. In the German-speaking world, however, about one person in five still uses broad dialect in the home and with neighbours and workmates, the standard being employed only on formal occasions or when dealing with those ignorant of the local dialect. In Germany itself, such speakers are to be found mainly in country districts and in some smaller towns, notably in the north where the dialects, collectively known as *Plattdeutsch*, i.e. Low German, are in many respects closer to Dutch than to German, and then in Swabia and Bavaria in the far south. Dialects related to the Swabian extend throughout Switzerland, where dialect-speaking is universal, while dialects of the Bavarian type are prevalent in Austria. A Franconian dialect is the ubiquitous spoken medium in Luxemburg. These various dialects differ from standard German so much that they are not immediately comprehensible to outsiders. To take an extreme case, we imagine that a North German could require up to a couple of months' residence in Bern in order to be able to follow a conversation between two local Swiss.

Such diversity, in former times even more marked than today, has not failed to make an impress on the standard language, which has been obliged to accept a significant number of regional synonyms as optional alternatives. The standard written language (*Hochsprache*, *Hochdeutsch*) endeavours to limit and reduce the number of such synonyms, but its spoken counterpart (*Umgangssprache*) freely admits regionalism from any quarter, many of which regularly find their way into print, especially of course in publications for local readers. These matters may now claim our attention.

Regional synonyms

Regional synonyms are not entirely unknown in English. In the north, throstle is commonly heard instead of thrush, children are endearingly called bairns. In the Midlands a broomstick is called a stale and is so marked in shops. In certain districts they 'wipe' the dishes after washing up, which sounds odd to those who 'dry' them. Such things are, however, rather exceptional. But not so in German, where a multitude of nouns and, to a lesser extent, of other parts of speech vary from place to place. One may think in terms of three to four thousand items of vocabulary, a novel prospect for anyone conditioned by such a highly standardized language as English.

How does the native speaker cope with such diversity? He will normally employ the expression which comes naturally to him, but through the media, by meeting people from other parts of the country, and from literature, he will also be familiar with the more commonly occurring alternatives. The rest must be guesswork. When persons from different districts meet, they automatically feel for common ground, each avoiding expressions assumed to be unfamiliar to the other. A few words of explanation can usually set to rights an occasional lapse.

The many regionalisms are naturally part of the local scenery, and may be called upon. The magazine *Spiegel* printed the opening of an interview with the Austrian chancellor Kreisky as follows: (Spiegel) *Herr Kanzler, wie sieht die Lage aus?* (Kreisky) *Schiach schaut's aus.* Every reader of course understood the question 'Chancellor, how are things looking?' and in the reply most readers would identify *schaut* as the southern (and Austrian) colloquial equivalent of *sieht*. But we suspect that relatively few had come across the dialect word *schiach* before. No matter! A broad Austrian idiom strikes an appropriate opening note, and from the Chancellor's subsequent remarks anyone could guess that the word in question must mean 'awful'.

The following illustrations are intended to give some further indication of the current situation and the problems associated with it.

Examples with nouns

It is at once noticeable that culinary terms may vary greatly; in fact cookery books often supply a glossary. The local distribution of the words may be complex. Take the expressions used for bread roll. In the northern half of the country *das Brötchen* is the most widespread term. But from Hamburg to the Danish frontier *die Semmel* is in use as well, and the same applies to an area corresponding to the southern half of the GDR. In Berlin and environs, however, the local word is *die Schrippe*. South of the Main, *Brötchen* virtually disappears. The common use of *Semmel* is the GDR continues southwards, becoming the most usual term in Bavaria and exclusive in Austria. In the western parts of South Germany *der Weck* or *Wecken* predominates, often in the diminutive form *das Weckele*, giving *das Weggli* in Switzerland. To these add two minor names: *das Rundstück* as a third term occurring in the area from Hamburg to the Danish frontier, and *das Kipfel* used beside *Semmel* in a small area south of Würzburg. Of these terms, *Brötchen* and *Semmel* must be regarded as *hochdeutsch* (in the above sense), the remainder being acceptable regionalisms. It may be noted that *Kipfel* is also found in Austria, especially in the variant form *Kipferl*, but now the roll in question is crescent-shaped; it has the same specialized sense in its Swiss form *Gipfel*. In Germany this variety is generally called *das Hörnchen*, in Bavaria colloquially *das Hörndl*. In Austria *das Weckerl* (cf. *Weck* etc. above) denotes a roll so shaped that it can be easily broken in two.

Vegetables often go under local names. Thus, beside the standard name *die Kartoffel* 'potato', in use over the greater part of Germany, there are many other names of which the following are important regionally: widespread in the north *die Tüffel*, in Bavaria and Austria almost universally *der Erdapfel*, in Switzerland *Herdapfel*, and lastly in Swabia *die Grumbeere* usually in the dialect form *Grumper*, in origin *Grundbirne* lit. 'ground pear'. But there are cases where, as yet, there simply is no overall standard. In an area centered on Berlin the carrot is called *die Mohrrübe*, but in Mecklenburg and the rest of the north the imprecise term *die Wurzel* lit. 'root' is ubiquitous, often in the Low German form *Wortel*. Throughout the centre the usual word is *die Möhre*, further south *die gelbe Rübe*, in Switzerland the dialect diminutive form *das Rüebli*. Finally, *die Karotte* is widespread in Austria; it also appears sporadically in Germany. All these words are found in print.

The names of utensils for culinary purposes are likewise often quite diverse. The pot for boiling, etc. is most commonly called *der Topf*, but in the north *der Pott* may be the more familiar word, in Upper German *der Hafen*, in some parts of Bavaria *der Weitling*. We can mention here that the spout of a kettle, coffee pot, etc. can be formally termed *der Ausguß*. This is a thoroughly bookish word, having moreover several other meanings, such as outlet, sink, drain, gutter, but which nevertheless has its justification in the written standard since in the ordinarily spoken language there is no one term with a claim to leading status, only a throng of regionalisms, some of them making a very outlandish impression on outsiders. The most widespread, relatively speaking, appear to be *der Schnabel* found in the far south, including Austria and Switzerland, and *die Tülle* common in the north; both are frequently seen in print. More in the centre the most typical term is *die Schauze* lit. 'snout'; it extends into the north-west, where it is current in the Low German form *Schnute*. In Thuringia they say *die Schneppe*, to the west of that province *die Schnaube*, on the Middle Rhine and in the Mosel valley *die Zotte* or *Zutte*. All areas of the everyday vocabulary are affected. In not a few cases one notices a north–south contrast. For example, northern *der Bordstein* '(pavement) kerb', southern *Randstein*, both with standard status. And the pavement itself: northern *der Bürgersteig*, southern *der Gehsteig* or *der Gehweg* or *das Trottoir*, all equally acceptable in standard writing. In the north a funeral is called either *die Beerdigung* or *das Begräbnis*, but in the south often *die Leiche*. Whereas in this case the two northern words are both acceptable in standard use, the southern equivalent remains purely regional, doubtless since the word in question already exists in the standard language with the meaning 'corpse'. Compare further *das Pferd* 'horse' with typically southern colloquial *der Gaul* or *das Roß*; in the standard language, however, *Gaul* and *Roß* are only used in the specialized senses of nag and steed respectively. The terms *das Bein* and *der Fuß* are distinguished in the north and in standard language as leg and foot, but in the south *Fuß* can embrace both meanings. In familiar southern use *die Fliege* 'fly' is often replaced colloquially by *die Mücke* (or dialect *Mucke*), elsewhere meaning midge, for which the south mostly uses *die Schnake*, in Austria *die Gelse*—to be perfectly explicit, one can use the regionally neutral *Stechmücke*.

Quite often the north and centre go together against the far south: *die Miete* 'rent', *die Mütze* 'cap', *das Streichholz* 'match', southern *der Zins*, *die Kappe*, *das Zündholz*, all with standard status. Similarly *der Schlips* 'tie', southern *die Krawatte*, but in this case the latter is felt to be stylistically superior, hence it is the usual term in the trade. Conversely, the south and centre may join forces against the north, a notable example being *die See* 'sea', proper to the North German coast, elsewhere *das Meer*, cf. *Nordsee* 'North Sea', *Ostsee* 'Baltic', but *Mittelmeer* 'Mediterranean'.

Exceptional distribution is seen in compounds of the type *die Kopf-*, *Zahnschmerzen* (pl.) and *das Kopf-*, *Zahnweh* 'headache, toothache'. The latter occur both in the north and in the south, the former driving a broad wedge between them in the centre. The type *-schmerzen* is preferred in medical articles, in advertisements for pain-killers and the like, but both types are standard. As a simplex *Weh*, having the additional sense of grief, is a somewhat emotive word proper to high style. Under its influence, speakers who naturally say, e.g. *Kopfschmerzen*, feel *Kopfweh* to be a rather elegant term.

Even a brand-new article can occasionally acquire different regional names, as blue jeans. Whereas *die Blue Jeans* (*Bluejeans*) is commonly used in Germany and Switzerland, also abbreviated *Jeans*, in Austria these have been modified to *die Blue Jean* (*Bluejean*) or simply *Jean*, after the analogy of *Hose* beside pl. *Hosen* (p. 54). Side by side with the Americanism, a synonym *Nietenhose* has arisen, which is also widely used, sometimes in the form *Niethose*; in East Germany the latter is so prevalent that it could be regarded as the standard term in that part of the world.

Examples with verbs

After nouns, verbs are the most susceptible to regional variation. Let us start with *klingeln* 'ring' (doorbell, etc.), the most widely used word and general in the north. But elsewhere it has competitors, in west-central areas giving way to *schellen*, which in turn continues into the south, when it faces *läuten* to the east as the commoner term in Bavaria and also in Austria. All three verbs are acceptable in standard language. Beside the formal and literary word *saugen* 'suck' one finds numerous popular expressions, the chief of which is *lutschen*, also in standard use. Among regional synonyms are: in central areas *nutschen*, also *nuckeln* or *nuppeln*, more to the south commonly *schnullen*, in Bavaria and Austria *zuzeln*. Standard *sich prügeln* 'have a fight' is commonly replaced in familiar style in the north by *sich keilen* or *sich kloppen*, in Bavaria and Austria by *sich raufen*. The overall standard word *sehen* 'see, look' is, in this second sense, very widely replaced in colloquial use by *gucken* (when it is pronounced *kucken* due to contamination from the Low German synonym *kieken*); in Swiss German *lugen* is the popular term, in Bavarian–Austrian *schauen*. It may be noted that in strictly standard language the simplex *schauen* is entirely synonymous with *sehen*, differing only in that it is then a purely literary word with high stylistic value: *der Reisende schaute die Wunder Indiens* 'the traveller beheld the wonders of India'.

There are many terms for chatting or gossiping, as widespread *quatschen* and *schwatzen* or *schwätzen*; more in the south is *tratschen*. Among northern expressions are: in the eastern part *quasseln*, to the west *klönen* and *schnacken*, in the far north-west *praten*. The north–south contrast, so often seen with nouns, reappears among the verbs, as northern *lecken* 'lick', *pflügen* 'plough', *pflücken* 'pick', southern *schlecken*, *ackern*, *brechen*. The former are the usual standard words, but the southern regionalisms are also admissible in good style, indeed *brechen* is then poetic. Characteristically Bavarian–Austrian is the use, in compounds, of *sperren* instead of *schließen*, e.g. *ab-* or *zusperren* 'lock (up)', *aufsperren* 'unlock', otherwise *abschließen*, etc. Instead of the main word *anzünden* 'light, set fire to', the term *anstecken* is preferred in the north and centre; it often appears in print. The standard verb *ziehen* 'pull' may be replaced in the north by *trecken*, hence regionally *der Trecker* for the more general term *der Traktor*.

Adjectives and other parts of speech

Among adjectives one may consider the synonyms of the overall standard term *schnell* 'fast, quick': in northern use *rasch* or colloquially *fix* are often preferred, in the south *geschwind*, which sounds rather elegant to speakers from other parts—another synonym *hurtig* is essentially a literary word. The Low German dialect form *oll* corresponding to standard *alt* 'old' has become well known outside its home area, but only in substandard use: *mein Oller* 'my old man', *meine Olle* 'my missus'. In familiar style Low German *lütt* 'little' often replaces *klein* locally, but such use remains purely regional.

We next note the adverbial *dieses Jahr* 'this year' which in the far south, including Austria and Switzerland, is ordinarily replaced by *heuer*, a regionalism permissible in standard language; the same applies to the derivate adjective *heurig*, otherwise *diesjährig*. The interrogative *nicht wahr?* is regularly replaced in the south by *gelt?* or *gell?*, e.g. *Sie kommen, nicht wahr (gelt? gell?)* 'you're coming, aren't you?', and such use may appear in print, though hardly in literary work. The particle *eben* 'just' is proper to the north and centre, the southern word is *halt*, also admissible in written use, p. 114. Stylistically rather than regionally differentiated are *nur* 'only' and the more colloquial *bloß* (p. 112), but a third synonym *man*, occurring in certain contexts, e.g. *laß das man!* 'just leave it! don't bother!', is confined to northern districts and not seen much in print. The same applies to the preposition *mang* (acc., dat.) 'among', also adverbial *mitten'mang* 'among them', common in the colloquial of the north beside standard *unter, mitten'drunter*.

SYNTAX

A note on translations

Apart from a handful of obvious exceptions, the German examples in this book are always original. Except where idiom had clearly to be matched by idiom, the English translations have been kept as literal as possible, allowing for reasonable style. In the nature of the matter, however, many German sentences are ambiguous when quoted in isolation, particularly as far as the tenses of the verb are concerned. Thus *sie hilft den Kindern* regularly means 'she helps, or is helping, or will help the children', the exact equivalent being determined by the wider context. Further, *sie half den Kindern* has precisely the same meaning as *sie hat den Kindern geholfen* so that either can equally well be translated 'she helped, or was helping, or has helped, or has been helping'. In giving one translation in such cases, the choice was unavoidably discretionary. See also 'A note on the English verb', p. 230.

German word order, being freer than English, may also pose problems, especially when a sentence is lifted out of its context. When not explicitly dealing with this subject, we have naturally endeavoured to use examples where word order in the two languages is fixed. But not always succeeding, our examples and their translations are sometimes perforce arbitrary in this respect.

13. Nouns

NOMINATIVE

THE nominative is the case of the subject: *der Apfel fällt nicht weit vom Stamm* 'the apple never falls far from the tree'. It is also the case of the predicative noun linked to the subject by the verbs *sein*, *werden*, or *bleiben*, e.g. *er ist ein guter Verlierer* 'he is a good loser', *er wurde ein gefährlicher Fanatiker* 'he became a dangerous fanatic' (see also pp. 297 f.), *er blieb zeitlebens unser treuer Freund* 'he remained our true friend all his life'. It is used in the vocative sense: *lieber Onkel!* 'dear uncle!', and in exclamations: *großer Gott!* 'good Lord!'.

A free nominative appears in postal addresses: *sie wohnen Maurerstraße 1 (eins)* 'they live at 1 Wall St'; the case is seen unequivocally in suitable instances: *sie wohnen Breiter Weg 2* 'they live at 2 Broad Way'.

Two (or more) unqualified nouns in the singular governed by a preposition remain uninflected: *ohne Glaube und Gesetz* 'without faith and law', *zwischen Patient und Arzt* 'between patient and doctor', *in Gedanke, Form und Stil* 'in thought, form, and style', also in phrases of the type *von Mensch zu Mensch* 'from one human being to another' and *Buchstabe für Buchstabe* 'letter by letter', further in idioms like *eine Seele von Mensch* 'a kind soul' alternatively *eine Seele von einem Menschen*. The uninflected form may be necessary to avoid confusion with the plural: *vor Konsonant* 'before consonant', *vor Konsonanten* only 'before consonants', in which connection cf. *Soldat spricht zu Soldat* lit. 'Soldier speaks to Soldier' (wartime radio programme). It is likewise the rule when forming part of a person's title: *der Standpunkt von Bundespräsident Weizsäcker* 'the standpoint of Federal President W.', but *ein Bericht von unserem Berliner Korrespondenten, Hans Schlüter* 'a report from our Berlin correspondent, H.S.' Book titles and the like remain unchanged: *Thomas Mann veröffentlichte 1913 seine Novelle "Der Tod in Venedig"* 'Th. M. published his short novel "Death in Venice" in 1913', but informally e.g. *haben Sie den "Tod in Venedig" gelesen?* 'have you read "Death in Venice"?'

Nouns used with proper names as titles do not, in general, decline: *Onkel Toms Hütte* 'Uncle Tom's Cabin', and compare further *Kanzler Brandts Amtsperiode = die Amtsperiode des Kanzler Brandt* 'Chancellor Brandt's period of office', thus different from *die Amtsperiode des sozialistischen Kanzlers Brandt* 'the period of office of the Socialist Chancellor, Brandt', further *die Schwester dieses (jenes) Fräulein Hausmann* 'the sister of this (that) Miss H.' Compare also: *er erhielt eine Botschaft von Genosse Stoph* 'he received a message from Comrade S.', *ich möchte Kollege Jacobi sprechen* 'I'd like to speak to "colleague" J.' Exceptionally, the term *Herr* is always declined: *haben Sie Herrn Zeidler besucht?* 'have you visited Mr Z.?'

Lastly, the nominative is used absolutely: *der Vater lag auf dem Heu, der Sohn neben ihm schlafend* 'the father was lying on the hay, the son asleep beside him'. Compare 'Accusative absolute', p. 148.

See also under 'Apposition', pp. 163 ff.

ACCUSATIVE

Accusative as case of direct object

The accusative is, above all, the case of the direct object: *sie liebt den Blumengarten* 'she loves the flower garden', *sie verloren ihren Einfluß* 'they lost their influence', (slangy) *er hat seine Leber kaputtgetrunken* 'he has ruined his liver with drink'.

The accusative occurs in certain cases after verbs compounded with prepositions governing the dative: *der Meister bildet die Lehrlinge aus* 'the master craftsman trains the apprentices', *wir fügen einen Durchschlag bei* 'we enclose a carbon copy', *haben Sie das Wort nachgeschlagen?* 'have you looked the word up?', *sie hat die Mahlzeit zubereitet* 'she has prepared the meal', also *ein Kellner löst den anderen ab* 'one waiter relieves the other'. In other examples the dative is used, see 'Dative after verbs compounded with a preposition', p. 159.

The accusative occurs with certain impersonal verbs, pp. 279 f.

Cognate accusative

As in other languages, a number of intransitive verbs may take an object which repeats the notion of the verb: *sie singt ein Lied* 'she sings a song', *kannst du Walzer tanzen?* 'can you waltz?' Examples from English and German do not necessarily correspond idiomatically: *er betet das Vaterunser* 'he is saying the Lord's Prayer', (rather elevated style) *sie klagte ihm ihr Leid* 'she told him her troubles'. By an extension of this principle, instances occur in which the object no longer stands in close relationship to the verb: *Sie laufen Gefahr, ihr Geld zu verlieren* 'you run the risk of losing your money', but again idiom in the two languages can differ: *er mußte Rede und Antwort stehen* 'he had to explain himself'.

Double accusative

A very small number of verbs may govern two accusatives: *ich will ihn Mores lehren* 'I'll give him a piece of my mind', *kannst du mich die Vokabeln abfragen?*', can you test me on the vocab. (to see if I've learnt it)?', *das kosten einen* (but often *einem*) *viel Mühe* 'that costs one a lot of effort'. As the alternative dative in the last sentence shows, the language strives to avoid repeating the same case: compare *er verband mich* 'he bandaged me', *er verband meine Wunde* 'he bandaged my wound', but in combination *er verband mir die Wunde* 'he bandaged my wound'.

In other examples the second accusative is the predicate of the first: *sie nannten mich einen Gauner* 'they called me a crook', *ich sehe es als meine Pflicht an* 'I see it as my duty'.

Elliptic accusative

Examples are commonest in conventional greetings and wishes: *guten Morgen* 'good morning', *gute Nacht* 'good night', *schönen Sonntag* say, 'have a nice Sunday'. Taking leave of an acquaintance who will be going home it may be appropriate to add *schönen Gruß zu Haus* which amounts to 'give my regards to those at home'. A holidaymaker sends *einen l. (lieben) Gruß aus den Ferien* lit. 'an affectionate greeting from the holidays'. And once a year the customary *einen guten Rutsch (ins Neue Jahr)* something like 'a good start (to the New Year)'. Similarly *besten Dank* 'thanks very much', also *keinen Augenblick länger* 'not a moment longer', *nicht einen Schritt weiter* 'not one step further'. These accusatives are objects of verbs unexpressed, as *ich wünsche (Ihnen) einen guten Morgen, ich sage (Ihnen) besten Dank*.

Adverbial accusative

The accusative forms adverbial expressions of place, time, and quantity. The first of these concerns movement along a path: *er geht seinen eigenen Weg* 'he goes his own way', *die Sterne ziehen lautlos ihre Bahn* 'the stars move silently in their courses'. The accusative is here often accompanied by an adverb of direction: *wir fuhren den Fluß hinauf (hinunter)* 'we travelled up (down) the river', *der Dampfer segelte die Küste entlang* 'the ship sailed along the coast'—but notice *segelte an der Küste entlang* 'hugged the coast'.

In the second use, the accusative regularly expresses duration of time: *er hielt einen Augenblick inne* 'he paused for a moment', *die Eule schläft den ganzen Tag* 'the owl sleeps all day'; the idea of duration may be reinforced by an adverb: *den ganzen Tag über* or *hindurch* 'the whole day through'. The accusative also expresses a period or point in time: *ich habe vorige Woche viel gearbeitet* 'I worked a lot last week', *er kommt den 13. (dreizehnten) März* 'he's coming on the 13th of March', but prepositional phrases are used as well: *in der vorigen Woche, am 13. März.*

Thirdly, the accusative of quantity: *es mißt einen Meter* 'it measures one metre', *es wiegt einen Zentner* 'it weighs one hundredweight', *das Thermometer ist einen Grad gestiegen* 'the thermometer has gone up one degree', alternatively *um einen Grad* 'by one degree'. Perhaps we may accommodate here colloquialisms like *das geht dich einen Schmarren* ('rubbish') *an*, a crude equivalent of *das geht dich nichts an* 'that's none of your business', more crudely *es geht dich einen Dreck* ('filth') *an* 'that's no bloody business of yours'.

Accusative with adjectives

An offshoot of the adverbial accusative is seen in expressions of the type *einen Monat alt* 'one month old', *einen Meter lang* 'one metre long', *einen Katzensprung entfernt* 'a short distance away' (lit. 'cat's jump'), *mein Bruder war einen Kopf größer als ich* 'my brother was a head taller than me', alternatively *um einen Kopf* 'by a head'.

The accusative is likewise found with such frequently used adjectives as *gewohnt, los, müde, satt, wert*, e.g. *er war schwere Arbeit gewohnt* 'he was used to hard work', *den Schnupfen wird sie gar nicht los* 'she just can't get rid of her cold', *ich bin es müde* 'I'm tired of it', *wir haben diesen Kerl satt* 'we're fed up with this fellow', *nicht das Papier wert, auf dem es geschrieben ist* 'not worth the paper it's written on'. These adjectives were formerly construed with the genitive, relics of which remain in compounds like *lebensmüde* 'tired of life, (humorous) ready for suicide' and in certain idioms, e.g. *es ist nicht der Mühe wert* 'it's not worth the effort'. Compare *du bist mir eine Antwort schuldig* 'you owe me an answer' with *er ist des Verbrechens schuldig* 'he is guilty of the crime'.

Accusative absolute

This construction is typically associated with either a past participle: *sie trat hinaus, einen Mantel umgeworfen* 'she stepped outside, a coat thrown over her shoulders', or else with a prepositional phrase: *er stand vor der Tür, den Schlüssel in der Hand* 'he stood in front of the door, the key in his hand'. The fixed expression *gesetzt den Fall, daß* 'supposing that' is another example of this use, nevertheless *gesetzt der Fall, daß* is often found, too. Compare 'Nominative absolute', p. 146.

Omission of accusative object

The direct object may in certain circumstances be understood: *sie zeigen euch* 'they'll show you', *sag ihm!* 'tell him!'. In German, however, such omissions are possible in examples where English idiom requires the object to be mentioned: *er gibt mir* 'he'll give me it, them, something, etc.', *sie leiht uns* 'she'll lend us it, etc.', *nehmen Sie nur!* 'just take it, etc.' or *nehmen Sie sich!* often corresponding to our 'help yourself!', and compare *es läßt (einiges) zu wünschen übrig* 'it leaves something to be desired', where the object is optionally, but very often, omitted.

GENITIVE

It may be noted at the outset that a construction involving the genitive will, broadly speaking, belong rather to the written than to the spoken language, the latter being prone to substitute other constructions, p. 154.

Genitive with nouns

The genitive is the case which, above all, denotes possession: *das Geld des Mannes, der Ring der Frau* 'the husband's money, the wife's ring', *das Studierzimmer des Gelehrten* 'the scholar's study', *das private Vermögen der Königin* 'the queen's private fortune'. In this, its main function, the genitive faces competition from *von* + dat., etc., below.

A genitive dependent on a noun has a number of other functions, more or less associated with the above, as in the following examples: *die Völker der Erde* 'the peoples of the earth', *das Venedig des Nordens* 'the Venice of the North', *die Pflege der Zähne* 'the care of the teeth', *eine Person dieses Namens* 'a person of this name', *der Held des Tages* 'the hero of the day', *der König der Könige* 'the king of kings', *die Kunst des Schreibens* 'the art of writing', *ein Strahl der Hoffnung* 'a ray of hope'. Understandably, idiom in the two languages occasionally differs: *ein Ding der Unmöglichkeit* 'a physical impossibility', *auf halber Höhe des Berges* 'half way up the hill', *Dozent der Mathematik* 'lecturer in mathematics'.

Partitive genitive

This is essentially a literary construction: *die Hälfte meines Königreichs* 'half of my kingdom', *keines seiner Kinder* 'none of his children', *die hübschere der beiden Frauen* 'the prettier of the two women', *das schwierigste aller Probleme* 'the most difficult of all problems', also after numerals: *drei der Soldaten* 'three of the soldiers'; the construction is reflected in the term *unsereiner* 'the likes of us', p. 222. The spoken language, however, prefers prepositional phrases, p. 154.

The genitive was formerly used after nouns denoting quantity, but apposition is now the rule if the former genitive is unqualified: *ein halbes Pfund Hammelfleisch* 'half a pound of mutton', *ein Schlückchen Wasser* 'a sip of water', similarly *eine Tasse Kaffee* 'a cup of coffee'. But should it be qualified, the genitive may, in literary style, remain: *eine Tasse heißen Kaffees* 'a cup of hot coffee', though here, too, apposition is the practice of the spoken language: *nichts trinke ich lieber als eine Tasse heißen Kaffee* 'there is nothing I like better (to drink) than a cup of hot coffee', by the same token (literary) *eine Menge neuartiger Ideen* 'a large number of novel ideas', (popular) *eine Menge tolle Angebote* 'lots of great offers'. This genitive was once usual after *viel*, of which occasional relics survive in set expressions: *sie macht viel Aufhebens* (or *Wesens*) *um nichts* 'she's making a fuss about nothing' and *ohne viel Federlesens* (but locally *Federlesen*) 'without beating about the bush', further *zuviel des Guten* 'too much of a good thing', similarly in connection with *genug* in the idiom *er ist Manns genug* 'he's man enough', also in strictly literary-style expressions like *genug der vielen Worte* 'enough has been said', and lastly the idiomatic *hier ist meines Bleibens nicht* (*länger*) 'this is not the place for me to stay (any longer)'.

Notice the peculiar word order in (essentially literary) expressions of the type *der Erklärungen gibt es viele* 'many are the explanations', *aller guten Dinge sind drei* 'all good things come in threes'.

Genitive with adjectives

A genitive is seen to be dependent on an adjective in a limited number of essentially literary words, among them *bewußt, habhaft, kundig, mächtig, würdig*, thus *er war sich seines Fehlers bewußt* 'he was aware of his error', *die Polizei konnte des Verdächtigen nicht habhaft werden* 'the police were unable to apprehend the suspect', *sie ist des Ungarischen kundig* or *mächtig* 'she has a command of Hungarian', *sie haben sich des Vertrauens würdig erwiesen* 'they have shown themselves worthy of trust'. Examples of the construction are also found with *gewiß* and *sicher*, as *ich bin dessen gewiß* or *sicher* 'I am certain (sure) of it'. In the case of *bar*, the genitive follows: *bar jeder Hülle* 'without a stitch of clothing'. In a few instances the genitive, facing competition from the accusative, survives only in certain idioms, p. 148.

Various constructions are found with *voll*. The genitive is acceptable in elevated language: *ein Glas voll duftenden Honigs* 'a jar of fragrant honey', but more ordinarily *ein Glas voll von* or *mit* (*duftendem*) *Honig*. If 'honey' is not further qualified, juxtaposition is possible: *ein Glas voll Honig*—an invariable form *voller* may also be used: *ein Glas voller Honig*.

Genitive with verbs

Two constructions are distinguished. In the first the genitive is the sole object of the verb, in the second one is dealing with a genitive-cum-accusative object.

In the older language a large number of verbs took the genitive as the sole object. Only a few remain today, all essentially literary words, as *bedürfen* 'need, require': *es bedurfte keiner Erklärung* 'it required no explanation'. Then *gedenken*, especially in solemn contexts: *in seiner Rede gedachte der Minister der großen Leistungen des Verstorbenen* 'in his speech the minister recalled the great achievements of the deceased'. The verb *harren* can occasionally be taken up in speaking: *wir harren der Dinge, die da kommen sollen* 'we are patiently awaiting events'.

In other cases the genitive survives in certain phrases. While *entbehren* is now normally construed with the accusative, e.g. *wir können seine Hilfe entbehren* 'we can do without his help', the genitive remains in *dieses Gerücht entbehrt jeder Grundlage* 'this rumour is without any foundation'. Nowadays regularly *er spottet über mich* 'he mocks me', on the other hand the idiom *das spottet jeder Beschreibung* 'that defies description'. Another isolated instance is *seines Amtes walten* 'to discharge the duties of one's office', e.g. jocularly *walte deines Amtes!* more or less 'get on with it!'

Turning now to the second construction, one sees that a number of verbs govern the accusative of the person and the genitive of the thing. This is a traditional arrangement which has survived better than the construction with the genitive as sole object. The background is again literary: *sie klagten ihn des Betrugs an* 'they accused him of fraud', less formal style substituting *wegen Betrug*. The corresponding passive runs *er wurde des Betrugs (wegen Betrug) angeklagt* 'he was accused of fraud'. Similarly other verbs from the same semantic field, as *beschuldigen* 'blame for', *überführen* 'find guilty', *verdächtigen* 'suspect'—these, however, do not have a less formal substitute. Here, too, verbs of depriving, e.g. *sie haben ihn seines Geldes beraubt* 'they have robbed him of his money', *er wurde seines Amtes enthoben* 'he was relieved of his office', *dann trat Herakles, der irdischen Unvollkommenheiten entkleidet, in die Reihen der unsterblichen Götter ein* 'then H., divested of earthly imperfections, stepped into the ranks of the immortal gods'. Another verb so treated is *würdigen*, e.g. *sie würdigte ihn keines Blickes* 'she did not deign to look at him'. The construction may now be confined to certain idioms: *man hat mich eines Besseren belehrt* 'I have been corrected', otherwise e.g. *man hat mich darüber belehrt* 'I have been instructed in the matter'.

Certain reflexive verbs are also involved, the reflexive pronoun representing the accusative: *sie hat sich seiner angenommen* 'she has taken him under her wing', *sie bedienten sich unseres Wagens* 'they made use of our car', *der Feind hatte sich der Festung bemächtigt* 'the enemy had seized the stronghold', *er erfreut sich bester Gesundheit* 'he enjoys the best of health', *ich kann mich des Eindrucks nicht erwehren, daß* . . . 'I cannot help feeling that . . . ' As elsewhere, the old may survive side by side with the new: (elevated) *ich kann mich noch jenes Tages entsinnen* or *erinnern* 'I can still remember that day', (ordinary) *an jenen Tag*.

Genitive in exclamations

This genitive has its place in high style: *o des Jammeranblicks!* 'oh, miserable sight!', *o weh der verlorenen Sieben!* 'alas for the lost seven!' But one such expression has passed into common speech: *leider Gottes!* 'most unfortunately!'

Predicative genitive

The genitive occurs predicatively in a number of set phrases: *er ist guter Dinge* 'he is in good spirits', *ich bin ganz ihrer Ansicht* 'I am quite of your opinion', *sie sind gleichen Alters* 'they are of the same age', *wir sind der festen Überzeugung, daß* . . . 'we are of the firm opinion that . . . '

Adverbial genitive

The genitive forms adverbial expressions of place, time, and manner, but all rather limited in their range. The first occurs in written style in connection with the words *Ort* and *Weg*: (officialese) *höheren Orts* lit. 'at a higher place' i.e. 'at a higher level', (elevated literary) *er geht seines Weges* 'he goes his way', ordinarily *seinen Weg*. The construction is recognized in a number of petrified forms now purely adverbs: *geradewegs* (also *geraden-, gerades wegs*) 'directly', *rechts*, *links* 'on (or, to) the right, left', alternatively especially in speaking *rechter*, *linker Hand*. In the case of *keineswegs* 'by no means' one no longer thinks spontaneously of the literal meaning.

Expressions of time are found with the genitive of *ein*, e.g. *eines Morgens* 'one morning', *eines Montags* 'one Monday', *eines Herbstes* 'one autumn', *eines Jahres* 'one year', analogically *eines Nachts* 'one night', further *eines schönen Tages* 'one fine day' distinct from *an einem schönen Tag* 'on a fine day'. In literary style the genitive is used with the corresponding definite article: *des Abends* 'in the evenings, of an evening', *des Sommers* 'in summertime', alternatively and normally in the spoken language *am Abend* or *abends*, *im Sommer*. Notice also (in written language) *dieser Tage* 'in the last, or next, few days'. The present construction is easily identified in such words as *mittlerweile* 'meanwhile', *jederzeit* 'at any time' and (rather formal) *derzeit* 'at the present time'.

The genitive of manner is common in essentially literary style after verbs of motion or rest: *sie ging leichten Schrittes vorbei* 'she went by with a light step', *schweren Herzens saß er da* 'there he sat with a heavy heart', alternatively *mit leichtem Schritt, mit schwerem Herzen*. Further in a number of set phrases: *allen Ernstes* 'in all seriousness', *meines Erachtens* 'in my opinion', *er kehrte unverrichteter Dinge zurück* 'he returned without having achieved anything'. The underlying genitive is likewise seen in such adverbs of manner as *jedenfalls* 'in any case', *keinesfalls* 'under no circumstances', *gewissermaßen* 'to a certain extent', *größtenteils* 'for the most part', *begreiflicherweise* 'understandably'.

Position of the genitive

In the medieval language the genitive preceded the noun it qualified, as it still does in English 'the engineer's work, a stone's throw'. In German this arrangement survives in two, albeit very different areas. Firstly, in everyday familiar use with personal or near-personal names: *Petras Puppe* 'Petra's doll', *Peters Freund* 'Peter's friend', *Lehmanns Vorgarten* 'Lehmann's (or Lehmanns') front garden', *Muttis Geldbörse* 'mummy's purse', also in connection with geographical names, stylistically neutral: *Deutschlands Grenzen* 'Germany's frontiers'; an alternative construction is *von* with the dative, below. Secondly, the genitive may precede in high style, particularly in poetry: *des Wandermüden letzte Ruhestätte* 'the weary wanderer's last resting place', and often in proverbs: *jeder ist seines Glückes Schmied* 'everyone is the architect of his own fortune'. A few instances of this archaic word order have become clichés, e.g. *der langen Rede kurzer Sinn* 'the long and short of it', and as an exclamation *das ist des Rätsels Lösung!* 'that's the answer! that explains it!'

Except as above the genitive follows the noun it qualifies. Firstly, with personal names in somewhat elevated style: *die Puppe Petras* 'Petra's doll', *ein Freund Peters* 'a friend of Peter's', in geographical names, still stylistically neutral: *die Grenzen Deutschlands* 'the frontiers of Germany'. Secondly, in average written style: *die Geldbörse der Mutter* 'the mother's purse', *die letzte Ruhestätte unseres teuren Freundes* 'our dear friend's last resting place'; in the spoken language these genitives are most commonly replaced by *von* with the dative.

The position of the genitive *Gottes* frequently shifts. Its original place before the noun is hallowed by tradition and often occurs side by side with more recent order after the noun, thus 'before God's throne' is either *vor Gottes Thron* or *vor dem Thron Gottes*, and similarly with *Christi* (p. 55): *Christi Leiden* or *das Leiden Christi* 'Christ's Passion'.

Expressing possession in the spoken language

The genitive, ubiquitous in print, is to a large extent absent from colloquial speech where, in its most characteristic function as the case of possession, it is commonly replaced by *von* 'of'. Thus, although one tends to write *das Geld des Mannes, der Ring der Frau* 'the husband's money, the wife's ring', one tends to speak *das Geld vom Mann, der Ring von der Frau*, or using another conversational construction, *dem Mann sein Geld, der Frau ihr Ring* (on which see further below). The colloquial type *Petras Puppe* (above) may alternatively be *die Puppe von* (or *von der*) *Petra*, also *Petra* (or *der Petra*) *ihre Puppe* 'Petra's doll'—on the use of the article with personal names, see pp. 186 f. Compare further *die Haushaltsgehilfin von Petras Mutter* as the most typical equivalent of 'Petra's mother's home help'.

It will be understood that there is no absolute line of demarcation between written and spoken language. Colloquial usage must often be admitted to novels and plays; it is introduced into many forms of journalism. And vice versa, through listening to news reports and the like, and through reading in general, there is a tendency to imitate more formal style in conversation, especially among educated people. Attitudes in such matters are bound to be more or less subjective. An excessive use of the genitive in conversation may strike some as an affectation, others find a constantly recurring *von* rather childish, while many would outlaw the construction *dem Mann sein Geld* altogether.

We have just seen how the typically literary construction exemplified in *das Geld des Mannes, der Ring der Frau*, tends to be modified in conversational German. On the other hand, such examples as *das Studierzimmer des Gelehrten, das private Vermögen der Königin*, not to speak of *die Völker der Erde*, etc., etc., p. 149, can hardly be changed. They will be spoken as they are written, for by their very nature they belong to a level of expression above that of the unsophisticated colloquial. They cannot be colloquialized. If taken into the spoken language they remain, so to speak, invariable literary quotations.

The construction *dem Mann sein Geld*

This is a construction with roots in the spoken language in which the possessor appears in the dative and the person or thing possessed is qualified by the possessive pronoun; it was referred to above in the examples *dem Mann sein Geld, der Frau ihr Ring* 'the husband's money, the wife's ring'. Although known everywhere, it is regarded as substandard. Nevertheless, it may be used for some special effect by speakers who would normally avoid it. It could add, say, a touch of sarcasm: *ach immer (der) Tante Emma ihre Wehwehchen!* 'oh! always Aunt Emma's aches and pains!' The construction is no stranger to print, naturally in imitation of popular idiom: (Grimm) *was war's so dunkel in dem Wolf seinem Leib!* 'how dark it was in the wolf's belly!', (Brecht) *das mit dem Kippernikus seinem Drehen* 'that about Tipper Nick's revolving'. In spite of its present lowly status the construction is traditional and recalls old-fashioned English 'Fred Moffat his book'. It can be used with pronouns: *es war nicht mein Fuß, sondern ihm seiner* 'it wasn't my foot, but his'.

Expressing possession, a stylistic summary

As shown above, possession can be expressed by four different constructions, each having its own stylistic value. The differences may be followed in the possible variations within a single sentence: (highest style, e.g. biblical) *in meines Vaters Hause sind viele Wohnungen* 'there are many dwelling places in my Father's house', (average literary style) *im Hause meines Vaters sind viele Wohnungen* 'there are many flats in my father's house', (usual colloquial) *im Haus von meinem Vater . . .*, (substandard) *in meinem Vater seinem Haus . . .*, so passing from the sublime to the . . ., well almost.

DATIVE

Dative as case of indirect object

The dative is, first of all, the case of the indirect object. It normally precedes the direct object unless the latter is a personal pronoun: *sie gibt dem Kellner ein Trinkgeld* 'she gives the waiter a tip', but *sie gibt es dem Kellner* 'she gives it to the waiter', and similarly *sie gibt ihm das Trinkgeld*, but *sie gibt es ihm*. See further under 'Word Order'.

When verbs governing both a direct (acc.) and an indirect (dat.) object are used in the passive, the dative object remains unchanged, thus active: *der Geschäftsführer bot dem Arbeitslosen eine Stelle an* 'the manager offered the unemployed man a job', passive: *dem Arbeitslosen wurde eine Stelle vom Geschäftsführer angeboten* 'the unemployed man was offered a job by the manager', alternatively *es wurde dem Arbeitslosen . . .*, pp. 194 f.

In the case of some verbs the indirect object may be replaced, optionally, by a prepositional phrase, more or less as in English: *sie senden die Säcke an Sie* 'they are sending the sacks to you', an alternative to *sie senden Ihnen die Säcke* 'they are sending you the sacks', and similarly *er hat einen Brief an seinen Onkel geschrieben* 'he has written a letter to his uncle' beside *er hat seinem Onkel einen Brief geschrieben* 'he has written his uncle a letter'.

After some nouns the place of the direct object is, as in English, taken either by an infinitive: *wir haben ihm geraten, die Zimmer möbliert zu vermieten* 'we have advised him to let the rooms furnished', or else by a surbordinate clause: *ich verspreche Ihnen, daß ich den Vertrag unterzeichne* 'I promise you that I will sign the agreement', with which compare *wir haben es ihm geraten* 'we have advised him in the matter', *ich verspreche es Ihnen* 'I promise you (it)'.

See also under 'Dative after verbs compounded with a preposition', pp. 159 f.

Dative as case of direct object

A considerable number of verbs—about a hundred—govern the dative as the sole object. Many are common words, including *danken* 'thank', hence *ich danke dir* 'I thank you', and notice the construction in sentences of the type *niemand wird es dir danken* 'no one will thank you for it', structurally comparable to e.g. *ich habe es dir zu verdanken* 'I owe it to you'. Other verbs governing the dative include *dienen* 'serve', *folgen* 'follow', *gefallen* 'please', *gehorchen* 'obey', *gehören* 'belong', *gelingen* 'succeed', *helfen* 'help', *passen* 'fit', *schaden* 'harm', *schmeicheln* 'flatter', *trauen* 'trust'. Some of these have opposites: *mißfallen* 'displease', *mißlingen* 'fail', *mißtrauen* 'mistrust'. Further examples: *nützen* 'be of use', cf. *es wird ihm nichts nützen* 'it will get him nowhere', *fehlen* or *mangeln* 'be lacking' in two constructions: *ihm fehlt der Mut* 'he hasn't the courage', *es fehlt ihm an Mut* 'he hasn't enough courage', further *gratulieren* 'congratulate', *imponieren* 'impress', and *passieren* or *geschehen* 'happen' 3rd person only: *was ist dir passiert?* 'what has happened to you?', *mir ist eine Panne passiert* 'I've had a breakdown'. Also common are *begegnen* 'meet (by chance)' and *bekommen* 'agree with (of food)', as are several verbs prefixed with *ent-*, e.g. *er entkam seinen Verfolgern* 'he escaped his pursuers', *sein Bericht entspricht nicht den Tatsachen* 'his report does not correspond to the facts', *sie ist kaum den Kinderschuhen entwachsen* 'she is hardly more than a child'. Other examples are found among impersonal verbs, as *mir graut vor* (+ dat.) 'I have a horror of', pp. 279 ff.

A small number of verbs which can govern a direct (acc.) and an indirect (dat.) object nevertheless frequently suppress the accusative object so that then the verb appears to be governing the dative only, e.g. *ich glaube Ihnen* for *ich glaube es Ihnen* 'I believe you', *sie hat ihm verziehen* for *sie hat es ihm verziehen* 'she has forgiven him (for it)', compare *antwortet er dir?* 'does he answer you?' with *was antwortet er dir?* 'what answer does he give you?'

Verbs taking a direct object in the dative form impersonal passives, p. 249: active *man hilft mir* 'one helps me', passive *es wird mir* or *mir wird geholfen* 'I am helped', similarly *es wurde mir* or *mir wurde geantwortet* 'I was answered', further *wem ist damit gedient?* 'who is helped by that?' The perfect participles of these verbs cannot be otherwise used in a passive sense, except for *gefolgt, geschmeichelt*, which commonly occur in such contexts as *er verließ den Tatort, gefolgt von einem Polizeibeamten in Zivil* 'he left the scene of the crime followed by a policeman in plain clothes', *er fühlt sich geschmeichelt* 'he feels flattered'.

Dative of interest

The dative of interest is found in various syntactical environments. It is often attached to a verb with an accusative object: *er repariert ihr den Kühlschrank* 'he is repairing the refrigerator for her', *sie öffnete ihm die Tür* 'she opened the door for him'. It may be reflexive: *hol dir einen Teller!* 'fetch yourself a plate!', sometimes expendable: *möchtet ihr (euch) den Obstgarten ansehen?* 'would you like a look at the orchard?', *ich habe es (mir) aufgeschrieben* 'I've written it down', *hast du es (dir) überlegt?* 'have you considered it?' The construction is regularly found with a verb accompanied by an adverb: *es steht Ihnen gut* 'it suits you well', or by a prepositional phrase: *sie wollten ihren Kindern nicht zur Last fallen* 'they did not want to become a burden to their children', *das kann allen zum Vorteil gereichen* 'that can be to the advantage of all'. Equally common are examples associated with the verb 'to be': *es ist ihm ein Rätsel* 'it is a mystery to him', *es war mir ein Bedürfnis, Ihnen zu schreiben* 'I felt I (really) had to write to you'. Less usually, the dative is connected to a verb without any of the foregoing adjuncts: (literary style) *er lebt seiner Arbeit* 'he lives for his work', (saying) *dem Glücklichen schlägt keine Stunde* 'those who are happy do not notice the passage of time'.

Ethic dative

Whereas the dative of interest (above) directly concerns the subject, the ethic dative refers to some other person or persons, normally the speaker. The construction has a pronounced emotional content and is common in the spoken language; close translation is scarcely possible: *du bist mir ein komischer Kerl* 'you are a funny sort of chap, that's for certain', *komm uns nicht mit diesen faulen Ausreden!* 'don't come here with weak excuses like that! We know you', *ihr red't mir nicht so!* 'don't you let me hear you talk like that!'

Possessive dative

The dative commonly functions as a possessive adjective, particularly in reference to parts of the body: *mir frieren die Füße* 'my feet are cold', *sie putzt sich die Zähne* 'she's cleaning her teeth', *das will mir*

nicht aus dem Sinn 'I can't put it out of my mind', *die Idee ging ihm durch den Kopf* 'the idea went through his head'.
See also 'The construction *dem Mann sein Geld*', pp. 154 f.

Dative with adjectives

The dative is very often dependent on an adjective. One distinguishes, in the first place, a group of mostly common adjectives, simple root words such as *böse* 'cross', *fremd* 'strange', *hold* 'gracious', *klar* 'clear', *neu* 'new', *recht* 'right', further *leicht* 'light, easy' and its opposite *schwer* 'heavy, difficult', and *lieb* 'dear, kind' with its near-synonym *teuer* 'dear, expensive'. Usage is most often predicative: *sei mir nicht böse* 'don't be cross with me', *das Glück war ihnen hold* 'fortune smiled on them', *das wird allen klar* 'that will be clear to all', *unserem Nachbar war das nicht neu* 'it was no news to our neighbour', *die Wahl fällt einem leicht (schwer)* 'one finds it easy (difficult) to choose'. Other examples appear under 'Impersonal verbs', p. 280. Attributive use is found in more literary style: *ein mir liebes (teures) Bild* 'a picture dear to me'.

A second group consists of adjectives corresponding to verbs which themselves govern the dative; they include *dankbar* 'grateful', *dienlich* 'serviceable', *nützlich* 'useful', *schädlich* 'harmful', cf. *danken* 'thank', *dienen* 'serve', *nützen* 'be of use', *schaden* 'harm', also *behilflich* 'helpful' beside *helfen* 'help', p. 156. Sample sentences: *wir sind ihnen dankbar* 'we are grateful to you', *können wir jetzt denen behilflich sein, die uns zuvor geholfen haben?* 'can we now be of help to those who helped us before?', *er überbrachte eine der Polizei nützliche Information* 'he brought a piece of information useful to the police'. A third group comprises a number of past participles functioning as adjectives, thus *die ihm angeborenen Eigenschaften* 'his innate qualities', *wir sind Ihnen sehr zu Dank verpflichtet* 'we are very much obliged to you', *ist er seinem Gegner gewachsen?* 'is he a match for his opponent?'

There remains a not inconsiderable number of miscellaneous examples, a few of which we may illustrate: *es ist mir egal* 'it's all the same to me', *es kann ihm nicht gleichgültig sein* 'he cannot be indifferent to it', *das geschah aus mir unerklärlichen Gründen* 'that happened for reasons inexplicable to me', *es war ihnen nicht möglich, nach Nürnberg zu fahren* 'it was not possible for them to travel to Nuremberg', *das war ihr selbstverständlich* 'that was for her a matter of course'.

Two final observations. Firstly, when an adjective qualified by *genug* is negated, a dependent phrase of the type *für mich* may be optionally replaced by the dative: *die Jacke war für mich* or *mir nicht groß genug* 'the jacket wasn't big enough for me', and likewise if an adjective is qualified by *zu*, hence *diese Übersetzung ist für die Anfänger* or *den Anfängern zu schwierig* 'this translation is too difficult for the beginners'. Secondly, the construction with *für* can, in some instances, be used as an alternative to the dependent dative: *es ist ihm wichtig* 'it is important to him', *es ist für ihn wichtig* 'it is important for him'. In all cases the prepositional phrase may follow the adjective, thus also *es ist wichtig für ihn*. Where nouns rather than pronouns are concerned, the use of the dative is more likely to occur in the written than in the spoken language.

Dative after verbs compounded with a preposition

In this construction the preposition determines the case of the object: *der Boxer konnte dem Schlag ausweichen* 'the boxer was able to dodge the blow', *wir wohnten der Gerichtsverhandlung bei* 'we attended the court hearing', *sie steht ihm in nichts nach* 'she is his equal in all respects', *der Gewinn fällt dem Staat zu* 'the profit goes to the state', also *du gehst mir ab* 'I miss you', where *ab* is literally 'from' (p. 302). Side by side with such examples are others in which, vice versa, the verb determines the (accusative) case of the object, see 'Accusative as case of direct object', p. 146. See also the last paragraph below.

One also finds a dative dependent on a preposition when the complement is the direct object in the accusative: *sie rissen ihm den Mantel ab* 'they tore the coat off him', *sie warf ihm einen Handkuß zu* 'she blew him a kiss', *ich habe es ihm nachgeschmissen* 'I flung it after him', *man mißt der Angelegenheit große Bedeutung bei* 'one attaches great importance to the matter', *das schlägt dem Faß den Boden aus!* 'that knocks the bottom out of the barrel!' i.e. 'that's the last straw!' And similarly with certain verbs having the prefix *ent-*, originally a preposition meaning 'out of': *das Gericht entzog ihm die Fahrerlaubnis* 'the court withdrew his licence to drive'. In accordance with current trends an explanatory preposition may sometimes be redundantly added: *wir haben ihrem Brief* or *aus ihrem Brief entnommen, daß der Fall erledigt ist* 'from your letter we gathered that the case has been settled', cf. *wir haben daraus entnommen, daß . . .* 'we gathered that . . .'

The preposition *mit* occurs with two verbs: *er hat es mir mitgeteilt* 'he has informed me about it' (originally 'shared it with me'), *ihm ist von angeblichen Freunden arg mitgespielt worden* 'he has been shabbily treated by supposed friends'.

Certain prepositions govern either the dative or the accusative (p. 299), hence e.g. (dat.) *Mängel haften diesem Werk an* 'there are flaws in this work' beside (acc.) *die Lufthansa fliegt über vierzig Städte an* 'L. flies to over forty cities'. However, there has been a tendency here for the dative to spread at the expense of the accusative: *ist Ihnen etwas Verdächtiges aufgefallen?* 'did you notice anything suspicious?', *ich kann es mir kaum vorstellen* 'I can hardly imagine it'. In the case of *ein* lit. 'into' the original accusative object survives in a number of idioms, as *darauf gehe ich jede Wette ein* 'I'll bet anything on that', but more generally the dative is now used: *fällt Ihnen nichts Gescheiteres ein?* 'can't you think of something more sensible?'

The preposition *wider* takes the accusative (p. 295), but verbs compounded with it govern the dative: (Oscar Wilde) *ich kann allem widerstehen, nur nicht der Versuchung* 'I can resist everything, except temptation'.

Dative after verbs compounded with an adverb of place

This construction has some similarity with that illustrated in the previous section: *sie eilen den anderen voraus* 'they hurry on ahead of the others', *wir sind ihm zuvorgekommen* 'we stole a march on him'; practically the same *wer weiß, was einem noch bevorsteht?* 'who knows what is in store for one?'

Dative replacing genitive

Given that a sequence of two genitives in *-(e)s* is felt to be inelegant, the second may be replaced by the dative: *infolge seines Bruders jähem Tode* (for *jähen Todes*) 'as a consequence of his brother's sudden death', *während Herrn Hillmanns langem Gespräch* (for *langen Gesprächs*) 'during Mr H.'s long conversation'.

The dative sometimes substitutes for a genitive in apposition, p. 165.

ADJECTIVES SUBSTANTIVIZED

All adjectives, including participles, can in principle be substantivized. Great numbers of them are regularly so treated; others can be transformed at will. There are certain parallels with English, sometimes in the plural: *die Tapferen* 'the brave', sometimes in the (neuter) singular: *das Schöne* 'the beautiful', i.e. 'that which is beautiful', *das Schöne daran* 'the beauty of it', *alles vom Schönsten und Besten* 'everything of the very best', *er tut sein Bestes* 'he does his best'. But German goes far beyond such limited parallels. Unlike English, the plural may be used without the article: *Tapfere* 'brave ones'. The words can equally well occur in the singular: *das muß eine Tapfere sein* 'that must be a brave woman', *so ein Schöner!* 'such a handsome man!', *diese Schöne* 'this beautiful woman, this beauty', also without an article: *komm her, Schönste* 'come here, darling'.

We further illustrate the range and scope of these formations, noting that compounds, often participial, are of very common occurrence. The examples are quoted in the plural simply for convenience; any of them could as easily be singular, and appear in any grammatical case: *Leichtsinnige, Klarsehende, Schwergeprüfte* 'people who are reckless, clear-sighted, sorely tried'. Many examples are, or can be, terms of a specific or technical nature, e.g. *Kranke* means not only 'people who are ill', but often also 'patients', hence such words as *Krankenhaus* 'hospital', *Krankenwagen* 'ambulance'. Other examples: *Heilige* 'saints', *Nächste* 'neighbours' (in the sense of one's fellow creatures), *Schwarze* 'blacks', further based on present participles: *Reisende* 'travellers' (including commercial travellers), *Trauernde* 'mourners', *Überlebende* 'survivors', and on perfect participles: *Abgeordnete* 'members of parliament', *Abgesandte* 'emissaries', *Angestellte* 'employees' (not manual workers), *Bekannte* 'acquaintances', *Beschäftigte* 'employees' (in a wide sense), *Delegierte* 'delegates', *Gelehrte* 'scholars', *Geliebte* 'lovers, mistresses', *Verlobte* 'fiancés, fiancées', *Verwandte* 'relatives'. Other standard expressions: *Erziehungsberechtigte* 'guardians (of children)', *Nichtzurechnungsfähige* 'persons not responsible for their own actions (owing to their mental condition)', *Steuerpflichtige* 'persons liable to tax', *Versetzungsgefährdete* 'children in danger of not being put up (into the next class)'. Not infrequently, such formations are related to the nouns ordinarily used, in which case they are more formal and stylistically elevated, e.g. *Lehrende* 'teachers', *Studierende* 'students' beside the commonplace *Lehrer*, *Studenten*, but notice only *Lernende* 'learners'.

There are a few special cases: *Vorsitzende* 'chairmen' has no corresponding participle. Occasionally a formation has no feminine: *Geistliche* 'clergymen', *Weise* 'sages'. The terms *Beamte(r)* 'official, (approximately) civil servant' and *Gesandte(r)* 'envoy' follow the above masculine declensions, but the feminine forms are *Beamtin*, *Gesandtin*. Notice *Elektrische* 'tram' and *Illustrierte* '(illustrated) magazine', both feminine, originally adjectives qualifying *Straßenbahn*, *Zeitschrift*; likewise feminine are *Gerade* 'straight line' and *Parallele* 'parallel (line)', alternatives to *gerade, parallele Linie*, and in the same way *die Rechte, Linke* are often used as abbreviations of *die rechte, linke Hand*. Lastly, *Junge(s)* 'young animal or bird' is neuter, cf. *Tier* 'animal' n.

On rare occasions, the regular plural ending *-e* could be confused with the fem. sg.; it is then altered to *-en* to avoid the ambiguity: *Mutters neue Illustrierte* 'mother's new magazine', *Mutters neue Illustrierten* 'mother's new magazines'.

The use of the strong genitive plural is somewhat restricted, being often replaced by *von* + dative: *die Ansichten von Gelehrten* 'the opinions of scholars'. But occurrences are to be expected in contexts of a more technical nature and therefore conducive to the use of the genitive case: *die wachsende Anzahl Ausreisewilliger* (or *von Ausreisewilligen*) 'the growing number of those wishing to leave (the country)'. The genitive also comes more easily when qualified by an adjective: *die Ansichten namhafter Gelehrter* 'the opinions of noted scholars'.

Great play is made of the neuter singular substantivization, again leading to usages unknown in English, and sometimes testing the ingenuity of the translator. But the basic sense is always clear enough, e.g. *Unglaubliches war geschehen* 'what happened was unbelievable'. Other examples: *er hat Hervorragendes geleistet* 'his achievements have been outstanding', *man darf nicht auf Unsicheres bauen* 'one must not build (or, rely) on something which is uncertain (or, insecure)', *das ist das Merkwürdige* 'that is the strange thing', *wir sind um ein Bedeutendes weitergekommen* 'we have taken an important step forward', *Besseres gibt es nicht* 'there is nothing better', *sie hatten Schlimmes durchgemacht, doch sollte noch Schlimmeres kommen* 'they had had a bad time of it, but worse was to come'. Lastly, a poetic line to speak for itself; an attempted translation might be felt as a desecration:

Und alles Getrennte findet sich wieder

To return to the mundane, we note among clichés: *Genaueres* or *Näheres* 'further particulars', *alles Gute* (*Schöne, Liebe*) 'all the best' (in conventional greetings), *Unzutreffendes streichen* 'delete which is inapplicable', and more concretely *das Kleingedruckte* 'the small print'. In some examples, a neuter noun is understood: *Gefrorenes* 'ice-cream' (now Austrian, but everywhere known in the variety *Halbgefrorenes*), *Gehacktes* 'minced meat', *Eingemachtes* 'preserved fruit', *Erspartes* or *Erübrigtes* 'savings', cf. *Eis* 'ice', *Fleisch* 'meat', *Obst* 'fruit', *Geld* 'money', all neuter.

Notice nom. acc. *nichts Gutes* 'nothing good', dat. *nichts Gutem*, and similarly: *etwas* (especially in the colloquial also *was*) *Gutes* 'something good', further *etwas ganz* (also *was ganz*, and informally *ganz was*) *Gutes* 'something quite good'.

In medieval German, abstract concepts like the above were expressed by the uninflected neut. sg. adjective. Examples survive in the modern language, but have become true substantives, e.g. *Gut* originally '(the) good' but now 'goods, treasure, estate', also *Licht* 'light', *Recht* 'right, law', *Übel* 'evil', thus different from the more recent formations *das Gute, Lichte, Rechte, Üble* 'the good, the good thing', etc. Both modes of formation are regularly seen in the names of colours: *(das) Blau* 'the blue colour' (*sie war ganz in Blau gekleidet* 'she was dressed all in blue') or *Grün* 'green colour, greenery, (golf) green' contrasting with *das Blaue, Grüne* 'the blue (in the abstract

sense), the blue thing', etc. The two formations are also found with
the names of languages: *(das) Deutsch* and *das Deutsche*. The former,
the pure substantive, can always be used, the latter only with the
definite article and in more technical or elevated style: *im heutigen
Deutsch* or *Deutschem* 'in present-day German'. The noun *Deutsch* is
not inflected (p. 54): *die Mängel meines Deutsch* 'the deficiencies of
my German, my shortcomings in German', similarly *meines Englisch*,
etc. Notice *in Deutsch*, sometimes *in deutsch*, an innovation modelled
on English usage, for more traditional *im Deutschen, auf deutsch*, and
naturally *in Englisch*, etc., too.

The substantivized adjective may be variously qualified: *berühmte
Heilige* 'famous saints', *das oben Angeführte* 'the above mentioned',
glücklich Verheiratete 'happily married people', *ein vom Tode
Gezeichneter* 'a man with the mark of death upon him', *die auf diese
Weise Hintergangene* 'the woman who was deceived in this way'. See
also 'Incapsulation', p. 338.

Given the ease with which an adjective or participle can be
transformed into a noun, it is not surprising that ad hoc creations
abound, e.g. (taking plural forms for convenience) *Herbeigeeilte*
'people hurrying up to the scene', *Trostspendende* 'people offering
consolation', *Zaubergewaltige* 'people with mighty powers of magic'.
Lines from Nietzsche's poem *Dem unbekannten Gott* 'To the
unknown God' will say the rest:

> *Ich will Dich kennen, Unbekannter,*
> *Du tief in meine Seele Greifender,*
> *Mein Leben wie ein Sturm Durchschweifender,*
> *Du Unfaßbarer, mir Verwandter!*

APPOSITION

In general, a noun in apposition appears in the same case as the noun
(or pronoun) to which it refers: *Heinz, der zweite Sohn, wurde
Tischler* 'H., the second son, became a carpenter', *er begrüßte seinen
Freund, den Schullehrer* 'he greeted his friend, the school-teacher',
wir erwarten ihn Sonntag, den 11. (elften) or *am Sonntag, dem 11.*
'we are expecting him (on) Sunday, the 11th', *zwischen Celle, einer
Stadt mit schönen Fachwerkhäusern, und Lüneburg breitet sich die
Heide aus* 'the Heath lies between C., a town with beautiful half-
timbered houses, and L.', *die Werke Shakespeares, des größten
Dramatikers der Weltliteratur, gehören zum Repertoire aller berühmten
Bühnen* 'the works of Sh., the greatest dramatist in world literature,
are part of the repertoire of all famous theatres (lit. stages)'.

Apposition is regular in such expressions as *die Stadt Düren* 'the
town of D.', *das Land Hessen* 'the province of H.', *die Insel Rügen*

'the island of R.', hence *die Insel Man* 'the Isle of Man', further *der Fall Böhm* 'the Böhm case' (but *der Fall des Herrn B.* 'the case of Mr B.'), similarly (*die*) *Villa Hammerschmidt* 'Hammerschmidt's Villa' and, finally, the pattern *der Monat Januar* 'the month of January'.

The same practice occurs after nouns qualified by a numeral: *eine verschwiegene Pension — genau das richtige für zwei, drei Tage ungestörte Liebe* 'a secluded guesthouse—exactly the right thing for two or three days of love undisturbed', *"ich war bei gut zwei Dutzend harten Demos dabei, ohne daß ich was abgekriegt habe", sagte der Student* ' "I've been in quite two dozen rough demos without getting into trouble", the student said'. The adjective qualifying the dative noun in apposition is usually weak: *Solschenitzyn wurde zu acht Jahren sibirischen Straflager verurteilt* 'Solzhenitsyn was sentenced to eight years' penal servitude in Siberia'. Apposition is further common after *Art* 'kind, sort': *diese Art Leute gefällt mir nicht* 'I don't like people of this kind'. The word may, however, be used with *von*, as locally in the spoken language: *eine Art von Unterschlupf* 'a sort of hide-out' for more general *eine Art Unterschlupf*, or it may appear stylistically superior, e.g. for sentence rhythm: *nach Ansicht der Sozialdemokraten brauchen wir eine neu zu schaffende Art von Verhältniswahlrecht* 'according to the Social Democrats we need to work out a new type of proportional representation'.

The conjunctions *als* and *wie* are often involved in appositions: *Emir Abdullah wurde als Prinz eingesetzt* 'Emir A. was installed as prince', *er begrüßte ihn wie einen alten Freund* 'he greeted him like an old friend', the *wie*-clause being a shortened version of *wie er einen alten Freund begrüßen würde* 'as he would greet an old friend'. But in such a sentence as *man fühlt sich wie ein Ausländer* 'one feels like a foreigner', the nominative is regular, the *wie*-clause being a truncation of *wie ein Ausländer sich fühlt* 'like a foreigner feels' (p. 321), hence also *in Zeiten wie diese* (*es sind*) 'in times like these (are)', *nach einer Schlacht wie jene* (*es war*) 'after a battle like that (was)', though case agreement is here equally common: *in Zeiten wie diesen*, etc. Notice that the nominative is used after *als* in cases like *das ist der Politiker, der sich als ehrlicher Makler ausgab* 'that is the politician who claimed to be an honest broker', and there is a strong tendency for the nominative to be used in other appositions as well, e.g. *beachtlich war auch der Einfluß Miltons als politischer Schriftsteller* 'considerable, too, was M.'s influence as a political writer'. On the other hand, agreement is general after comparatives: *in weniger als einem halben Jahr* 'in less than half a year'.

There are various other exceptions to the general rule of case agreement. An unqualified singular noun is now left in the nominative:

er interviewte Dr. Lederer, Dozent an der Handelsschule 'he interviewed Dr L., lecturer at the Commercial College', *wir erhielten ein Schreiben von Herrn Hoffmann, Vorsitzender des Sportvereins* 'we received a communication from Mr H., chairman of the Sports' Club'. There is a temptation to put the dative instead of the genitive when the genitive antecedent itself is preceded by a dative: *man sieht es am Beispiel Japans, diesem* (for logically correct *dieses*) *industriellen Riesen Ostasiens* 'one sees it illustrated in the case of Japan, that industrial giant in East Asia'. Apparently the preposition (here *an* with the dative) exercises a remote effect and in so doing conveniently prevents an accumulation of genitives.

Apposition is also found in connection with expressions of quantity, etc., see under 'Partitive genitive', pp. 149 f, and 'Singular for plural', pp. 310 f; it may be used after the numerals 100, 1,000, p. 77.

14. Adjectives

We first illustrate the regular use of the three types of declension: weak, strong, mixed, and then refer to significant exceptions to the general rules.

WEAK DECLENSION

The adjective is preceded by the definite article *der, die, das*, or by *dieser, -e, -es* 'this', likewise by *jener* 'that', *jeder (jeglicher)* 'each, every', then *derselbe (der nämliche, der gleiche)* 'the same', and *derjenige* . . . , *der* 'that . . . who, which': *dieser starke Tee* 'this strong tea', *nach jener berühmten Schlacht* 'after that famous battle', *jeder solche Fehler* 'every such error', *dieselben schönen Häuser* 'the same fine houses', *die Taten derjenigen mutigen Widerstandskämpfer, die* . . . 'the deeds of those courageous resistance fighters who . . .' Also *solcher* 'such': *mit solchem unerhörten Elan* 'with such extraordinary dash', but strong forms are also found in the plural: *solche gute* or *guten Nachrichten* 'such good news', etc.

This declension is also found after *welcher, -e, -es* 'which, what': *welcher weiße Stein?* 'which white stone?', *welche bewundernswerten Errungenschaften!* 'what admirable achievements!'; similarly after *irgendwelcher* 'of some sort or another'.

Weak inflexion is regular after *all* 'all' and its bookish synonym *sämtlich*, e.g. *alles* (or *sämtliches*) *verfügbare Geld* 'all available money', naturally commoner in the plural: *alle* (or *sämtliche*) *modernen Fabriken* 'all modern factories', *aller guten Dinge sind drei* (proverbial) 'all good things come in threes'. Likewise after *beide* (and of course after *die beiden*) 'both': *beide* (or *die beiden*) *hohen Türme* 'both (the) high towers'. On use with dative nouns in apposition, see p. 164.

STRONG DECLENSION

The adjective is unqualified: *lautes Geschrei* 'loud shouting', *niedrige Stühle* 'low chairs', *mit heißem Wasser* 'with hot water'.

The adjective is qualified by a word without a declensional ending, e.g. *viel* 'much', *mehr* 'more', *wenig* 'little', *weniger* 'less': *viel lautes Geschrei, mehr niedrige Stühle, mit wenig (weniger) heißem Wasser*, and similarly after the uninflected forms *manch, solch, welch*, e.g.

manch guter Geselle 'many a good fellow' (high style), *solch freudiges Widersehen* 'such a joyous reunion', *welch glücklicher Zufall!* 'what a lucky chance!'

The adjective is qualified by a proper name in the genitive: *Kanzler Schmidts politischer Erfolg* 'Chancellor Schmidt's political success', or by an ordinary noun, as may occur in literary style: *Des Kaisers neue Kleider* 'The Emperor's New Clothes'.

Strong forms are also found after *dessen, deren* (formal, officialese, p. 192): *dessen (deren) schlechter Gesundheitszustand* 'his (her, their) poor state of health'.

MIXED DECLENSION

The adjective is preceded by the indefinite article *ein, eine, ein*, or similarly inflecting word, i.e. *kein* 'no, not a, not any' or a possessive adjective: *mein, dein, sein, ihr (Ihr), unser, euer* 'my, etc.' (p. 60), e.g. *ein (kein) geringer Unterschied* 'a (no) slight difference', *auf deiner linken Schulter* 'on your left shoulder', *dank seines großen Glückes* 'thanks to his (or, its) great good fortune', *ihre reichen Bekannten* 'her (or, their) rich acquaintances'.

VARYING GENITIVE SINGULAR

The adjectives *aller, -e, -es* 'all' and *jeder* 'each, every', also *mancher* 'many a', *einiger* and *etlicher* 'some' (p. 215) form the gen. sg. masc. neut. in *-es* instead of *-en* when used before a substantivized adjective, and also before any other noun making its genitive in *-en*. Contrast *die Wurzel allen Übels* 'the root of all evil' with *die Ablehnung alles Fremden* 'the rejection of everything foreign (or, unfamiliar)', further the adverbial genitive *jeden Falls*, now written *jedenfalls* 'in any case', but *die Gefühle jedes Menschen* 'the feelings of each person'. This termination may be adopted by some in other contexts, too. Historically speaking, the ending *-es* is the older, hence in archaizing style *die Wurzel alles Übels*.

INFLEXION AFTER NUMERAL ADJECTIVES, ETC.

Inflexion in these cases is not entirely stabilized, there being some vacillation between strong and weak declension. To begin with the plural, adjectives following *andere, einige* and synonymous *etliche, mehrere, viele, wenige*, now take the strong ending in the nom. acc., e.g. *andere alte Freunde* 'other old friends', *viele frohe Stunden* 'many happy hours', though after *manche* weak forms are by no means unusual as well. Usage in the genitive is particularly unsettled: *der*

Verlust etlicher seltener (or *seltenen*) *Exemplare* 'the loss of some rare specimens', *der Einsatz mehrerer neuer* (or *neuen*) *Maschinen* 'the introduction of several new machines', and similarly with the inflecting numeral (p. 76): *die Mutter zweier gesunder* (or *gesunden*) *Kinder* 'the mother of two healthy children'. It may be recalled that such genitives are essentially literary forms not supported by daily colloquial use, p. 154. Those who prefer the sequence *-er, -er* will reason that this is grammatically correct, while those who incline to *-er, -en* are following a trend in the language according to which the termination of the first attributive is sufficient to indicate the grammatical case, the second then taking the weak ending after the pattern of *der* (or *dieser*, etc.) *gesunden Kinder*.

It is even less easy to formulate practice for the singular, but one can affirm that, whatever individual preferences may be in given cases, the weak form will always be acceptable: *mancher reiche Bürger* 'many a rich citizen', *mit einigem gesunden Menschenverstand* 'with some (a modicum of) common sense'—except, of course, after the uninflected forms *viel, wenig, manch* (p. 166), where strong declension is the rule.

The inflexions of the adjective after *folgend* also correspond to the above pattern: pl. *folgende schwierige Fälle* 'the following difficult cases', sg. *folgendes unerwartete Ereignis* 'the following unexpected event'. Should the optional alternative with the definite article be used, the weak declension is required, the article taking precedence in all such matters, hence *die folgenden schwierigen Fälle*, etc., and by the same token *wenig Geld* 'little money', *das wenige Geld* 'the little money'.

INFLEXION AFTER PERSONAL PRONOUNS

Descriptive adjectives frequently occur after a personal pronoun in the nominative case. In the singular, strong inflexion is the rule: *ich armer Tor* 'I poor fool'. In the plural, endings are mostly weak: *wir deutschen* (but not uncommonly also *deutsche*) *Männer* 'we German men' and always *ihr deutschen Männer* 'you German men', correspondingly *wir Deutschen* (or *Deutsche*), but only *ihr Deutschen*. In the rarely occurring oblique cases, weak declension prevails: *mir armen Toren* 'to me poor fool'.

DESCRIPTIVE ADJECTIVES STANDING TOGETHER

Two or more descriptive adjectives take the same endings: *der gute preiswerte Stoff* 'the good, inexpensive material', dat. *dem guten preiswerten Stoff(e)*, etc.; should the adjectives not be qualified, then *guter, preiswerter Stoff*, etc. In the latter case, there is a tendency to avoid a repetition of *-em* in the dat. sg., hence in spontaneous language *aus gutem preiswerten Stoff*. When the formal rule is followed, the adjectives are often separated by a comma: *aus gutem, preiswertem Stoff*. The same applies to the genitive plural: *die Verwendung guter preiswerten* (*guter, preiswerter*) *Stoffe* 'the use of good, inexpensive materials'. In the spoken language one often hears, e.g. *mit frischer grünen Farbe* 'with fresh green paint' instead of the prescribed *mit frischer grüner Farbe*, following the principle that one distinctive ending suffices to indicate the grammatical case, the second adjective then being weak after the analogy of *mit der grünen Farbe*.

NOUN UNDERSTOOD

If the noun is understood, the adjective inflects according to rule: *ist englisches Bier stärker als deutsches?* 'is English beer stronger than German?', *diese Hemden sind schmutzig, ihr braucht saubere* 'these shirts are dirty, you want clean ones', *sein Bruder ist der Gescheitere* 'his brother is the cleverer one', *ich möchte einen Gebrauchtwagen, könnten Sie mir einen preiswerten besorgen?* 'I should like a used car, could you get hold of a cheap one for me?'

ADJECTIVE NOT INFLECTED

Adjectives are not inflected when used predicatively: *der Turm ist hoch, die Türme sind hoch* 'the tower is, the towers are high', or when in apposition: *die Wasserbüffel, stark und gutmütig, lassen sich auch von Frauen und Kindern leiten* 'the water buffaloes, strong and good-natured, allow themselves to be led by women and children, too'.

In a few cases a descriptive adjective occurs without an ending. We first note an archaic uninflected nom. acc. neut. sg. surviving in a few set phrases, as *lieb* and *ruhig* in the everyday idioms *sich lieb Kind machen* 'to ingratiate oneself' and *ruhig Blut bewahren* 'to keep calm', hence the often heard elliptical *nur ruhig Blut!* 'just keep calm!', further with *gut*, commonly e.g. *auf gut Glück* 'on the off chance', *ein gut Teil* 'a good part (portion, amount)', and the proverbial *gut Ding will Weile haben* 'to do a good job needs time'. Notice an analogous use with a masculine noun: *sie sind wieder gut Freund* 'they are (good) friends again'.

Adjectives relating to towns, countries, etc. are invariable when forming names: *Schwäbisch Hall*, sometimes hyphenated *Deutsch-Landsberg*, or written as though part of a compound *Windischgrätz*. By analogy, such modern terms as *Britisch-Indien* or *Französisch-*

Westafrika. A well-known item: *Kölnisch Wasser* 'eau de Cologne'. It will be remembered that all these names are neuter, p. 55.

The adjectives *ganz* and *halb* do not inflect before geographical names: *in ganz München* 'in all Munich', *durch halb Europa* 'through half Europe', except of course when qualified by the article: *aus der ganzen Schweiz* 'from all Switzerland' (*die Schweiz*, p. 55). The idiom *ich bin ganz Ohr* 'I am all ears' is presumably a perversion of *ich bin ganz still* 'I am quite still'.

The adjective *einzig* remains uninflected before another adjective: *die einzig mögliche Antwort* 'the only possible answer', equally so when the latter is substantivized: *das einzig Vernünftige dabei* 'the only sensible thing about it'.

Notice instructions of the type *groß A*, *klein b*, as when dictating.

In certain usages *manch*, *solch*, *welch*, also *all*, remain unchanged, see under these words.

Observe the idiomatic use of *eigen* 'own' preceded by a possessive pronoun: *zehn Häuser nennen sie ihr eigen* lit. 'ten houses they call their own' = 'they own ten houses', where the uninflected adjective is virtually a noun. The same applies when, occasionally, two adjectives make an invariable pair: *sie gingen gemeinsam durch dick und dünn* 'they went together through thick and thin', *haben Sie es schwarz auf weiß?* 'have you it in black and white?', further *gleich und gleich gesellt sich gern* 'birds of a feather flock together'.

DEFECTIVE ADJECTIVES

Many adjectives are syntactically defective: some occur only predicatively, or only predicatively and adverbially, others only attributively, etc.; reference has already been made to adjectives which cannot be used as adverbs, p. 67.

Adjectives which cannot be used attributively are, of course, uninflected. We instance first of all certain essentially literary words: *gewahr*, *habhaft*, cf. *er wurde der Schwierigkeiten gewahr* 'he became aware of the difficulties', *die Polizei konnte des Täters nicht habhaft werden* 'the police could not catch (lay hands on) the culprit'. Other examples: *abhold*, *verlustig* (always construed with the verb *gehen* 'to go'), *vorstellig*, cf. *er war jedem Pomp und Gepränge abhold* 'he disliked any sort of pomp and circumstance', *eines Teils seines Vermögens verlustig gehend* 'losing part of his fortune', *sie wurden bei der zuständigen Behörde vorstellig* 'they made representations to the appropriate authority'. Similarly *gewillt*, e.g. *das Zebra ist nicht gewillt, als Lasttier zu dienen* 'the zebra is not prepared to serve as a beast of burden' (being untamable), and *getrost*, e.g. *seid getrost!* 'be comforted!', also adverbial: *man kann getrost sagen* 'one can confidently say'.

Other examples are colloquialisms, such as *fit* 'fit', also *topfit* 'as fit as can be', *futsch* 'broken, busted, lost'. Notice *fehl* and *quitt* in expressions like *diese Ansichten sind fehl am Platz* 'these views are out of place', *nun sind wir quitt* 'now we're evens'. Sometimes the adjectives occur in pairs, as *recht und billig* 'right and proper', and amounting to the same thing *null und nichtig* 'null and void'.

Four adjectives which were originally nouns belong here; their use is typically idiomatic. The first two: *feind* 'hostile, opposed to' (*Feind* 'enemy'), very common in the colloquial *spinnefeind*, e.g. *die beiden sind sich* (dat.) *spinnefeind* 'the pair of them hate each other like poison', and *schade* 'regrettable' (*Schade*, now *Schaden* 'damage'), *es ist sehr schade, daß er nicht kommt* 'it's a great pity that he's not coming', *es ist zu schade zum Wegwerfen* 'it's too good to throw (or, be thrown) away', *meine Zeit ist mir dafür zu schade* 'I don't waste my time on that'. In the other two examples, *schuld* (*Schuld* 'guilt') and *angst* (*Angst* 'fear'), the transition from noun to adjective has only been partially carried through, although the words concerned are always written with a small initial. Thus we have *ich bin* (or *habe*) *an allem schuld* 'I'm to blame for everything', when *bin . . . schuld* is felt as literally meaning 'am . . . guilty', but *habe . . . schuld* is still clearly 'have . . . guilt'. The phrase *mir ist angst* 'I am afraid' is literally 'to-me is fear', but in the popular extension *mir ist angst und bange* 'I'm scared stiff' the original noun is co-ordinated with the adjective *bange* 'fearful', also e.g. *er macht mir angst und bange* 'he scares me stiff'.

Conversely, certain adjectives can only be found in attributive use and, as an obvious consequence, occur in practice solely in the inflected forms. A small group consists of adjectives in *-ig* formed from adverbs: *der, die, das heutige, morgige, gestrige* 'pertaining to today, tomorrow, yesterday', cf. *die heutige Mode* 'today's fashion', *das morgige Wetter* 'tomorrow's weather', *die ewig Gestrigen* 'those who persist in acting as though they were living in the past', also *diesjährig* or (Upper German) *heurig* (from local *heuer* 'this year'), cf. *die diesjährige* or *heurige Ernte* 'this year's harvest'. Equally common are *dortig* and *hiesig*, cf. *das dortige (hiesige) Postamt* 'the post office of that place, at your end (here, at this end)', and *obig*, as *(die) obige Adresse* 'the above address'. To these add *recht* and its opposite: *die rechte, linke Straßenseite* 'the right, left side of the street'. A second group is made up of adjectives having no positive, as *äußere* 'outer, exterior', set out on p. 65. And finally, all superlatives (p. 63), though an uninflected (adverbial) form may appear in composition: *bestmöglich* 'best possible'.

Participles used as adjectives are generally defective, see the following.

PARTICIPLES USED AS ADJECTIVES

Present participles

These are purely adjectives, and decline accordingly. Nevertheless they are, as a class, defective to the extent that (apart from certain exceptions, below) they cannot be used with the verb 'to be', nor can they, of course, be compared.

But all may be used attributively (though not normally *seiend* 'being' or *habend* 'having' except in composition, e.g. *wohlhabend* 'well-to-do'). Examples: *grollender Donner* 'rolling thunder', *eine steigende Tendenz* 'a tendency to rise', *schallendes Gelächter* 'roaring laughter, roars of laughter', *verhungernde Menschen* 'people starving (to death)'. Such usage is thus in principle parallel to English, but as the examples show, English may prefer or require different constructions in given cases. Adverbial use is likewise commonplace: *überraschend schnell* 'surprisingly quick(ly)', *schweigend verließ sie das Zimmer* 'she left the room without saying a word', *wir haben Ihren Entwurf an die kompetente Stelle befürwortend weitergeleitet* 'we have forwarded your draft to the proper authority, adding our recommendation'.

In numerous instances, the participle has come to be felt as an ordinary adjective, e.g. *aufregend* 'exciting', *bedeutend* 'important', *befriedigend* 'satisfactory', *dringend* 'urgent', *empörend* 'revolting', *glänzend* 'brilliant', *lärmend* 'noisy', *passend* 'suitable', *reizend* (rather a lady's word) 'charming', *strahlend* 'radiant', *überzeugend* 'convincing', *vermögend* or *wohlhabend* 'well-to-do', and naturally enough all participles with the negative prefix *un*-: possible formations from the preceding are *unbedeutend, unbefriedigend, unpassend, unvermögend* 'unimportant', etc., also *unwissend* 'ignorant', though not its positive *wissend* 'knowing'. Such participles are in no way defective. They are freely used with the verb 'to be': *er ist sehr wohlhabend*, and may be compared: *aufregend*, comp. *aufregender*, superl. *der aufregendste*.

See further under 'Incapsulation', p. 338.

Perfect participles

As in English, the perfect participle of a transitive verb may be used as an adjective, though as with the present participle, English may prefer or require other constructions in given cases. The participle is common in the attributive position: *beeidigter Zeuge* 'sworn witness', *eine versäumte Gelegenheit* 'a chance missed', *das abgehobene Geld* 'the money withdrawn'; it is likewise usual in other functions, as the following may illustrate: *er kam erschöpft an* 'he arrived exhausted', *wir waren alle sehr verärgert* 'we were all very much annoyed', *über den Kurswechsel enttäuscht, traten sie aus der Partei aus* 'disappointed by the change of policy, they left the party'. Passive sense is, of course, regular, but there are a handful of exceptions such as *ein gelernter Arbeiter* 'a skilled tradesman', the colloquial idiom *ein studierter Mann* 'a man with a university education', similarly (substantivized) *der Geschworene* 'the juror' and the humorous *ungegessen*, used adverbially: *komm ungegessen, du kannst bei uns essen* 'don't have anything to eat before you come, you can have a meal with us'.

The perfect participle of the intransitive verb conjugated with *sein* can also be used adjectivally: *die aufgegangene Sonne* 'the sun which has (or, had) risen', *verwelkte Blumen* 'faded flowers', *sie sieht verwelkt aus* 'her looks have faded'. On predicative use: *die Blumen sind verwelkt* 'the flowers are (or, have) faded', see further pp. 245 f.

Many perfect participles have come to be felt as ordinary adjectives, though most of them remain ambivalent, as they are still in use as participles proper. In adjectival use, a considerable semantic change is often evident, e.g. *er hat sie nach Hause geschickt* 'he has sent her home', *er ist recht geschickt* 'he is quite skilled', *sie hat fünfzig Kilo gewogen* 'she weighed 50 kilos', *sie ist ihm gewogen* 'she is well-disposed towards him', further *man hat das Kind ausgelassen* 'the child has been left out', *das Kind ist ausgelassen* 'the child is boisterous', *der Lehrer hat aufgeschlossen* 'the teacher has opened up (lit. unlocked)', *der Lehrer ist aufgeschlossen* 'the teacher is open-minded'. Other examples: *bekannt* perf. part. 'confessed'—adj. '(well-)known', *erbaut* 'built—edified', *geziert* 'adorned—affected', *zerstreut* 'scattered—absent-minded'. Notice perf. part. *verdorben* 'spoilt', but isolated adj. *verderbt* 'corrupt(ed)' and numerous such adjectives, e.g. *verfrüht* 'premature', *verlogen* 'mendacious', *verqualmt* 'full of smoke'. All negative participles are pure adjectives: *ungelernt* 'unskilled', *ungebunden* 'unbound, unrestrained', some with a figurative sense only, as *ungehalten* 'annoyed', *ungezogen* 'rude, illbred', and some (like certain other adjectives, p. 18) with no positive, e.g. *unbescholten* 'of stainless character, with no previous convictions', *unverhofft* 'unexpected'.

COMPARATIVE AND SUPERLATIVE

In the case of a few common adjectives, German often uses the comparative in an absolute sense, i.e. without any implication of comparison: *eine größere Summe* 'a rather large sum of money', *eine ältere Dame* 'an elderly lady', *ein jüngerer Herr* 'a youngish gentleman', *eine bessere Scheune* 'a glorified barn', these in addition to the true comparative meanings 'a larger sum', etc. It can happen that the absolute sense is the more usual one: *die neueren Sprachen* generally '(the) modern languages', or indeed the only one: *seit längerer Zeit* 'for quite some time now'.

As in English, two usages are possible with the comparative in predicative position: *welcher Brunnen ist tiefer* or *der tiefere?* 'which well is deeper, or the deeper?' The predicative superlative likewise exists in two forms: *welcher Brunnen ist am tiefsten* or *der tiefste?* 'which well is deepest, or the deepest?' The former is, of course, always used when there is no comparison with others: *der Garten ist jetzt am schönsten* 'the garden is at its best now'. But it is also regular when the items compared are in the same category: *Bronze ist härter als Kupfer oder Zinn, aber Eisen ist am härtesten* 'bronze is harder than copper or tin, but iron is the hardest', i.e. *das härteste Metall* 'the hardest metal', also *die Lufthansa ist am pünktlichsten, sagte er* 'L. is the most punctual, he said', *die pünktlichste Fluglinie* 'the most punctual airline' being understood.

A relationship between two comparatives is expressed by *je . . . desto* or *um so*, e.g. *je unwirtlicher die Städte, desto (um so) stärker wird der Baudruck auf den Grüngürtel* 'the more inhospitable the towns, the stronger the pressure becomes to build in the green belt'. In elevated style also *je . . . je*, as *je mehr er mir es versicherte, je* (but normally *desto, um so*) *weniger glaubte ich es* 'the more he assured me, the less I believed it'; the construction is petrified in the phrase *je länger, je lieber* 'the longer the better', substantivized as *das Jelängerjelieber* 'the honeysuckle'.

15. Adverbs

FROM ADJECTIVE TO ADVERB

As already noted (p. 67) the uninflected adjective can, in the vast majority of cases, readily function as an adverb: *sie seufzte tief* 'she sighed deeply', *er steckt tief in Schulden* 'he is deeply in debt', *wir waren tief enttäuscht* 'we were deeply disappointed'. Such use is particularly extensive, often occurring where English requires an adverbial phrase or other idiom: *Bismarck starb 83jährig* 'B. died at the age of 83', *literarisch hinterließ Heines Tod eine große Lücke* 'H.'s death left a large gap in the literary scene', *die Angelegenheit könnte telephonisch* (or *fernmündlich*) — *brieflich, postlich — erledigt werden* 'the matter could be dealt with over the telephone—by letter, through the post', *diese Namen stehen stellvertretend für viele andere* 'these names are representative of many others', *wie geht es Ihnen gesundheitlich?* 'how is your health?' Sometimes translations have to be very free, e.g. *die Römer drangen erobernd in Gallien ein* 'the Romans penetrated into Gaul, overcoming the inhabitants as they advanced', (notice in a supermarket) *das Mitbringen von Hunden ist lebensmittelpolizeilich verboten* 'dogs not allowed in this store by order of the food inspector'. As with adjectives (pp. 173 f) the comparative adverb is occasionally used absolutely, everyday examples being *näher*, e.g. *Sie kennen ihn näher?* 'you know him rather well?', and *öfter* or less formally *öfters* (with secondary *-s*): *wir sahen uns öfter(s)* 'we saw each other quite often'.

ADVERBS OF TIME, PLACE, ETC.

In addition to adverbs formed from adjectives, German, like other languages, possesses a considerable number of original adverbs. Some refer to time or place, such as *gestern* 'yesterday', *heute* 'today', *morgen* 'tomorrow', or *oben* 'above', *unten* 'below', *hinten* 'behind', *vorn* 'in front'. Others are described as adverbs of quality, comparison, affirmation, and so on, e.g. *sehr* 'very (much)', *zu sehr* 'too much', *gleichsam* 'as it were', *allerdings* 'by all means'.

We may note that the indefinite adverb *irgendwo* 'somewhere, anywhere' is sometimes replaced in the spoken, but rarely in the literary language by (unstressed) *wo*, e.g. *ich finde meinen Bleistiftspitzer nicht, ich muß ihn wo liegen gelassen haben — hast du ihn wo gesehen?* 'I can't find my pencil-sharpener, I must have left it lying around somewhere—have you seen it anywhere?'. This unstressed word cannot stand at the head of a sentence, hence only *irgendwo muß ich ihn liegen gelassen haben*.

In general, however, these adverbs are more of lexical than grammatical concern and need not occupy us further here. Only the adverbs of direction form a notable exception; to these we now turn.

ADVERBS OF DIRECTION

Of particular interest to the foreign student are, in the first place, the adverbs *her*, *hin*, lit. 'hither, thither': *hin und her* 'backwards and forwards', *kommen Sie her!* 'come here!', *gehen Sie hin!* 'go there!', *wo kommen Sie her?* 'where are you coming from?', *wo gehen Sie hin?* 'where are you going to?', more formally *woher kommen Sie? wohin gehen Sie?* These adverbs have the same function in noun formations: *auf dem Herweg* 'on the way here', *auf dem Hinweg* 'on the way there'. They may be freely added to a prepositional phrase, so reinforcing the notion of movement: *der Luftzug kommt von der Tür her* 'the draught comes from the door', *die Armee bewegte sich nach der Stadt hin* 'the army moved towards the town'. Notice the redundant *hierher*, *dorthin*, hence *kommen Sie hierher! gehen Sie dorthin!*

In certain connections the directional differentiation is lost: *der Hund lief vor (neben, hinter) dem Radfahrer her* 'the dog ran along in front of (beside, behind) the cyclist', *der alte Herr fiel tot hin* 'the old gentleman fell down dead', similarly in figurative use: *sie fielen über das Essen her* 'they pitched into the food', *die Verhandlungen mit den Luftpiraten zogen sich endlos hin* 'the negotiations with the hijackers went on endlessly', also in noun formations: *der Hergang* 'the course (of events)', *Hingang* 'passing, decease', and when used in a temporal sense: *es ist schon lange her* 'it is a long time since (it happened)', *hin und wieder* 'now and again'.

It is convenient to mention here a comparable use of *zu* as a means of expressing motion towards a goal: *er kam (ging) auf mich zu* 'he came (went) up to me'.

Compound forms

An innovation in German has been the evolution of adverbs of direction compounded with (unstressed) *her*, *hin*, similarly reflecting the perspective of the speaker. The commonest are *her-*, *hinüber* 'across, over', *her-*, *hinaus* 'out', *her-*, *hinein* 'into', *her-*, *hinauf* 'up', *her-*, *hinunter* with the essentially literary synonyms *her-*, *hinab* 'down'. They are used as separable prefixes: *er springt (über den Zaun) herüber* 'he jumps over (the fence)'—towards the speaker, *er springt (über den Zaun) hinüber*—away from the speaker, *er springt über den Zaun* being of course neutral. Similarly *sie kommt die Treppe herunter* 'she comes downstairs', *sie geht die Treppe hinauf* 'she goes upstairs'.

It is important to observe that, as a general rule, the primary adverbs (*über*, *aus*, *ein*, etc.) are themselves no longer freely employable as adverbs of direction, but are purely verbal prefixes bound to the verb in question. Only occasionally do relics of their earlier use remain, as in the expressions *auf und ab*, *ein und aus*, e.g. *er springt auf und ab* 'he jumps up and down', *in 'dem Haus geht der Arzt ein und aus* 'the doctor goes in and out of that house'. Certain verbs may use the old mode beside the new: *er tritt ein* 'he walks in, enters', neutral from the perspective of the speaker, to this extent contrasting with alternative *er tritt herein* or *hinein*, further *er tritt ins Zimmer ein* no different from *er tritt ins Zimmer* 'he walks into, enters the room', again contrasting with the alternatives *er tritt ins Zimmer herein* or *hinein*. This verb also occurs in figurative senses, as *er trat in den Verein ein* 'he joined the club', *Schwierigkeiten sind eingetreten* 'difficulties have arisen'. Loss of the literal sense has, in fact, been a common fate of verbs compounded with the primary adverbs of direction. One says *er kommt (aus dem Loch) heraus* 'he comes out (of the hole)', *er geht (in das Loch) hinein* 'he goes in (into the hole)', but *kommt aus*, *geht ein* can today only have figurative meanings, e.g. *mein Vetter kommt mit seinem Gehalt gut aus* 'my cousin manages well on his salary', *der Baum geht ein* 'the tree is dying'. Whereas one can still say *treten Sie ein* 'come in', one can only say *kommen Sie herein*, in the same way only *gehen Sie hinaus* 'go out', *gehen Sie aus* having a figurative meaning 'go somewhere for pleasure, have an evening out or the like'.

In spite of the clear distinction between *her* and *hin*, illustrated above, there are instances of compounds being formed with only one or the other. The following occur with *her* only: *herbei* 'up to (a spot)', (literary) *hernieder* 'down from above', *herum* 'around', *hervor* 'forth, out'; with *hin* only: *hindurch* 'through', *hinweg* 'away, off'. It will be seen that in some cases the directional force has been lost; sometimes the adverb is used simply as a verbal prefix, often in figurative senses: *sie kamen herbeigeeilt* 'they came rushing up'—*furchtbare Blitze zuckten hernieder* 'dreadful flashes of lightning streaked down'—*sie sitzen um den Tisch (herum)* 'they sit round the table' with which compare the tongue-twister *in Ulm und um Ulm und um Ulm herum*, further *du kommst nicht drum herum* 'you can't avoid it', also colloquially replacing *umher*, e.g. *sie schleichen herum*, higher style *umher* 'they prowl around'—*die Erde bringt Früchte hervor* 'the earth brings forth fruits', *die Katze kroch hinter dem Kachelofen hervor* 'the cat crept out from behind the (tiled) stove', *solche Bemerkungen mußten Widerspruch hervorrufen* 'such remarks were bound to invite contradiction'—*das Wasser fließt durch die Röhre (hindurch)* 'the water flows through the pipe'—*die Pest raffte ihn hinweg* 'the plague carried him off', commonly in association with *über*, e.g. *er hat sich über alle Anweisungen hinweggesetzt* 'he has ignored all instructions'.

In addition to the common adverbs of direction mentioned in the first paragraph above, there are two pairs with less universal application: *her-, hinan*, and *her-, hinzu*. Of the first, only *heran* is in everyday use. It may lose the directional distinction, thus beside *komm nur heran!* 'just come closer!' one could say, e.g. *ich konnte nicht (an den Lichtschalter) heran* 'I couldn't get near (the light switch)'; it is often used figuratively: *die heranwachsende Generation* 'the rising generation'. Its formal opposite is a somewhat rare, literary word: *der Jäger stieg den Berg hinan* 'the hunter ascended the hill'. As regards the second pair, *herzu* is a literary word, an alternative to the more mundane *herbei* (above), generally occurring in association with certain verbs: *er eilte herzu* 'he hurried along (to the spot)', while *hinzu*, similarly used, embodies the idea of joining: *er eilte hinzu* 'he hurried along (to join the others)' from which use has arisen the common meaning 'in addition': *erschwerend kommt hinzu, daß er zahlungsunfähig ist* 'an additional difficulty is that he is insolvent'.

It is, on occasion, hard to decide in which direction things are going: is 'I have swallowed a fishbone' to be *ich habe eine Gräte herunter-* or *hinuntergeschluckt*? Since nobody is sure, either will do. In figurative use, directional differences tend to be blurred, if not lost altogether. One can equally well put *die Preise werden herauf-* or *hinaufgesetzt* 'the prices are going up'. Or one of the alternatives may have become standard: *halt dich aus der Angelegenheit heraus* 'keep out of the affair', *er zog seinen Aufenthalt hinaus* 'he extended his stay'.

Although the literary language is at pains to distinguish the adverbs according to the speaker's perspective, the language as ordinarily spoken today ignores the distinction. In the north the forms with *her* have been generalized, hence *herauf und herunter* 'up and down' instead of *hinauf und herunter*. Before a vowel, except in the case of (the literary word) *herab*, the element *her* is commonly reduced to *r*, hence also *rauf und runter*, and *geh rüber* 'go across' just like *komm rüber* 'come across', and such abbreviations are acceptable in informal writing, too. Compare further *wir müssen hier rein* 'we've got to go in here', *wieviel Kilometer hast du runter?* 'how many kilometres have you done?', *du hältst das Ding verkehrt (rum)* 'you're holding the thing the wrong way round', *ich mache mich an die Arbeit (ran)* 'I'm starting the job', *sie haben ihn rausgeschmissen* 'he's been chucked out' whence *Rausschmeißer* 'chucker out'. In the south, locally, the forms with *hin* have sometimes been generalized, and similarly reduced to *n*, e.g. *naus* for *hinaus*. But such abbreviations are not normally seen in print, and indeed northern forms are now widespread in southern use as well.

There is no harm in mixing the styles, if it helps: (from the visitors' book at a mountain inn) *im Nebel zogen wir hinauf, / benebelt wieder runter* 'in the fog we went up, befogged "tipsy" (we came) down again'.

16. Articles

By origin the definite article (p. 57) is a weakened form of the general demonstrative *der*, *die*, *das*, the indefinite article (p. 58) a corresponding weakening of the numeral *ein*. The articles in English are of comparable provenance. Usage in the two languages largely coincides, but can differ to the extent that the one language may need or prefer an article in cases where the other does not; less commonly, one language may require the opposite article to the other. It is chiefly these differences we seek to illustrate.

Survivals from the pre-article stage

In the oldest German, articles occur more sparingly than they do now, and the same applies to English. The reason is that this part of speech was then a relatively new phenomenon still in the process of establishing itself. It had been unknown in the parent Germanic language, and many relics of that pre-article stage remain even today, as in stereotype pairs like *Vater und Sohn* 'father and son', *Haus und Hof* 'house and home'. Some such pairs are found together with a particular preposition; in many cases these, too, will go back to ancient times, others will have arisen by analogy later: *bei Tag und Nacht* 'by day and night', *über Berg und Tal* 'over hill and dale', *unter Dach und Fach* 'under cover, safely', *mit Kind und Kegel* 'with bag and baggage, with the whole family' (*Kegel* originally 'illegitimate child'), *hinter Schloß und Riegel* 'behind bars', *in Hülle und Fülle* 'in plenty', compare also *es geht um Kopf und Kragen* (*Kragen* here 'neck'), another way of saying *es geht um Leben und Tod* 'it is a matter of life and death'. Another survival of ancient syntax is seen in pairs like *Seite an Seite* 'side by side', *Wort für Wort* 'word for word', *Fehler um Fehler* 'mistake after mistake', *Auge um Auge* 'an eye for an eye', further in phrases of the type *von Jahr zu Jahr* 'from year to year', and similarly *von Anfang bis Ende* 'from beginning to end'.

The use of the definite article has, to some extent, spread to personal names (pp. 186 f., 190), but since these are by their nature definite they traditionally appear without such qualification: *Ilse*, *Ulrich*. Where, in certain contexts, appellatives approach the status of proper names, they may be used without the article, e.g. in business correspondence: *Schreiber dieser Zeilen* 'the writer of these lines', *Überbringer der Dokumente* 'the bearer of the documents'. Close to these are the names of professions and the like which, as the complement of the verb 'to be', are similarly treated: *er ist Maurer* 'he is a bricklayer', *er blieb einfacher Matrose* 'he remained an ordinary seaman', *sie möchte Serviererin werden* 'she would like to become a waitress'. Here also *er ist Vater, sie ist Mutter* (*zweier Kinder, von zwei Kindern*) 'he is a father, she is a mother (of two children)', further *ich spreche als Freund* 'I speak as a friend', and commonly with names of nationalities: *sie ist Französin* 'she is French', but see also p. 189.

More archaic syntax and some innovations

Archaic syntax is further attested in numerous idioms where a noun is governed by a preposition, prominently among them those with *zu*, sometimes in its otherwise rare sense of rest at a place: *zu Haus* 'at home', *zu Pferd* 'on horseback', *zu Wasser und zu Lande* 'on land and sea', at other times with its usual meaning 'to': *zu Asche* 'to ashes', *zu Markt* 'to market', compare also the expression *zu Fall bringen* 'bring about someone's downfall' and a few more like it: *zu Kopf steigen* 'go to one's head', *zu Kreuz kriechen* 'eat humble pie', *zu Wort kommen* 'get a chance to speak'. In *zu Bett* both senses are potentially present: *er liegt krank zu Bett* 'he lies ill in bed', *sie bringt ihr Kind zu Bett* 'she puts her child to bed'. Examples with other prepositions: *auf Erden* 'on earth', *bei Tisch* 'at table', *nach Haus* 'home(wards)', *über Nacht* 'overnight', in terms associated with shipping: *auf Deck* 'on deck', *an Bord* 'on board', *über Bord* 'overboard', together with such expressions as *vor Anker liegen* 'lie at anchor', *an Land gehen* 'go ashore', *in See stechen* 'put to sea', *sich über Wasser halten* 'keep one's head above water'. Notice the mining terms *über Tage, unter Tage* 'above ground, underground', whence *Tagebau* 'open-cast mining'.

Although the two languages are in broad agreement on essentials, they often go their separate ways in matters of detail. Original syntax is preserved in English 'in heaven, in hell' whereas German has introduced the article: *im Himmel, in der Hölle*. By and large, German is less conservative in this respect than English and there are many more examples of this contrast, cf. *in die Schule* 'to school', *in der Schule* 'at school', *nach der Kirche* 'after church', *aus dem Gefängnis* 'out of prison', *vor dem Parlament* 'before parliament', *zur See* 'at sea', *mit der Bahn, mit dem Zug, mit der Fähre, mit dem Flugzeug* 'by rail, train, ferry, plane'. Furthermore, the use of the article is generalized in German: *die Hölle auf Erden* 'hell on earth'. It may also be observed that not all the forms mentioned in the previous paragraph are exclusive; alternatives are available for a few of them. Beside *zu Bett* one meets *im* or *ins Bett* as the case may be, innovating constructions employing the article, and doubtless commoner today. The phrase *zu Markt* is less usual than *auf den Markt*, while the idiom *auf Erden* (where *Erden* is the old inflected dative) belongs to lofty, especially biblical style: *der Himmel auf Erden* 'heaven on earth', otherwise *auf der Erde*.

Analogical formations

The preservation of so large a number of traditional phrases not using the article led to many analogical formations so that the pattern preposition plus noun remained productive. Both languages are affected, but again examples need not overlap, though they more often do so: *auf Kredit* 'on credit', *aus Versehen* 'by mistake', *außer Betrieb* 'out of order' (as a machine), *bei Versagen* 'in case of failure', *in Wirklichkeit* 'in reality', *nach Bedarf* 'as required', *ohne Unterstützung* 'without support', *vor Gebrauch* 'before use'. Compare *ein Zimmer mit Lage nach Süden* 'a room facing south' and such expressions as *in Erscheinung treten* 'become visible, appear', *in Schach halten* 'keep in check', *sich in Szene setzen* 'show off' and colloquialisms like *mit Rad fahren* 'go by bike', *auf Dienst gehen* 'go to work'.

The article is also frequently missing when the noun is qualified by an adjective: *auf geheimnisvolle Weise* 'in a mysterious way', *auf offener Strecke* 'on an open stretch' (of road, etc.), *aus erster Hand* 'at first hand', *aus eigenem Antrieb* 'of one's own accord', *bei guter Gesundheit* 'in good health', *bei strömendem Regen* 'in (the) pouring rain', *in tiefster Not* 'in most dire distress', *in weiter Ferne* 'a long way off', *mit großem Erfolg* 'with great success', *mit reicher Beute* 'with a good bag (catch, haul)', *nach kurzer Zeit* 'after a short time', *nach langjährigem Gebrauch* 'after years of use'. The construction may have a formal ring: *ein Haus mit schönem Garten* 'a house with (a) beautiful garden' beside ordinary *mit einem schönen Garten*. A noun with a dependent genitive likewise often appears without an article: *nach Art des Hauses* 'after the custom of the house', *in Gegenwart* (but synonymous *im Beisein*) *von Zeugen* 'in the presence of witnesses', *gegen Ende des Jahres* (= *gegen Jahresende*) 'towards the end of the year', also in apposition: *gegen Ende Mai* 'towards the end of May'.

Other constructions without an article

In several idioms the complement of the verb 'to be' is commonly used without an article: *das ist Sache der Polizei* 'that is a matter for the police', *es ist Mode* (*Sitte*) *geworden* 'it has become the fashion (custom)' and the same may apply to the direct object of a verb: *Hand anlegen* 'lend a hand', *(festen) Fuß fassen* 'find one's feet', *Familie haben* 'have a family (children)', often in agreement with English: *Schritt halten* 'keep pace', *Hilfe leisten* 'render aid', *Wurzel schlagen* 'take root'.

There is a marked tendency not to put an article when two or more nouns are brought together. Whereas one finds e.g. *im Krieg* 'in war', *im Frieden* 'in peace', when occurring separately, they are generally coupled as *in Krieg und Frieden*; one sits *beim Kaffee* 'having coffee', but *bei Kaffee und Kuchen* 'having coffee and cake'. The practice applies equally to proper names: *am Rhein* 'on the Rhine', *an der Donau* 'on the Danube', but usually combining as *an Rhein und Donau*, and similarly *Rhein, Main und Donau sind für die Binnenschiffahrt wichtig* 'The Rhine, Main, and Danube are important for inland navigation'.

Use with names of substances

Practice differs here from English in that the article may appear in general statements: *nur der Wein wird besser, wenn er anfängt, alt zu werden* 'only wine improves when it starts to get old'. Nevertheless the article is frequently omitted: besides *das Geld regiert die Welt* 'money rules the world', also (saying) *Geld regiert die Welt*, similarly *(das) Gold ist teurer als (das) Silber* 'gold is dearer than silver'. In such cases, the examples without the article could actually be felt as having a higher stylistic value, compare the proverbial *Reden ist Silber, Schweigen ist Gold* 'speech is silver, silence is golden'.

In certain usages, however, the article is obligatory where English may omit it: *Amphibien laichen im Wasser* 'amphibians spawn in (the) water', *man kann nicht von der Luft leben* 'one can't live on air', *es steht vorerst nur auf dem Papier* 'so far it's only on paper'.

Use with abstract nouns

It is most noticeable that abstract nouns in German often take the definite article in circumstances where English has none. But then again, usage may on occasion correspond exactly, while at other times options feasible in the one language are not matched in the other. Certain indications could be given, incidentally, under other headings in this chapter. Thus articles may be necessary to mark grammatical case (p. 188), they are regularly omitted when nouns are coupled together (above). It is, however, scarcely possible to formulate digestible rules to cover the whole field, for one is dealing with an idiomatic and to a large extent lexical problem, when each case must be taken on its own merits. The overall situation is further complicated by usage in the south which may reflect a local preference for the article, p. 190. With such intractable material, we felt the best practical course was to illustrate typical uses of sample nouns—*Freiheit, Glück, Liebe, Mut*—in this way conveying some impression of a complex and subtle reality.

F r e i h e i t——compare the general statement *in unserem Land herrscht Freiheit* 'there is freedom in our country' with the reply to a specific question: *warum nimmt man diese Chaoten nicht in Schutzhaft?*

— *in unserem Land herrscht die Freiheit* 'why aren't these anarchists taken into protective custody?—there is freedom in our country' i.e. 'the freedom to be an anarchist'. Similarly *der Kampf um Freiheit geht weiter* 'the struggle for freedom continues' is a general statement, *der Kampf um die Freiheit geht weiter* is specific, so that one now envisages concrete demands for, say, freedom of speech or action, hence the article is also used when such things are spelt out: *der Kampf um die Freiheit der Rede, des Handelns*. Further, as a general truth: *überall streben die Unterdrückten nach Freiheit* 'the oppressed everywhere strive for freedom', but *wir werden ihnen die Freiheit geben* 'we shall give them their (now specific!) freedom' or likewise *wir werden ihnen zur Freiheit verhelfen* 'we shall assist them to gain their freedom'. Other contrasting examples: (Böll) *Freiheit wird nie geschenkt, immer nur gewonnen* 'freedom is never given, (always) only won', (Virchow) *die Freiheit ist nicht die Willkür, beliebig zu handeln* 'freedom is not licence to act as one pleases'. The same distinction between the general and the specific can be made when the noun is qualified by an adjective: *(die) politische Freiheit steht auf dem Spiel* 'political freedom is at stake', *es geht um die Einschränkung persönlicher* or *der persönlichen Freiheit* 'it is a question of limiting personal freedom', with English style ignoring the nuances.

Examples involving idioms: *dort liegt der Weg in die Freiheit* 'there lies the way to freedom', *die Menschen (Tiere) wurden in Freiheit gesetzt* 'the people (animals) were set free', *die ehemalige Kolonie wurde in die Freiheit entlassen* 'the former colony was granted its freedom', *die Franzosen leben in Freiheit* 'the French live in freedom', *dieser Vogel kann nur in (der) Freiheit (= in freier Wildbahn) leben* 'this bird can only live in the wild'.

G l ü c k——*das Glück hat uns verlassen* 'luck has deserted us', *ihm lächelt das Glück* 'fortune smiles on him', *das Glück ist dem Kühnen immer hold* 'fortune favours the brave', *welch ein Glück!* 'how fortunate!', *ein Glück, daß du einen Korb mitgebracht hast* 'a good job you brought a basket with you', *wir hatten das Glück, es mit eigenen Augen zu sehen* 'we had the good fortune to see it with our own eyes', *da hat sie Glück gehabt* 'that was a stroke of luck for her', *ich wünsche Ihnen Glück* 'I wish you luck'—*sie erlebten zwei Jahre ungetrübten Glückes* 'they had two years of perfect bliss', *um das ungetrübte Glück der letzten zwei Jahre beneide ich Sie* 'I envy you the perfect bliss of these last two years'—*auf Glück oder Unglück* 'for better or for worse', *auf gut Glück* 'on the off chance', *zum Glück* 'fortunately', *die Jagd nach dem Glück* 'the pursuit of happiness', *du kannst von Glück reden, daß dir das gelungen ist* 'you can count yourself lucky that you managed to do it', *die Braut strahlte vor Glück* 'the bride was radiant with happiness', *wir hatten Glück im Unglück* 'we were lucky that it wasn't much worse'.

L i e b e——*es war Liebe auf den ersten Blick* 'it was love at first sight', *(die) Liebe zum Vaterland ist uns anerzogen* 'we have been taught to love our country', *(die) Liebe zwischen den beiden ist längst gestorben* 'love between the two died long ago', (Menge) *nun aber bleiben Glaube, Hoffnung, Liebe, diese drei, die größte unter ihnen aber ist die Liebe* 'but now are left faith, hope, and love, these three, but the greatest of these is love'—*tun Sie mir die Liebe* 'do me a favour', *eine Liebe ist der anderen wert* 'one good turn deserves another'—*ein Wort der Liebe* 'a word of love', *ein Wort von Liebe* 'a word about love', *Werke der Liebe* 'deeds of charity'—*(die) platonische Liebe* 'Platonic love', *(die) geschlechtliche Liebe* 'sexual love'—*sie haben aus Liebe geheiratet* 'they married for love', *er entbrannte in Liebe zu ihr* 'he fell madly in love with her', *sie hatte kein Glück in der Liebe* 'she had no luck in love', *von der Liebe kann man nicht leben* 'the flames of love won't boil the pot', *sie tun alles mit Liebe* 'they do it all with loving care', *sie tun alles aus Liebe* 'they do everything just for love', *nichts geht über die Liebe* 'there's nothing greater than love'.

M u t——*im letzten Augenblick verließ ihn der Mut* 'courage left him at the last moment', *dazu fehlt ihr der Mut* 'she hasn't got the courage (to do it)', *dazu gehört Mut* 'that takes courage', (cliché) *nur nicht den Mut verlieren!* 'don't lose heart', *er bekam wieder Mut* 'he picked up courage', *wird er den Mut aufbringen?* 'will he muster the courage?', *das macht uns Mut* 'that gives us courage'—*er schöpfte neuen Mut* 'he drew fresh courage', *er hat einen unbezwinglichen Mut* 'he has indomitable courage'—*sie verteidigten sich mit dem Mut der Verzweiflung* 'they defended themselves with the courage of desperation'.

Article with nouns denoting parts of the body

Whereas English uses the possessive pronoun in sentences like 'shut your eyes and open your mouth!', German normally responds with *mach die Augen zu und den Mund auf!*, the articles being understood as referring to the person addressed. At the same time it is quite permissible to make up the sentence *mach deine Augen auf und deinen Mund zu!* which will, however, usually involve some modification of the sense, as when emphasis is placed on 'your'.

If the definite article does not refer back to the subject, a dative of interest is of course required: *sie trat ihm auf den Fuß* 'she stepped on his foot', alternatively *sie trat auf seinen Fuß*. The construction with the dative is also found in many cases where the article actually refers back to the subject, as in such everyday sentences as *ich wasche mir die Hände, putze mir die Zähne, kämme mir die Haare, lasse sie mir schneiden* 'I'm washing my hands, cleaning my teeth, combing my hair, having it cut'. But not all sentences follow this pattern, and the possessive pronoun may be an alternative, as above; indeed it may be the only possible form: *ich wasche meine Hände in Unschuld* 'I wash my hands of it'.

Article with nouns denoting items of clothing and the like

In certain respects practice is comparable to that found with nouns denoting parts of the body (above). The article alone may suffice: *man trägt den Hut auf dem Kopf* 'one wears one's hat on one's head', *nimm den Hut ab* 'take your hat off'. Generally, however, the precise sense depends on the context: *sie zieht die Schuhe an* can mean either 'she's putting the shoes on' or 'she's putting her (own) shoes on', synonymous with (similarly ambiguous) *sie zieht sich die Schuhe an*, but *sie zieht ihr die Schuhe an* (northern English) 'she's putting her her shoes on'. A possessive pronoun may appear: *sie zieht ihre Schuhe an*, a sentence most likely to occur when the stress is on 'her', i.e. somebody else's. Many everyday sentences are per se ambiguous: *ich ziehe mir das Hemd über* 'I'm putting my (or, the) shirt on', *nimmst du dir den Schal um?* 'are you putting your (or, the) scarf on?', others tend to occur in contexts where only one meaning is usual: *ich putze mir die Stiefel* 'I'm cleaning my boots', *setze dir die Brille auf!* 'put your glasses on!' Under this rubric, too, examples like *tragen Sie stets den Personalausweis bei sich* 'always have your identity card with you'.

Lewis Carroll wrote ' "Take off your hat," the King said to the Hatter. "It isn't mine," said the Hatter.' This needs to be in German *"Nimm deinen Hut ab," sagte der König zum Hutmacher. "Es ist nicht mein Hut"*, *sagte der Hutmacher*, in this way rescuing at least some of the original wit.

Article with proper names

Although proper names may commonly be used without a (definite) article, there are significant exceptions, as follows.

The article is needed when the name is qualified by an adjective: (Grimm) *der getreue Heinrich* 'faithful Henry', *die kluge Else* 'clever Elsa'. As with ordinary nouns (p. 188) the article may be used to indicate the genitive, a construction often found with classical names and the like: *die Kriegszüge des Alexander* 'Alexander's campaigns', *die Gedichte der Sappho* 'Sappho's poems'; it is the rule with names ending in -*s*, cf. *die Taufe des Johannes* 'the baptism of John', *das Ei des Kolumbus* 'the surprisingly simple solution to a problem'. Otherwise the construction is used when the name is accompanied by a title: *der Antrag des Fräulein Bosse* 'Miss Bosse's application', *der Wohnsitz des (Herrn) Professor Lehnert* 'Professor Lehnert's residence' (where *Herrn* is an optional addition to *Professor*). Such genitives occur in formal contexts; it will be noticed that the name itself is not inflected, similarly *des getreuen Heinrich* (above), often too *das Problem des gespaltenen Deutschland* rather than *Deutschlands* 'the problem of divided Germany'. The article may also indicate the dative: *er stellte Herbert der Helga vor* 'he introduced Herbert to Helga'.

The article is used descriptively. It occurs in colloquial style: *ist der Pohl da?* 'is P. there?', implying that Pohl is well known to those concerned. In the case of a female, however, the article is also apposite in formal style if needed to distinguish the sex: *die Brüning wurde für schuldig erklärt* '(the woman) B. was found guilty'. The article is further regularly employed in connection with the names of works of art or literature: *der Laokoon, die Emilia Galotti*, hence *eine Aufführung des Faust* 'a performance of F.' The article is likewise used with certain geographical terms, p. 55 f.

Miscellaneous examples of the use of the definite article

There is some preference for the article with the names of meals: *das Frühstück wird um acht Uhr eingenommen* 'breakfast is taken at eight o'clock'. In a less formal context use may be optional: *hast du (das) Frühstück schon bestellt?* 'have you ordered breakfast?' The article is always present after a preposition: *vor dem* or *vorm Essen* 'before eating, before a meal', *nach dem Mittagessen* 'after lunch', *beim Kaffeetrinken* 'at afternoon coffee', *zum Abendbrot* 'for supper'.

The article is commonly found with the names of months (p. 83): *der April war heuer kalt, aber im Mai wurde es wärmer* 'April was cold this year, but in May it got warmer'. Except with *in*, however, the article is unusual after prepositions: *das Wetter war kalt für April, aber seit Mai ist es recht warm* 'the weather was cold for April, but since May it has been quite warm'. The article is similarly common with the names of seasons: *der Frühling gilt als die beste Reisezeit* 'spring is regarded as the best time for travelling', *im Herbst fallen die Blätter* 'in autumn the leaves fall', but not in sentences of the type: *es ist Sommer* 'it is summer', *es wird bald Herbst* 'autumn will soon be here', cf. also *meine Frau geht Sommer wie Winter schwimmen* 'my wife goes swimming all the year round'.

The German definite article corresponds to the English indefinite in such idioms as *zehn Mark das Stück (das Pfund)* 'ten marks apiece (a pound)', also with expressions of time, e.g. *zweimal die Stunde (die Woche)* alternatively *in der Stunde (in der Woche)* 'twice an hour (week)'.

Certain nouns used in the plural in a general sense take the definite article where the corresponding English has no article at all: *die Geschmäcke sind verschieden* 'tastes differ', *die Mieten sind wieder gestiegen* 'rents have gone up again', *das verstößt gegen die guten Sitten* 'that offends against good manners'.

Article as indicator of case

An article, otherwise wanting, may be necessary to mark the dative case: *die meisten Engländer ziehen Tee dem Kaffee vor* 'most English people prefer tea to coffee'. The same is true of the genitive: *die Kaufkraft des Geldes* 'the purchasing power of money', though the meaning can equally well be 'of the money', depending on context as regularly with any such genitive. Occurrences of the genitive article with abstract nouns (p. 183) are particularly frequent: *der Tag der Arbeit* 'Labour Day', *die Stunde des Todes* 'the hour of death', *ein Jahrzehnt des Chaos* 'a decade of chaos'. Compare *er braucht Ruhe* 'he needs rest' with the same in higher style: *er bedarf der Ruhe*. An example in the plural: *das Guinness-Buch der Rekorde* 'the Guinness Book of Records'.

See also 'Article with proper names' above.

Article and preposition as inseparable unit

Most of the common prepositions can combine with certain forms of the definite article to produce contracted words. The forms concerned are sg. acc. *den* m., acc. *das* n., dat. *dem* m.n., dat. *der* f., the contractions being as follows.

Prepositions combining with *den* are *hinter, über, unter, vor* giving *hintern, übern, untern, vorn*.

Prepositions combining with *das* are *an, auf, durch, für, hinter, in, über, um, unter, vor* giving *ans, aufs, durchs, fürs, hinters, ins, übers, ums, unters, vors*.

Prepositions combining with *dem* are *an, in, von* giving *am, im, vom*, and *bei, hinter, über, unter, vor, zu* giving *beim, hinterm, überm, unterm, vorm, zum*.

Only *zu* combines with *der* giving *zur*.

Not all occurrences of contraction to be heard in ordinary speech are normally reproduced in writing. One may often hear (from *den*) *an'n, auf'n, durch'n, für'n, in'n,* (from dat. pl. *den*) *an'n, auf'n, aus'n, in'n, mit'n, nach'n, zu'n,* (from *das*) *gegen's,* (from *dem*) *auf'm, aus'm, nach'm*. Further discussion on p. 15.

As to the respective use of the contracted and uncontracted forms, it may be said that the former are, in the first place, optional variants of the latter: *an dem* or *am Fluß* 'by the river', *auf das* or *aufs Dach* 'on to the roof'. The contracted forms are, however, a great deal commoner and may be regarded more or less as the norm in spoken German. Indeed in many cases the contracted form has become the invariable standard: *am Anfang* 'in the beginning', *am Tag* 'by day', *am Leben* 'alive', *am Neckar* 'on the N.', also when giving dates: *am 13. (dreizehnten) Juni* 'on the 13th of June', and in superlative forms: *am besten*, and usually *aufs beste* 'best' (pp. 63, 68), further *aufs Haar* 'to a T', *Hand aufs Herz* 'cross my heart', *fürs Auge* 'for the eye', i.e. 'to look at, admire', *fürs Leben* 'for life', *im Ernst* 'in earnest', *im voraus* 'in advance', *ins Freie, im Freien* 'into, in the open (air)'.

Many examples are associated with idiomatic phraseology: *sie sind ihr ans Herz gewachsen* 'she has taken them to her heart', similarly *ans Werk gehen* 'set about a job', *übers Herz bringen* 'find in one's heart', *ums Leben kommen* 'lose one's life', *ins Fäustchen lachen* 'laugh up one's sleeve' and other phrases using the diminutive, p. 128, further *zur Sprache bringen* 'bring up (for discussion)' and expressions of the type *das ist zum Lachen (Weinen)* 'that's ridiculous (something to cry about)' and *zum Krüppel werden* 'become a cripple' (pp. 297 f.), and lastly in tavern names and suchlike: *(Gasthaus) zur Scharfen Ecke* 'Sharp Corner Inn', *(Apotheke) zum Weißen Schwan* 'White Swan Pharmacy'.

Indefinite article

Differences between the two languages in respect of this article are less complex than in the case of the definite article. A few of these differences have already appeared above, as in the observation (p. 181) that names of professions, nationalities, etc. are found without an article in sentences like *ich bin Engländer* 'I'm English'. An article may, however, be used: *ich bin ein Engländer* 'I'm an Englishman' when there will generally be an added nuance, say, 'hence I am as I am, I can't help it because I'm English'. When, on a memorable occasion in Berlin, President Kennedy said *ich bin ein Berliner*, he conveyed the sentiment 'I'm one of you', whereas *ich bin Berliner* means rather baldly 'I am a Berliner (having been born and bred in that city)'.

The indefinite article is found in German in sentences of the type *er trägt den Titel eines Professors* 'he bears the title of professor', *sie hat die Stelle einer Bibliothekarin inne* 'she holds the position of librarian'.

See further under 'Articles in Southern German' below.

Generalizing use of articles

Both languages having evolved the generalizing use of the article, both definite and indefinite. But developments have sometimes been divergent, as may be seen from the examples to follow.

In certain sentences it is the definite article which has become standard in German: *der Mensch denkt, Gott lenkt* 'man proposes, God disposes', *der Mensch ist sterblich* 'man is mortal'. It is possible after *als*, though more often omitted, e.g. *die Schlange gilt als das Sinnbild* (or simply *als Sinnbild*) *der Falschheit* 'the serpent is regarded as the symbol of falsity'. In other instances the two articles are virtually synonymous: *der (ein) Mensch ist manchmal ein gefährliches Wesen* 'man (a human being) is sometimes a dangerous creature', *soll die (eine) Frau dem (einem) Mann untertan sein?* 'is the (a) woman to be subservient to the (a) man?'. If such sentences are construed in the plural, the definite article (unless required to denote the case, p. 188) will be optionally omitted: *(die) Menschen sind manchmal gefährliche Wesen,* and *sollen (die) Frauen den Männern untertan sein?* Compare further *man muß (die) Menschen nehmen, wie sie sind* 'one must take people as they are', and likewise synonymous *(die) Leute.* Lastly, there are times when the indefinite article alone is possible: *sogar ein Kind weiß das* 'even a child knows that'.

Articles in southern German

The southern colloquial makes freer use of the articles than is usual elsewhere. The definite article regularly appears before Christian names: *der Joseph, die Maria,* and before surnames: *der* or *die Huber,* hence e.g. *hast du den Joseph gesehen?* 'have you seen J.?', further *ich habe es von der Frau Kammenhuber gekauft* 'I've bought it from Mrs K.'

But more surprising is the use of the indefinite article: *wir haben ein gutes Fleisch zu Mittag* 'we're having a nice piece of meat for dinner', otherwise *ein gutes Stück Fleisch,* further *der Bauer hat dort ein Heu liegen* 'the farmer has some hay lying over there', otherwise just *Heu.* Such use may be extended to abstract nouns: *um die Hausaufgaben gut zu machen, muß man eine Ruhe haben* 'to do one's homework well one must have peace and quiet' instead of just *Ruhe,* and compare *mit den Kindern* (closer to dialect: *mit die Kinder*) *muß man eine Geduld haben* 'one must have patience with children' with standard *mit Kindern muß man Geduld haben.* This usage is sometimes found in local idioms unknown—and unappreciated—elsewhere: *ich hab so'n Schlaf* 'I'm so sleepy' i.e. *ich bin so schläfrig.*

17. Pronouns

PERSONAL PRONOUNS

First and second persons

THE use of the 1st person *ich* 'I', *wir* 'we' poses no problems for the English speaker, except perhaps to note that our employment, colloquially, of the plural for the singular is not paralleled in German, e.g. 'give us a kiss' has to be, say, *gib mir ein Küßchen*.

The 2nd person pronouns are more problematic. Sg. *du* and pl. *ihr* 'you' are essentially pronouns of familiarity. They are used between relatives and close friends, workmates and students, and other ranks. Children use them to each other and are so addressed by adults, until after an embarrassing phase of uncertainty somewhere in the middle teens, young people become old enough to be addressed as *Sie*, the girls tending to reach maturity also in this respect a little before the boys. Some closed organizations, such as trades unions and left-wing political parties, may employ these pronouns in their internal business.

If one speaks to animals or objects, *du* and *ihr* are the required pronouns, and where English has 'thou', German has correspondingly *du*. The familiar forms are found in fairy tales and the like, in biblical and older historical contexts, the polite form *Sie* not developing until the seventeenth century: *da sagte Kyrus zum König der Lyder: Fordere, was du willst, ich will es dir sofort erfüllen* 'then Cyrus said to the king of the Lydians: Ask for whatever you want, (and) I will fulfil your wish at once', *Calgacus sprach: Wenn ihr daher jetzt in die Schlacht zieht, denkt an eure Vorfahren und an eure Nachkommen* 'C. spoke: So when you now go into battle, think of your forebears and of your descendants'. If a polite form is required, then *Ihr*, e.g. *der Spiegel antwortete: Frau Königin, Ihr seid die Schönste im Land* 'the mirror answered: you, O queen, are the fairest in the land'.

In other circumstances, the pronoun of address is the polite, respectful *Sie*, singular or plural. Its meaning is literally 'They', hence the construction with the 3rd person plural verb: *Sie sind* 'you are'. Locally in Upper German, *Ihr* (regularly with the 2nd person plural verb) rather than *Sie* may be heard when more than one person is being spoken to.

Using *du* is called *(das) Duzen*, a term in very common use: *sie duzen sich* 'they say *du* to each other'; it has given rise to such expressions as *Duzbruder* 'intimate friend, pal', also *Duzschwester*. The opposite of *Duzen* is *Siezen* 'saying *Sie*'.

Notice the idioms *wir beide* 'both of us', *ihr* (or *Sie*) *alle* 'all of you'.

The genitive of these pronouns is essentially a bookish form, found chiefly after a handful of adjectives and verbs governing this case: *sie hat sich meiner angenommen* 'she has befriended me', *ich schäme mich deiner* 'I'm ashamed of you' (ordinarily *wegen dir*, or *deinetwegen*, p. 73), *ihr seid euer nicht mehr mächtig* 'you are no longer in control of yourselves'; also before numerals: *wir waren unser vier* 'there were four of us', further (slightly formal) clichés of the type *das ist unser beider (unser aller) Hoffnung* 'that is what both of us (all of us) hope', and compare *wir beide*, etc., above. As the genitive of the object, the pronoun is qualified by *selbst* '-self', p. 209: *die Überschätzung deiner selbst in gefährlichen Situationen kann zur Katastrophe führen* 'overestimation of yourself in dangerous situations can lead to catastrophe'.

Third person

The 3rd person pronoun is modified in the singular for gender: *er* 'he', *sie* 'she', *es* 'it', but in the plural uniformly *sie* 'they', as in English. Since German, however, retains grammatical gender, e.g. *der Spiegel* 'the mirror', *die Wand* 'the wall', *das Bett* 'the bed', the corresponding singular pronouns are *er*, *sie*, *es* respectively, whereas English knows only 'it': *wir haben einen neuen Spiegel gekauft; er war ganz schön teuer* 'we have bought a new mirror; it was pretty expensive', *die Wand ist frisch gestrichen, und ich finde sie sehr schön* 'the wall has just been painted, and I think it is very nice', *aber das Bett ist altmodisch; es paßt nicht mehr so recht ins Zimmer* 'but the bed is old-fashioned; it doesn't really look right in the room any more'.

As with other persons (above), the genitive of the 3rd person pronoun is essentially a bookish form and used in the same way: *o Herr, erbarme dich seiner (ihrer)!* 'O Lord, have mercy on him (on her, them)!', *es* (also *sie*, in literary style only) *waren ihrer vier* 'there were four of them', *ich bin mir dessen bewußt* 'I am conscious (or, aware) of it'. This last is, in formal style, also used attributively: *im neunzehnten Jahrhundert entstand der Sozialismus. Dessen Ziel bestand darin, das wirtschaftliche und politische Leben nach den Bedürfnissen der Gesamtheit zu gestalten* 'socialism arose in the nineteenth century. Its aim was to organize economic and political life in accordance with the needs of society as a whole'. Such usage proliferates in officialese: *Frau Fuhrmann und deren Adoptivsohn wurde eine Sozialwohnung zugewiesen* 'Mrs F. and her adopted son were allocated a council flat'.

The 3rd person pronoun is necessary in comparative clauses

introduced by *wie* '(such) as, like': *ein Weihnachtsstollen, wie ihn meine Großmutter gebacken hat, den gibt's nicht mehr* 'a Christmas fruit cake like my grandmother used to bake, that's a thing of the past'. Usage in the two languages may, however, coincide: *das Haus, wie ich es in Erinnerung habe, war geräumig und doch leicht, sauber zu halten* 'the house, as I remember it, was spacious and yet easy to keep clean'.

In the nature of things, the 3rd person pronoun can only be used in reference to someone or something already mentioned or implied. It has thus, inherently, the quality of a demonstrative. In fact, the boundary between it and a demonstrative proper is not always clear cut, so that *er, sie, es* are not infrequently replaceable by the general demonstrative *der, die, das*. The form *dessen* (above), the only one available for the gen. neut. sg. of the personal pronoun is, of course, properly the demonstrative. See further pp. 201 ff.

Extended use of *es*

The functions of *es*, like those of its counterpart 'it', are far-reaching. Practice in the two languages often agrees, but just as often differs.

We first note that *es* occurs as the subject of a construction with the verb 'to be' and a noun predicate, whether singular or plural: *nun kommt jemand — es ist der Briefträger, die Eierfrau, das Kind von nebenan* 'now someone's coming—it's the postman, the woman who sells eggs, the youngster from next door', *wer sind diese Menschen? — es sind Türken*, or *Türken sind es* 'who are these people?—they are Turks'. Notice further: *wer ist es? wer ist da? — ich bin es (bin's), wir sind es (sind's), es ist Ihre Schwester, es sind seine Eltern* 'who is it? who is there?—it's me, it's us, it's your sister, it's his parents', *waren Sie es?* 'was it you?', *wer glaubst du, war es, sie oder ich?* 'who do you think it was, her or me?', *du warst es also* 'so it was you', *es war mein Bruder* (or *mein Bruder war es*), *der mir den Fußball kaufte* 'it was my brother who bought me the football'.

Like its English counterpart, the pronoun often anticipates an infinitive: *es ist nicht leicht, immer auf dem Posten zu sein* 'it's not easy to be always on your toes'. In this function *es* may be the object: *ich kann es nicht aushalten, täglich genau dasselbe zu tun* 'I cannot stand doing exactly the same thing every day', but the use of the pronoun is then generally optional: *wir konnten (es) kaum vermeiden, ihm die Wahrheit zu sagen* 'we could hardly avoid telling him the truth'. A *daß*-clause may be similarly anticipated: *es liegt auf der Hand, daß die Schulden zurückgezahlt werden müssen* 'it is obvious that the debts will have to be repaid'; with *es* as the object: *er hat es geschafft, daß der Mietpreis heruntergesetzt wurde* 'he has managed to get the rent reduced', but again the use of the pronoun is, as a rule, optional: *er hat (es) nicht verheimlicht, daß alles Geld aufgebraucht war* 'he has not concealed the fact that all the money was used up'. Other clauses may be anticipated in the same way: *man darf es ihm nicht verübeln, wenn er angesichts so vieler Enttäuschungen jetzt endgültig absagt* 'one must not blame him if, in view of so many disappointments, he now calls the arrangements off', *ich begreife (es) nicht, warum der Unfall nicht früher gemeldet wurde* 'I cannot comprehend why the accident was not reported earlier'.

The pronoun also appears as the substitute for a substantival or adjectival predicate: *er ist ein Dieb, ich bin es nicht* 'he is a thief, I am not', *du bist glücklich, sie ist es auch* 'you are happy, she is too'. Reference may be to a whole clause, either as a subject: *es ist schon lange her, seitdem ich ihn das letzte Mal sah* 'it's a long time since I last saw him', or as an accusative object: *er wird denselben Fehler wieder machen, ich sehe es kommen* 'he will make the same mistake again, I see it coming'. The dative object is expressed by the demonstrative, p. 203.

As an object, *es* is used in many idioms without regard to an antecedent, thus moving away from its pronominal function proper, in principle as in English. And indeed, idioms in the two languages sometimes coincide: *man macht es sich leicht (schwer)* 'one makes it easy (difficult) for oneself', or more or less coincide: *sie hat es in sich* 'she has it in her', though the German can also refer to things, e.g. *dieses Getränk hat es in sich* 'this drink has a kick in it'. But more often the wording of the respective idioms is quite different: *er wird es weit bringen* 'he will go far', *die Deutschen nehmen es mit Vorschriften sehr genau* 'the Germans are very strict about regulations', *er hatte es auf ihr Geld abgesehen, also wollte er es sich mit ihr nicht verderben* 'he was out for her money, so he wanted to keep on good terms with her'.

The pronoun is widely used as a sentence-opener, *es* in this function often corresponding to 'there': *es kommt eine Zeit, wo man sagen muß: genug ist genug* 'there comes a time when one has to say: enough is enough'. Comparison with parallel sentences construed without *es* reveals differences of emphasis or style. The sentence *es waren viele junge Menschen anwesend* 'there were many young people present' is a neutrally couched statement, whereas the alternative *viele junge Menschen waren anwesend* places an emphasis on the subject which, in the spoken language, could be brought out further by affective stressing. In other instances, however, the construction helps to highlight the subject: *es wird 'dies nicht das erste Mal sein* 'this won't be the first time', contrasting with the alternative which, however, will tend to be differently stressed: *dies wird nicht das 'erste Mal sein* 'this won't be the 'first time', although the stressing '*dies wird nicht das erste Mal sein* is not excluded. In many cases, the presence of *es* produces more elevated style. It can be poetic, as *es scheint die Sonne* 'the sun shines', while *die Sonne scheint* is the ordinary, prosaic statement. Or it can carry a note of formality: in the *Bundestag* one could hear the announcement *es spricht der Bundeskanzler* 'the Federal Chancellor will speak'. The degree of formality is not necessarily excessive: *die Mutter sagte zum Kind: sei ruhig, es spricht der Vater* 'the mother said to the child: be quiet, father's speaking', and is often quite slight: *es folgt der Wetterbericht* 'the weather report follows'. The verb may be in the passive: *es werden neue Wohnungen* (alternatively *neue Wohnungen werden*) *gebaut* 'new flats are being built', *es wurde den Gefangenen* (beside *den Gefangenen wurde*) *die Freiheit geschenkt* 'the captives were given their freedom'.

Regarding *es* in impersonal constructions see pp. 200, 249, 278 ff.

Reflexive pronoun

The 3rd person pronoun has an invariable reflexive form *sich*; it functions both as an accusative: *man sieht sich im Spiegel* 'one sees oneself in the mirror', and in the dative: *strickt sie sich einen Schal?* 'is she knitting herself a scarf?', *sie kamen wieder 'zu sich* 'they came to again'. One notices that *sich* is properly an accusative (being formed like *mich*, *dich*) and its use was, in fact, originally confined to this case, the dative having the non-reflexive pronoun. This older practice remains locally in Upper German, where one can hear, e.g. *wollen Sie Ihnen die Fotos anschauen?* 'do you want to have a look at the photographs?' for standard *wollen Sie sich*, etc. Its genitive *seiner* is used in connection with *selbst* '-self': *man ist seiner selbst nicht mehr mächtig* 'one is no longer in control of oneself', cf. p. 192.

The reflexive pronoun is often used in a reciprocal sense: (as an accusative) *sie haben sich gesucht und gefunden* 'they have sought for, and found, each other', said of those who are well matched, (as a dative) *sie reichen sich die Hände* 'they shake (each other's) hands', *sie sind sich ähnlich* 'they are like one another'. Reciprocal *sich* is not infrequently strengthened by *gegenseitig* 'mutually': *sie betrogen sich gegenseitig* 'they deceived each other'. A few intransitive verbs are commonly found with reciprocal *sich*, thus *sie streiten sich* 'they quarrel'. One party can be made the subject and the second joined by *mit*, hence *sie streitet sich mit ihm* 'she quarrels with him'. By analogy, transitive verbs may be affected: *sie versteht sich mit ihm* 'she gets on with him', further *sie schreibt sich mit ihm* 'she corresponds with him'. In these last examples the pronoun has, of course, lost its reciprocal character and become purely reflexive again.

The present pronoun occasionally occurs in reciprocal use after a preposition; it is customary to say, e.g. *sie teilten den Gewinn unter sich* 'they divided the profit among themselves', but generally speaking reciprocal *sich* is replaced by *einander* in such cases. The two pronouns may often be used as alternatives, see further p. 209.

The 1st and 2nd person pronouns have, of course, no special reflexive (or reciprocal) form, hence *ich sehe mich im Spiegel* 'I see myself in the mirror', *strickst du dir einen Schal?* 'are you knitting yourself a scarf?', etc. etc.

See also 'Reflexive Verbs', pp. 277 f.

Pronoun replaced by adverbial form

The 3rd person pronoun is, by and large, not used with the undermentioned prepositions when reference is to inanimate objects or concepts. Instead the adverb *da* is combined with the preposition, thus *damit* 'with it, with them', before vowels *dar-*, as *darauf* 'on it, on them' (acc. or dat.), literally 'therewith, thereon'. The other combinations are *daran* ('at, by'), *daraus* ('out of'), *dabei* ('at, by'), *dadurch* ('though'), *dafür* ('for'), *dagegen* ('against'), *dahinter* ('behind'), *darin* ('in'), *danach* ('after'), *daneben* ('beside'), *darüber* ('over'), *darum* ('about, around'), *darunter* ('under'), *davon* ('of, from'), *davor* ('before'), archaizing *dawider* ('against'), *dazu* ('to'), *dazwischen* ('between'); in a few contexts *darein*, see below. Examples: *sehen Sie den Baum (die Bäume)? — dahinter fließt der Bach* 'do you see the tree (the trees)?—the stream runs behind it (them)', *diese neue Idee (diese neuen Ideen) — was halten Sie davon?* 'this new idea (these new ideas)—what do you think of it (them)?', *wir sind damit zufrieden* 'we satisfied with it, with them, with things', *der Schuß ging daneben* 'the shot missed'. The above is invariable practice when reference is to the content of a phrase: *er hat Zeit verloren, aber er macht sich nichts daraus* 'he has lost time, but he doesn't mind'.

Contrary to usual practice, the combination *darunter* is in regular use for living beings too: *viele Vogelarten waren zu sehen, darunter* (commoner than *unter ihnen*) *Zugvögel aus dem hohen Norden* 'many sorts of birds were to be seen, among them migrants from the far north'.

In the present connection, the stress falls on the prepositional element: *da'mit, da'rauf*, etc., as a consequence of which *dar-* may contract to *dr-*, hence *drauf*, etc., common in speaking, but uncontracted forms are preferred in the written language. Nevertheless, in a number of cases, only contracted forms are possible, as in the idiomatic *ich bin dran* 'it's my turn', *es geht drunter und drüber* 'things are topsy-turvy', *mit allem Drum und Dran* 'with all the trimmings', and such terms as *Draufgänger* 'dare-devil', *Draufgeld* 'part payment in advance'. The combination *darein* seen, for instance, in the formal-sounding *sich dareinfinden* or *-fügen* 'to submit, resign oneself (to it, etc.)', is purely literary and relatively infrequent; contracted *drein*, on the other hand, is common and universal in such expressions as *dreinreden, dreinschauen*, e.g. *sie will in alles dreinreden* 'she wants to interfere in everything', *er schaut traurig drein* 'he has a sad look'. Comparable to the above, but of much less frequent occurrence, are analogous formations based on *hier*, e.g. *hiermit* 'with it, with them, herewith': *hiermit melde ich mich vom Kurs ab* 'I herewith withdraw from the course'. Stress may again fall on the prepositional element, but is in practice commonly distributed more or less equally over both syllables: *'hier'mit*.

The stress can also be placed on the first element of the above combinations (except *dazwischen*), thus *'damit, 'darauf*, similarly *'hiermit*, when the words take on a demonstrative sense, p. 204.

In colloquial style the compound adverb may, in given cases, be split, so that e.g. *ich weiß nichts davon* 'I don't know anything about it' can become *da weiß ich nichts von*, a formulation commonplace in the north. In another variation, the adverbial element is duplicated: *da weiß ich nichts davon*, and by yet another development in the opposite direction, may be suppressed altogether: *ich weiß nichts von*.

Other uses of adverbial replacement

A number of intransitive and reflexive verbs are joined to a noun (or pronoun) complement by a preposition: *er trachtet nach Ruhm* 'he aspires to fame', *man kann sich auf ihn verlassen* 'one can rely on him', *sie haben sich zu besseren Arbeitsleistungen verpflichtet* 'they have undertaken to improve their working standards'. Such verbs may be joined to an infinitive, in which cases the preposition combines with *da(r)-* as the representative of this infinitive, sometimes compulsorily: *er trachtet danach, berühmt zu werden* 'he aspires to become famous', *man kann sich darauf verlassen, ihn dort anzutreffen* 'one can rely on finding him there', but more often optionally: *sie haben sich (dazu) verpflichtet, ihre Arbeitsleistungen zu verbessern* (translation as above)—whether the use of the adverbial combination will be compulsory or not, is a lexical matter, so that each case has to be considered individually. Where use is optional, it may be said that the presence of the adverbial combination tends to add a touch of formality to the style. The word normally bears no appreciable stress, but emphatic stress may occur in certain examples, p. 204.

A *daß*-clause is also often anticipated in the above manner: *ich zweifle nicht (daran), daß er Erfolg haben wird* 'I don't doubt that he will be successful'. To a lesser extent, adjectives and nouns are associated with these constructions: *ich bin davon überzeugt* 'I am convinced of it', *ich bin (davon) überzeugt, daß sich alles zum Besten wenden wird* 'I am convinced that all will turn out for the best', *dies ist die Garantie für die Ware* 'this is the guarantee for the goods', *das neue Verfahren bietet die Garantie (dafür), daß die Ware kostengünstig erzeugt werden kann* 'the new process guarantees that the goods will be produced at low cost'. In given instances, both infinitive and *daß*-clauses are possible alternatives: *die Mannschaft war stolz (darauf), das Spiel gewonnen zu haben*, or *daß sie das Spiel gewonnen hatte* 'the team was proud to have won the match', or 'that they had won the match'.

Interrogative clauses, too, are frequently involved: *wir haben uns (danach) erkundigt, wie die Produktion weiterlaufen würde* 'we enquired how production would continue', *der Laie ist oft außerstande, (darüber) zu urteilen, ob eine bestimmte politische Entscheidung zurecht besteht oder nicht* 'the layman is often not in a position to judge whether a certain political decision is right or not', *sie hat sich gedanklich damit beschäftigt, wer es gewesen sein könnte, und was es zu bedeuten hätte* 'she pondered over who it could have been and what it might mean'. A relative clause, however, should not be so anticipated, see next section.

Exceptions to replacement rule

Deviations from the general rule that the 3rd person is not used with (most of the common) prepositions when reference is to inanimate objects (p. 196) are by no means infrequent, both in writing and speaking. The construction with the independent pronoun may be preferred for clarity: *der Roboter hat zwei Greifer, und mit ihnen kann man die verschiedensten Arbeitsvorgänge ausführen* 'the robot has two grabs, and with them the most diverse operations can be carried out'. The formulation *mit ihnen* makes it clear that the two grabs, rather than the robot as such, are at the centre of interest, whereas *damit* would be ambiguous. The differing constructions can imply different emphasis: *in der guten Stube stand ein Tisch und auf ihm* (or *darauf*) *ein große Vase* 'in the parlour stood a table and on it a large vase'. The formulation *auf ihm* draws attention to the pronoun and through it to its antecedent, so that one sees the whole table, so to speak, but in the case of *darauf*, it is the element *-auf* 'on' which determines the emphasis, so that attention is concentrated on the surface of the table. At this point we recall that an adverbial compound has sometimes developed an additional sense, e.g. *darauf verließ er das Zimmer* 'thereupon he left the room'. As a consequence, the independent pronoun may be necessary to express the primary sense unequivocally: *die Barbaren nahmen Baumstämme und überquerten auf ihnen den Fluß* 'the barbarians took tree trunks and on these crossed the river'—*darauf* in this position and context would be uncomfortably close to the secondary meaning 'thereupon, then'. The very intimate connection of the independent pronoun with its antecedent can be exploited stylistically: *die "Germania" des Tacitus gilt als ein Meisterwerk lateinischer Prosa; klar und übersichtlich ist in ihr die Gliederung des Stoffes* 'Tacitus' *Germania* is regarded as a masterpiece of Latin prose; in it the presentation of the material is clear and well set out.'

The adverbial compound should not be used as the antecedent of a relative clause; occasional occurrences may be seen as lapses rather than an alternative construction, hence regularly *die Chronik schweigt über das, was nachher geschah* 'nothing is known (lit. the chronicle is silent, a standard idiom) about what happened afterwards', *hatte sie etwa unter dem zu leiden, was die Leute über sie sagten?* 'had she perhaps to suffer because of what people said about her?' When the dependent clause precedes, the above construction is, of course, not apposite, thus e.g. *was nachher geschah, 'darüber schweigt die Chronik*, cf. p. 204.

Whereas most common prepositions are freely used in the adverbial forms, oddly enough *ohne* and *seit* are not so combined: *ohne das* 'without that', *seit dem* 'since that'.

Omission of pronoun

The 1st person singular is occasionally omitted, though users of the language may not be fully aware of the omission: *bitte* 'please; don't mention it' lit. '(I) beg', *danke* 'thank you', *bedaure* 'sorry (but no)'. Also *sage und schreibe,* an expression of indignation: *er verlangt für sein Haus sage und schreibe eine Viertelmillion* 'he's asking for his house, would you believe it, a quarter of a million', and particularly in this case the ordinary speaker does not understand the literal meaning, i.e. '(I) say and (I) write'. On the other hand, ellipsis is evident enough in such phrases as *wünsche guten Morgen* '(I) wish you good morning', *gratuliere zum Geburtstag* '(I) congratulate you on your birthday' = our 'many happy returns'.

In familiar colloquial, the (enclitic) 2nd person singular is frequently dropped: *hast recht* 'you're right', *wirst sehen* 'you'll see', *kannst mir glauben* 'you can believe me, take my word for it', *bist bereits ein großes Mädel* 'you're already a big girl', *machst schon wieder Dummheiten* 'you're up to your silly tricks again'. It is likewise not uncommon for the 3rd sg. neut. pronoun to be suppressed in casual speech, as often in English: *geht nicht* 'doesn't go, doesn't work', *läßt sich machen* 'can be done', *wird gemacht* 'it'll be done', *hat Zeit* 'there's (plenty of) time', *ist mir schon recht* 'all right by me', *freut mich auch* 'I'm glad, too', *fragt sich nur wieviel?* 'the question is just how much?'

In non-initial position the 3rd neut. sg. pronoun is dropped in the case of certain impersonal verbs, see *passim* under 'Impersonal

Verbs'. The practice is also found in other impersonal constructions as follows. It is the rule in the case of sentence-opening *es*, p. 194: *es steht in diesem Buch, daß der Planet Pluto erst 1930 entdeckt wurde* 'it says in this book that the planet Pluto was only discovered in 1930', but *in diesem Buch steht, daß . . .* 'in this book it says that . . .', similarly *es ist unsicher*, or *unsicher ist, ob er kommen kann* 'whether he can come is uncertain'. Such omission is frequent with an impersonal reflexive: *es stellte sich heraus, daß er sein Geld verspielt hatte* 'it turned out that he had lost his money gambling', but *er hatte sein Geld verspielt, wie sich herausstellte* 'as it turned out', similarly *Goslar ist eine Stadt, in der sich gut lebt* 'G. is a good town to live in'; further in such structures as *darüber läßt sich streiten* 'it's something one can argue about'. In a non-reflexive construction the pronoun may be retained, but with a tendency nowadays to suppress: *es könnte dann passieren* or *dann könnte (es) passieren, daß wir zuviel Zeit verlieren würden* 'it could then happen (then it could happen) that we would lose too much time'. Omission is the invariable rule in the case of the impersonal passive, examples on p. 249.

The reflexive pronoun is often omitted before the present participle, cf. *eine Mutter opfert sich für ihre Kinder auf* 'a mother sacrifices herself for her children', *eine für ihre Kinder sich aufopfernde Mutter* 'a mother sacrificing herself for her children', but *eine aufopfernde Mutter* 'a devoted mother', hence analogically e.g. *aufopfernde Pflege* 'devoted care'.

Pronoun compounded with *-gleichen, -wegen, um . . . willen*

Sample usages: *unseresgleichen hat es manchmal schwer* 'people like us sometimes find the going hard', *mit seinesgleichen wollen wir nichts zu tun haben* 'we don't want to have anything to do with the likes of him', *nur euretwegen sind wir so früh gekommen* 'we have only come so early because of you', virtually the same as *nur um euretwillen* 'only for your sake', this latter being, however, mainly a literary form; *meinetwegen* may have a special sense: *meinetwegen kann er es behalten* 'he can keep it, I don't mind'.

POSSESSIVE PRONOUNS AND ADJECTIVES

Examples of the forms, pp. 70 f.: (ordinary formations) *das ist euer Geld (eures), aber wo ist meins* 'that is your money (yours), but where is mine?', *kommt deine Frau? meine nicht!* 'is your wife coming? mine isn't!', *ihre Schiffe sind anders als unsere* 'their ships are different from ours', *es war das Ende seiner Laufbahn — und meiner* 'it was the end of his career—and mine', (alternative, less usual formations) *in einer Gesellschaft wie der unseren* (or *der unserigen*) *hat fast jeder mit dem*

Finanzamt zu tun 'in a society like ours almost everyone has to deal with the tax office'.

There are occasional survivals of an otherwise obsolete use of the uninflected pronoun: *alles, was mein ist, ist auch dein* 'all that is mine is yours, too', further *Die Rache ist unser* (recent book title) 'Vengeance is ours' after the biblical *die Rache ist mein*, not unlike *Dein ist das Reich und die Kraft und die Herrlichkeit* 'Thine is the kingdom and the power and the glory'.

In given contexts, these pronouns are treated as nouns proper and written with a capital letter: *die Meinen* (or *die Meinigen*) 'my family', *jedem das Seine* 'to each man his lot', *er verwechselte Mein und Dein* (but also written *mein und dein*) lit. 'he mixed up mine and yours', a euphemism for 'he took what did not belong to him'.

DEMONSTRATIVE PRONOUNS AND ADJECTIVES

The general demonstrative

The general demonstrative is *der, die, das*. It is used substantivally and adjectivally; in the former case it follows the declension set out on p. 71, in the latter its forms are those of the definite article. It usually bears a full stress, the meaning being 'this' or 'that' according to context; for exceptions, see p. 202. The owner of a house points to it and says *das ist mein Haus*. If he is standing right in front of the property, the translation will be 'this is my house', if he is some distance away, then 'that is my house' is the appropriate equivalent. Further examples: *unser Garten ist weniger gepflegt als der unseres Nachbarn* 'our garden is less well cared-for than our neighbour's (that of our neighbour)', *dieses Bier ist stärker als das, was Sie trinken* 'this beer is stronger than what you're drinking', *dort fand ich all das, was ich mir wünschte* 'there I found all I wished for'. Notice everyday clichés of the type *die Frage ist nämlich die: wo nehmen wir denn das Geld her?* 'you see the question is: where are we going to get the money from?' and *der mit dem Schnurrbart* 'the one with the moustache', *die mit der Handtasche* 'the one with the handbag'. As a stressed word, the pronoun commonly occurs at the head of the sentence, both as the subject: *der hat alle Hände voll zu tun* 'this/that one has got his hands full', and frequently also as the object: *das kann ich glauben* 'this/that I can believe', *denen kann nicht mehr geholfen werden* 'these/those can no longer be helped', (elevated style) *dessen (deren) entsinnt er sich nicht* 'this/that (these/those) he no longer recalls'.

The alternative short forms *des* (gen. sg. masc. neut.) and *der* (gen. sg. fem., gen. pl.) are required before a genitive or corresponding construction with *von*, thus *der Ton Ihres Schreibens sowie des Ihrer*

Frau Schwester überraschte mich sehr 'the tone of your letter and that of your sister greatly surprised me', *trotz seiner Einwände und der von seinen linken Parteifreunden wurde die Politik des rechten Flügels mehrheitlich gebilligt* 'in spite of his objections and those of his party friends on the left, the policy of the right wing won majority approval'. These short forms are, historically speaking, the primary forms which survive best in the construction just illustrated. Otherwise they are archaic: *wes das Herz voll ist, des geht der Mund über* 'out of the abundance of the heart the mouth speaketh'. The genitive plural form *derer* is applicable when antecedent to a relative pronoun: *es waren Landsleute derer, die wir vorhin gesehen hatten* 'they were compatriots of those (whom) we had just seen'.

The forms compounded with *-wegen, um . . . willen* (p. 73) are, except for *deswegen*, confined to literary style: *der Hof war zu verkaufen, und dessentwegen* (more ordinarily *deswegen*, or *deshalb*) *waren wir dorthin gereist* 'the farm was for sale and on that account we made the journey there', *es gibt viele Renntiere hier in Lappland, und um derentwillen* (more ordinarily *wegen ihnen*) *sind wir hergekommen* 'there are a lot of reindeer here in L., and we have come here because of them'.

From demonstrative to personal pronoun

In numerous contexts, the general demonstrative pronoun approaches very close to the personal pronoun (and is then often needed in the English translation): *er erzählte von seinen Flitterwochen; die hatten die Neuvermählten im Harz verbracht* 'he spoke about his honeymoon; the newly-weds had spent it in the Harz', (or it is optional): *jemand hat den Teller zerbrochen; das muß er gewesen sein* 'somebody has broken the plate; that (it) must have been him'. In other contexts, the demonstrative quite loses its stress and becomes *de facto* a personal pronoun. Thus *'was ist das? was 'ist das? 'wer ist das? wer 'ist das?* are the normal equivalents of "what is it? what 'is it? 'who is it? who 'is it?', the demonstrative sense only emerging when *das* is stressed: *was ist 'das? wer ist 'das?* 'what is this/that? who is this/that?'. Further: *du kennst Otto Hager, oder? — er* (or *der*) *hat mir einmal von seiner Schwiegermutter erzählt — bist du ihr* (or *der*) *jemals begegnet?* 'you know O.H., don't you?—he was once telling me about his mother-in-law—have you ever met her?' The demonstratives often have a colloquial ring (as in the last sentences) and such usage is particularly common in the spoken language; in fact, in some districts, expressions like *es sieht (schaut) nach Regen aus* 'it looks like rain' are regularly given as *das sieht (schaut) . . .* At the same time the demonstrative, being basically more emphatic than the personal pronoun, can be used to lend weight: (Arabian Nights) *wenn ihr mir nicht gehorcht, so wecke ich den Geist, meinen Gemahl, und der wird euch töten* 'if you do not obey me, then I shall waken the spirit, my consort, and h e will kill you'.

The genitive is here a special case. It is naturally not a constituent of colloquial style on the lower levels (p. 154), nevertheless it is often heard in the speech of educated persons: *es waren derer* (replacing *ihrer*) *vier* 'there were four of them'. Attributive use is also commonplace: *ich war mit Frau Krüger und deren* (replacing *ihrem*) *Mann im Theater* 'I was at the theatre with Mrs K. and her husband'. Such usage has been lifted from the written language, p. 192. The genitive may, however, have a special syntactic function, as follows. Since the demonstrative, unlike the personal, pronoun is never reflexive, it can be employed to avoid ambiguity: *sie zog zu ihrer Tante in deren Wohnung* 'she moved into her aunt's flat'; in less formal style: *sie zog zu ihrer Tante* (or *zur Tante*) *in die Wohnung*. Notice the implication that the aunt remained in residence, not explicit in the English translation; correspondingly imprecise German would be *sie zog in die Wohnung ihrer* (or *der*) *Tante*.

Although the nom. acc. *es* is regularly used in reference to the content of a clause (p. 194), the dative cannot be so employed, only the demonstrative being possible: *obwohl man ihn vor den Germanen warnte und zur Vorsicht riet, schenkte dem Varus keinen Glauben* 'although warned against the Germans (Germanic tribesmen) and advised to be cautious, V. gave no credence to such things (lit. to it, to this/that)'.

Adjectival use

In adjectival use the general demonstrative is much more prevalent in the spoken than in the written language where it is relatively rare, the reason being that its forms are only distinguished from those of the definite article in that they bear a stress, a feature not normally indicated in writing. Thus *die 'Seite* means 'the side', but *'die Seite* 'this side' or 'that side'. For instance, giving directions on the street one might say *gehen Sie geradeaus, aber bleiben Sie immer auf 'der Straßenseite*. The sentence will be accompanied by a gesture showing which side of the street is meant, since as an utterance, pure and simple, the sense is indifferently 'go straight on, but keep on this side of the street, or on that side of the street'. It would be possible to show the stress in print by using spaced type: *auf d e r Straßenseite*, but this device is not often resorted to, so that in actual practice the above sentence is hardly likely to appear in writing at all, since *auf der Straßenseite* would be understood as 'on the side of the street'; to convey the meaning unambiguously, other words must be used, see below. All the same, such use of the demonstrative adjective is not unknown in print, in contexts where the meaning is not in doubt: *am besten vermeidet man Leute von der Sorte* 'it is best to avoid people of that sort', *trinkt man um die Zeit Kaffee?* 'does one have coffee at this/that time (of day)?', *es wurde der und der Name genannt* (each *der* stressed) 'such and such a name was mentioned'. The reader recognizes the clichés and, if reading out, stresses the demonstratives accordingly. Similarly *in dem Zimmer essen wir, in dem anderen sehen wir fern* 'in this/that room we have our meals, in the other we watch television'.

Pronoun replaced by adverbial form

The replacement, under certain conditions, of the personal pronoun by an adverbial formation, e.g. *da'mit, da'rauf*, has already been discussed, p. 196. The demonstrative may also be replaced under the same conditions and by the same adverbs, but now stressed on the first element: *'damit, 'darauf* 'with this/that, with these/those, on this/that, etc.', similarly *'hiermit* 'with this, with these'.

Usage is quite common in written language, too, for although the accentuation is not shown in print, the word order frequently implies the demonstrative sense. This is notably the case in initial position: *'davon bin ich überzeugt* 'of this/that I am convinced', *'damit sind wir zufrieden* 'we are satisfied with this/that, etc.', *'darauf kommt es an* 'it depends on this/that, etc.' contrasting with *es kommt darauf* (or very commonly *drauf*) *'an* 'it depends (on it), etc.', *'hiermit bin ich einverstanden* 'I am in agreement with this, these matters'. The context itself often indicates the emphatic, demonstrative sense: *es geht nicht 'darum, den Kindern etwas zu verbieten, sondern 'darum, sie zu schützen* 'it is not a question of forbidding children to have (or, to do) something, but of protecting them', *man kann den Wärmeverlust nur 'dadurch erklären, daß das Dach nicht genügend abgedichtet ist* 'one can only explain the loss of heat by the fact that the roof is not sufficiently insulated'.

The specific demonstratives

We have seen that the general demonstrative (p. 201) is indifferently 'this' or 'that'. If, however, the speaker or writer feels a need to differentiate, that is, to be specific, the demonstrative can be suitably qualified: *der hier* 'the one here, this one', *der Laden hier* 'this shop', *der dort* 'the one there, that one', *der Laden dort* 'that shop'. Further *der da, der Laden da*, but in these cases the sense varies, *da* being the general demonstrative adverb, basically indicating the direction in which one is pointing, fluctuating, so to speak, between the poles *hier* and *dort*. In this connection there is a noticeable regional variation; in the north *da* is commonly associated with *dort*, in the south more usually with *hier*.

dieser, jener

In addition to the above-mentioned idioms, 'this' is often represented by *dieser, diese, dieses* (*dies*); in certain circumstances, 'that' corresponds to *jener, jene, jenes*.

Examples: *dieser* 'this one', *dieser Laden* 'this shop', or emphasized: *dieser hier, dieser Laden hier*, in the south often *dieser da, dieser Laden da*. Notice that *dies* is syntactically comparable to *das*, e.g. *wessen Bücher sind das?* — *dies hier sind meine, und das dort sind seine* 'whose books are they?—these are mine, and those are his'.

In the light of the foregoing, one may state that *dies (hier)* and *das (dort)* typically express the contrast between 'this' and 'that' in the spatial sense. In a few contexts, however, this sense is absent, only the concept of difference remaining: *wir plauderten über dies und das* 'we chatted about this and that'. It is this sort of contrast which is also brought out by *dies* and *jenes*, hence alternatively *wir plauderten über dies und jenes*, and compare the expression *aus diesem und jenem Grund* 'for one reason or another'. But, in general, such usage belongs to literary style: *die beiden Enten tauchten immer wieder unter, bald diese, bald jene* 'the two ducks were continually diving, now this one, now that one', less formally *bald die eine, bald die andere*. In another contrastive use an element of spatial difference is present in examples where the sense is equivalent to 'the latter . . . the former': *Sie werden gewiß von Albert Einstein und Max Planck gehört haben; dieser stellte die Quantentheorie auf, jener die spezielle und allgemeine Relativitätstheorie* 'you will certainly have heard of A.E. and M.P.; the latter propounded the quantum theory, the former the special and general theory of relativity'. A direct spatial contrast is less usual today, and then only in choice diction: *ich möchte einen Strauß Astern, und was kosten jene* (lesser mortals *die*) *Dahlien dort?* 'I should like a bunch of asters, and what do those dahlias cost?' A relic of the once commoner spatial difference remains in the terms *diesseits* 'on this side (of)', *jenseits* 'on that (= 'yon') side (of)', also as nouns *das Diesseits* 'this life, this world', *das Jenseits* 'the hereafter, the life to come'.

Finally, *jener* occurs independently: *die Schriftstellerin Annette von Droste-Hülshoff wurde in jenem Landhaus geboren* 'the writer A. v. D.-H. was born in that country-house', i.e. the one already referred to, or which is known about, different then from *in dem Landhaus dort* 'in that country-house (there)', the one being pointed out. Other examples: *der Geschichtslehrer erzählte gern von jenem unvergeßlichen Tag, an dem Wellington und Blücher die Franzosen bei*

Waterloo besiegten 'the history teacher loved to tell of that unforgettable day on which W. and B. defeated the French at Waterloo', *es war jene Jugendliebe, die er nie vergessen konnte* 'it was that early love he could never forget'. It will be observed that no contrast with *dieser* is implied in these sentences; indeed, the latter can actually replace *jener* in less formal style: *es war diese Jugendliebe*, etc.

'derjenige

Used substantivally, this pronoun may replace the general demonstrative, for the most part optionally, in three constructions. Firstly, in connection with a relative clause: *der Redner richtete seinen Appell an diejenigen* (or *die*), *die für die Entwicklungshilfe verantwortlich sind* 'the speaker directed his appeal to those who are responsible for development aid', *seine Worte waren eine Warnung an die Adresse derjenigen* (or *derer*), *die einen härteren Kurs verlangen* 'his words were a warning addressed to those who are demanding a tougher line'. In this usage the pronoun may start the sentence: *diejenigen, die für die Hilfe verantwortlich sind, hörten aufmerksam zu* 'those who are responsible for aid listened attentively'. In the above the present pronoun will usually be preferred, the general demonstrative often giving the repetitive *die, die*. At a pinch, the construction referred to on p. 326 would be an acceptable alternative: *die für die Hilfe verantwortlich sind, hörten aufmerksam zu.*

Secondly, the pronoun may represent a preceding noun in connection with a preposition: *nicht das Haus mit dem Schieferdach wollte er übernehmen, sondern dasjenige* (or *das*) *mit dem Strohdach* 'it was not the house with the slate roof he wanted to take over, but the one with the thatch'. Thirdly, it occurs in sentences of the type *die Kralle war scharf wie diejenige* (or *die*) *einer Katze* 'the claw was sharp as that of a cat'. In both these constructions, however, the use of the present pronoun is confined to formal or technical style; the last might be found, for instance, in a textbook on zoology. Otherwise, the general demonstrative (here in brackets) is the norm.

Lastly, the pronoun may be used adjectivally; it qualifies a noun followed by a relative clause: *der Kriminalbeamte befragte diejenigen* (or *'die*) *Personen, die sich in unmittelbarer Nähe des Tatorts befanden* 'the detective questioned those persons who were in the immediate vicinity of the scene of the crime'. The general demonstrative is again the alternative normally heard in conversation, the demonstrative sense being indicated by the stress.

On the twice stilted, but now jocular *derjenige, welcher*, see p. 323.

der'selbe

Like its English counterpart 'the same', *der'selbe*, *die'selbe*, *das'selbe* is properly the pronoun of identity. Usage in the two languages is closely comparable: *dasselbe gilt für uns* 'the same applies to us', *seine Frau hat wieder dieselbe Frisur* 'his wife has the same hair style again', *ihre Nachbarin hat auch dieselbe (die gleiche) Frisur* 'her neighbour has the same (the identical) hair style, too', *sind das dieselben?* 'are they the same?', *das Kleid? — es war dasselbe, das sie schon immer getragen hatte* 'the dress?—it was the same as she had always worn'. As a substitute for a personal pronoun, usage again corresponds in both languages: *nach Erhalt desselben* 'on receipt of (the) same'.

Contraction with a preposition is possible (p. 188), e.g. *am selben* (= *an demselben*) *Abend* 'on the same evening', *ins selbe* (= *in dasselbe*) *Kino* 'into the same cinema'. The contracted forms predominate in the spoken language, and are by no means uncommon in writing as well.

solch ('derartig, so)

Also inflected *solcher, -e, es* 'such'. In adjectival use this word occurs only as an attributive. Before a descriptive adjective in the singular, invariable *solch* followed by the strong inflexion is the norm: *solch dummes Zeug* 'such nonsense'; in the plural, however, this use is associated with high style: *solch malerische Dörfer* 'such picturesque villages', the inflected form being more commonplace: *solche malerischen* (also *malerische*, p. 166) *Dörfer*. In the singular, it is most often found together with *ein*, which either precedes or follows: *an solch einem Tag, an einem solchen Tag* 'on such a day', the latter being perhaps commoner. If *ein* is not used, the phrase tends to have a more literary character: *an solchem Tage*. At the same time, *ein* may be omitted in many everyday contexts, differences often being regional: *ich habe (einen) solchen Durst, Hunger* 'I am so thirsty, hungry', *(ein) solches Wetter hatten wir seit langem nicht* 'we have not had weather like this for a long time'. The present pronoun is common in exclamations: *ein solches Glück!* 'such good luck!', stylistically more elevated *solch ein Glück!* 'such good fortune!' Occasionally, uninflected *solch* appears before a nom. acc. sg. masc. or neut.: *solch Zahn* 'such a tooth', *solch Messer* 'such a knife', adding a nuance, say, 'such a (remarkable, odd) tooth', etc.

The demonstrative *derartig* is synonymous (though not always interchangeable) with *solch*, e.g. *an einem derartigen Tag* 'on such a day' or more literally 'on a day like this/that'. The same may be expressed by *so*, hence *an so einem Tag*, and this is the everyday formulation in spoken German. Cf. further *ein so schöner Tag*, ordinary colloquial *so ein schöner Tag* 'such a lovely day', parallel to *ein solch* (informally *ein solcher*) *schöner Tag, solch ein schöner Tag*, also stylistically more elevated *so schöner Tag, solch schöner Tag*. But observe that *solch* and *so* cannot alternate in such sentences as these: *kein solcher Unterschied* 'no such difference', when followed by an adjective: *kein so großer Unterschied* 'no such big difference'. Nor can idioms of the type 'the idea as such' be otherwise expressed than by *die Idee als solche*.

Less usually, *so* may stand directly before the noun, for the most part in various vernacular phrases, e.g. *das sind so* (or *solche*) *Sachen* 'things like that happen' (a hackneyed comment); also before pronouns: *so einer, so jemand* = *ein solcher* 'such a one', *so etwas*, especially in the spoken language *so was* 'something like it, some such thing', whence colloquial *so etwas* (or *so was*) *von* 'such' used attributively: *so was von* (= *eine solche, so eine*) *Schlamperei* 'such a sloppy job'. In ordinary talk the words *so ein* frequently contract to *so'n*, whence the substandard pl. *so'ne* 'such', e.g. *das sind so'ne Sachen* (as above).

Substantival use is, of course, commonplace: *das ist ein schönes Lineal — hast du ein solches?* 'that's a nice ruler—have you one like it?', *schaut euch diese großen Äpfel an! wir haben keine solchen in unserem Garten* 'look at these large apples! we have none like them in our garden', *mit solchem hat man seine liebe Not* 'one has no end of trouble with suchlike'.

Predicatively, *solch* is variously replaced, e.g. *die Wege sind derart* (or *so*) *beschaffen, daß sie nur mit einem geländegängigen Wagen befahrbar sind* 'the roads are such that they can only be negotiated by a cross-country vehicle'. Altogether solutions are often more a lexical matter than a grammatical one, for while *solch* and 'such' play the same basic roles in their respective languages, their idiomatic application can vary considerably: *er kaufte sich eine Villa, eine solche, die sonst nur sehr vermögende Leute kaufen* 'he bought himself a villa such as only very wealthy people buy', *wir haben zwar einen Bericht vom Institutsdirektor, möchten aber auch gern einen solchen von Ihnen* 'we have, it is true, a report from the director of the institute, but we should also much appreciate one from you', *es war, wie in einem solchen . . . hm . . . solchen Parkhaus* 'it was like in one of those . . . hm . . . those multi-storey carparks'.

der'gleichen

Invariable *der'gleichen* is in everyday use as a substantive: *dergleichen ist mir öfters passiert* 'that sort of thing has often happened to me', *dergleichen habe ich noch nie gesehen* 'I've never seen the likes of that', *er hat nichts dergleichen gesagt* 'he said nothing of the sort', *und dergleichen* or *und dergleichen mehr* 'and the like, and so on', often abbreviated to *u. dgl. (m.)*. Adjectival use is confined to more formal style: *dergleichen* (or, as ordinarily, *solche*) *Pflanzen sind jetzt sehr selten geworden* 'such plants have now become very rare'.

THE PRONOUN *SELBST, SELBER*

Literally 'self', these words correspond to 'myself, yourself, etc.' used emphatically. They do not decline and always bear a full stress: *ich selbst* 'I myself', *wir sahen den Mann selbst* 'we saw the man himself', *man darf nicht immer nur an sich selbst* (or simply *an 'sich*) *denken* 'one must not always think only of oneself'. The alternative *selber*, thus *ich selber*, etc., has a colloquial ring and appears in print when this effect is desired: (advertisement) *Möbel zum Selbermachen* 'furniture you can make yourself'. When used with abstract nouns, however, *selbst* is likely to be the preferred form, as more in keeping with the higher stylistic quality of such modes of expression: *sie ist die Güte selbst* 'she is goodness itself', and the same naturally in phrases proper to literary diction: *jeder muß zu sich selbst finden* 'each one must find himself'. The German words are not necessarily associated with a noun or pronoun: *die Tür schließt von selbst* 'the door shuts on its own', *das versteht sich von selbst = das ist selbstverständlich* (*selbst-* in casual pronunciation ['zɛlp-]) 'that is a matter of course, that is self-evident'.

As in English, the present pronoun may be variously separated from the word it qualifies depending on context and emphasis, though resources in the two languages do not necessarily overlap. Consider the following possible interpretations: *ich selbst fahre morgen ab* 'I myself (and not, e.g. my assistant) leave tomorrow', *ich fahre selbst morgen ab* 'as for myself, I leave tomorrow', *ich fahre morgen selbst ab* 'I leave tomorrow myself' (stressing that tomorrow is when I myself leave). Notice *unser kleines Töchterchen kann sich schon selbst anziehen* 'our little daughter can already dress herself' i.e. 'by herself'.

On *selbst* as an adverb, see p. 264.

THE PRONOUN *EIN'ANDER*

The reciprocal pronoun *ein'ander* 'each other, one another' is indeclinable. It often occurs as an alternative to a personal pronoun: *wir sind einander* (or *uns*) *im Weg* 'we are in each other's way', *sie lieben einander* (or *sich*) *sehr* 'they love one another very much', *einander* being stylistically the more elevated. But, except as mentioned on pp. 195 f., the present pronoun alone can be used with a preposition, to which it is joined orthographically; the stress remains on the pronoun, thus *vonein'ander*, etc.: *wir haben lange nichts voneinander gehört* 'we have heard nothing from one another for a long time'. Many other everyday phrases are involved, sometimes answering to quite differently worded English idioms, as *wir reden aneinander vorbei* 'we are talking at cross-purposes', *sie war ganz durcheinander* (familiar) 'she was quite confused'—often substantivized: *ein heilloses Durcheinander* 'total confusion'—*seid glücklich miteinander* 'be happy together', *zweimal nacheinander* 'twice in succession'.

INTERROGATIVE PRONOUNS AND ADJECTIVES

wer, was

To begin with, sentences showing the case forms, p. 71: *wer hat sich krank gemeldet?* 'who has gone sick?', *wer sind diese Ausländer?* 'who are these foreigners?', *wen haben Sie gesehen?* 'who have you seen?', *wem haben Sie geholfen?* 'who have you helped?', *mit wem treffen sie sich?* 'who are they going to meet?', *was kommt als nächstes?* 'what comes next?', *was sind Ihre Bedingungen?* 'what are your conditions?' (see p. 212), *was haben Sie gefunden?* 'what have you found?'. As far as *was* is concerned, its genitive is met with only in literary style: *wessen können sich die Spanier rühmen?* 'of what can the Spaniards boast?'. As the genitive of *wer*, however, *wessen* is a spoken as well as a literary form, e.g. *wessen Platz ist das?* 'whose seat is it?', although *wem gehört der Platz?* lit. 'who does the seat belong to?' doubtless represents the commoner construction actually used in questions of this type.

There is no operational neut. sg. dat., the syntactical niche being filled by the interrogative adjective *welcher* and a noun in the dative: *aus welchem Anlaß beehren Sie uns mit Ihrem Besuch?* 'to what (lit. from what cause) do we owe the honour of your visit?'

The pronouns *wer, was* are singulars. However, the notion of plurality can be conveyed by the use, in apposition, of neut. sg. *alles* 'all'—we recall that this form is often used in a plural sense, pp. 219 f.: *wer hat sich alles krank gemeldet?* 'what people have gone sick?', *was haben Sie alles gefunden?* 'what things have you found?'

A neut. sg. substantivized adjective is very often used in apposition to *was*, e.g. *was gibt es Neues?* 'what is the news?'; the words in apposition need to be separated: *was haben Sie Interessantes zu berichten?* 'what matters of interest have you to report?'

Original interrogative use shifts, almost imperceptibly, to the exclamatory, witness *wer hätte das geglaubt!* 'who would have believed it!' With *was* the break is more tangible: *was haben wir geschuftet!* 'how we have slaved!', i.e. with the same meaning as *wie haben wir geschuftet!* or with different word order *wie wir geschuftet haben!*, whence by analogy (mainly colloquial) *was wir geschuftet haben!* Compare further *was Sie nicht sagen!* 'you don't say!', *was sie nicht alles für ihre Schönheit tut!* 'the things she does for her appearance!' For another semantic shift, see pp. 326 f.

Pronoun replaced by adverbial form

Especially in the literary language, the pronoun is not as a rule used with (most of the common) prepositions when reference is to inanimate objects or to concepts. Instead the adverb *wo*, before a vowel *wor-*, is prefixed to the preposition, thus *womit?* 'with what? what with?', *worauf* 'on what? what on?' (acc. or dat.), lit. 'wherewith? whereon?'. The prepositions in question are among those which similarly combine with *da(r)-*, p. 196. The stress falls on the prepositional element: *wo'mit, wo'rauf.* Examples in context: *woran ist er gestorben?* 'what did he die of?', *worum handelt es sich?* 'what is it about?', *worüber sprechen Sie?* 'what are you speaking about?', *wovon soll man leben?* 'what is one to live on?'. In casual speech, such combinations can generally be replaced by the preposition concerned plus *was*, hence very colloquially *von was soll man leben?*, etc., and for special emphasis *was* can, of course, be stressed.

In certain instances, however, the combined forms have a more restricted meaning than the independent prepositions so that the two are then not, or not always, interchangeable. The combination *wovon*, mentioned above, cannot be used when any idea of motion is involved, 'where from?' being *von wo?* or *woher?* Compare further *wozu macht er das?* 'what is he doing that for?', but 'where to?' is *wohin?* The combination *wodurch* means 'in what way?', the literal sense 'through what?' being rendered *durch was?*

The combination *wofür?* 'for what purpose? why?' is widely replaced in substandard language by *für was?*, not unlike our 'what for?'. In the same way *weswegen* 'on what account? why?' (where *wes-* is a relic of the original gen. sg., see p. 71) often becomes *wegen was?* Indeed, *was* itself can acquire this meaning in colloquial style: *was lachst du denn?* 'what are you laughing for?'

welch

Also inflected *welcher? welche? welches?* (p. 71) 'which?, what?', the traditional adjectival interrogative: *welcher Verkäufer hat sie bedient?* 'which assistant served you?', *welches Auto möchten Sie* 'which car would you like?', *in welchem Laden haben Sie es gekauft?* 'in which shop did you buy it?', *welche guten Engel werden uns beistehen?* 'what good angels are going to help us?', *unter welchen Umständen würden Sie einen Vertrag unterzeichnen?* 'under what conditions would you sign a contract?'

As with *wer*, *was* (p. 210), the interrogative can shift to the exclamatory: *welche gewaltigen Fortschritte sind erzielt worden!* 'what enormous advances have been made!', the intonation alone distinguishing this sentence, if spoken, from the corresponding question. With an exclamation, however, different word order is possible and indeed more usual: *welche gewaltigen Fortschritte erzielt worden sind!* It is in such exclamatory sentences that uninflected *welch* occurs, as optionally before an adjective: *welch wunderschöne Gemälde das sind!* 'what beautiful pictures those are!', and always in the combination *welch ein*, thus *welch ein Genie!* 'what a genius!', further *welch* (or *welch ein*) *großes Genie!* 'what a great genius!', *mit welch einer* (or *welcher*) *Hingabe sie den kranken Bruder pflegte!* 'with what devotion did she nurse her sick brother!' The uninflected form may also be used before a masc. or neut. sing. noun: *welch* (or *welcher*) *Eigensinn!* 'what obstinacy!', *welch* (or *welches*) *Glück!* 'what good fortune!' These exclamatory constructions are proper to literary style, the spoken language substituting *war für*, below.

Substantival use is also commonplace: *da sind die Hefte — welches (welche) wollen Sie haben?* 'there/here are the exercise books— which one (which ones) do you want?', *ich habe mit einer der Schwestern gesprochen — mit welcher?* 'I have spoken to one of the sisters—to which one?' As with other pronouns, the neut. sg. can be employed regardless of gender or number: *er weiß anscheinend nicht, welches die Äpfel und welches die Birnen sind* 'he doesn't know, apparently, which are the apples and which the pears'. Compare *welches sind Ihre Bedingungen?* 'what are your conditions?', *welche sind Ihre Bedingungen?* 'which are your conditions?', further the general question: *welches ist der höchste Berg Deutschlands?* 'which is Germany's highest mountain?', different from *welcher ist der höchste Berg?* which implies that the speaker is actually looking at various mountains as he asks the question. In examples such as the above *welches* may be replaced, less elegantly, by *was*, p. 210.

war für

The interrogative *was für* 'what kind (or, sort) of? what?' functions as an uninflecting attributive adjective. It is used not only before a noun, but also before the pronoun *einer* 'someone', pl. *welche* (pp. 222, 215); notice that it does not affect the case: *was für ein Mensch ist er?* 'what kind of person is he?' Similarly, and with the same sense: *was für einer ist er?* In the plural: *was für Menschen sind sie? was für welche sind sie?* 'what kind of people are they?'. The words *was für* may separate as follows, giving a modified construction: sg. *was ist er für ein Mensch? was ist er für einer?*, pl. *was sind sie für Menschen? was sind sie für welche?* Other examples: *was für Brot möchten Sie kaufen? was möchten Sie für Brot kaufen?* 'what sort of bread would you like to buy?', *was für Bücher lesen Sie? was lesen Sie für Bücher?* 'what sort of books do you read?' This latter construction is the usual one in simple colloquial style, witness Little Red Ridinghood: *Großmutter, was hast du für große Augen!* 'Grandmother, what big eyes you've got!'

The present idiom is common in prepositional phrases: *in was für eine Lage wird sie versetzt?* 'what sort of a position will she be placed in?', *mit was für einem Menschen haben wir es zu tun?* 'what sort of a person are we dealing with?', *von was für einer Seuche wurden die Tiere befallen?* 'what sort of a disease were the animals affected by?'

In colloquial or unpretentious written style, *was für?* may occur as an alternative to *welcher?* 'which, what?': *was für neue Ideen hast du? was hast du für neue Ideen?* (or *welche neuen Ideen hast du?*) 'what new ideas do you have?', *es fehlt ein Ersatzteil — was für einer?* (or *welcher?*) 'there's a spare part missing—which one?', *ich habe ein Paar Handschuhe verloren — was für welche?* (or simply *welche?*) 'I've lost a pair of gloves—which ones?'

Finally, the present idiom is used in exclamations. It may be found in literary use, e.g. *was für wunderschöne Gemälde das sind!* 'what beautiful paintings these are!', though stylistically less elevated than *welch wunderschöne Gemälde*, p. 212. It is more typically an informal expression, rooted in the colloquial, and at the simpler levels separable: *was das für wunderschöne Gemälde sind!* It is, as one would expect, constantly heard in conversation: *was für ein großer Unterschied!* 'what a big difference!', *was für herrliches Wetter!* 'what glorious weather!', *was für tolle Preise!* 'what fantastic (i.e. fantastically low) prices!', and similarly with the indefinite pronoun: *er hat ein Problem und was für eines!* 'he has a problem and what a problem!'

Pronoun in a subordinate clause

As in English, interrogative pronouns are common in subordinate clauses, the finite verb being characteristically at the end: *wer kann erraten, wer (welcher Herr) gestern bei uns war?* 'who can guess who (which gentleman) was at our house yesterday?', *wir möchten wissen, wen (welches Mädchen, was für ein Mädchen) er heiraten wird* 'we would like to know who (which girl, what sort of girl) he is going to marry', *wer in eurer Familie bestimmt, welches Fernsehprogramm eingeschaltet wird?* 'who in your family decides which television programme is put on?', *ich habe nicht gesehen, mit wem er hereingekommen ist* 'I didn't see who he came with', *können Sie mir bitte sagen, wessen Unterschrift das ist?* 'can you please tell me whose signature it is?—an archaic gen. sg. *wes* survives in the common expression *wes Geistes Kind*, e.g. *endlich erkennen wir, wes Geistes*

Kind er ist 'at last we recognize what his (true) opinions are'—*sie fragt, wozu ich das Geld brauche* 'she is asking what I want the money for', *nicht jeder begreift, was Armut bedeutet* 'not everyone understands what poverty means'. In certain instances the subordinate clause may precede, e.g. *was Armut bedeutet, begreift nicht jeder*, also *das begreift nicht jeder*.

INDEFINITE PRONOUNS AND ADJECTIVES

etwas, was

The meanings are basically 'something, anything': *etwas liegt vor der Tür* 'something is lying in front of the door', *liegt etwas daneben?* 'is anything lying beside it?', *ich glaube, ich sehe etwas Kleines, jedenfalls nicht etwas sehr Großes* 'I think I see something small, at any rate not something very large'—the pronoun is not otherwise used in a negative context, hence e.g. our 'I don't see anything' is given as *ich sehe nichts* e.g. 'I see nothing'. Notice the everyday expression *so etwas* 'something/anything like this/that, this/that sort of thing'. The pronoun is often found in the partitive sense: *ich möchte etwas von Ihrem Kuchen* 'I should like some (often with the nuance 'a little') of your cake'. The more indefinite *irgend etwas* 'something or other, etc.' can also, in principle, be used in constructions such as the above: *irgend etwas liegt vor der Tür*, etc.

The pronoun is regularly used as an attribute; the meaning is again 'some', often with the nuance 'a little': *wir könnten etwas Bargeld gut gebrauchen* 'we could do with some ready money', *man muß etwas Geduld haben* 'one has to have some patience'; in a given context 'a little' may be the only meaning: *sie spricht etwas italienisch* 'she speaks a little Italian'. Finally, the pronoun may be transformed into a noun: *sie hat ein gewisses Etwas, was der anderen abgeht* 'she has a certain something which the other one lacks'.

The form *was* is an extremely common substitute for *etwas* in the sense 'something, anything', preponderating in the spoken language; it is always unstressed: *dort brennt was* 'something's burning over there', *hast du was für mich?* 'have you anything for me?', *das Kind spielt mit was* 'the child's playing with something', *hat es was geholfen?* 'has it helped a bit?', *sie bekommt was Kleines* 'she's going to have a baby'. It will be apparent that, except in such expressions as *so was*, *was Kleines* (= *so etwas*, *etwas Kleines*, above), the pronoun in this sense cannot stand first in the sentence, for then it would necessarily be taken for an interrogative, e.g. *was brennt dort?* 'what's burning over there?' With *irgendwas* for *irgend etwas* the limitation just mentioned does not, of course, apply: *irgendwas brennt dort* 'something or other is burning over there'.

wer, welcher

These words are substitutes for extinct *etwer* 'somebody, someone, anybody, anyone' and archaic *etwelcher* 'some, any'. They are thus comparable to *was* (p. 214), and are likewise always unstressed, nor can they stand at the head of the sentence. Examples: *er glaubt, er ist wer* 'he thinks he's somebody', *siehst du wen?* 'do you see anybody?', *hat es wem genützt?* 'has it been of use to anyone?' This pronoun competes, essentially on a simple colloquial level, with the standard term *jemand* (p. 217). The compound *irgendwer* 'somebody or other' similarly competes with *irgend jemand*, but unlike the simplex *wer*, the compound has achieved a degree of literary status. A third synonym with comparable ranking is *irgendeiner*, p. 222.

Although adjectival in origin, *welcher* in the present connection is used substantivally: *haben Sie mit dem Wagen wieder Ärger? wie ich höre, hatten Sie gestern welchen* 'are you having trouble with the car again? you had some yesterday, so I hear', *er sucht Mörtel; haben wir welchen?* 'he's looking for plaster; have we any?', *führen Sie Kühlschränke? — ja, wir haben welche* 'do you stock refrigerators? — yes, we have some'.

The compound *irgendwelcher* 'some or other, etc.' may be employed in the same way: *er wird seine Gründe haben — ja doch, irgendwelche wird er wohl haben* 'he'll have his reasons—yes, of course, he'll have some or other, I daresay'. It is, however, more prominent as an attributive: *wir konnten die Zollkontrolle ohne irgendwelche Schwierigkeit* (or *Schwierigkeiten*) *passieren* 'we were able to go through the customs control without any difficulty at all', *der Arzt fragt: haben Sie irgendwelche Schmerzen?* 'the doctor asks: have you any pain?' See further p. 222.

Omission of object pronoun

The object pronoun is often omitted, optionally, in contexts like the following: *möchten Sie (etwas) von der Suppe?* 'would you like some of the soup?', *danke, ich habe schon (welche, etwas, etwas davon,* or simply *davon) gehabt* 'no, thank you, I've had some already'.

einiger, etlicher

These words mean 'some (but not much), a little', in the plural 'some (but not many), a few'. The former is the usual term, the latter less common and often felt to be old-fashioned and bookish. In Upper German, however, it is a living word in ordinary use, though facing competition from *einiger*. Examples: *das Häuschen lag in einiger (etlicher) Entfernung* 'the cottage lay at some little distance', *dazu gehört einiger (etlicher) Mut* 'some courage (understatement = 'a good deal of courage') is called for', *sie wird dir einiges (etliches) erzählen* 'she'll tell you a thing or two', *haben Sie noch Glühbirnen vorrätig? — jawohl, einige (etliche) sind noch da* 'have you any more electric bulbs in stock?*—to be sure, there are still a few left'; often together with *wenige*, e.g. *er teilte das Geheimnis mit einigen (etlichen) wenigen Freunden* 'he shared the secret with some few friends'.

jeder

Also sometimes *ein jeder* and as an occasional literary alternative *(ein) jeglicher*, all meaning 'each, every, each one, every one', also 'any, anyone'.

The pronoun *jeder* is the usual one: *jedes Kind (jedes der Kinder) bekam ein Geschenk* 'each child (each of the children) received a gift', *der Postbote stellt die Briefe jeden Tag zu* 'the postman delivers the letters every day', *der Gemüsehändler kommt jeden zweiten Tag* 'the greengrocer comes every second day', *am ersten jeden* (some use *jedes*) *Monats* 'on the first of each month', *jeder für sich* 'every man for himself', *jede Frau würde sich darüber freuen* 'any woman would be pleased with it', *schöner als jede Blume* 'fairer than any flower', *jede Menge Kartoffeln* 'any amount of potatoes', *ohne jeden Zweifel* 'without any doubt', *bei jedem Wetter* 'in all weathers'. Appositional use is common in sentences of the type *sie gaben ihm jeder eine Spende = jeder von ihnen gab ihm eine Spende* 'each of them gave him a donation'. Especially in the north, *jeder* can be used informally in the plural in expressions of time: *jede zehn Minuten* 'every ten minutes', otherwise and generally *alle zehn Minuten*, p. 219. Notice *jeder einzelne* 'each single one'. On substantival use in the genitive, see next paragraph.

In certain everyday contexts *ein jeder* is an optional alternative to *jeder*, e.g. *das weiß (ein) jeder* 'anyone knows that', *(ein) jeder könnte dasselbe behaupten* 'anyone could say the same', but by and large this form is associated with elevated style: *ein jedes Mal*, but generally simply *jedes Mal*, also written *jedesmal* 'each time', *er erinnert sich eines jeden*, ordinarily *an jeden* 'he remembers each one'. We now note that *jeder* cannot in any case be used substantivally in the genitive, *ein jeder* taking its place: *die soziale Sicherheit eines jeden* (= *jedes einzelnen*) *ist gesetzlich gesichert* 'the social security of each one (of each individual) is guaranteed by law'.

Examples of the purely literary synonym: *ohne jegliche* (normally *jede*) *Aussicht auf Verbesserung* 'without any prospect of improvement', *ein jeglicher* (living language *jeder*) *nach seiner Art* 'each after his kind'.

jedermann

A rather literary word corresponding in general to 'everyman', as in the title of Hofmannsthal's play *Jedermann*, but idiomatically also 'everyone'. In this latter sense it commonly occurs in the genitive in set phrases like *es ist nicht jedermanns Sache, nach jedermanns Geschmack* 'it is not everyone's line, to everyone's taste'.

jemand, niemand

The latter corresponds to 'no one, nobody': *niemand raucht* 'no one is smoking', the former to 'someone, somebody': *jemand hustet* 'someone is coughing', but 'anyone, anybody' may be equally appropriate in a question: *hast du jemand gesehen?* 'have you seen someone? have you seen anyone?', distinct from *hast du irgend jemand gesehen?* 'have you seen anyone at all?'

In English, the genitives 'someone's, no one's' are, of course, very often used. In German, the corresponding genitives occur much less frequently and essentially as literary forms: *jemand(e)s — niemand(e)s — Verantwortung* 'someone's—no one's—responsibility'. For 'it must be someone's responsibility' we suggest normally *irgend jemand muß verantwortlich sein*, for 'it's nobody's business', let us say *es geht niemand was an*, and so on.

The present pronouns can freely take the inflexion *-en* in the accusative and dative, e.g. also *hast du jemanden gesehen?*, and details on these forms and their stylistic relevance are given on p. 72. Here it may suffice to notice again the (usually invariable) expressions *jemand (niemand) anders* 'someone (no one) else' and their inflecting, Upper German masculine variants *jemand (niemand) anderer*. This difference is paralleled when the pronouns are used with an adjective: *jemand Frisches* (Upper German *Frischer*) *ist in die Wohnung eingezogen* 'someone new has moved into the flat'. In the oblique cases, however, the (original) masculine declension is still widespread: *sie will niemand Armen heiraten* 'she doesn't want to marry anyone poor', *darf ich mal mit jemand Vernünftigem reden?* 'may I have a word with someone sensible?'

The pronouns *einer* (p. 222) and *wer* (p. 215) may be found instead of *jemand*, while *keiner* is a common alternative to *niemand*, e.g. *ich habe keinen* (= *niemand*) *gesehen* 'I've seen no one'.

beide

Substantival and adjectival use may be considered together: *beide (beide Söhne) waren anwesend* 'both (both sons) were present', *die Ansprüche von beiden* (*von beiden Söhnen*, more formally *beider Söhne*) 'the claims of both (both sons)'. The pronoun may be preceded, optionally, by the definite article, when it regularly takes the weak ending: *die beiden* 'both', *die beiden Söhne* 'both (the) sons'. It may likewise be qualified by a (preceding NB!) demonstrative or possessive, e.g. *diese beiden* 'both these', *diese beiden Söhne* 'both these sons', *seine beiden* 'his two', *seine beiden Söhne* 'both his sons'.

When qualified by a personal pronoun, *beide* in most cases retains the strong ending: *wir beide* 'both of us', *für euch beide* 'for both of you', but usually *ihr beiden* 'both of you', cf. the use of the weak adjective after this particular pronoun, p 168. The same is usual after *wir*, too, when in the attributive position: *wir beiden Arbeitslosen* 'we two unemployed'. It will be seen that English idiom quite often requires 'two' or other equivalent rather than 'both': *welcher von* (or *von den) beiden?* 'which of the two', *keiner von* (or *von den) beiden* 'neither of the two, neither of them', *alle beide* 'both of them'.

Although the present pronoun is dual in number, there exists nevertheless a substantival neut. sg. *beides* having the same wide range of application as other neut. sg. pronouns: *sie hat beides: Schönheit und Reichtum* 'she has both: beauty and wealth'.

Lastly, we notice that English 'both . . . and' is, in the German of today, rendered *sowohl . . . als (auch)*, the older construction *beides . . . und*, not unknown to the writers of the classical period, being now quite extinct.

all

Also inflected *aller, -e, -es* (p. 61), used substantivally and adjectivally; we begin with the latter.

Occurrences in the inflected singular have, in general, a literary flavour: *jetzt hat aller Zwist ein Ende* 'now all strife is at an end', *nicht für alles Geld der Welt* 'not for all the money in the world', *allen Ernstes* 'in all seriousness', *in aller Bescheidenheit* 'in all modesty', *zu allem Unglück verlor die Witwe auch noch ihren Sohn* 'most unfortunately the widow lost her son, too'. This pronoun was formerly used in contexts where today only *jeder* would be possible; a relic survives in the proverb *aller Anfang ist schwer* 'every beginning is hard'. The two pronouns may still occasionally be interchangeable: *er hat allen* (or *jeden) Grund, argwöhnisch zu sein* 'he has every reason to be suspicious'.

Usage in the plural, on the other hand, is not so much associated with literary style (except, of course, in the genitive, p. 149): *alle Kinder mögen Süßigkeiten* 'all children like sweets', *wir haben alle leeren Flaschen zurückgebracht* 'we have returned all the empty bottles', *alle seine Freunde sind gekommen, alle anderen sind weggeblieben* 'all his friends came, all the others stayed away', *ein hoher Prozentsatz aller Erwachsenen leidet unter rheumatischen*

Beschwerden 'a high percentage of all adults suffer from rheumatic complaints'. Translation into English may again require 'every': *alle Augenblicke* 'every so often', similarly *alle zehn Minuten* 'every ten minutes' overlapping with local *jede zehn Minuten*, p. 216. As a result of the close semantic affinity between the two pronouns, the plural *alle* is virtually interchangeable with the singular *jeder*, e.g. *alle Tische* 'all (the) tables', *jeder Tisch* 'each, every table'. Compare further the everyday expression *auf alle Fälle* in varying idiomatic contexts: *wir sind auf alle Fälle gewappnet* 'we are ready for all eventualities', *wir werden auf alle Fälle* (= *auf jeden Fall*) *vorbeischauen* 'we'll drop in to see you in any case', where English requires yet another pronoun.

Uninflected *all* followed by the definite article is widely used, both in the singular and plural: *all das Geld* 'all the money' (less formal than *alles Geld* above), *all die anderen* 'all the others' (= *alle anderen* above), *ich habe genug von all dem Schieben und Drängen* 'I've had enough of all the shoving and pushing', *wir brauchen wirksamen Schutz vor all den schädlichen Abgasen* 'we need effective protection from all the noxious fumes'. Where appropriate, the inflected form *alle* occurs as a common alternative: *all/alle die Hilfe* 'all the help', *all/alle die Ideen* 'all the ideas', also *alle die anderen* (see above).

The uninflected form is similarly used before demonstratives: *all das* (exceptional alternative *alles das*, cf. *das alles* below) 'all that', *all dies(es) Geld* 'all this money', *ich bin mir all dessen bewußt* 'I am aware of it all', *mit all 'dem Geld* 'with all that money', *all/alle diese Ideen* 'all these ideas', *wir gedenken mit Stolz all jener Patrioten, die für eine gerechte Sache stritten* 'we remember with pride all those patriots who struggled in a just cause'. It likewise occurs before possessives: *all sein Geld* 'all his money', *mit all unserem Geld* 'with all our money', *all/alle meine Hilfe* 'all my help', *all/alle Ihre Ideen* 'all your ideas'. When in such use *all* and *alle* are plural alternatives, a certain difference of meaning emerges: *all diese (Ihre) Ideen sind Unsinn* 'all these ideas (of yours) are nonsense' is a general, sweeping statement, contrasting with, say, *alle diese (Ihre) Ideen müßten aufgegriffen werden* 'all these ideas (of yours)—i.e. emphatically every idea—should be taken up'.

In substantival use only inflected forms play any part: *das alles* (= *all das, alles das*) 'all that', *Ende gut, alles gut* 'all's well that ends well', *hat die Ziege alles gefressen?* 'has the goat eaten it all, or everything?', *ich muß mich mit allem abfinden* 'I have to put up with everything', *alle sind gekommen* 'all have come, every one has come', *vor aller Augen* 'in the sight of all', *das ist unser aller Wunsch* (rather formal) 'that is what we all wish', *sie versuchte, ihren Willen mit allen Mitteln durchzusetzen* 'she tried by every means to get her own way'. As with other indefinite pronouns, the neut. sg. has a considerable

range of application, hence: *alles Ausreden!* 'nothing but excuses!',
bei schönem Wetter ist alles unterwegs 'when the weather is fine,
everybody is out and about', *es sind alles Seeleute* 'they are all
seamen', less formal than *sie sind alle Seeleute*.

When two pronouns are involved, they may be separated giving
some slight difference of emphasis: *sie sind alle gekommen* 'they have
all come', *sie alle sind gekommen* 'all of them have come', compare
also *sie können mich alle gern haben* 'I don't give a damn about the lot
of them', further *das wird alles zu prüfen sein* 'that will all have to be
checked', *das alles wird zu prüfen sein* 'all that will have to be
checked'.

In conclusion, as a curiosity, a much-used colloquial word *alle*
meaning 'used up' or the like; it occurs predicatively: *der Honig ist alle*
'the honey has been used up, there is no honey left', *die Erbsen sollen
alle werden* 'the peas are to be finished off'. Such things are mostly
heard in the northern and central parts of the country. Alternatively,
one could say, e.g. *es ist kein Honig mehr da, wir sollen die ganzen
Erbsen aufbrauchen.* The term is of unknown origin and may well
have nothing to do with the pronoun discussed in this section.

Notes on the use of ganz

It will be appropriate to append here some notes on the part played by
this word. It is an adjective and means primarily 'whole': *die ganze
Maschine* 'the whole machine', a meaning in the nature of things close
to *all* 'all' and which leads to a degree of interchange: *mit seiner
ganzen Macht = mit all seiner Macht* 'with his whole might, with all his
might'. Such overlapping is not necessarily the same in both
languages. In English one may say 'the whole, or all the family', in
German only *die ganze Familie*, and likewise in comparable collectives:
die ganze Schule 'the whole school, all (the) school', further in
expressions of time: *die ganze Woche* 'the whole week, all (the)
week', cf. also *von ganzem Herzen* 'with all my (etc.) heart,
wholeheartedly'. Notice the idiom: *wieviel sind aufgekreuzt? — ganze
drei!* 'how many turned up? — a mere three!'

Altogether *ganz* has a much wider range than 'whole'. Except in
general statements: *alle Wege führen nach Rom* 'all roads lead to
Rome' and in set phrases (as in the first paragraph of the section *a l l*),
the pronoun *all* is, by and large, replaceable by *ganz*, especially in
colloquial style. Thus one regularly finds *das ganze Geld* 'all the
money', *meine ganze Hilfe* 'all my help', cf. *all das Geld, all/alle Hilfe*
(p. 219), also in the plural: *die ganzen Schwierigkeiten* 'all the
difficulties'. Use in the plural may be rather inelegant, however, since
here the basic sense 'whole', properly a singular sense, is more
obtrusive, e.g. *die ganzen Kartoffeln* 'all the potatoes' lit. 'the whole

potatoes' as opposed to, say, *die halben Kartoffeln* 'the half-potatoes' (on this phrase, see also p. 81), further *die ganzen Fenster* lit. 'the whole windows' easily imagined as contrasting with *die zerbrochenen Fenster* 'the broken windows'. Occasionally the use of the two terms contrasts idiomatically: *die ganze Welt* 'the whole world' literally and figuratively, but *alle Welt* only figuratively, as *alle Welt weiß davon* 'everybody knows about it', cf. also *wo in aller Welt bist du gewesen?* 'where on earth have you been?'

The adjective is frequently substantivized: *das Ganze* 'the whole'.

man, einer, sie

The pronoun *man* (originally meaning 'man') may be appropriately translated 'one': *man kann vieles voraussehen, was man doch nicht verhindern kann* 'one can foresee many things which one cannot prevent'. The numeral *ein* supplies the oblique cases (acc. and dat.): *echte Freunde lassen einen nicht im Stich* 'real friends don't leave one in the lurch', *ein bißchen Bewegung tut einem gut* 'a little exercise does one good'. The possessive *sein* takes the place of a genitive: *man muß auf seinem Recht bestehen* 'one must insist on one's rights'. The English construction 'one' belongs, roughly speaking, to somewhat elevated style; in popular use 'you' is generally preferred. But German *man* embraces both levels, and 'you' could be substituted for 'one' in translating the sample sentences above. Sometimes 'people' or 'they' are suitable equivalents: *in China benützt man Eßstäbchen* 'in China people (or, they) use chopsticks'. By comparison with English, the present construction is particularly prominent, the more so since it often corresponds idiomatically to our passive: (a notice) *man spricht polnisch* 'Polish spoken', see further p. 248.

The traditional pronoun *man* faces a degree of competition from a relative newcomer *einer*, a slightly substandard colloquialism, formed after the analogy of the oblique *einen*, *einem* above: *und das soll einer wissen?* 'and is one (or, a chap) supposed to know that?'. Notice the indispensable idiom *sieh mal einer an!* 'just look at this/that! what a surprise!', syntactically obscure, but which nevertheless seems to belong here. The present pronoun is distinct from *einer* 'someone', p. 222.

In the same way as English may have 'they', German can also use the 3rd pl. *sie* as an indefinite pronoun, especially in spoken style: *sie machen ihm am Arbeitsplatz Unannehmlichkeiten* 'they are making difficulties for him at work', a little less formal than *man macht*, etc. While not in itself substandard, this use of *sie* is nevertheless very common in slangy speech: *sie haben mir meine Uhr geklaut* 'they've pinched my watch, my watch has been pinched'.

irgendein(er), *irgendwelcher*

These pronouns inflect like their respective simplexes, pp. 58, 71; their meanings are 'some, some one (or other), etc.' Examples of the first: *er hat irgendeinen Tisch zu verkaufen* 'he has some table or other for sale', *aber ich brauche einen Stuhl — irgendeiner genügt* 'but I want a chair—any old one will do'. This pronoun is very close to the second one which, in casual conversation at any rate, often replaces it: *er hat irgendwelchen Tisch zu verkaufen*, though the two pronouns do, properly speaking, convey different shades of meaning: *sie lebten von der Hand in den Mund ohne irgendwelche Möglichkeit, ihr Los zu verbessern* 'they were living from hand to mouth, without any possibility of improving their lot', *da bot sich irgendeine unverhoffte Gelegenheit* 'then some unexpected chance or other presented itself', i.e. one single, specific chance. It hardly needs mentioning that only *irgendwelcher* can be used in the plural: *er hat irgendwelche Tische zu verkaufen* 'he has tables of some sort or another for sale'. Cf. p. 215.

einer 'someone, etc.'

Except after *was für* (p. 212) not particularly common owing to easy confusion with the numeral 'one', p. 71. But in suitable contexts, such confusion is excluded: *es muß doch einer das Fenster zerbrochen haben, es kann ja nicht der Wind gewesen sein* 'someone must have broken the window, it can't have been the wind', *sie möchte einen mit Geld heiraten* 'she would like to marry someone with money', *du bist mir alles gewesen, was einer einem sein kann* 'you have been to me all that anyone can be to anyone', and now two sayings: first, the perennial puerility *mein letzter Wille — eine mit 'ner Brille* 'my last will and testament (but interpretable as 'the last thing I want')—someone (female) with a pair of spectacles', and second, the well-worn misquotation *wenn einer eine Reise tut, dann kann er was erzählen* 'when somebody goes on a journey, he has a lot to talk about'. In all these sentences the present pronoun could be replaced by *jemand*; indeed, the last example was originally *wenn jemand eine Reise tut . . .* (Claudius 1789).

   Notice (chiefly literary) *unsereiner* (lit. 'of-us one') = *einer wie wir* 'one like us': *unsereinen kennt die Welt nicht mehr* 'the world no longer takes notice of people like us'. In colloquial style, the inflected pronoun is commonly replaced by invariable *unsereins*, e.g. *mit unsereins springt man nicht so um* 'you can't ride roughshod over people like us'.

   Cf. *irgendeiner* (in the previous section); on *einer* = *man*, see p. 221.

kein, keiner

There is a clear formal distinction: *kein* is the adjective, *keiner* the pronoun, both inflecting, pp. 62, 72. We recall that the nom. acc. neut. sg. pronoun is *keines* or *keins* and note that the latter is dominant in the spoken language: *ich hab' keins* 'I have none'. Other examples: *auf seinesgleichen ist kein Verlaß* 'there is no relying on the likes of him', *wir haben dazu keine Lust* 'we don't feel like (doing) it', *wir geben auf keinen Fall nach* 'on no account will we yield', *keiner von beiden konnte ihr helfen* 'neither of them could help her', *er kam mit keinem gut aus* 'he got on well with no one'.

In adjectival use *kein* lit. 'no' very often corresponds, alternatively, to 'not a, not any' and is in fact the usual equivalent of these English words: *es ist überhaupt kein Problem* 'it is no (or, not a) problem at all', *sie wollte Äpfel kaufen, aber sie sah keine schönen* 'she wanted to buy some apples, but she saw no nice ones (or, did not see any nice ones)'. By a use unparalleled in English idiom, *kein* can substitute for *nicht* in expressions of time: *er war keine* (or *nicht*) *zehn Minuten bei uns* 'he wasn't with us ten minutes'.

The masculine singular of the present pronoun may alternate with *niemand* (p. 217), when it will be the commoner of the two, especially in the language as ordinarily spoken: *keiner* (or *niemand*) *glaubt ihm* 'no one believes him', *ich sehe keinen* (or *niemand*) *anderen* 'I see no other one, no one else', *die Post darf keinen* (or *niemand*) *Vorbestraften beschäftigen* 'the postal services are not allowed to employ anyone with a criminal record'. A further (colloquial) substitution is *kein Mensch*, e.g. *kein Mensch glaubt ihm* 'no one believes him'.

viel

The basic meanings are straightforward: sg. *viel* 'much, a lot, a good deal', pl. *viele* 'many'.

When used as a substantive in the singular and not qualified by an inflecting word, *viel* is then most commonly uninflected: *sie hat viel zu sagen* 'she has much to say', *es wird nicht viel dabei herauskommen* 'not much will come out of it'. Naturally enough, its function is frequently that of an adverb: *ich habe viel versucht* 'I've tried a lot' i.e. 'often'. Now inflected forms occur as well: nom. acc. *vieles*, dat. *vielem*. These always retain their pronominal function and may therefore, in given contexts, contrast with the uninflected form in its adverbial function: *ich habe vieles versucht* 'I've tried a lot (of different things)', cf. further *ich bin mit vielem, doch nicht mit allem einverstanden* 'I agree with many things, though not with all'. Such considerations apart, the inflected forms will be more suitable in literary diction: *vieles* (rather than *viel*) *harrt noch der Aufklärung* 'much awaits clarification', likewise idioms of the type *um vieles besser* 'much better', in ordinary style simply *viel besser*. Whereas the plural sense 'many things' is sometimes implicit in the inflected forms, plurality is brought out unequivocally by *vielerlei*, p. 78: *willst du gut deutsch lernen, dann mußt du viel und vielerlei lesen* 'if you want to learn German well, you have to read a good deal, and also many sorts, of German'.

The singular pronoun is likewise common in adjectival use, when it is nearly always uninflected: *viel Glück im Neuen Jahr* 'A Happy New Year', *wir hatten so viel schwere Arbeit* 'we had so much hard work', *er gab sich viel Mühe* 'he went to a very great deal of trouble', *sie praktizierte mit viel Erfolg* 'she practised (as a doctor) with much success'. Everyday exception: *vielen Dank* 'many thanks'—otherwise inflexions are rare and restricted to more literary style: *vieles Schöne* 'much that is beautiful', e.g. *wir wünschen Dir vieles Schöne*, but more ordinarily *viel Schönes*, idiomatically something like 'we wish you all the very best'.

As a plural substantive the pronoun takes the regular (strong) endings: *viele sind berufen* 'many are called', *er war nur einer unter vielen* 'he was but one among many', and may also do so when used adjectivally: *viele Kinder* 'many children', *die Ansichten vieler Fachleute* 'the opinions of many experts', *in vielen Fällen* 'in many cases'. In this latter use, however, nom. acc. *viele* is most often replaced by the uninflected form in the spoken language: *viel Kinder* 'a lot of children', and the same is not infrequently heard in examples of the dative as well: *es war ein Bericht mit viel Fehlern* 'it was a report with many mistakes'. The uninflected form can be found in print, too.

The attributive pronoun may be qualified by an inflecting word—the definite article or a demonstrative or possessive pronoun, when it takes the appropriate inflexions: *was hat er mit dem (diesem, seinem) vielen Geld gemacht?* 'what has he done with all the (this, his) money?', *die vielen Leute!* 'so many people!'

soviel, zuviel, wieviel

Firstly, *so'viel* 'so much, so many, such a lot (of), as much, as many' is invariable: *nimm, soviel du kannst* 'take as much as you can', *das Pferd frißt doppelt soviel Heu* 'the horse eats twice as much hay', *ich habe soviel Briefe zu beantworten* 'I have so many letters to answer'. But with emphatic stressing: *'so viel* (two words) *'so* much, etc.' the rules are as for *viel* (above): *selbst ein Pferd kann nicht so viel fressen* 'even a horse cannot eat *so* much', *woher nehme ich die Zeit, so viel (or viele) Briefe zu beantworten?* 'where do I find the time to answer *so* many letters?'

Secondly, *zu'viel* 'too much, too many' is also unchanged: *das ist zuviel des Guten* 'that's too much of a good thing', *viel zuviel* 'much too much', *sie haben zuviel Sachen in diesem kleinen Zimmer* 'they have too many things in this small room'. Then with emphatic stressing: '*zu viel* (two words) '*too* much, etc.': *das ist schon viel, aber noch nicht zu viel* 'that's a lot, but still not too much', *ich habe zu viel* (or *viele*) *Briefe zu beantworten* 'I have too many letters to answer'.

Uninflected *wieviel* 'how much, how many' is used both in questions and exclamations; in the interrogative, pl. also *wie viele?* (two words). The stress is commonly *wie'viel*, but '*wieviel* is equally possible in the same way as our 'how *much*' can become '*how* much'. The uninflected form predominates in the spoken language and is quite usual in the written style, too: *wieviel hast du?* 'how much (or, how many) have you?', *wieviel Pfennig hat die Mark?* 'how many pfennigs are there in a mark?', *wieviel Tage hat die Woche?* 'how many days are there in a week?', *wieviel Sorgen Kinder machen!* 'how much worry children cause!' The interrogative pl. *wie viele* is appropriate in formal style when a precise number is required: *wie viele Tage noch bis Weihnachten?* — *dreizehn* 'how many days still to Christmas?—thirteen'. Even so, the uninflected form is pretty general with nouns denoting quantity or measurement: *wieviel Tonnen wiegt die Lok?* 'how many tons does the engine weigh?', *wieviel Kilometer sind es bis Nürnberg?* 'how many kilometres is it to Nuremberg?'

wenig

The meanings: sg. *wenig* '(a) little', pl. *wenige* '(a) few'.

Several comparisons with *viel* (p. 233) suggest themselves. Used substantivally in the singular and similarly unqualified, *wenig* also generally remains unchanged: *sie hat wenig zu sagen* 'she has little to say', *es wird wenig dabei herauskommen* 'little will come out of it'. This word, too, may have an adverbial function: *ich habe wenig versucht* 'I haven't tried a lot' i.e. 'not often'. Inflexions are, however, even less usual than is the case with *viel*, and when they do occur they have a literary flavour, in which connection notice idioms such as *weniges Gute*, e.g. *er kann weniges Gute* (more ordinarily *wenig Gutes*) *berichten* 'he can report little that is good', and expressions of the type *um weniges höher*, e.g. *sein Angebot ist um weniges höher* (simpler style *ein wenig höher*) 'his offer is a little higher'. Otherwise invariable *wenig* is the general rule: *man muß sich manchmal mit wenig abfinden* 'one has to be content at times with a little', and equally so in adjective use: *sie kann nur wenig Dänisch* 'she knows only a little Danish', *die Gefangenen gingen mit wenig echter Begeisterung an die Arbeit* 'the prisoners set about the job with little real enthusiasm', *er war ein wenig schöner Anblick* 'it was not a very pleasant sight'.

As a plural substantive the pronoun takes the regular (strong) endings: *wenige sind auserwählt* 'few are chosen', *die Geschichte ist wenigen bekannt* 'the story is known to few', and may also do so when used adjectivally: *wenige Kinder* '(a) few children', *in wenigen Fällen* 'in a few cases'. In this latter use, however, nom. acc. *wenige* is most often replaced by the uninflected form in colloquial German, hence *wenig Kinder*, and this may be found in print, too. It also very commonly occurs in the dative as well: *ich versuche, mit möglichst wenig Worten, möglichst viel zu sagen* 'I am trying to say as much as possible with as few words as possible'.

The attributive pronoun may be qualified in the same way as *viel*, taking the appropriate terminations: *was hat er mit dem (diesem, seinem) wenigen Geld gemacht?* 'what has he done with the (this, his) small amount of money?'

The expression *ein wenig* is invariable: *hast du Geld? — ein wenig* 'have you any money?—a little', *ein wenig Geld* 'a little money', similarly *ein klein wenig* 'just a little'.

Cf. *paar*, p. 227.

sowenig, zuwenig, wie wenig

The first two may be compared, in principle, with *soviel, zuviel* (p. 224), being likewise uninflected and having the stress on the second component: *so'wenig* 'so little, such a little, as little', *zu'wenig* 'too little': *sie ißt sowenig, weil sie abnehmen will* 'she eats so little because she wants to lose weight', (cynical saying) *die Rente ist zum Leben zuwenig, zum Sterben zuviel* lit. 'the pension is too little to live on, (but) too much to die of'. Then with emphatic stressing: *'so wenig, 'zu wenig* (two words) '*so* little, *too* little', rules as for *wenig* above: *sie hatte so wenig gegessen, daß ihre Gesundheit gefährdet war* 'she had eaten so little that her health was endangered', *infolge der anhaltenden Dürre hatten die Tiere zu wenig Wasser, um zu überleben* 'as a consequence of the prolonged drought the animals had too little water to survive'. The term *'ebensowenig* 'just as little, etc.' is written as one word even though the first component always bears the stress: *der qualifizierte Lehrer verdiente ebensowenig wie der ungelernte Arbeiter* 'the qualified teacher earned just as little as the unskilled labourer', but it is divided when the second component is inflected: *heute kamen ebenso wenige* (or *ebensowenig*) *Gäste wie gestern* 'just as few guests came today as yesterday'.

Unlike *wieviel* 'how much' (p. 224), *wie wenig* 'how little' is never written as one word, regardless of stress; it is commonly *wie 'wenig*, but also *'wie wenig*, cf. our '*how* little': *es ist merkwürdig, wie* '*wenig man in der nichtjüdischen Welt vom jüdischen Volk weiß* 'it is remarkable how little the Gentile world knows about the Jewish people', *wenig schon, aber ich weiß nicht* '*wie wenig* 'a little certainly, but I don't know how little'.

bißchen

The word is invariable. It is used adjectivally: *mit dem bißchen Geld, das er verdient, kann er sich kaum über Wasser halten* 'with the bit of money he earns he can hardly keep his head above water', very commonly in the form *ein bißchen*, thus *ein bißchen Käse* 'a bit of cheese', *ein bißchen Kaffee* 'a drop of coffee', stylistically often 'a little': *mit Kindern muß man ein bißchen Geduld haben* 'one must have a little patience with children', also qualifying an adjective: *ein bißchen laut* 'a bit loud'. Notice the negative use: *kein bißchen Brot im Haus* 'not a bite of bread in the house', *kein bißchen weise* 'not a bit wise (in the ways of the world)'. Substantival use is commonplace: *möchten Sie ein bißchen?* 'would you like a bit?' The present term is close to *wenig* (pp. 225 f.) and may be likewise qualified by uninflected *klein*, e.g. *sein klein bißchen Geld* 'his little bit of money'.

paar

An invariable expression: *die Busse fahren alle paar Minuten ab* 'the buses leave every few minutes', *sie genoß die paar Monate, die ihr verblieben waren* 'she enjoyed the few months that were left to her', in many contexts *ein paar*, e.g. *hast du ein paar Mark mit?* 'have you a few marks on you?', *sie wird in ein paar Tagen hier sein* 'she will be here in a few days', *wir gingen mit ein paar Freunden* 'we went with a few friends'. The present expressions are often interchangeable with *wenige* (p. 226), e.g. from the sentences above: *die wenigen Monate* 'the few months', *in wenigen Tagen* 'in a few days', with a slight change of meaning *mit wenigen Freunden* 'with few friends'.

The pronoun *ein paar* is naturally distinct from its source *ein Paar* 'a pair', e.g. *ein Paar Schuhe* 'a pair of shoes', nevertheless it cannot be used in contexts in which the original meaning is inherent—'I need a few shoes' will be *ich brauche einige Schuhe* or, if 'few' is to be emphasized, *einige wenige Schuhe*. On the other hand the sentence *ein paar Schuhe wurden weggeworfen* is unambiguously 'a few shoes were thrown out', clearly different from *ein Paar Schuhe wurde weggeworfen* 'a pair of shoes was thrown out', similarly *diese paar Schuhe* 'these few shoes', but *dieses Paar Schuhe* 'this pair of shoes'.

ander

The pronoun 'other', pp. 62, 72.

Examples: *der andere (ein anderer) Freund, die andere (eine andere)*

Freundin 'the other (another) friend' (masc., fem.), *kein anderer als der Teufel selbst* 'none other than the devil himself', *ein Wort gab das andere* 'one word led to another', *alles andere* 'everything else', *etwas anderes* 'something else', *alle anderen* 'all (the) others'—notice *wir (ihr) anderen* 'we (you) others'—*am anderen Tag* 'next day', *unter anderem* 'inter alia, among other things', *ich hielt sie für jemand anders*, or *anderen* (p. 72) 'I mistook her for someone else', *wir sind anderer Meinung* 'we are of a different opinion', *man hat mich eines anderen belehrt* 'I have been told something else', *ein anderes Mal* 'another time', alternatively *ein andermal* corresponding to a regional use of the uninflected nom. acc. neut. sg., e.g. *ein ander Messer* for standard *ein anderes Messer* 'another knife'.

manch

Also inflected *mancher, -e, -es*, p. 61: sg. 'many a (but not too many a)', pl. 'some' i.e. rather more than *einige*, but less than *viele*. The inflected forms are those most often found: *mancher arme Junge hat es in der Welt weit gebracht* 'many a poor boy has got on well in the world', *manche Leute teilen ihre Ansicht* 'some people share your view', *wir hatten in manchen Fällen gute Resultate* 'we had good results in some cases'. The neut. sg. has the usual range of application, *manches läßt sich noch nicht absehen* 'some things cannot yet be foreseen', *er mag in manchem recht haben* 'he may be right in some ways'. When used with a noun qualified by an adjective, *manche* pl. will be often more appropriately rendered by 'many a': *wir haben manche glückliche* (or *glücklichen*) *Stunden in seiner Gesellschaft verbracht* 'we have spent many a happy hour in his company'.

Uninflected *manch* occurs only as an attributive. It is commonest when it forms the pronoun *manch einer*, a variant of *mancher* 'many a one', the difference being essentially regional: *manch einer* (or *mancher*) *muß sich sein Leben lang plagen* 'many a one has to struggle hard all his life', also *manch ein* 'many a': *manch eine* (a little more formal than *manche*) *Hausfrau hat eine Karriere außerhalb ihrer vier Wände* 'many a housewife has a career outside her own four walls'. Otherwise such usage belongs to high style: *sie hatten manch Schönes* (more ordinarily *manches Schöne*) *gesehen* 'they had seen much that was beautiful'—but not so much as *vieles Schöne, viel Schönes*, p. 224—and is often found in poetry: (Goethe) *manch bunte Blumen sind an dem Strand, / meine Mutter hat manch gülden Gewand* 'many a gay flower grows by the shore, / my mother has many a golden raiment'.

The present term may be strengthened by *so*, moving it close in meaning to *viele*, as *ich bin ihr so manches Mal in der Stadt begegnet* 'I have met her in the town a good many times'. In the south *gar* may substitute for *so*, e.g. *gar mancher wird sich wohl ins Fäustchen lachen* 'a lot of people will now be laughing up their sleeve', but such use is otherwise a feature of high style.

-gleichen

Invariable *meinesgleichen* 'one like me, my equal(s)', etc. (p. 73) are treated as singulars: *meinesgleichen denkt nicht so* 'a person like me doesn't think like that', *er sagte, er habe unseresgleichen sein Lebtag nicht gesehen* 'he said he had never seen the likes of us in all his born days', *sie verkehrte nur mit ihresgleichen* 'she associated only with people like herself'. Further *dergleichen* 'of that sort', p. 208.

18. Verbs and their uses

A note on the English verb

As languages descended from a common parent, English and German once possessed identical verbal systems. But during the subsequent, separate evolution of the two languages many differences arose. While German remains by and large more conservative, English has made two important additions to the common stock. It has developed, firstly, the so-called continuous tenses, e.g. *he is (was, will be, etc.) playing*, which express a special aspect of the action: *he is playing football* is not quite the same as *he plays football*. These new tenses have enriched the English verb, enabling it to convey shades of meaning beyond what is conceivable in the more traditional German system, which in this instance can offer only *er spielt Fußball*, of itself innocent of the nuances implicit in the two English 'equivalents'. If German needs to bring out the continuous aspect, other devices are available, as explained on p. 246. Secondly, English has introduced emphatic tenses with *do*, as *I do see*, the emphasis being, however, ordinarily lost in questions and negative statements, thus *what do you say?* for archaic *what say you?* or *I don't know* instead of old-fashioned *I know not*. It will be noticed that German usage here corresponds to the older English style: *was sagst du? ich weiß nicht.* The emphatic conjugation as such is, of course, absent from German, although a periphrasis with *tun* is possible, see pp. 246 f.

Apart from such innovations on the English side, the languages may still differ significantly in the idiomatic application of the tenses they have in common, as may be seen from the relevant discussion *passim* below. This is a further reason why translations of so many German sentences in this book have necessarily been arbitrary in respect of the English 'equivalent' tense.

The Indicative

Introductory

The indicative is the mood which makes a statement about a fact: *die Lampe steht (stand) auf dem Tisch* 'the lamp stands (stood) on the table'; it is also found in a type of conditional clause, see p. 263.

The indicative can occur instead of the usual preterite subjunctive when certainty or a high degree of probability is implied: (story) *schon die nächste Welle konnte die wertvolle Kiste über Bord befördern* 'the very next wave could sweep the valuable chest overboard', (magazine) *doch da die Ägypter sich das Treffen so sehr wünschten, wollten wir keine Spielverderber sein. Vielleicht kam ja etwas dabei heraus* 'but since the Egyptians were so keen on the meeting we didn't want to be spoilsports. Very possibly something would come out of it'.

In subordinate clauses the indicative is often an optional alternative to the more formal subjunctive, especially in the spoken language; see *passim* below.

PRESENT TENSE

This tense has the same basic function as the English present, i.e. to express present time: *sie arbeitet im Augenblick an einem neuen Projekt* 'she is working at the moment on a new project', or to state a general truth: *die Politiker wachen erst auf, wenn es längst zu spät ist* 'politicians only wake up when it's far too late'. It is likewise regular in timeless statements, as in proverbial style: *der Ertrinkende klammert sich an einen Strohhalm fest* 'a drowning man clutches at a straw'.

But other uses require comment. We notice first the use of the present to denote an action which began in the past and has continued up to the present: *ich habe seit Wochen Zahnschmerzen* 'I have had toothache for weeks', *vor fünfzehn Jahren haben wir das Häuschen gekauft, solange besitzen wir es schon* 'we bought the little place fifteen years ago, we have owned it for that long', *jetzt ist sie über zwanzig Jahre tot* 'she has been dead now for over twenty years'.

The present tense regularly expresses an instruction: *nach drei Wochen stellt der Lehrer die Listen auf* 'after three weeks the teacher will make out the lists', *überzählige Formulare werden dem Büro zurückgegeben* 'surplus forms are to be returned to the office'. In the 2nd person the present can express a peremptory command: *du bleibst zu Hause!* 'you're staying at home!', *ihr macht, daß ihr fortkommt!* 'you (lot) push off!', *Sie schreiben ihm unverzüglich!* 'you will write to him without delay!'

The present historic, adding vividness to the narrative, is particularly common both in writing and speaking, much more so than in English: (memoir) *er reicht mir ein dickes Buch, das erste Drehbuch, das ich in meinem Leben in der Hand halte* 'he passed me a thick book, the first script I had (ever) held in my hand in my life'. Sometimes the tenses switch: (from a verbatim report about a stolen car) *ich wollte meine Freunde nach Hause fahren; wir gehen zur Tür, und da sehe ich, daß der Wagen weg ist* 'I wanted to drive my friends home; we went to the door, and then I saw that the car had gone'. This use of the present commonly provides variation in historical writing in a way that is impossible in English: *die Prinzessin ist dreizehn Jahre alt, als ihre Mutter stirbt* 'the princess was thirteen years old when her mother died', *damals ist Jerusalem eine Stadt, die von Ägypten abhängig ist* 'at the time Jerusalem was a city which was dependent on Egypt', with switching of tenses: *obwohl das Konzil von Konstanz das Schisma zu beseitigen vermag, stiftete es gleichzeitig durch die Verfolgung der Hussiten einen Anlaß zu erneuter religiöser Unruhe* 'although the Council of Constance was able to overcome the Schism, at the same time it caused renewed religious unrest through the persecution of the Hussites', *Herschel wurde in Hannover geboren, ist also von Geburt Deutscher, lebte aber später ausschließlich in England* 'H. was born in H., and was therefore a German by birth, but later lived exclusively in E.'

In a few examples, present time is expressible by the present of *sein* with the simple infinitive: *Mutter ist einkaufen* 'Mother is out shopping', *ist sie Obst einkaufen?* 'is she out buying fruit?', *Vater ist arbeiten* 'Father is at work', elliptic for *einkaufen gegangen* 'gone shopping', *arbeiten gegangen* 'gone to work'.

An expression such as *wir kommen, um Ihnen zu gratulieren* 'we are coming to congratulate you' is also used when the sense is 'we have come to congratulate you'.

Present as indicator of future time

In point of fact, the pure feature is most commonly expressed by the present tense. Or, put in another way, the German present is far commoner in this function than is the case in English, which more usually requires, or at least prefers, a future tense rather than the present (continuous). The German present is, first of all, the normal tense when an adverbial expression makes it evident that future time is indicated: *tschüs bis auf morgen! Ich warte vorm Postamt auf dich. Wir essen ein Kleinigkeit im Schnellimbiß und gehen dann ins Kino* ' 'bye till tomorrow! I'll wait for you in front of the post-office. We'll have a bite of something in the snack-bar and then go to the cinema', *vielleicht setzt man ihm eines Tages ein Denkmal* 'perhaps they will put up a monument to him some day', *lange dauert es ja doch nicht mehr* 'it won't last much longer anyway', *bald ist Weihnachten* 'Christmas will be here soon'. A conditional clause may likewise make it clear that future time is involved: *falls der Plan mißlingt, gibt es Ärger* 'if the plan goes wrong, there'll be trouble'.

The present tense is usual after *wann?* 'when?': *wann haben Sie Zeit?* 'when will you have time?' It often denotes compliance with a request or the like: *nehmen Sie bitte Platz, wir rufen den Betriebsleiter* 'please take a seat, we'll call the manager', *na gut, ich gebe ihm Bescheid* 'all right, I'll let him know'. In these matters one may learn from a slip sometimes made by Germans when speaking English. Easily missing the lightly pronounced ' 'll', they tend to say 'we call the manager, I let you know', using the present as they would in German. Actually, this (simple) present was permissible in older English, and a single relic of the practice remains: instead of 'I'll tell you what' many still say 'I tell you what' just as Germans have *ich sage dir was*.

A present tense closely following a future tense will itself take on a future meaning: *Paulus sagte, alle werden am Leben bleiben, nur das Schiff geht verloren* '(St) Paul said, all shall survive, only the ship will be lost'.

In other examples, the context sufficiently indicates the future: *beeilen Sie sich! — sonst kommen Sie zu spät* 'hurry!, or you'll be too late', *der Ursprung dieser Völker liegt im dunkeln und bleibt es wohl auch* 'the origin of these peoples is obscure and will most likely remain so'. Notice the different renderings of the same German present in the following: *es ist Zeit, daß Georg heiratet — ach! der heiratet nie* 'it's time George got married—oh! he'll never marry'.

Present tenses with future meanings are equally prevalent in subordinate clauses: *wir sehen nicht, daß sich die Situation in Zukunft bessert* 'we don't see the situation getting better in the future', *es ist unwahrscheinlich, daß die Regierung darauf eingeht* 'it is unlikely that the government will consent to it', *im Anschluß an den Vortrag möchten wir Sie zu einem Empfang einladen, wo Sie auch Gelegenheit haben, den Künstler persönlich kennenzulernen* 'after the recital we should like to invite you to a reception where you will also be able to meet the artist personally', *weiß jemand, wann er kommt?* 'does anybody know when he'll be coming?'

Any future tense is prone to acquire a modal nuance (p. 234) and such is also evident when the present functions as a future in questions like *welches brave Mädchen hilft der Mutti beim Abwaschen?* 'which good little girl wants to help Mummy with the washing-up?', similarly (personal advertisement) *Ralf, 25 Jahre alt, sportlicher Typ, sucht nettes natürliches Mädchen für gemeinsame Freizeitgestaltung. Wer meldet sich?* 'Ralph, 25 years old, athletic type, wishes to meet pleasant, unsophisticated girl to share leisure-time pursuits. Who would like to reply?'

From the foregoing it follows that the English person speaking German must be on guard against an inclination to put *werden* whenever future time is involved, since this will often add an unwarranted modal nuance, see under 'Auxiliary *werden*', pp. 234 f.

FUTURE TENSE

Modals as future auxiliaries

In the oldest periods of English and German there was no future tense
as such; the present tense sufficed, since future meaning, when not
self-evident from the context, could be brought out by adverbs of
time. Such practice survives to a large extent in modern German,
accounting for the section 'Present as indicator of future time' above.

It will be pertinent to consider the linguistic implications of the
banal observation that future time is never with us, we are always
waiting for it. Unlike the present or the past, the future has no real
existence, it exists only in the mind, and this has determined how the
future is to be expressed in language. Now an event envisaged as
taking place in the future may be regarded as the result of a desire ('I
will drown') or of a decision ('and nobody shall save me') and such
views led to the once purely modal 'will' and 'shall' becoming future
auxiliaries as well.

In German, the corresponding *wollen* and *sollen*, primarily auxiliaries
of mood, have been similarly used as markers of future time; today
they are generally replaced in this function by *werden*. Nevertheless
they may still occur in contexts where a modal nuance is scarcely
tangible: *die Misere will kein Ende nehmen, was soll aus der
Menschheit werden?* 'there is no end to the misery, what shall become
of mankind?' to all intents and purposes the same semantically as *die
Misere nimmt kein Ende, was wird aus der Menschheit werden?* In
particular, the 1st person of *wollen* is common as a future auxiliary,
especially in North Germany: *ich will mal sehen, was ich machen kann*
'I'll see what I can do', *es ist schon spät, wir wollen jetzt gehen* 'it's
already late, we'll be going now', alternatively *ich werde mal sehen . . .
wir werden jetzt gehen*. The teacher in a Berlin school announces *wir
wollen jetzt eine Arbeit schreiben* 'we'll have a test now', but it never
occurs to any pupil to mutter *wir wollen nicht* 'we don't want to', for in
this context *wollen* is understood as a future auxiliary devoid of modal
shading. In Vienna, however, the teacher says *wir werden eine Arbeit
schreiben*. If he were to use *wollen*, the class might well protest that it
didn't want to! There is likewise some interchange between *wollte* and
würde, p. 290. Lastly, it is noteworthy that *wollen* is the only auxiliary
possible for the future infinitive: *es scheint schneien zu wollen* 'it looks
as if it's going to snow'.

Auxiliary *werden*

Except as above, the future tense is formed by the auxiliary *werden*
with the infinitive: *wir werden sehen, wie es geht* 'we shall see how

things go', *was wird er bloß sagen?* 'whatever will he say?', *er wird seine Behinderung überwinden, weil er sie überwinden will* 'he will overcome his disability because he wants to overcome it'. This tense is usual when a contrast with the present is implied: *wenn die Bohrung durchgeführt ist, werden wir mehr über die Beschaffenheit der Erdkruste wissen* 'when the drilling is completed we shall know more about the nature of the earth's crust', or when making a formal announcement: *eine weitere Versammlung wird in acht Tagen abgehalten* 'a further meeting will be held in a week's time'.

But how easily modal nuances can attach themselves to a future tense becomes clear from other examples: (Menge 1926) *siehe da, die Hütte Gottes ist bei den Menschen! und er wird bei ihnen wohnen, und sie werden sein Volk sein* 'behold, the tabernacle of God is with men, and he will dwell with them and they shall be his people', where a prophetic ring is quite inseparable from these future forms. In many cases the modal aspect has become more important than the temporal one, conveying notions of intention, assurance, or promise and the like. Should a future tense have such modal force, it may well stand in contrast to a present tense with a non-modal connotation: *wir beide werden später darüber sprechen* beside *wir beide sprechen später darüber* 'the two of us will speak about it later', the auxiliary *werden* carrying an additional element of assurance (or suchlike) absent from the simple present—one might even translate 'will indeed', similarly *er wird bald fertig sein* 'he will be finished soon', i.e. with a hint of 'I promise you', whereas *er ist bald fertig* is the matter-of-fact 'he'll be finished soon'.

The nuances mentioned above may be inherent in questions, too: *wann wird er gehen?* could almost be translated 'when does he intend to go?', but no such modality is present, of course, in the alternative *wann geht er?* 'when is he (or, will he be) going?' In other types of question, however, quite a different nuance can appear: in the form *sprechen wir beide später darüber?* 'will the two of us be speaking about it later?' the questioner's expectancy that the matter will actually be discussed is greater than in the alternative *werden wir beide später darüber sprechen?*, where the auxiliary adds an element of uncertainty or hesitation; this form of the question could therefore be felt as more deferential, or more polite. The same again in principle in *wird sie kommen?* 'will she come?' where the question is wide open, the answer can be equally *ja* or *nein*. On the other hand, *kommt sie?* implies some expectancy that she will be coming.

It not infrequently happens that a modal nuance is no longer truly perceptible; instead the auxiliary carries a touch of emphasis: *wann wirst du endlich begreifen* (beside *begreifst du endlich*), *daß wir Geschäftsleute sind und keine Wohltäter?* 'when are you going to understand that we are in business and not a benevolent society (lit. businessmen and not benefactors)?'—the slight difference is often scarcely reproducible in a written translation, as in the present case.

By a further development of its emphatic function, *werden* can be used in energetic commands: *du wirst Ruhe geben!* 'be quiet (or else)!' A supposition is commonly expressed by *werden*, e.g. *sie wird wohl in Braunschweig sein* 'she will most likely be in Brunswick'.

EXPRESSING PAST TIME

Preterite and Perfect

The preterite is the oldest tense known for the expression of past time, in German as in English; the perfect (and more so the pluperfect, p. 243) are, in both languages, later developments encroaching on the territory of the primeval preterite. The use of these tenses in German today, with their frequent interchangeability, often so puzzling to the foreign learner, is best understood against the historical background.

The perfect came into being as the means of characterizing a past action the effect of which continues into the present, the present tense of the finite verb in the periphrasis, e.g. *ich h a b e gekauft* 'I h a v e bought', providing the link. The original function of the tense is well preserved in English: 'I have bought a bicycle' contains a nuance absent from 'I bought a bicycle'. In German, however, this refinement has meanwhile become obscure, for the following reasons. In the later Middle Ages, the perfect in the spoken language of the south began to replace the preterite regardless of the precise shade of meaning, the process of replacement being more or less completed by the beginning of modern times. In this way the south reverted to the primordial position of having just one tense to express past time, the only difference being that it was now the perfect, not the preterite, which performed this function. This continues to be the general practice in the unsophisticated colloquial of the south, so not *ich ging, ich sagte*, but only *ich bin gegangen, ich habe gesagt*, not even *ich hatte*, but *ich habe gehabt*, hence also not e.g. *ich hatte ihn gesehen*, but *ich habe ihn gesehen gehabt* 'I had seen him'. Formal exceptions are the preterite subjunctives of auxiliary verbs: *hätte, wäre, würde*, with the modals *dürfte, könnte, möchte, müßte*, also *bräuchte*, not felt to be tenses in the same way as the indicatives.

In the modern period, the above simplification of the past-tense system spread to the spoken language of the north, too, but never becoming exclusive. The auxiliaries *hatte, war, wurde* remained, as did the modals *durfte, konnte, mochte, mußte, sollte, wollte*, all standard today. A handful of other very common preterite forms, such as *ging, sagte, kam, dachte, sah, fand*, also persisted. But the one-time semantic difference which separated these from the perfect is no longer truly perceptible, any preference for the one or the other being a matter of idiom.

In literary style, however, and in conscious opposition to developments in the spoken language, the preterite was retained as the narrative past tense, recounting events as they occurred; the perfect automatically continued its original function of linking the past with the present. This arrangement is commonly observed today: (preterite) *der Wecker rasselte. Gerhard schreckte aus dem Schlaf, sprang aus dem Bett und eilte ins Badezimmer* 'the alarm went off. G. awoke with a start, jumped out of bed and hurried into the bathroom', (perfect) *bedeutende Teile der gotischen Bibelübersetzung sind auf uns gekommen* 'considerable portions of the Gothic translation of the Bible have come down to us', *Ruhe ist wichtig für jemanden, der sein Alter erreicht hat* 'rest is important for someone who has reached his age'. Formally this is just as in English. But appearances are deceptive. With the extension, in so many respects, of the southern colloquial perfect to the rest of the country, the traditional distinction between the two tenses was no longer anywhere supported by the more vital spoken language, so that feeling for semantic nuances was weakened and became uncertain. Usage in literary style, as illustrated above, is today maintained by convention, especially by the convention that the preterite is to be used as the narrative past tense, rather than by any genuine appreciation of traditional shades of meaning such as are perceived in English. Thus any notion that the German perfect links the past with the present is in fact produced, not by the tense itself, but by the context.

In the language of today, preterite and perfect alike simply denote past time as such, differences in use being functional, not meaningful. We have just noticed a difference of this sort within the literary language. An equally striking contrast is seen in the different use of the tenses as between literary and spoken language. For example, one might hear in ordinary conversation: *Bertha hat die Wäsche im Hof aufgehängt. Ich habe* (southern *bin*) *am Fenster gestanden und habe beobachtet, wie Rudolf auf sie zugelaufen ist und seine Hand auf ihre Schulter gelegt hat* 'B. was hanging out the washing in the yard. I was standing by the window and observed how R. ran up to her and placed his hand on her shoulder'. But one would expect to read: *B. hing die Wäsche im Hof auf. Ich stand am Fenster und beobachtete, wie R. auf sie zulief und seine Hand auf ihre Schulter legte.* The sentences now sound like a piece of narrative from a printed work.

It is of the utmost importance to appreciate that the difference between a German preterite and a perfect, aside from the occasional use of the latter as a substitute for a future perfect or a pluperfect (p. 242), is not at all a matter of meaning. And we may also repeat: neither of the German past tenses has the power of denoting anything more subtle than just past time as such—it will have been noticed that German leaves unexpressed the nuance contained in the continuous forms 'was hanging, was standing' required in the English translation above. It follows, too, that the English learner must resolutely resist the temptation to automatically equate, e.g. *legte* with 'laid' and *hat gelegt* with 'has laid', since the English tenses convey aspects of meaning which the German verb of itself is unable to express. German indifference in this respect is further underlined by the now widespread use of a pseudo-pluperfect as a third tense denoting past time pure and simple, p. 241. Only the context will determine which English tense is idiomatically appropriate, as may be amply seen from the examples in the paragraphs to follow as well as elsewhere in this book.

We have seen that there is a contradiction between the inherited conventions of traditional literary style and the actual practice of the language as spoken. In the nature of the case the two can hardly be expected to remain exclusive, particularly as the tenses concerned are in general no longer distinguished in point of meaning and therefore potentially interchangeable. And, indeed, contamination on a wide scale, with frequent switching of tenses, is now the order of the day. There are still no hard and fast rules governing these innovations, but one can discern tendencies.

The succinct preterite may seem more elegant or economical than the slightly unwieldy perfect: *keine seiner Schriften blieben erhalten* 'none of his writings have been preserved' in preference to *sind erhalten geblieben*, though both are equally acceptable. The auxiliaries are often so treated: (police report) *die Namen der beteiligten Personen wurden geändert* 'the names of the persons involved have been altered' shorter than *sind geändert worden*. One hears daily on radio or television *Sie sahen (hörten) soeben* . . . 'you've just been watching (listening to) . . .' In ordinary use the variants *das Buch erschien* and *ist erschienen* may follow conventional rules, but in a formal announcement the preterite is as regular in German as the perfect in the corresponding English: (advertisement) *in der Reihe "rowohlts monographien" erschien als Band 260 eine Darstellung Simone de Beauvoirs* 'a portrayal of S. de B. has appeared as volume 260 in the series "rowohlts monographs" '.

Developments are far from one way only. There is always the possibility of the preterite being replaced by the colloquial perfect, adding thereby a touch of variety to the style without necessarily making it too lax for literary purposes. Admittedly, feelings in the matter differ, southerners tending to be more partial to this tense than other writers, but the usage is widespread: (biography) *zu jener Zeit hat Marie einige Wochen bei Kasimir gewohnt. Da er unter dem Verdacht stand, an dem Attentat an Alexander II. mitgewirkt zu haben, hat er aus Rußland fliehen müssen, ist in Genf revolutionärer Publizist geworden, später in Paris Student der Medizin und schließlich Arzt* 'at that time M. lived for a few weeks with K. Since he was suspected of having been involved in the plan for the assassination of A., he had to flee from Russia, becoming a revolutionary journalist in Geneva, later a medical student in Paris and finally a doctor'. Another, say northern, author might well have employed only preterite forms: *wohnte, mußte, wurde.*

The written language is thus no longer rigidly bound to the older conventions. There is a new feeling for stylistic effects to be gained by varying the tenses, in which sentence rhythm, too, can play a part. In view of the high degree of interchangeability, the situation is fluid and personal choice largely the decisive factor: (newspaper comment) *es hat Mißstimmungen gegeben, als er der Pressekonferenz fernblieb* 'there were ill-feelings when he stayed away from the press conference', (theology text-book) *endete die römische Gefangenschaft mit dem Tod des Paulus, oder ist er noch einmal freigekommen? Hat er seinen Plan, nach Spanien zu reisen, noch ausführen können?* 'did Paul's imprisonment in Rome end with his death, or was he again set free? Was he able to carry out his plan to travel to Spain?', (feature article) *in Wolfenbüttel hat ein Herzog namens Julius, der von 1568 bis 1589 sein Herzogtum regierte, den Grundstock für eine weltberühmte Bibliothek gelegt. Julius, der in Köln und Löwen studiert hat, sammelte seit frühester Jugend Bücher* 'in W. a duke by the name of J., who ruled his duchy from 1568 to 1589, laid the foundations of a world-famous library. J., who studied in Cologne and Louvain, was from his earliest youth a collector of books'. It is not difficult to deduce that alternative variations would be permissible, too. If changes occasionally seem infelicitous, they do at least prove the point: the *Prisma-Verlag* asked its readers on a postcard (Question 1) *welches unserer Bücher l a s e n Sie?* 'which one of our books have you read?', (Question 2) *h a b e n Sie schon andere Bücher aus unserem Verlag g e l e s e n?* 'have you already read other books published by us?'

The more informal the style, the closer to the spoken word, the more often will the perfect be required. In writing to small children, for instance, almost every verb will be, appropriately, in the perfect (grandmother to grandson, printed in a colour supplement) *Lieber Kai, Du hast mir vorhin am Telefon eine Frage gestellt, die ich so schnell nicht gut beantworten konnte, deshalb bekommst Du nun noch einen Brief, den Dir die Mama vorlesen wird. Du hast erzählt, daß Du einen ganz großen Regenwurm gefunden hast. "Das ist gut", habe ich gesagt, "weil Du sorgsam mit ihm umgegangen bist und ihn in die Erde zurückgelegt hast"* 'Dear Kai, a little while ago you asked me a question over the phone that I couldn't answer properly at once, so now you are getting a letter which Mummy will read out to you. You told me that you found a great big worm. "That is right", I said, "because you treated it carefully and placed it back in the earth" '. Here the only example of a preterite is the modal *konnte* 'could'; a southern writer might well have avoided this, putting *die ich so schnell nicht gut habe beantworten können*. Other passages in familiar style may show a mixture of tenses: (East German comic paper) *schon der Vater war Straßenbahner, und wir Geschwister sind alle linientreu geblieben. Bloß mit Otto ging es abwärts, der ist zur U-Bahn abgewandert* 'our father himself was a tramwayman and we, the children (lit. 'brother(s) and sister(s)'), all remained true to the line (overtones of *Parteilinie* 'party line'). Only with Otto did things go downhill. He migrated to the Underground'—essentially a North German spoken style, with the common preterites *war, ging*, but otherwise using perfect forms. In conclusion, an idiomatic nicety: the perfect *ich habe vergessen* is also necessary when English may optionally have the present, e.g. *wo hast du den Teller hingelegt? — ich habe vergessen* 'where have you put the plate?—I forget'.

A note on the preterite in spoken style

To describe the preterite as the past tense typically used in writing (above) does not mean that it doesn't occur in speaking as well. We have already noted that relics of the old preterite survived in colloquial use in the north. But more importantly, the printed word can and does affect the spoken word. So much information today comes from newspapers and magazines, everyone listens to news and reports on radio or television, where the formal preterite is commonplace. Inevitably, conversational style takes up elements proper to literary diction, including in fair measure the narrative preterite. In this respect the north is more receptive than the south, though even there the preterite, especially of the more commonly used verbs, may slip into ordinary speech; in particular *war* 'was' has generally re-established itself. And of course educated people from any part of the country can talk like a book if the need arises.

Given its prevalence in the written as opposed to the colloquial language, a feeling often develops that the preterite is more 'correct' than the perfect and hence socially superior. Erich Kästner in *Als ich ein kleiner Junge war* represents his (ambitious) mother as saying to him when he was still a little boy *er kratzte dich schon, als ihr noch im Kinderwagen saßt* 'he was scratching you when you were still in your prams'. Most mothers would have said *er hat dich schon gekratzt, als* (or *wie*) *ihr noch im Kinderwagen gesessen habt* (southern *seid*), and compare the letter from grandmother to grandson, above.

Pseudo-pluperfect

The preterite and perfect have hitherto been spoken of as the two tenses expressing past time pure and simple and note has been taken of the instability arising from such duplication. As if that were not enough, we have now to consider a third tense with the same function, a newcomer relatively speaking, which came into being as follows. The persistence of the auxiliaries *war*, *hatte* as equivalents of *ist gewesen*, *hat gehabt* (p. 236) led in certain areas to a conflation of forms giving *war gewesen*, *hatte gehabt*, outwardly pluperfects, but in practice simply expressing past time like the forms from which they had sprung: *was war das gewesen?* (otherwise *was war das?*, especially southern *was ist das gewesen?*) 'what was that?', similarly *er hatte keine Zeit gehabt* (otherwise *er hatte keine Zeit*, esp. south. *er hat keine Zeit gehabt*) 'he had no time'. By the same token the sentences *er war in die Arbeit gegangen, sie hatte das Mittagessen gekocht* can be used to mean 'he went to work, she cooked the dinner'. This being so, the conversational sequence on p. 237 could also be heard as *Bertha hatte die Wäsche im Hof aufgehängt. Ich hatte (war) am Fenster gestanden und hatte beobachtet, wie Rudolf auf sie zugelaufen war und seine Hand auf ihre Schulter gelegt hatte.*

But more than this. A third pluperfect could now appear: *ich hatte zugesagt gehabt* (otherwise *ich hatte zugesagt*, esp. south. *ich habe zugesagt gehabt*) 'I had agreed'. Needless to say, such developments have lessened sensitivity to the original meaning and use of the traditional pluperfect (p. 243), for these colloquialisms are now quite widespread and may be reproduced in print.

Past tenses of *sein* with infinitive

In a few examples, past time is expressible by the past tenses of *sein* with the simple infinitive: *gestern abend waren wir tanzen* 'last night we went to a dance, or were out dancing', the same sense with the usual past tense variations (perfect and pseudo-pluperfect) *gestern abend sind* (or *waren*) *wir tanzen gewesen*; likewise in questions: *wart ihr eislaufen?* 'did you go skating, or have you been skating?'

On the origin of the construction, see p. 232.

Further remarks on interchangeable past tenses

It has been seen how the spoken language can affect the written style, and vice versa, encouraging fluctuation in the use of tenses. This matter is strikingly illustrated in ordinary letter-writing. One can imagine a homely missive starting *Liebe Inge, der Winter kam diesmal sehr früh, seit Ende November hatten wir bitter kaltes Wetter; ab und zu schneite es sogar vor Weihnachten* 'Dear Inge, winter has come very early this time, since the end of November we have had bitterly cold weather; it was snowing on and off even before Christmas'. But another writer could well put *der Winter ist . . . gekommen, seit Ende November haben wir . . . gehabt, ab und zu hat es . . . geschneit*. A third might prefer to ring the changes, say like this: *der Winter kam . . . seit Ende November hatten wir . . . ab und zu hat es . . . geschneit*, a fourth like this: *der Winter ist . . . gekommen, seit Ende November hatten wir . . . ab und zu schneite es . . .*, and so on. The pseudo-pluperfect is also in the running: *war . . . gekommen, hatten . . . gehabt, hatte . . . geschneit*, making possible yet more permutations. So chaotic is the situation at this level. But the chaos is not difficult to live with, once its mechanisms are understood.

Perfect refers to future perfect time

Just as the present tense can denote future time, so can the perfect express future perfect time. The concept of futurity will be indicated by an accompanying adverb or be evident from the context: *noch eine Stunde und wir haben es geschafft* 'one hour more and we'll have finished it', *bis du zurückkommst, habe ich schon abgewaschen* 'by the time you get back I'll have done the washing up', *bald wird der sechste Kontinent nicht mehr als weißer Fleck auf unseren Landkarten erscheinen, und der forschende Mensch hat eines der letzten Geheimnisse der Erde entschleiert* 'soon the sixth continent will no longer appear as a white patch on our maps and the explorer man will have unveiled one of the earth's last secrets'. Alternatively, the regular future perfect tense may be used, see below.

Perfect for pluperfect

In the same way as the historic present can express past time in vivid style, so can the perfect do duty for the pluperfect: *die lateinischen Quellen stellen die Kelten als ein unterentwickeltes Volk dar. In der Tat haben diese jedoch bereits im vierten Jahrhundert vor unserer Zeitrechnung Italien überwältigt und Rom geplündert* 'the Latin sources represent the Celts as an underdeveloped people. In actual fact, however, they had overcome Italy and plundered Rome as early as the fourth century before our era'.

Future perfect

German and English correspond in the use of this tense: *wird die Zeit kommen, in der alle reaktionären Regierungen verschwunden sein werden?* 'will the time come when all reactionary governments will have disappeared?' The auxiliary *werden* can, of course, carry the usual nuances (p. 235), e.g. *noch eine Stunde und wir werden es geschafft haben* 'one more hour and we will (surely) have finished it'. But the perfect can also be used, above.

Like the simple future, the future perfect commonly expresses a supposition: *sie wird wohl in Braunschweig gewesen sein* 'she will very likely have been in Brunswick'.

Pluperfect

In its original function, this tense is used like the corresponding English: *sie hatten nicht bemerkt, daß keine Butter mehr da war* 'they hadn't noticed that there was no butter left', *bis der Vater nach Hause kam, waren die Kinder schon schlafen gegangen* 'by the time the father returned home, the children had already gone to bed'.

As in English, a logical distinction between pluperfect and preterite is not always made, notably in subordinate clauses, so that the tenses are then interchangeable: *als der Bankbeamte die Schriftstücke geprüft hatte* or *prüfte, stellte er fest, daß eine Quittung fehlte* 'when the bank clerk (had) checked the documents, he found that a receipt was missing'. But German is more lax than English: (Grimm) *als das Mädchen eine Zeitlang bei der Frau Holle war, wurde es traurig* 'when the girl had been with Frau Holle for a while, she became sad'. And matters in German are further complicated by the development of a pseudo-pluperfect denoting past time pure and simple, p. 241.

The auxiliaries *haben* and *sein*

The perfect system is formed with the auxiliaries *haben* 'have' and *sein* 'be'. Their distribution is somewhat complex, though certain main rules emerge as follows.

Apart from a small number of exceptions, all transitive verbs, including reflexives, are conjugated with *haben*, thus *ich habe den Arzt nicht wieder aufgesucht, da ich mich bereits erholt hatte* 'I didn't go to the doctor again since I had already recovered', likewise most impersonal verbs: *es hat geregnet* 'it has been raining', but e.g. *es ist ihr gelungen* 'she has succeeded'. Further, many intransitive verbs in so far as these are imperfective: *er hat gut gearbeitet* 'he has worked well', *sie hatte festgeschlafen* 'she had slept soundly'. On the other hand, perfective intransitives are conjugated with *sein*, e.g. *du bist gefallen* 'you have fallen', *er wird gekommen sein* 'he will have come', *ihr wart verschwunden* 'you had disappeared', *sie waren aufgewacht* 'they had wakened up', *das Rohr ist geplatzt* 'the pipe has burst' (p. 250), as well as numerous others, thus *sie ist sich gleichgeblieben* 'she has not changed', *die Trauben sind in der Sonne gereift* 'the grapes have ripened in the sun'.

Certain verbs are both transitive and intransitive: *die Seeluft hat seinen Heuschnupfen geheilt* 'the sea air has cured his hay fever', *die Wunde ist geheilt* 'the wound has healed', or *er hat mich getreten* 'he has kicked me', *ich war zur Seite getreten* 'I had stepped to one side'. A regional difference may appear, the north using *haben*, the south *sein*, hence *sie hat* or *ist auf einen spitzen Stein getreten* 'she has stepped on to a sharp stone', likewise the verbs *hocken, liegen, sitzen, stehen*, p. 245. One may compare *ich bin ihm begegnet* with *ich habe ihn getroffen*, both meaning 'I have met him', though the former carries the nuance 'I happened to meet him', whereas the latter is neutral, like English 'meet'; but by contrast only *der Botschafter ist in Lissabon eingetroffen* 'the ambassador has arrived in Lisbon'. Intransitive verbs can be made transitive by adding inseparable prefixes, with *haben* as the regular auxiliary: *Magellan ist als erster um die Welt herumgesegelt* 'M. was the first to sail round the world', *Magellan hat als erster die Welt umsegelt* 'M. was the first to circumnavigate the globe', the latter type then stylistically the more elevated.

Verbs of motion—aspective differences

Verbs of motion can be regarded as perfective or imperfective, the former when the action is conceived as beginning or ending (conjugation with *sein*), the latter when the action is considered as simply taking place (conjugation with *haben*). This distinction was formerly observed, but most verbs now take *sein* only, regardless of aspect. But the old difference is preserved in a few cases, as *tanzen*, thus *sie hat wunderbar getanzt* 'she danced wonderfully', but *sie ist durch den Saal getanzt wie eine Fee* 'she danced through the (ball-)room like a fairy'. Notice that *folgen* now takes *sein* in its literal sense, but preserves the conjugation with *haben* in its figurative sense: *das Kind ist mir gefolgt* 'the child followed me', *das Kind hat nicht gefolgt* 'the child did not do as it was told'.

In other examples aspective differences may be retained, too, though not so exclusively, in line with the tendency for *sein* to take over from *haben*. Such fluctuation occurs in e.g. *rudern* 'row' and *segeln* 'sail': *wir haben oft gerudert (gesegelt)* 'we have often rowed (sailed)', but *wir sind über den See gerudert (gesegelt)* 'we have rowed (sailed) across the lake'; similarly *schwimmen* 'swim' may still be heard with *haben* in imperfective use: *haben Sie heute geschwommen?* 'have you been for a swim today?'. But also *wir sind oft gerudert (gesegelt), sind Sie heute geschwommen?*

In other cases a verb which does not of itself specifically express movement will nevertheless be conjugated with *sein* if motion is implied: *er ist weggeeilt* 'he hurried away', but *er hat damit geeilt* 'he hurried with it'. Among other examples are *er ist die Treppe hinuntergepoltert* 'he clattered down the stairs' and various expressions for decamping: *er ist ausgerissen* 'he has made off', *er ist abgehauen* or *getürmt* 'he has cleared off'.

A number of developments are peculiar to certain verbs. Thus *fahren* 'go (in a vehicle)' acquired a transitive sense 'drive (car, etc.)' so needing *haben*, e.g. *er hat einen Fiat gefahren* 'he drove a Fiat', and *fliegen* 'fly' followed suit: *er hat die Boeing geflogen* 'he flew the B.' Compare *es ist gelaufen* 'it has run' with *das Rad hat sich heiß gelaufen* 'the wheel has run hot'. But transitive compounds of *gehen* retain *sein*, e.g. *sie sind die Rechnungen durchgegangen* 'they have gone through the accounts', *wir waren ein großes Risiko eingegangen* 'we had taken a big risk'.

Aspective differences with other verbs

Aspective differences are generally well preserved in the case of intransitive verbs, compare *die Flüchtlinge haben gehungert* 'the refugees went hungry', (Chinese proverb) *ein guter Artz ist niemals verhungert* 'a good doctor never died of hunger', *ich habe gefroren* 'I was freezing', *ich bin durchgefroren* 'I'm frozen (through)', *das Wasser ist gefroren* 'the water has frozen', *der Teich war zugefroren* 'the pond was frozen over', further *die Bäume sind aufgeblüht* or *erblüht* 'the trees have burst into blossom', *die Bäume sind verblüht* 'the trees have finished blossoming'. Quite exceptionally, all verbs compounded with *aus* in the sense of 'to the end' take *haben*, hence *die Bäume haben ausgeblüht = sind verblüht*.

The verbs hocken *'crouch',* liegen *'lie',* sitzen *'sit'* stehen *'stand'*

These verbs are conjugated with *haben* in the north, with *sein* in the south: *ich habe* or *bin gehockt* 'I have crouched', *ich habe* or *bin gelegen* 'I have lain', etc. The standard language prefers *haben*, but southern writers often use their naturally spoken *sein*. Indeed, only the latter is possible in association with the adjectival use of *gelegen*, e.g. *Bonn ist am Rhein gelegen* 'B. lies on the Rhine', further in the compounds *über-, unterlegen*, e.g. *unsere Truppen waren dem Feind überlegen* (*unterlegen*) 'our troops were superior (inferior) to the enemy'.

The compounds *aufsitzen* 'mount (a horse)' and *absitzen* 'dismount' are always conjugated with *sein*, thus *der Jockey ist aufgesessen* 'the jockey has mounted the horse', but *aufsitzen* when meaning 'sit up' is treated like the simplex: with *haben* in the north, *sein* in the south, so *wir haben* or *sind die halbe Nacht aufgesessen* 'we sat up half the night'.

The compounds *aufstehen* 'get up, arise', *entstehen* 'come into being, arise', *auferstehen* 'rise (as from the dead)' are conjugated with *sein* only, e.g. *Christus ist auferstanden* 'Christ has risen'. The compound *erstehen* commonly means 'buy, get' and as a transitive verb regularly takes *haben*, thus *er hat eine neue Schreibmaschine erstanden* 'he has bought a new typewriter'.

EXPRESSING THE CONTINUOUS ASPECT

Not possessing continuous tenses, the German verb cannot by itself characterize a continuing action, p. 230. Nevertheless, this aspect is often brought out by the addition of *eben* or *gerade* 'just': *sie wäscht sich eben* or *gerade* 'she is (just) getting washed', alternatively *sie ist (eben, gerade) dabei, sich zu waschen*. The aspect may be further expressed by the construction *am* or *beim* with the substantivized infinitive: *er ist am* or *beim Rasieren* 'he is shaving'; an object joins with the infinitive to form a compound: *als Sie uns suchten, waren wir am* or *beim Birnenpflücken* 'when you were looking for us, we were picking pears'. Of the two, *beim* is the more widespread and more literary form, *am* is the usual idiom in the north-west. With a few verbs a third variant *im* is found, e.g. *neue Galaxien sind im Entstehen* (= *im Entstehen begriffen*) 'new galaxies are in the making'. It goes without saying that the aspect is less consistently expressed in German than it is in English, and is often ignored: *was macht sie? — sie wäscht sich* 'what's she doing?—she's getting washed'.

EMPHASIZING THE VERB

German has no equivalent to the English emphatic conjugation with 'do', but a comparable emphasis can be obtained by the use of particles, e.g. *ich hasse ihn doch* 'I do hate him', *er hat es ja für möglich gehalten* 'he did think it possible', *es gibt sie eben noch, die Liebesgeschichten* 'they still do exist, those (true) love stories'.

German does, however, have a periphrastic conjugation using *tun* 'to do', regularly heard in the spoken language of various districts up and down the country. But it is largely a redundant formation, not conveying any special nuance to distinguish it semantically from the ordinary conjugation: *wo tun die Kinder spielen? — sie tun auf der Straße spielen* equals *wo spielen die Kinder? — sie spielen auf der Straße* 'where are the children playing?, where do the children play?—they are playing, they play on the street'. But since the construction enables the infinitive to be placed at the head of the sentence and so achieve a degree of emphasis by virtue of the word order, it does have a certain justification. It is in this form that the construction is most widely used and enters the standard language:

schmerzt der Zahn noch? — ja, schmerzen tut er wohl 'does the tooth still hurt?—yes, it does indeed hurt', also *kostet das Zimmer im Ritz viel? — gewiß, viel verlangen tut man schon* 'does the room in the Ritz cost a lot?—to be sure, they do indeed ask a lot'.

VERB OMITTED

The omission of a finite verb is noticed in the proverb *Ende gut, alles gut* 'all's well that ends well' and in a number of clichés: *wer da?* 'who goes there?', *was tun?* 'what is to be done', *so weit Götting* 'that is what G. has to say', *doch 'damit nicht genug* 'but that is not all' (then the writer or speaker goes on to give more details), *danke schön — gern geschehen* 'thank you very much—you're welcome', colloquially also *mal sehen* for *ich werde mal sehen* 'I'll (just) see' and *Hauptsache* for *die Hauptsache ist*, e.g. *Hauptsache wir bleiben im Rennen* 'we stay in the race, that's the main thing'. Other examples remind one of telegram style: (on an envelope) *falls Adressat verzogen, bitte mit neuer Anschrift an den Absender zurück* 'if addressee has moved, please return to sender with new address'.

An occasional feature of literary style is the optional suppression of the auxiliaries *haben* and *sein* in subordinate clauses: *das Haus, das viele Jahre leer gestanden (hatte,* southern *war), bekam unerwartet neue Mieter* 'the house which had stood empty for many years unexpectedly had new tenants', *die alte Freundin, wie vertraut sie einst gewesen (ist,* or *war), wirkte jetzt doch etwas fremd* 'the old friend, familiar though she once was, now seemed rather remote'.

The Imperative

The imperative expresses a command: familiar sg. *komm her!* pl. *kommt her!*, polite *kommen Sie her!* 'come here!', and also an entreaty: familiar sg. *sei so gut!* pl. *seid so gut!* polite *seien Sie so gut!* with an often heard, substandard colloquial alternative *sind Sie so gut!* 'be so kind!', whence by analogy also substandard familiar sg. *bist du so gut!* pl. *seid ihr so gut!*

In the spoken language of the south the pl. *kommt!* may occur locally in polite address as well, the form *kommen Sie!* being then reserved for the singular only.

In emphatic use the pronouns *du, ihr* may be added: *komm du her! kommt ihr her!*

In the 1st person plural: *gehen wir!* 'let us go', originally subjunctive as still seen in *seien wir!* 'let us be!' An alternative construction using indifferently *laß* or *laßt uns* with the infinitive is, in general, of a more literary character: *laß(t) uns gehen! laß(t) uns sein!* Notice traditional *lasset uns beten* 'let us pray'.

Commands may be expressed by other means: by the present indicative (p. 231), the infinitive (pp. 254 f.), the perfect participle (p. 258), or by a clause introduced by *daß* (p. 274), in written style by the present subjunctive also (pp. 260 f.).

An unexplained use of the imperative occurs in the everyday expression *sieh mal einer an!* 'just look at this/that! what a surprise!', see p. 221.

The Passive

The passive construction is formed with the auxiliary *werden* and the perfect participle, p. 88. It will be practical to distinguish between the personal and the impersonal passive, and begin with examples of the former: *zusätzliche Schreibkräfte werden eingesetzt* 'additional secretarial staff are being engaged', *der Sachschaden muß behoben werden* 'the material damage must be made good', *Herr Möller wurde vom Facharzt behandelt* 'Mr M. was treated by the specialist', *der Angeklagte war gesehen worden, als er versuchte, durch das halboffene Fenster des Hauses einzusteigen* 'the accused had been seen trying to enter the house through the half-open window'.

A personal passive in German is only possible with transitive verbs governing an accusative; in other cases the impersonal passive (below) is required. By comparison with English usage, the German passive is of relatively infrequent occurrence, and is in any case more typical of the written language, especially when technical, and so tends to sound rather more formal. The spoken language, at its simplest level, in most cases employs an active construction, the agent in the passive construction being now the subject: *der Facharzt hat Herrn Möller behandelt*; in the absence of an agent, the impersonal pronoun *man* will commonly be used: *man hatte den Angeklagten gesehen*. At the same time, through the influence of the printed word, passive structures enter the spoken language to a greater or lesser extent, depending on the educational status of the speaker and the subject under discussion. Indeed it is not difficult to find cases where the passive is the normal mode of expression: *Ihre Nummer wird ausgerufen* 'your number will be called out', *die Ehe wurde geschieden* 'the marriage was dissolved'. See also under 'Impersonal Verbs' below.

Exceptionally, a few transitive verbs lack a passive voice. Thus, *bekommen* and *kriegen* 'get, obtain, receive' cannot be so used, although other verbs with the same meanings, as *empfangen, erhalten* readily form a passive. Notice *ich weigere mich hineinzugehen* 'I refuse to enter', but *der Eintritt wird mir verweigert* 'I am refused entrance'.

Impersonal passive

The impersonal passive characteristically describes activity not necessarily attributable to a particular agent: *es wird gebaut* 'building is going on, men are building', *es ist überall nach ihm gesucht worden* 'people have been looking for him everywhere'. At the same time, in suitable examples, an agent may be mentioned: *es ist überall nach ihm von der Kriminalpolizei gesucht worden* 'the CID has been looking for him everywhere'. The impersonal subject *es* may only stand at the head of the sentence; it does not appear in other positions: *hier wird gebaut* 'building is going on here'. The construction is much used and quite often heard in ordinary conversation, especially in simple sentences like the above-mentioned *es wird gebaut, hier wird gebaut*.

The impersonal passive has spread to intransitive verbs which cannot otherwise form a passive: *auf der Party wurde viel gelacht und geflirtet* 'at the party there was a lot of laughing and flirting', (notice in a second-hand clothing shop) *bei uns darf gestöbert werden* 'in this shop you may rummage around'.

Lastly, all verbs governing a dative object require this construction: *es wird mir geraten* or *mir wird geraten* 'I am advised', p. 156.

Passive with *sein*

Whereas the passive formed with *werden* denotes an action: *die Strümpfe werden gewaschen* 'the stockings are being washed', the passive with *sein* as auxiliary expresses a state: *die Strümpfe sind gewaschen* 'the stockings are washed' i.e. 'have been washed'. Compare further: *der Laden wird um 8 Uhr geöffnet* 'the shop opens at 8 o'clock', *der Laden ist um 8 Uhr geöffnet* 'the shop is open at 8 o'clock'. Notice *jedes Mädchen möchte verheiratet sein* 'every girl would like to be married'—the concept 'get married' is expressed actively: *jedes Mädchen möchte heiraten* lit. 'to marry'.

Since English always forms the passive with the verb 'to be', it cannot distinguish the different types of passive in certain contexts: 'we were assigned to the same group' could be either *wir wurden* or *waren derselben Gruppe zugeteilt*, German here conveying nuances absent from English. It frequently happens that English idiom requires, or prefers, a perfect where the German logically uses the present: *die Herkunft der Etrusker ist nicht geklärt* 'the origin of the Etruscans has not been explained' (but *ist ungeklärt* 'is unexplained', the negative participle being adjectival), *hier ist ein Werk geschaffen, das seinesgleichen sucht* 'here a work has been created that is without parallel', *seit die Scharfmacher zurückgedrängt sind, entwickeln sich die Beziehungen zwischen den beiden Staaten positiv* 'since the extremists have been pushed into the background, relations between the two states are developing in a positive way'. By the same token, the English pluperfect may correspond to a German preterite: *das Urteil war vollstreckt* 'the sentence had been carried out', *die neuen Abgeordneten waren gewählt* 'the new representatives had been elected'.

The few verbs which can only denote a state, and not an action, are naturally conjugated with *sein*, e.g. *in dieser Flasche ist Schwefelsäure enthalten* 'hydrochloric acid is contained in this bottle'. We recall that a number of perfect participles are habitually used as adjectives (p. 172) and these, too, take *sein*, thus *er ist vom Teufel besessen* 'he is possessed of the devil'. But there are borderline cases, the participle being ambivalent: *das Rohr ist geplatzt* 'the pipe is, or has, burst' (p. 243).

The Infinitive

The infinitive occurs in two forms, as in the English: the simple *betteln* 'beg' and the prepositional *zu betteln* 'to beg', their respective use in the two languages being, in general, quite close. Historically speaking, the simple infinitive is the primary one, so that in cases where the two forms compete, or simply quietly coexist, we have the old side by side with the relatively new. It will be practical to begin the discussion with the prepositional form.

Prepositional infinitive

This form occurs as the complement of a verb: *sie fingen an, Fragen zu stellen* 'they began to ask questions'. It also commonly appears as the complement of a noun: *er hatte nicht die Absicht aufzugeben* 'he had no intention of giving up', or an adjective: *ich war bereit zu verhandeln* 'I was ready to negotiate'. See further under 'The construction *um zu*, etc.', pp. 253 f.

Special uses, in general alternating with the simple infinitive, will be referred to *passim* below.

Simple infinitive

The simple infinitive is best preserved when its connection with the finite verb is particularly intimate. This is naturally the case after *werden* in the future periphrasis: *ich werde kämpfen* 'I shall struggle' and after modal auxiliaries which require an infinitive to complete the sense: *ich darf wohl sagen* 'I dare say', *du kannst tun oder lassen, wie du willst* 'you can take it or leave it, as you like', *möge der Frieden erhalten bleiben!* 'may the peace be maintained!', but not after *vermögen*, thus *ich vermag, keinen Unterschied zu erkennen* 'I am unable to perceive any difference'. On use with *brauchen* 'need', see pp. 290 f.

The simple infinitive may still be found with other verbs, as *lernen* 'learn', notably in the expression *kennenlernen*, e.g. *ich lernte ihn kennen, ich habe ihn kennengelernt* 'I (have) got to know him', with which compare *sie lernte gut kochen, sie hat gut kochen gelernt* 'she (has) learnt to cook well', but which may also be expressed *sie lernte (hat gelernt), gut zu kochen.* Similarly with *lehren* 'teach': *sie lehrt ihn deutsch sprechen* 'she is teaching him to speak German', but *sie lehrt ihn, die Worte richtig auszusprechen* 'she is teaching him to pronounce the words correctly', the prepositional infinitive occurring when the connection between the finite verb and the infinitive is not so close. Overlapping is occasionally found: *er lehrte mich bescheiden sein*, or *bescheiden zu sein* 'he taught me to be modest'. For occasional use with *sein* 'to be', see pp. 232, 241.

The simple infinitive survives to some extent after certain verbs of motion. We notice in the first place *gehen* 'go': *sie geht einkaufen* 'she's going shopping', *wir gehen aus essen* 'we're going out for a meal', *er geht schlafen* 'he's going to bed' ('he's going to sleep' is *er ist beim* (or *am*) *Einschlafen*), further *sie werden spazierengehen* 'they will be going for a walk'. Some of these idioms have become productive: *wollt ihr spazierenfahren?* 'do you want to go for a drive?', *sie führt ihren Hund spazieren* 'she's taking her dog for a walk', *die Eltern hatten sich schlafen gelegt* (= *waren schlafen gegangen*) 'the parents had gone to bed'. The same construction is found with *kommen* 'come': *kommst du mit uns spielen?* 'are you coming to play with us?', *sie kommt dich besuchen* 'she is coming (or, has come, p. 232) to visit you', *wirst du mir helfen kommen?* 'will you come to help me?', alternatively *wirst du kommen, mir zu helfen?*, and as a third possibility (p. 253) *wirst du kommen, um mir zu helfen?* In all these sentences, *gehen* could be substituted for *kommen*.

The present construction is regular with the object of *hören* 'hear' and *sehen* 'see': *hörst du ihn rufen?* 'do you hear him calling?', *wir haben die Kinder spielen gesehen* 'we have seen the children playing', also after *fühlen* or *spüren* 'feel': *man fühlte (spürte) den Frühling herannahen* 'one felt spring approaching'. The same again with *lassen* in its various meanings: *er ließ es dort hängen* 'he left it hanging there', *die Sache wurde fallen gelassen* 'the matter was allowed to lapse', *sie läßt ihn gewähren* 'she lets him have his own way', *das habe ich mir sagen lassen* 'that's what I've been told', *eine Dame läßt man nicht warten* 'one doesn't keep a lady waiting', *wir müssen die Reparaturen machen lassen* 'we must have the repairs done'. Further with *machen* 'make', though now ordinarily confined to the two expressions *glauben machen* and (without an object) *von sich reden machen*, e.g. *kannst du sie glauben machen, daß alles in Ordnung ist?* 'can you make her believe that everything is in order?', *er machte von sich reden* 'he caused quite a stir', and likewise the archaizing *heißen* 'command, bid': *er hieß ihn schweigen* 'he bade him be silent'. Certain other idioms contain the simple infinitive after this pattern, e.g. *er schickt die Frau arbeiten* 'he sends his wife out to work', *sie legt das Kind schlafen* 'she is putting the child to bed', cf. *sich schlafen legen* above.

The simple infinitives *hängen, liegen, sitzen, stehen*, are regularly used in conjunction with the verb *finden* 'find': *ich habe meinen Regenmantel in deinem Schrank hängen gefunden* 'I have found my raincoat hanging in your wardrobe', *Sie finden den Schlüssel unter der Fußmatte liegen* 'you'll find the key lying under the doormat', *wir fanden das Baby am Boden sitzen* 'we found the baby sitting on the floor', *man findet ihn immer im Wirtshaus an der Theke stehen* 'one will always find him in the public house standing by the bar'. These infinitives are corruptions of earlier (and logical) present participles, still found with other verbs: *man fand ihn betend, schlafend, weinend* 'he was found praying, sleeping, weeping'. The simple infinitive used after *bleiben* 'remain' is of the same origin: *es bleibt hängen* 'it remains hanging' or 'it gets stuck', *sie ist sitzen geblieben* 'she has remained seated', also 'she has been kept down (in school)' or 'she has been left on the shelf'.

The verb *haben* occurs with an infinitive and an accusative object, although only a few infinitives are involved, usually *hängen, liegen, sitzen, stehen* (as after *finden* above), also *wohnen*, e.g. *sie haben einen Farbfernseher in der Ecke stehen* 'they have a colour television standing in the corner', *er hat Verwandte in Kiel wohnen* 'he has relatives living in Kiel'. However, the prepositional infinitive is normal in the spoken German of some places in the north, as Berlin, where in an office the following was overheard in reference to a pretty typist: *Sie haben einen netten Käfer dort zu sitzen* 'you have a nice bird sitting over there'. Notice also the common idiom *er hat gut reden* 'It's all very well for him to talk'.

The simple infinitive occurs as the complement of *heißen* or *nennen*, e.g. *nun heißt es großzügig sein* 'now the call is to be generous', *das nenne ich arbeiten* (also *gearbeitet*, p. 259) 'I call that working'.

The infinitive often comes close to a noun and may therefore more naturally take the simple form: (W. Busch) *Vater werden ist nicht schwer, / Vater sein dagegen sehr* 'to become a father isn't difficult, / to be a father, on the other hand, (is) very (difficult)'. None the less there is a tendency to insert the preposition, both constructions being acceptable in good style: *Bücher (zu) schreiben ist nicht immer leicht* 'to write books is not always easy'. The borderline nature of the infinitives here is illustrated by the use, alternatively, of the verbal noun in English: 'writing books is not always easy'.

It will have been noticed that only accusative objects have appeared in the preceding examples. Dative objects require the prepositional infinitive: *er gab mir zu essen und zu trinken* 'he gave me to eat and drink'. A sole exception is allowable in the case of *helfen* and then only when the subject performs the same action as the person in the dative: *ich helfe dir tragen* 'I'll help you with the carrying', *ich helfe dir den Koffer tragen* 'I'll help you (to) carry the suitcase'. Otherwise the preposition is prescribed: *ich helfe dir, dich aus der Affäre zu ziehen* 'I'll help you (to) pull out of the affair'.

Other uses in the next section.

The construction *um zu*, etc.

Traditionally, purpose could be expressed by the prepositional infinitive, e.g. *zu lesen*, but this has now been largely replaced by *um zu lesen* '(in order) to read': *ich brauche meine Brille, um das Kleingedruckte zu lesen* 'I need my glasses (in order) to read the small print'. But the older construction may survive, as not uncommonly in colloquial use: *er hatte nicht die Kraft aufzustehen* 'he hadn't the strength to get up', though in writing one will be inclined to use the more purposeful *um aufzustehen*. At the same time, there may be hesitancy in the written language, depending on how forcefully the notion of purpose is to be expressed, e.g. *Siegfried beeilte sich nun, (um) den Rat des Vaters zu befolgen* 'S. hastened now to follow his father's advice'. In other cases the older construction may be preferred in elevated style (Menge 1926) *ich bin nicht gekommen aufzulösen, sondern zu erfüllen* 'I have not come to destroy, but to fulfil'.

The present construction also expresses an unintended result: *er legte die Fahrprüfung ein zweites Mal ab, um nur wieder durchzufallen* 'he took the driving test a second time, only to fail again'. It further occurs optionally after adjectives preceded by *zu* 'too': *er war zu müde um aufzustehen*, but also simply *aufzustehen*. The construction also occurs, again optionally, in connection with *genug* or *genügend*, thus *haben wir genug Zeit* (or *Zeit genug*), *(um) den Zug zu erreichen?* 'have we enough time (time enough) to catch the train?', *die Firma war noch genügend zahlungskräftig, (um) alle Schulden zu begleichen* 'the firm was still sufficiently solvent to settle all the debts'.

Comparable constructions are *(an)'statt zu* and *ohne zu*, but whereas *um zu* can refer to the object in the same way as the traditional infinitive, e.g. *er schickte seinen Sohn, um die Post abzuholen* 'he sent his son to collect the post', the present idioms can only refer to the subject of the sentence: *statt* or *anstatt selbst die Post abzuholen, schickte er seinen Sohn* 'instead of collecting the post himself, he sent his son', *ohne einen Augenblick zu zögern, sprang der Angler in den Fluß, um den ertrinkenden Jungen zu retten* 'without hesitating a moment, the angler plunged into the river to rescue the drowning boy'.

Purpose may also be expressed by the verbal noun: *er hatte nicht die Kraft (er war zu müde) zum Aufstehen* equals *(um) aufzustehen* above; see 'Infinitives as nouns', p. 255. See also 'Final Clauses'.

Infinitive with passive meaning, passive participle

As a rule the simple infinitive has active meaning: *ich möchte ein Sparkonto eröffnen* 'I should like to open a savings account'. Occasionally, however, in association with certain verbs, the active infinitive can take on a passive meaning. Compare the sentences *er ließ seine Werkleute die Mauer bauen* 'he had his workmen build the wall' and *er ließ die Mauer von seinen Werkleuten bauen* 'he had the wall built by his workmen'. By the same token, *ich hörte es sagen* can mean either 'I heard it (e.g. a child) say' or 'I heard it said' depending on the wider context. Notice constructions of the type *es läßt sich machen* 'it can be done'.

The prepositional infinitive, too, usually has active meaning: *ich habe etwas Geld anzulegen* 'I have a little money to invest'. When used with the verb 'to be', however, it acquires a passive sense: *das Haus ist zu verkaufen* 'the house is to be sold'. Passive sense is likewise found with one or two other verbs, thus *es steht zu befürchten* 'it is to be feared', *es bleibt zu erwägen* 'it remains to be considered'. This usage led to a formation which may be called the passive participle: *das zu erwägende Problem* 'the problem to be considered', a corruption of *das zu *erwägene Problem*, and similarly *ein preiswert zu verkaufendes Haus* 'a house to be sold cheaply', further *die zu bewältigende Vergangenheit* 'the past one has to come to terms with', *stationär zu behandelnde Patienten* 'patients requiring treatment in hospital'. Though of regular occurrence in the written language, this idiom does not enter the language as ordinarily spoken. In everyday colloquial the concept *der zu bezahlende Betrag* 'the amount to be paid' would be rendered *der Betrag, der zu bezahlen ist*, or by some other paraphrase, say, *der Betrag, den man zu bezahlen hat*.

Infinitive as imperative

The simple infinitive frequently has the force of an imperative: *aufpassen!* 'pay attention!', *weitermachen!* 'carry on!', *nicht drängen!* 'don't push!', (advertisement) *Auflage fast vergriffen — rasch zugreifen!*

'edition almost exhausted—seize the opportunity without delay!' The reflexive pronoun is as a rule suppressed: *vorsehen!* 'watch out!', ordinary imperative *sehen Sie sich vor!* In rare cases, however, the pronoun is necessary for the sense, cf. (affective) *immer zusammensein! sich nie* (more elevated *nie sich*) *trennen!* 'always stay together! never be parted!'. In such a context *nie trennen!* could hardly fail to suggest the meaning 'never divide', so disturbing the style. In a boxing match, on the other hand, *trennen!* 'break!' is understandably adequate.

The present construction may be appropriate when talking to small children, especially in emotional situations: *Händchen geben! Fingerchen zeigen! nicht weinen!* 'give us your hand! show us your finger! don't cry!' It is conspicuous in notices and instructions (generally without an exclamation mark): *Nicht stürzen* 'this side up', *Durchfahrt freihalten* 'keep passage clear', *Coupon ausschneiden und auf frankierte Postkarte kleben* 'cut out coupon and paste on stamped postcard', *Kartoffeln und eine Zwiebel schälen, reiben, mit den genannten Zutaten vermischen* 'peel potatoes and one onion, grate, and mix with the ingredients mentioned', (seen at a filling station) *Nicht vergessen, Ölstand messen* 'don't forget, check the oil (level)', with suppression of reflexive pronoun: *bitte nicht mehr anstellen, die Kasse wird geschlossen* 'no further queuing please, the checkout is being closed', ordinary imperative *stellen Sie sich nicht mehr an!* Occasionally the prepositional infinitive may occur: beside *hereinkommen!* 'come in!' also *hereinzukommen!* It is elliptical for, say, *ich bitte Sie hereinzukommen*, with which compare: (letter) *bitte, das Fernbleiben meiner Tochter von der Schule am Montag zu entschuldigen* 'please excuse my daughter's absence from school on Monday'.

Infinitive in exclamations and questions

The simple infinitive appears in exclamations: *was! das alles übernehmen!* 'what! take over all that!', *jemanden deswegen verurteilen, geht doch nicht an!* 'to condemn someone for that is quite out of the question!', and in questions: *wozu sich weiter bemühen?* 'why bother further?'

Infinitives as nouns

The simple infinitive is basically a hybrid, having at one and the same time verbal and substantival character, and borderline cases have already been noticed, p. 252. Should the substantival overshadow the verbal character, the infinitive is written with a capital: *Schreiben ist Sprechen mit der Feder* 'writing is speaking with the pen', the status of noun proper being indubitably reached when used with an attribute, hence alternatively *das Schreiben ist Sprechen mit der Feder*, cf. also *das Bücherschreiben ist nicht immer leicht.* Such usage is a prominent feature on all stylistic levels: *Wissen und Können* 'knowledge and ability', *er mag das Rauchen nicht* 'he doesn't like smoking', *sowohl ihr Maschineschreiben als auch ihr Stenographieren haben sich verbessert* 'both her typing and her shorthand have improved', *es war ein letztes Aufflackern vor dem endgültigen Erlöschen* 'it was a last flickering before the final extinction'. Spontaneous creation of compounds is commonplace: *Zähneputzen abends ist besonders wichtig* 'cleaning one's teeth last thing at night is specially important', *das Gefeiertwerden bereitete ihm viel Freude* 'being fêted gave him much pleasure'. The substantivized infinitive is often used with a preposition and contracted definite article, as in the formation referred to under 'Expressing the continuous aspect', p. 246. Further examples: *danke fürs Zuhören* 'thanks for listening', *er nimmt seine Pillen vorm Schlafengehen* 'he takes his pills before going to bed', and the idioms *im Handumdrehen* 'in a jiffy', *vom Hörensagen* 'by hearsay'. Notice the highly productive type: *es ist zum Lachen* 'it is laughable', *es ist zum Kotzen* 'it's enough to make one sick', *es ist zu kalt zum Draußensitzen* 'it's too cold to sit outside', *die marode Wirtschaft hat die Regierung zum Umdenken bewogen* 'the ailing economy has induced the government to change their approach', with suppression of the reflexive pronoun (p. 255) *hier ist ein netter Ort zum Ausruhen* 'here is a nice place to take a rest'.

As a result of reiterated use, a considerable number of substantivized infinitives have tended to live a life of their own. They have thus been open to semantic changes which have, in varying degrees, isolated them from the verbs with which they are formally connected. Hence while verbal affinities are still tangible in *unser Hiersein* 'our being here', they are absent in *unser Dasein* 'our existence'. The term *Vermögen* 'ability', also in *Durchhaltevermögen* 'staying power', is still close to *vermögen* 'be able', but the association is severed in the secondary meaning 'assets, wealth' which will have developed via a special narrowing of the sense to 'ability to pay'. In given cases the substantivized infinitive can form a plural, e.g. *Abkommen* 'agreement, treaty', *Leiden* 'complaint, illness', *Versprechen* 'promise', pl. *Abkommen*, etc., and may actually denote a concrete object, as *Andenken* 'souvenir', *Essen* 'meal, food', *Schreiben* 'letter'. But at the same time the spontaneous substantivization of the infinitive in its literal meaning is always a possibility, thus *Übung im Schreiben* 'practice in writing', *übermäßiges Essen* 'excessive eating'.

The infinitives of a number of reflexive verbs are commonly used as nouns, when the pronoun is of course suppressed, thus *Benehmen* 'behaviour', *Vergnügen* 'enjoyment' beside *sich benehmen* 'behave', *sich vergnügen* 'enjoy'. But in the case of casually substantivized infinitives the reflexive pronoun may, very occasionally, be felt necessary for the sense: *das Sichärgern hat wohl selten jemandem geholfen* 'being annoyed will seldom have helped anyone'.

Infinitive instead of perfect participle

When compound tenses are used with a simple infinitive, an expected perfect participle is replaced by the infinitive in certain instances, above all and without exception, in the case of the modal auxiliaries. Thus *er hat es tun müssen* 'he has had to do it', contrasting with synonymous, elliptic *er hat es gemußt*, p. 291. Compare further *sie hat nicht schwimmen dürfen* 'she has not been allowed to swim', *wir hatten immer mit ihnen Geschäfte machen können* 'we had always been able to do business with them', *Leber habe ich nie gern essen mögen* 'I have never liked (to eat) liver', *du hättest hingehen sollen* 'you ought to have gone there', *Geld haben sie keines ausgeben wollen* 'they didn't want to spend any money'. On use with *brauchen* 'need', see p. 290. Under the influence of the present construction, the perfect participle of the modals has often been lost in the colloquial language in elliptic sentences also, thus *er hat es müssen* instead of *er hat es gemußt* as above. Such practice is widespread in the south.

The substitute infinitive is also found in connection with *lassen*, invariably so when the basic meaning is 'cause to': *wir haben die Mansarde renovieren lassen* 'we have had the attic renovated', and generally so in other cases: *sie hat sich in die Irre führen lassen* 'she has let herself be led astray', *das hätte ich mir nie träumen lassen* 'I should never have dreamt of it'. However, *lassen* frequently occurs together with such verbs as *fallen* 'fallen', *liegen* 'lie', *stehen* 'stand', also *stecken* as when used of a key, see specimen sentence below. With these, it forms compounds: *fallenlassen* 'let fall', *liegenlassen* 'leave lying', etc. In such cases the substitute infinitive is, we believe, commoner, but the participle remains an optional alternative: *hast du den Regenschirm irgendwo stehenlassen* or *stehengelassen?* 'have you left the umbrella (standing) somewhere?', *ich hatte den Schlüssel steckenlassen* or *steckengelassen* 'I had left the key in the door'. Finally, the infinitive is usual with *sehen* 'see': *ich habe den Unfall kommen sehen* 'I saw the accident coming', and often with *hören* 'hear': *hast du die Müllmänner vorbeigehen hören* or (equally common) *gehört?* 'have you heard the dustmen go by?'

The present substitution is likewise found in connection with the perfect infinitive: *sie wird ihn nicht haben sehen können* 'she won't have been able to see him', in contrast e.g. *kann sie sich erinnern, den Verdächtigen jemals gesehen zu haben?* 'can she remember ever having seen the suspect?'

Participles

The participles, both present and perfect, are by and large treated like adjectives, pp. 172 f. They often occur in apposition: *auf einem Klappstuhl hockend, die Beine in Decken gehüllt, betrachtete Maria die im Schnee spielenden Kinder* 'sitting on a folding-chair, her legs enveloped in blankets, M. watched the children playing in the snow'. The present participle may, as in English, take an object: *seine Experimente wieder aufnehmend, machte der Physiker eine bedeutende Entdeckung* 'taking up his experiments again, the physicist made a significant discovery'. Below we notice certain uses of the perfect participle.

Perfect participle after *kommen*

In a unique construction, the participle is obligatory in such sentences as *da kommen sie gelaufen* 'there they come running', *er kam ins Zimmer hereingeschneit* 'he just blew into the room'.

The idiom *verloren gehen*, etc.

Another construction involving the participle is seen in *verloren gehen*, e.g. *der Schlüssel ist verloren gegangen* 'the key has got lost' and syntactically comparable to *da liegt der Hund begraben* 'there's the rub' lit. 'there lies the dog buried'.

Perfect participle as imperative

By a striking development, the participle can be employed as a (generally vigorous) imperative, as in the military *stillgestanden!* 'attention!' more literally 'stand still!', originally *es wird stillgestanden!* —the present indicative may express this sort of command, p. 231. Similarly *aufgemacht!* 'open up!', *erst mal die Schuhe ausgezogen* 'first of all take off the shoes!', (slogan in a departmental store) *aufgepaßt! zugefaßt!* 'look here! seize the opportunity!', (book title) *Hereinspaziert ins alte Wien* 'Walk into Old Vienna'.

Other absolute uses of perfect participle

Elliptic expressions, closely related to those in the preceding paragraph, are seen in the everyday phrases *wohl gemerkt* 'mind you' and *offen gestanden* 'frankly speaking', also *strenggenommen* (one word) 'strictly speaking'. One imagines that *es sei* 'let it be' has been suppressed.

At times the participle stands for the verbal concept pure and simple: *gesagt, getan* 'no sooner said than done'. The English translation may need an adjective or noun: *das ist doch gelacht!* 'that's quite ridiculous', *versprochen ist versprochen* 'a promise is a promise'.

A small number of participles are regularly used in an absolute sense: *Bedienung inbegriffen* 'service included', *Rückporto beigelegt* 'return postage enclosed', *Provision abgerechnet* 'commission deducted', *falls verzogen, bitte mit neuer Adresse zurück* 'if moved, please return with new address', *sonn- und feiertags ausgenommen*, also *ausgenommen sonn- und feiertags* 'Sundays and holidays excepted'. Some examples indicate a condition: *angenommen, die Sache stimmt wirklich*, also *angenommen, daß die Sache wirklich stimmt* 'assuming (that) the matter is really in order', further *vorausgesetzt, (daß) der Regen kommt* 'provided (that) the rain comes', *zugegeben, (daß) die Preise steigen* 'granted (that) prices are rising'. Notice *gesetzt den Fall, der Zug hat Verspätung*, or *daß der Zug Verspätung hat* 'suppose (that) the train is late'.

Miscellaneous

The perfect participle occurs after verbs of receiving: *sie kriegt (bekommt, erhält) ihre Witwenrente wöchentlich ausgezahlt* 'she gets her widow's pension paid weekly', and also with other verbs: *wir glaubten uns gerettet* 'we thought we were saved', *er sah seinen Plan gefährdet* 'he saw his plan endangered', *der Kaiser hielt den Herzog gefangen* 'the emperor held the duke prisoner'. The participle is further found after *gehören*, more typically in southern use: *diese Tücher gehören gebügelt* 'these sheets want ironing'. It may also have a substantival function: *das nenne ich gearbeitet* (or *arbeiten*, p. 252) 'I call that working'.

The Subjunctive

Decline of the subjunctive

There are two basic tenses of the subjunctive, present and preterite, parallel to those of the indicative. In the earliest German the two moods were entirely distinct since their respective endings differed throughout. In the subsequent evolution of the language, however, the two sets of terminations tended to fall together. Wherever this happened the subjunctive lost its identity to the indicative, its functions passing largely to the modal auxiliaries. But so heavy is the hand of tradition that many authorities continue to print full subjunctive paradigms when the majority of the forms are no longer subjunctives at all. It is true that in a few cases (*passim* below) the old subjunctive function is discernible behind the modern indicative, but obviously not because of the form, but because of the construction. A verbal form, of itself, can only possess a subjunctive function if it possesses a subjunctive form, i.e. one which differs from its indicative counterpart, as in the 3rd singular, in other persons also in the preterite of strong verbs, especially those with a modifiable root vowel, and in the case of certain auxiliaries, in particular *sein* 'to be'.

Subjunctive in spoken German

Nowhere is the decline of the subjunctive more marked than in everyday speech. The present subjunctive, indeed, is no longer a characteristically colloquial form at all. At the simplest level of conversation it is as good as absent, save only in occasional relics, e.g. *Gott sei Dank!* 'thank God!' and (though no longer felt as such) in the polite imperative: *seien Sie vernünftig!* 'be (lit. may They be) sensible!' But as noticed elsewhere (p. 240), the printed word can and does affect everyday speech. As a consequence the 3rd sg. *habe, sei*, and the 3rd pl. *seien* may from time to time be heard as (essentially literary) alternatives to the more natural present indicative or preterite subjunctive (p. 264): *es sieht aus, als ob sie Geld habe*, but usually *hat* or *hätte* 'it looks as though she has money', *er führt sich auf, als ob er verrückt sei*, but usually *ist* or *wäre* 'he behaves as though he were mad', *sie führen sich auf, als ob sie verrückt seien*, but usually *sind* or *wären* 'they behave as if they were mad'. No other present subjunctives are likely to be encountered in ordinary conversation.

The preterite subjunctive has fared better than the present, but even so the only forms normally heard are the auxiliaries *hätte, wäre, würde*, with the modals *dürfte, könnte, möchte, müßte*, also *bräuchte*, further such verbs as *wüßte*, in educated speech, say, *ließe, ginge, käme, täte*. Other preterites would normally be colloquialized, e.g. literary *stünde er jetzt hier* 'were he now standing here' becoming in spoken language *würde er jetzt hier stehen* (p. 262) or in simpler style *wenn er jetzt hier stehen würde* 'if he were now standing here'.

The above remarks refer, as we have said, to pedestrian conversational language. In more formal circumstances, as when making a speech, literary usages can well dominate if the occasion calls for it. Vicki Baum had such a situation in mind when she wittily wrote *Preysing hörte mißvergnügt der Plädoyerstimme zu, die in vielen tadellosen Konjunktiven lauter unangenehme Dinge vorbrachte* 'P. listened with little joy to that court-room voice which, in many faultless subjunctives, raised nothing but unpleasant matters' (from *Menschen im Hotel*).

SUBJUNCTIVE IN MAIN CLAUSES

Present subjunctive

In essentially literary style the present subjunctive can come close to an imperative: *man nehme zwei Tabletten alle vier Stunden* 'take two tablets every four hours', similarly *wer von einer Kreuzotter gebissen wurde, schneide rasch entschlossen die Bißstelle auf, lasse die Wunde kräftig ausbluten, binde darauf das Glied oberhalb des Einschlags halbwegs fest und begebe sich stehenden Fußes zum nächsten Arzt* 'anyone bitten by an adder should immediately lance the area around the bite, allow the wound to bleed freely, thereupon bind the limb above the stricken part fairly tightly and proceed without delay to the nearest doctor'.

In a few contexts the subjunctive has concessive force: *wie dem auch sei* 'however that may be', *es koste* (or *koste es*), *was es wolle* 'cost what it may'. In some others it expresses a wish: *es lebe die Republik!* 'long live the republic!', *möge der Geist des Friedens bei uns bleiben!* 'may the spirit of peace remain among us!', although in another phrase the indicative can take over: *mag es genügen, zu sagen* 'suffice it to say', but alternatively *es genüge* (or *genüge es*), *zu sagen*. A plural form is, of course, possible with the verb 'to be': *deine Sünden seien dir vergeben!* 'your sins be forgiven (you)!'

Preterite subjunctive

This subjunctive traditionally expressed a wish, a prominent survival being pret. *möchte*, e.g. *er möchte Sie kurz sprechen* 'he would like a word with you'. In association with the particles *doch* or *nur*, either singly or together, the preterite subjunctive has the force of 'would that!': *könnten wir doch die Winterzeit verschlafen!* 'would that we could sleep through the winter-time!', *wäre ich nur in Grantchester!* 'would I were in G.!', *möchte* (but also *möge*, p. 285) *er doch nur kommen!* 'would that he might come!'

This tense can further be used to imply a certain reluctance or reserve: *ich hätte noch eine Frage* 'I have another question (if you don't mind)'. It is familiar in polite questions: *wäre das möglich?* 'would that be possible?', *hättet ihr dazu Lust?* 'would you like to?', alternatively (p. 262) *würde das möglich sein? würdet ihr dazu Lust haben?* Notice *bräuchte* (p. 291), now widespread: *wozu bräuchte er denn das?* 'what would he need it for?', and (only formally subordinate) *nicht, daß ich wüßte* 'not that I know of'.

Apparently related to the above is a special use illustrated by the following: *ja, das wäre meine Geschichte* 'yes, that is my story' (said just after telling it), *das hätten wir nun geschafft* 'we've got it done now' (the matter being just completed), the subjunctive here suggesting an element of modesty on the part of the speaker. Somewhat similarly in answer to enquiries: *jawohl, hier wäre noch Platz* 'yes (of course), there's still room here', where the mood of the verb conveys a touch of courtesy not implicit in the forthright *hier ist noch Platz.*

The subjunctive is standard in sentences containing *beinahe* (*beinah*) or *fast*, e.g. *beinahe* (*fast*) *wären sie zusammengestoßen* 'they nearly collided, or had nearly collided', *ich hätte es beinahe* (*fast*) *vergessen* 'I nearly forgot, or had nearly forgotten'. But the spoken language can, in pedestrian style, use the appropriate indicatives: *ich habe es beinah* (*fast*) *vergessen, ich hatte es beinah* (*fast*) *vergessen*.

Subjunctive force can lie behind *wollte* (and synonymous *wünschte*): (proverbial, from an apocryphal remark by Wellington at Waterloo) *ich wollte, es würde Nacht, oder die Preußen kämen* 'I wish it would get dark, or the Prussians would come'.

See further 'Conditional Sentences'; on the subjunctive in subordinate clauses, see *passim* below.

würde with the infinitive

In the contemporary language the preterite subjunctive is extensively replaced by a periphrasis consisting of the pret. subj. of *werden* + the infinitive in question. Thus *wenn ich es nur verstehen würde* may be preferred to the now more formal *wenn ich es nur verstünde* (*verstände*) 'if only I understood it'; likewise when the subjunctive has fallen together with the indicative: *wir hatten geglaubt, daß sie noch in Neapel wohnen würden* beside *wohnten* 'we had thought that they were still living in Naples'. Both constructions can well appear side by side: *stellen Sie sich vor, Luther würde noch leben und schriebe einen Brief an den Papst* 'imagine L. were alive and wrote a letter to the pope'.

The periphrasis may be regarded as normal in the spoken style. As already noticed (p. 260), only in the case of auxiliary verbs has the preterite subjunctive maintained itself to any extent in the language as ordinarily spoken, though even here the periphrasis is often used as well, in southern areas predominantly so: *ich würde gern noch eine Tasse Kaffee haben* beside *ich hätte gern noch eine Tasse Kaffee* 'I would like another cup of coffee', or *würde er dann glücklich sein?* in addition to *wäre er dann glücklich?* 'would he then be happy?' The logic of the language has inevitably involved *würde* itself: contrast literary *wenn er eines Tages Millionär würde*, but informally tautological *werden würde* 'if he one day became a millionaire'.

Since the preterite and pluperfect are not always logically distinguished, the construction under discussion may occur instead of the latter: *sie lachten und amüsierten sich, als ob sie sich ein Leben lang kennen würden*, a loose alternative to *gekannt haben würden* or *gekannt hätten* 'they laughed and had fun as if they had known each other all their lives'.

Conditional Sentences

Open condition

As in English, the indicative is the mood in open conditional sentences: *Sie müssen es uns sofort wissen lassen, falls er heute kommt* 'you must let us know immediately if he comes today', *sie konnte immer ihre Tochter anrufen, wenn sie sich nicht gut fühlte* 'she could always ring up her daughter if she didn't feel well'—the conjunctions *falls* and *wenn* being interchangeable. As in English the order of the clauses may be reversed: *wenn sie sich nicht gut fühlte, konnte sie* or (more emphatically) *sie konnte immer ihre Tochter anrufen*. Given this order, the main clause could be introduced by *dann* or (more literary) *so* 'then': *wenn sie sich nicht gut fühlte, dann (so) konnte sie immer ihre Tochter anrufen*. At the same time, unlike English, the 'if'-clause could be reconstrued: *fühlte sie sich nicht gut, (dann, so) konnte sie immer ihre Tochter anrufen*, also the (rather less usual) alternative *sie konnte immer ihre Tochter anrufen, fühlte sie sich nicht gut*.

A final example: *wenn er dir das erzählte, dann war es eine Lüge* 'if he told you that, then it was a lie' to be contrasted with *dann wäre es eine Lüge* below.

Unreal condition

The subjunctive is the characteristic mood in unreal conditional sentences. Examples using the preterite ('present conditional'): *es würde keine Kriege geben, wenn die Welt einsichtsvoll wäre* 'there would be no wars if the world were sensible', *sie wäre stolz, falls sie den Preis gewinnen könnte* 'she would be proud if she could win the prize'. The clauses may be varied as with the open condition. Firstly, they are reversible: *falls sie den Preis gewinnen könnte, wäre sie* (or more emphatically) *sie wäre stolz*. Secondly, the main clause can now be introduced by *dann* or (more literary) *so* 'then': *falls sie den Preis gewinnen könnte, dann (so) wäre sie stolz*. Thirdly, the 'if'-clause may be reconstrued: *könnte sie den Preis gewinnen, (dann, so) wäre sie stolz*, also the (rather less usual) alternative *sie wäre stolz, könnte sie den Preis gewinnen*, cf. our 'could she but win the prize'. Where appropriate the pluperfect ('perfect conditional') is used: *wir wären weggegeangen, wenn wir das gewußt hätten* 'we would have gone away if we had known that'.

Where a verb has no special subjunctive form, the corresponding indicative may do duty: *wenn er dir das erzählte, dann wäre es eine Lüge* 'if he told, or were to tell you that, then it would be a lie'.

The condition need not be expressed in so many words: *nie wäre sie allein ausgekommen* 'never would she have managed on her own', and naturally often in questions: *hätte es einen Ausweg gegeben?* 'would there have been a way out?' A nursery rhyme preserves forms now possible only in high literary style (*spielt(e)*, *sänge*, *spränge*, in normal use *spielen*, *singen*, *springen würde*, p. 262): *eine kleine Geige hätt' ich gern;/ alle Tage spielt' ich mir / zwei, drei Stückchen oder vier / und sänge und spränge gar lustig herum* 'I'd like to have a little fiddle; every day I'd play two or three tunes or four, and sing and jump around as merry as can be'. Frequently the conditional clause is replaced by an adverb or equivalent: *gegebenenfalls könntest du übernehmen* 'if need arises, you could take over', *mit neuen Maschinen ließe sich die Produktion verdoppeln* 'with new machines production could be doubled'. Conversely, 'if'-clauses can occur in isolation: *wenn wir nur die Chance hätten!* 'if only we had the chance!' coming very close to the volitive 'would that!', p. 261.

als ob-clauses

Clauses introduced by *als ob* 'as if, as though' arose from conditional clauses (*ob* originally 'if') and are therefore regularly construed with the subjunctive: *er benimmt sich, als ob er der Chef wäre* 'he behaves as if he was the manager', alternatively (mainly literary) *als wäre er der Chef*. Especially in spoken German, *als ob* may be replaced by *als wenn*, *wie wenn*, and in simple conversational style the subjunctive gives way to the indicative: *er benimmt sich, als ob (als wenn, wie wenn) er der Chef ist*. Hence beside *es sieht so aus, als ob sie nicht heiraten würde*, colloquial also *wird*, under the influence of which some would doubtless write *werde* 'it looks as though she won't marry'.

Concessive Clauses

Concessive clauses are of various sorts. We first mention one which is simply a variety of the conditional; it is introduced by *auch* (or *selbst*, *sogar*) *wenn* 'even if, even though': *auch wenn er mich darum bittet, ich werde ihm doch kein Geld leihen* 'even if he asks me for it, I (still) won't lend him any money'. The word order in the main clause is emphatic, as is possible in certain conditional sentences (above). In this construction it is the norm, and likewise regular after most types of concessive clause.

In an essentially literary variation of the above, *auch wenn* can appear as *wenn . . . auch*; observe that *auch* is quite unstressed: *wenn er mich darum auch 'bittet, ich werde ihm doch kein Geld leihen*. Notice that *auch* follows the pronoun (and here also a pronominal adverb); the same applies to a noun object, but only when qualified by the definite article or a demonstrative or a possessive: *wenn wir das (dieses, sein) Fahrrad auch gekauft hätten* 'even if we had bought the (this, his) bicycle'. Otherwise *auch* precedes the object: *wenn er auch keine Ahnung hat* 'even though he has no idea'; it similarly precedes the complement of the verb 'to be': *wenn er auch mein Freund wäre* 'even though he were my friend'. If *auch* stands before the object or complement and bears some stress, the concessive nuance is lost, the adverb taking on its literal meaning: *wenn er 'auch mich darum bittet* 'if he asks me, too, for it', *wenn wir 'auch das . . . Fahrrad gekauft hätten* 'if we had bought the . . . bicycle as well', *wenn er 'auch mein Freund wäre* 'if he were also my friend'.

As a further parallel to the conditional, the concessive clause may be construed without a conjunction, though only in a very elevated style: (Menge 1926) *müßt' ich auch wandern in finsterm Tal, ich fürchte kein Unglück* 'even though I walk in the dark valley, I fear no misfortune', in simpler style: *wenn ich auch wandere.* Further *fanden wir auch hier keine Pagoden, so wurden wir jedoch voll entschädigt vom Reiz dieser kleinen Ortschaft* 'though we found no pagodas here, we were nevertheless fully compensated by the charm of this small village'.

Linked to the above is a not uncommon literary construction, namely *und* introducing a conditional clause. It is applicable when the clause is intimately connected with a preceding noun or pronoun: *der Stuntman (er) würde es wagen, und wenn es ihm sein Leben kosten würde*, alternatively *und würde es ihm sein Leben kosten* 'the stuntman (he) would risk it, even if it cost him his life'.

Another common type of concessive clause is formed with an indefinite pronoun or adverb in association with one or more (unstressed) adverbs which follow immediately as *immer*, or at a distance as *auch*, or may take either position as when the aforesaid are used side by side, i.e. *auch immer.* Examples: *wo immer es ist, wir werden es finden* 'wherever it is, we shall find it', *wer dieser junge Herr auch sein mag, er muß zuerst die Aufnahmeprüfung bestehen* 'whoever this young gentleman is, he must first pass the entrance examination', *hoffen wir, daß solches sich nicht wiederholt, was auch immer in der Vergangenheit* (or *in der Vergangenheit auch immer*) *geschehen sein mag* 'let us hope that such things will not be repeated, whatever may have happened in the past'. Further: *wie* (or rather more formal *so*) *kalt das Wetter auch war, wir mußten trotzdem in die Arbeit gehen* 'however cold the weather was, we still had to go to work'. This construction is also found with an indefinite adjective: *welche* or *was für Probleme er auch hat, sie werden kaum auf diese Art und Weise gelöst* 'whatever problems he may have, they will hardly be solved in this way'. The adverb *auch* is optional in clauses introduced by *so sehr* 'however much' and *so wenig* 'however little': *so sehr er sich (auch) plagt, er kommt auf keinen grünen Zweig* 'however much he slaves away, he'll never get on', also in the common idiom *so leid es mir (auch) tut* 'much as I regret it'. The indicative is the usual mood, but the subjunctive may occur in elevated style: *was immer die Bedingungen auch seien* or *wären, wir werden sie annehmen müssen* 'whatever the conditions are, we shall have to accept them'.

Notice the concessive force of *noch so*, e.g. *er kann noch so viel Geld haben, glücklich ist er nicht* 'no matter how much money he has, he isn't happy'. This is very common spoken style, but has literary possibilities as well: *scheint die Sonne noch so schön, / sie muß am Ende untergehen* 'no matter how fair the sun may shine, in the end it has to set'.

Concessive clauses are often introduced by *obwohl* 'although' or by one of its less usual, bookish synonyms *obgleich*, *obschon*, very occasionally *obzwar*—all stressed on the second component. Sentences containing this type of clause differ from those above in that a following main clause has non-emphatic order, i.e. verb before subject: *obwohl er zurückhaltend ist und immer leise spricht, ist es unmöglich, ihn zu übersehen* 'although he is of a retiring nature and always speaks softly, it is impossible not to notice him'. The main clause can, of course, precede the concessive clause: *sie hat den Mann nicht wiedererkannt, obwohl sie ihn schon vorher gesehen hatte* 'she didn't recognize the man although she had seen him before'. The contrast between the concessive and the main clause can be heightened by the insertion of *so . . . doch* into the latter: *obwohl er seine Fehler hat, so ist er doch kein Schuft* 'although he has his faults, that doesn't make him a villain'. The above conjunctions are often replaceable by the more vigorous *trotz'dem* lit. 'in spite of the fact that', hence e.g. *trotzdem er zurückhaltend ist und immer leise spricht*, etc.

The present subjunctive may have concessive force, p. 261.

Indirect Speech

As in English, indirect speech is contained in a subordinate clause with or without the conjunction *daß* 'that': (average written style) *er behauptete, sie würde bald heiraten* or *daß sie bald heiraten würde*, (a typical spoken version) *er hat behauptet, daß sie bald heiraten wird* 'he maintained that she would be marrying soon'. The tense and mood of the subordinate verb (of which the above are merely samples) are subject to considerable and, at first sight, confusing variation. The task is therefore to discover what rationale there may be behind the apparent confusion, and we believe that a brief historical note will help put matters into perspective.

According to the original arrangement, the verb in the subordinate clause would be in the indicative if reference was to a fact, in the subjunctive if a supposition was expressed, sequence of tenses being the rule in both cases. But even in the earliest German known to us this equilibrium had already been disturbed at one significant point: after verbs of saying the subjunctive was generalized, regardless of whether a fact or a supposition was involved. Such practice spread to other verbs and in the course of time the (generally more distinctive) preterite superseded the present subjunctive, in this way becoming purely a marker of indirect statement, one of its typical functions today. But these developments were not exclusive. The indicative tended to survive after verbs expressing certainty. Furthermore, in the spoken language, a new construction emerged in which the indicative of direct speech is preserved unchanged in the subordinate clause. At the same time, in the written language, the 3rd sg. pres. subj., by now generally the only surviving part of this tense, came into regular use as the number-one indicator of subordination in reported statement.

INDIRECT STATEMENT

Indirect statement naturally follows verbs of saying, i.e. *sagen* 'say' and others, including *antworten* 'answer', *behaupten* 'maintain', *beteuern* 'solemnly declare', *erklären* 'explain', *erwähnen* 'mention', *erwidern* 'rejoin', *erzählen* 'tell', *feststellen* 'note, observe', *versichern* 'give an assurance', further the impersonal *es heißt* 'it is said, stated'. Associated with these in the present connection are such verbs as *denken* 'think', *erwarten* 'expect', *fühlen* 'feel', *fürchten* 'fear', *glauben* 'believe', *hoffen* 'hope', *hören* 'hear', *schreiben* 'write', *vernehmen* (high style) 'hear', *wünschen* 'wish', and some of these, too, will be illustrated below. Phrases may take the place of simple verbs, e.g. *der Ansicht* (*Auffassung, Meinung*) *sein* 'be of the opinion', *die Ansicht*, etc., *teilen* 'share the opinion', cf. *meinen* 'think, suppose, express an opinion'.

Spoken style

It is of prime importance to make a clear distinction between ordinary spoken use and conventional written style. We consider first the forms of the verb *sein*.

The spoken language chiefly employs two constructions. Firstly, it can use the indicative tense of direct speech unchanged regardless of the tense of the verb in the main clause, thus *Mutter sagt, "Das Frühstück ist fertig"* 'mother says, "The breakfast is ready" ' becomes indirect *Mutter* (present) *sagt*, (future) *wird sagen*, (past) *sagte* or *hat gesagt* or *hatte gesagt, daß das Frühstück fertig ist*. This construction is very widespread and the more usual one when the main verb is in the present or future. Alternatively, the subordinate verb may be used in the preterite subjunctive. This use is common when the main verb is in a past tense: *Mutter sagte*, etc., *daß das Frühstück fertig wäre*; it is generally felt to be more refined than the previous construction. Finally (under literary influence), but much less commonly, the pres. subj. *sei* could replace *wäre*. It may be stressed that neither of these subjunctives has here any modal force; they are just formal indicators of indirect speech. In these matters, the imperative as the main verb is the equivalent of the present tense: *sage, daß das Frühstück fertig ist*.

Should the verb in direct speech be in the future tense and the verb in the main clause in the present or future: *Mutter sagt* or *wird sagen*, *"Das Frühstück wird fertig sein"* 'mother says, or will say, "The breakfast will be ready" ', the indirect statement will be *Mutter sagt* (*wird sagen*), *daß das Frühstück fertig sein wird*—but never *würde* which has the sense 'would'. If the main verb, however, is in a past tense, then the subjunctive becomes possible: *Mutter sagte* (*hat, hatte gesagt*), *daß das Frühstück fertig sein wird* or *würde* 'mother said (etc.) that the breakfast would be ready'. At the same time *würde*, like Eng. 'would', may introduce an ambiguity.

If the verb in direct speech is a preterite or other past tense: *Mutter sagt*, etc., *"Das Frühstück war fertig* or *ist fertig gewesen* or *war fertig gewesen"*, the corresponding indirect constructions will be *Mutter sagt*, etc., *daß das Frühstück fertig war* (but not properly *wäre* which would equal *ist* above!) or *gewesen ist* or *gewesen war*, the last two alternatively *gewesen wäre*, rarely *gewesen sei*, i.e. ignoring the difference between perfect and pluperfect, and most usually heard, as we have said, when the main verb is in a past tense.

The above practice applies equally to *haben* 'have': *Vater sagt*, etc., *daß er eine neue Stelle hat*, alternatively *hätte*, rarely *habe* 'father says, etc., that he has a new job', and similarly with *werden* 'become' except that pres. subj. *werde* is not likely to be heard: *der Meteorologe sagt*, etc., *daß es kälter wird*, alternatively *würde* 'the weather man says, etc., that it is becoming colder'. The modals, too, alternate between pres. indic. and pret. subj., as do the few other verbs using a pret. subj. in ordinary speech, e.g. *wissen* 'know': *weiß*, *wüßte*.

With most other verbs, however, the rules are necessarily different from the foregoing to the extent that the preterite subjunctive is not heard in ordinary speech (p. 260), nor is it likely that anyone would be so pedantic as to form a present subjunctive of any of these verbs. The general pattern is thus as follows. When the verb in the main clause is in the present or future tense, it is followed in the subordinate clause by the indicative: *er sagt, daß sie später zurückfährt* 'he says that she will be returning later', *sie wird uns erzählen, daß sie uns nicht gesehen hat* 'she will tell us that she hasn't seen us'. If the main verb is in the past, the subordinate verb may also preserve the indicative tense of direct speech unchanged: *er hat geantwortet, daß er kein Geld verdient* (*verdient hat*) 'he answered that he earns (has earned) no money', but at the same time the indicative *hat* may be optionally replaced by *hätte*, rarely *habe*, in accordance with the rules given in the previous paragraph. A verb conjugated with *sein* will naturally have corresponding variants: *ich habe gedacht, daß ein Dachziegel heruntergefallen ist*, alternatively *wäre*, rarely *sei* 'I thought that a roofing tile had fallen off'. For *werden*, cf. *er hat geantwortet, daß er kein Geld verdienen wird*, alternatively *würde* 'he answered that he would earn no money'.

Written style

Turning to more literary language, one soon notices that far wider use is made of the subjunctive than is the case in ordinary speaking; indeed, it tends to act as a main indicator of subordination. Great play is made of the (3rd sg.) present subjunctive, leading to sentence structures never heard in everyday speech. Of course, not all writing is of a strictly literary character and more relaxed styles purposely admit colloquialisms. These matters need to be considered in some detail.

It will be recalled that the subjunctive is the traditional mood for the expression of a supposition. Accordingly the subjunctive is regular by ancient canon in certain subordinate clauses today, e.g. (with the once obligatory sequence of tenses) *er meinte, daß alles in Ordnung wäre* 'he supposed that all was in order'. If, on the other hand, reference was to a fact, the verb in the *daß*-clause was logically in the indicative: (Luther) *da er aber hörte, daß Archelaus . . . König war* 'when, however, he heard that A. was king'.

In more recent German this traditional difference has been obscured by a marked tendency to employ the subjunctive, in particular the (3rd sg.) present, as an indicator of indirect statement as such, regardless of modality or sequence of tense. Hence Menge (1926) modernizing Luther, puts *als er aber vernahm, daß Archelaus . . . König sei*, possible also *wäre*. By the same token one could modify the first sentence above to *er meinte, daß alles in Ordnung sei*. Now, as shown in the preceding section, the spoken language may use the indicative. Consequently the last sample sentence could be further varied to *er meinte, daß alles in Ordnung ist*. And so, at the expense of former precision, the language has developed a number of semantically undifferentiated, more or less interchangeable alternatives not unlike the plethora of past tenses discussed above. Consider the possible mutations in the following, any of which could, of course, actually occur: *er sagte uns* or *hat uns gesagt* or *hatte uns gesagt, daß er seinen Wagen gestern verkauft hat* or *hätte* or *habe*, or *verkaufte*, without the conjunction *er hat* or *hätte* or *habe seinen Wagen gestern verkauft* 'he told us (that) he sold his car yesterday'.

It will now be evident that a sentence like *er sagt, daß er krank sei*—to take an often-quoted example—will not differ in meaning from *er sagt, daß er krank ist* 'he says that he is ill'. It is a fiction to interpret the use of the subjunctive here as implying that the statement is to be treated as a supposition rather than an established fact, though some still teach that it ought to be. Nor would it matter here if *wäre* were substituted for *sei* (although in certain examples a formal ambiguity could arise, see 'Note on modality' below), since in these contexts a subjunctive does not convey any truly tangible modality. To so qualify the statement it is necessary to add explanatory words, e.g. *er sagt zwar, daß er krank ist* or *sei* or *wäre, aber ich kann ihm nicht so recht glauben* 'it is true, he says that he is ill, but I can't quite believe him'. And we repeat: the present tense form is the favourite convention used by the written language to characterize an indirect statement, e.g. *der General wußte, daß der Feind in der Nähe sei, und kam zu der Erkenntnis, daß die Stellung unhaltbar sei* 'the general knew that the enemy was nearby and came to the conclusion that the position could not be held'.

In sentences where *daß* is omitted (p. 273), the subordinate clause is particularly in need of a subjunctive to draw attention to its subordinate character, and in such cases this mood is the norm: *Mark Twain schrieb, es sei falsch, die Ameisen als Beispiele unermüdlichen Fleißes hinzustellen* 'M.T. wrote that it was wrong to describe ants as examples of indefatigable industry', *der Minister versicherte, er wolle bessere Beziehungen* 'the minister gave the assurance that he wished for better relations', *Jakob fürchtete, Esau werde sich an ihm rächen* 'Jacob feared Esau would take vengeance on him'.

As a further development of the above principle, the subjunctive regularly occurs in what are *de facto* main clauses, at the same time neatly indicating that the statements are reported: (judicial ruling that a postman may leave parcels with a neighbour if the addressee is not at home) *die Richter sagten: bei dem heutigen Postaufwand sei es nicht zu vertreten, daß unzustellbare Päckchen tagelang gelagert würden. Das führe zu hohen Kosten, die von der Gesamtheit getragen werden müßten. Wer unbedingt Wert darauf lege, seine Pakete nur persönlich in Empfang zu nehmen, könne ja den Absender veranlassen, sie postlagernd oder per Einschreiben aufzugeben* 'the judges said: in view of the high cost of the postal service today, it cannot be justified that undeliverable packets should be stored for days on end. That would lead to great expense, which would have to be borne by the community at large. Anyone attaching particular importance to taking delivery of his parcels in person could always instruct the sender to despatch them *poste restante* or by registered post'. One observes the preference for the present subjunctive, but pret. *würden* is regular, as explained in the following paragraph, and the same essentially in the case of *müßten*, p. 286. It may be noted that the verb in every subordinate clause forming part of the original direct statement will properly appear in the subjunctive: (newspaper) *der Kanzler werde sich mit dem amerikanischen Präsidenten über das Thema unterhalten, wenn dieser Anfang Mai die Bundesrepublik besuche, hieß es in Bonn* 'the chancellor, it was stated in Bonn, will be discussing the topic with the American president when he visits the Federal Republic at the beginning of May'. Should, however, a clause not forming part of the direct statement be inserted, as by way of comment, then its verb will regularly be in the indicative: *der Makler schrieb uns, daß Herr Mühsam, mit dem wir uns über den Hausverkauf bereits mündlich geeinigt hatten, an dem Geschäft nicht mehr interessiert sei* 'the agent wrote to us that Mr M., with whom we had already reached a verbal agreement about the sale of the house, was no longer interested in the transaction'.

The desire to use a subjunctive as a mark of subordination can, of course, only be satisfied if a distinct subjunctive form is to hand. For the present tense, the 3rd sg. is always available, but (except in the case of *sein* 'be') the other persons are wanting. Recourse can then be had to a distinct preterite subjunctive. This arrangement was recognized as appropriate in literary style and generally adopted, thus *ich stelle* (*stellte*) *mir vor, er habe die Mittel* 'I imagine (imagined) he has (had) the means', but *ich stelle* (*stellte*) *mir vor, sie hätten die Mittel* 'I imagine (imagined) they have (had) the means', (letter, educated style) *mein Mann sagte mir heute morgen, als ich ihn anrief, daß Bamberg völlig eingeschneit sei, und daß unsere beiden Söhne sich sehr darüber gefreut hätten* 'my husband told me this morning, when I rang him up, that B. was completely snow-bound and that our two sons were very pleased about it'. The need for a distinctive subjunctive can lead to the appearance of otherwise seldom used forms: *der Psychologe stellte fest, Eheleute sprächen miteinander im Durchschnitt sieben Minuten pro Tag* 'the psychologist noted that married couples speak to each other, on average, for seven minutes per day'. Should a distinctive subjunctive not be available, the preterite indicative may be taken in lieu: (newspaper) *Österreichs Politiker stellen gelegentlich fest, in ihrem Lande gingen die politischen Uhren anders als in der Bundesrepublik* 'Austria's politicians occasionally note that in their country the political clocks keep different time from those in the Federal Republic'.

In cases where both present and preterite subjunctive forms occur, the latter can be used optionally, too: *er schreibt (schrieb), er komme nicht* or *käme nicht* (or *würde nicht kommen*, p. 262) 'he writes (wrote) that he is not (was not) coming'. Given that the present has so little currency in the spoken language, the preterite is felt as the less formal and consequently may be preferred; it can also function as the main verb: (from a summary introducing a play) *Erna Sander bekommt Besuch. Ein Polizist warnt sie. Ein Mann hätte noch ein Hühnchen mit ihr zu rupfen* 'E.S. will be having a visitor. A policeman warns her. (And says) a man has a bone to pick with her'. If there are several dependent verbs in a sentence, a writer may choose to vary the options, as fancy takes him: (Ompteda, from H. F. Eggeling, Dictionary of Modern German Prose Usage (1961), 327) *er sann über sich selbst nach und meinte, daß er für sein Alter noch nicht gefestigt genug sei, daß ihm sichere Ansichten fehlten, daß er nicht genug Selbstzucht hätte, daß er unwissend sei, keinen rechten Glauben besäße, daß er in Menschen sich täusche und nie ein guter Offizier sein könnte* 'he thought about himself and concluded that, for his age, he was not yet sufficiently certain of himself, that he lacked firm opinions, that he had not enough self-control, that he was not knowledgeable, that he often misjudged people and could never be a good officer'.

Indicative in written language

In spite of the predominance of the subjunctive in written style, there is nevertheless a noticeable tendency to substitute indicative forms provided always that the conjunction *daß* is used to mark the subordinate clause, hence beside *er meint, es gehe*, the more natural *er meint, daß es geht* 'he thinks it will work' in writing, too.

Where a choice between the two moods is open, the indicative is the somewhat less formal: (magazine) *insofern teile ich die Auffassung von Herrn Sörgel nicht, daß eine geringere Wahlbeteiligung zu erwarten ist* 'I do not share Mr S.'s opinion in so far as he holds that a lower turnout at the polls is to be expected'. The indicative may be preferred to avoid a subjunctive which, being little used, sounds particularly stilted: (newspaper) *der Unterhändler sagte, er hoffe, daß die Vernunft siege und Verhandlungen beginnen* (instead of *begönnen, begännen*, preterite following practice described on p. 271), *um die Militarisierung des Weltraums zu verhindern* 'the negotiator said he hoped that reason would prevail and talks begin in order to prevent the militarization of space'.

The indicative is usual after verbs which of themselves express certainty. Such include *entdecken* 'discover', *erfahren* 'hear (a fact)', *herausfinden* 'find out', *sehen* 'see', *wissen* 'know' and the equivalent phrases *gewiß* or *sicher sein* 'be certain, sure': *Lavoisier fand heraus, daß es ein bestimmter Teil der Luft war, der sich mit dem Blei verband* 'L. found out that it was a definite part of the air which combined with the lead'.

It goes without saying that spoken idiom can be expected to break through in a piece avowedly close to conversational style: (comic paper) *"Gott sei Dank!", sagte der seekranke Passagier, als er erfuhr, daß das Schiff untergeht* ' "Thank God!", said the seasick passenger when he heard that the ship was sinking', the colloquial present indicative (p. 267) contrasting with preterite *war* in the sentence in the previous paragraph, this the more literary use observing the sequence of tenses.

Note on modality

We have seen that a preterite subjunctive can appear as a formal marker of subordination, the auxiliaries *hätte, wäre, würde* being common examples. But—in contrast to the colourless, bookish present tense forms *habe, sei, werde*—the preterites are central words in the language and retain, in other constructions, their original subjunctive force, notably in unreal conditional sentences. Such modality is thus potentially present in these subjunctives and may become tangible in what are otherwise ordinary subordinate clauses in indirect speech, thereby giving rise to ambiguity: *glauben Sie, wir hätten das gesagt?* can mean either 'do you believe we (had) said that?' or 'do you believe we would have said that?', the exact sense depending on the given context. Similarly *sie sagte, ihr Freund wäre gekommen* 'she said her friend had come' or 'she said her friend would have come'. On *würde*, see p. 268.

Omission of *daß*

Broadly speaking, the conjunction *daß* may be optionally omitted as long as the main clause does not contain a negative, thus possibly *ich sehe, du bist auf dem richtigen Weg* 'I see you are on the right track', but only *ich sehe nicht, daß du auf dem richtigen Weg bist*. There is a strong tendency to drop the conjunction when a subjunctive verb is used, since this on its own can amply indicate subordination: *Mutter sagte, das Frühstück wäre fertig* 'mother said breakfast was ready', *Vater sagte, er hätte eine neue Stelle* 'father said he had a new job', *der Meteorologe sagte, es würde kälter* 'the weatherman said it would become colder'; this construction often has stylistic value, see examples on p. 270. Otherwise, again broadly speaking, one may say that *daß* is less likely to be omitted than is 'that' in comparable clauses, for example where English tends to say 'I hear you like swimming very much' or 'do you think the bus has gone?' the corresponding German will most likely be *ich höre, daß du sehr gern schwimmst* and *glaubst du, daß der Bus schon weg ist?* Indeed, after certain verbs, as *entdecken, feststellen, herausfinden* (p. 273), the use of *daß* is obligatory.

Miscellaneous types of *daß*-clause

German *daß* has a wide range of functions comparable to English 'that', understandable in view of their common origin, but there are divergencies as well. These are our chief concern here.

Although the conjunction may, as in English, be used in a temporal sense, cf. *es war am 4. August 1914, daß Großbritannien zum ersten Mal gegen Deutschland in den Krieg zog* 'it was on 4 August 1914 that Great Britain first went to war with Germany', the meaning in German is also commonly 'since': *es ist noch keine Stunde, daß er hier war* 'it's not an hour since he was here'. Thus *daß* is the equivalent of *seit*, or *seitdem*, with which it may interchange stylistically: *es sind jetzt fünf Jahre, daß seine Arbeit abgeschlossen, und zumindest drei, seit die letzte Änderung für den Druck vorgenommen wurde* 'it is now five years since his work was completed, and at least three since the final alteration for the printer's copy (lit. for the printing) was made'.

Elliptic use is common, as in a few fixed exclamations: *daß Gott erbarm!* 'God have mercy!' more or less like our 'good heavens!', *daß ihn (doch) der Teufel hole!* 'the devil take him!', *daß ich nicht lache!* 'don't make me laugh!'. Wishes can be so expressed: *(ich wünschte,) daß ich das nie angefangen hätte!* 'I wish I'd never started it!'; and see further on p. 262. Other examples reflect the speaker's surprise or annoyance, or a range of other responses depending on the general context. Thus *daß sie immer spät kommt!* could stand for, say, *komisch*, or *ärgerlich, daß sie immer spät kommt!* 'odd, or what a nuisance, that she's always late!—es ist komisch (ärgerlich), daß sie immer spät kommt* would, of course, be the same in full statement form—likewise e.g. *(entsetzlich), daß so was am hellichten Tag passieren kann!* 'appalling, that such a thing can happen in broad daylight!'.

Ellipsis is further present when, in spoken German, a (rather imperious) command is expressed by a clause introduced by *daß*, the main clause (say, *ich verlange* 'I insist') being understood: *daß du sofort Ruhe gibst!* 'be quiet at once!', *daß ihr nicht drein redet!* 'don't interfere!', *daß Sie es sich nur nicht überlegen!* 'only don't change your mind!', *daß Sie das bitte nicht verlieren!* 'mind you don't lose it, please!'

The conjunction may be preceded by a preposition, as follows:

(a n) '*s t a t t   d a ß*——'instead of': *(an)statt daß er eine Lehre macht, versucht er sich mit Gelegenheitsarbeiten durchzuschlagen* 'instead of taking up an apprenticeship he is trying to get by with casual jobs'. The same is commonly expressed by an infinitive construction: *(an)statt eine Lehre zu machen*, etc.

'*a u ß e r   d a ß*——'except': *alles war in Ordnung, außer daß ich meine Geldbörse verlor* 'everything was in order except that I lost my purse'. Cf. *außer*, p. 316.

'*o h n e   d a ß*——'without': *sie arbeiten beide im Geschäft, ohne daß viel dabei herauskommt* 'they both work in the business without it showing much profit'. The verb in the subordinate clause occasionally appears in the subjunctive, as in elevated style: *die Spezies starb aus, ohne daß man den Grund dafür zu erkennen vermöchte* 'the species died out without one being able to detect the reason for it'. When only one subject is involved, the present construction is commonly replaced by a prepositional infinitive: *er zog aus der Wohnung aus, ohne daß er die Schlüssel abgab* or usually *ohne die Schlüssel abzugeben* 'he moved out of the flat without handing in the keys'.

Cf. also *als daß*, p. 277, *kaum daß*, p. 319.

INDIRECT QUESTION

The evolution of the indirect question has run closely parallel to that of the indirect statement, thus in literary style: *sie erkundigten sich, wie der Redakteur eine solche Veränderung zu bewerkstelligen beabsichtige* 'they enquired how the editor proposed to bring about such a change', (newspaper) *was sei das für ein Bundeskanzler, fragte Strauß, der sich krampfhaft bemühe, von Honecker empfangen zu werden?* 'S. asked what sort of a Federal Chancellor is he who makes such frantic efforts to be received by H.?', *ich fragte im Fundbüro an, ob man die Handtasche gefunden habe* or *hätte*, in the spoken language commonly *ich habe im Fundbüro angefragt, ob man die Handtasche gefunden hat* 'I enquired at the lost property office if the handbag had been found', similarly *frage nach, wer sonst noch kommen wird* 'ask about who else will be coming'; such indicative forms are not unusual in writing, too.

As in other examples of indirect speech, the subjunctive can appear in what are virtually main clauses: (newspaper) *kaum hatte der Referent seine Rede beendet, bohrten die Zuhörer nach: wie es denn um die SPD stehe und ob sie noch regierungsfähig sei?* 'the (official) speaker had scarcely concluded his remarks when his listeners began to press him: how did things stand with the SPD (*Sozialdemokratische*

Partei Deutschlands) and was it still capable of governing?' In this connection we note that phrases introduced by *ob* are, in spoken German, regularly used elliptically, when they become direct questions: *ob er das Fenster zugemacht hat?* 'I wonder if he has shut the window?', *ich frage mich* 'I ask myself' or similar words being understood.

SUBORDINATE PAST SUBJUNCTIVES IN ASSOCIATION WITH NEGATIVES

Past (preterite and pluperfect) subjunctives are commonly found in certain subordinate clauses in association with negatives: *ich hab' heute nicht einen einzigen Kunden gehabt, der nicht die neue Kreditkarte vorgezeigt hätte* 'I've not had a single customer today who hasn't produced the new credit card', alternatively *hat*, but written style at least shows a distinct preference for the subjunctive. Other examples: *wir kennen niemanden, der jetzt in der Lage wäre, diese Aufgabe zu übernehmen* 'we know no one who is now in a position to take over this assignment', *sie ging vorbei, ohne daß sie mich auch nur einmal angeschaut hätte* (= *ohne mich auch nur einmal anzuschauen*, p. 275) 'she passed by without even once looking at me', also expressions of the type (*es war*) *nicht* (*so*), *daß er krank gewesen wäre* '(it was) not that he was ill', not forgetting the set phrase *nicht, daß ich wüßte* 'not that I know of', p. 261.

Final and Consecutive Clauses

Final clauses are commonly introduced by *da'mit*. The indicative is customary in subordinate clauses when the verb in the main clause is in the present or future: *seine Frau arbeitet auch* (*wird auch arbeiten*), *damit mehr Geld ins Haus kommt* 'his wife works (will work) as well so that (= in order that) more money comes into the house'. When the main verb is a past tense, however, the subordinate verb may, in literary style, appear in the subjunctive, present or preterite indifferently: *seine Frau arbeitete auch, damit mehr Geld ins Haus komme* or *käme* (or *kommen würde*, p. 262), alternatively pret. indic. *kam*. But in the language as ordinarily spoken, the subordinate verb most commonly remains in the present indicative: *seine Frau arbeitete*, or more usually *hat gearbeitet, damit mehr Geld ins Haus kommt*, but pret. *kam* could also be heard, at least in the north.

The conjunction *daß* may have similar force, chiefly in the spoken language: *seine Frau arbeitet auch, daß mehr Geld ins Haus kommt*.

Purpose may also be expressed by means of infinitive constructions, see 'The construction *um zu*, etc.', p. 253.

Consecutive clauses are commonly introduced by *so 'daß*, the verb in the subordinate clause being generally in the indicative, its tense determined by the same considerations as in final clauses: *seine Frau arbeitet auch, so daß mehr Geld ins Haus kommt* 'his wife works as well so that (= with the result that) more money comes into the house', etc. The conjunction *daß* can, on its own, have consecutive force, as typically in vivid statements like the following: *sie klopfte den Teppich, daß der Staub flog* 'she beat the carpet with the result that the dust rose in clouds', also in everyday language: *er trinkt, daß es ein Jammer ist* 'it's a crying shame the way he drinks'. With correlative *so* (or equivalent) in the main clause, the conjunction is again simply *daß*, just like Eng. 'that': *es war noch im Mai so (derart, dermaßen) kalt, daß der Teich zufror* 'it was still so cold in May that the pond froze over'. The verb in the subordinate clause occasionally appears in the subjunctive, as in elevated style: *die Flüchtlinge waren so sehr abgemagert, daß wir sie kaum wiedererkannt hätten* 'the refugees were so emaciated that we hardly recognized them again'.

In literary style *als 'daß* with the preterite subjunctive is a much-used conjunction when correlative *zu* figures in the main clause: *es ist zu kalt, als daß wir spazierengehen könnten*, but possible also present tense *können* 'it is too cold for us to take a walk'; the spoken language substitutes *es ist uns zu kalt, um spazierenzugehen* or *zum Spazierengehen*, p. 256.

Reflexive Verbs

On the conjugation, see pp. 103 f.

Some reflexive verbs have a non-reflexive counterpart from which they are distinguished semantically: *ich habe mich versprochen* 'it was a slip of my tongue', *ich habe versprochen* 'I have promised', *das Lager befindet sich zwei Kilometer von hier* 'the camp is situated two kilometres from here', *der Gast hat nicht über den Gastgeber zu befinden* 'the guest should not pass judgement on the host'. Other reflexives may be compared with corresponding non-reflexive transitive forms: *es ändert sich* 'it changes', *es ändert nichts* 'it changes nothing', *die Räder drehen sich* 'the wheels turn', *sie drehen die Räder* 'they turn the wheels'. The reflexives *sich legen* 'lie down', *sich setzen* 'sit down', *sich stellen* '(go and) stand' are the verbs of motion paired with *liegen* 'lie', *sitzen* 'sit', *stehen* 'stand'. The verb *baden* used intransitively means either 'bathe' or 'take a bath', used reflexively it has only the latter meaning; *ich habe gebadet* and *ich habe mich gebadet* are, in practice, used quite indiscriminately. The reflexive *sich stürzen* is different from *stürzen* in that it denotes an intentional action: *er stürzte sich vom Felsenrand* 'he threw himself off the edge of the cliff', also figuratively: *er stürzte sich in Schulden* 'he ran into debt', but non-reflexive: *er stürzte vom Pferd* 'he fell from his horse'.

Reflexive verbs are close to intransitive verbs. This circumstance has led to some movement from one category to the other leaving a certain amount of overlapping, as may be seen in cases where reflexive and intransitive forms exist side by side. Though the meaning of each pair is basically the same, a degree of semantic specialization or at least of idiomatic differentiation will generally be present. Thus *sich irren* 'err', but *irren* commonly 'wander (aimlessly)' though sometimes 'err' too, stylistically more elevated than the reflexive variant; *eilen* and *sich eilen* are identical in meaning, yet not always interchangeable: *ich eile hinaus* 'I hurry out', but *eile dich!* (also *beeile dich!*) 'hurry!' The reflexive *sich flüchten* is standard in the cliché *er flüchtet sich in die Öffentlichkeit* 'he resorts to publicity', but *flüchten* is the commoner term, e.g. *die Zivilbevölkerung flüchtete vor den heranrückenden Truppen* 'the civilian population fled before the approaching troops', *das Eichhörnchen ist auf den Baum geflüchtet* 'the squirrel made off up the tree', but also *hat sich auf den Baum geflüchtet* more in local use.

Reflexives used impersonally

Especially noteworthy is the large number of impersonal reflexives, e.g. *es gehört* or *schickt sich* 'it is proper', *es tut sich was* 'something's brewing'. These forms often approach the passive sense. A semantic difference may still be tangible: *eine Tür öffnet sich* 'a door opens', *eine Tür wird geöffnet* 'a door is opened'. But in not a few instances the reflexive verb has to all intents and purposes the same meaning as the passive: *wie erklärt sich das? wie wird das erklärt?* 'how is that explained?', *das Rätsel löste sich, das Rätsel wurde gelöst* 'the riddle was solved'—'the riddle solved itself' would be *das Rätsel löste sich von selbst*—and one translates *es versteht sich* by 'it is understood'. In fact a reflexive construction having purely passive sense occurs commonly, though always in association with an adverb: *so ein Gedicht lernt sich leicht* 'a poem like that is easily learnt' or (English idiom disguising the passive) 'easy to learn', similarly *die Bücher verkauften sich gut* 'the books sold well'. Out of this developed another much used impersonal construction: *es sitzt sich hier bequem* 'it's comfortable sitting here'—or *hier sitzt sich bequem*, p. 200.

Impersonal Verbs

The oldest group of impersonal verbs, in German as in English, consists of those which denote natural phenomena, e.g. *es regnet, hagelt, schneit* 'it rains, hails, snows, it is raining, etc.', *es friert* 'it is freezing', *es blitzt* 'it's lightning', *es stürmt* 'it is blowing a gale', further *es ebbt, flutet* 'the tide is ebbing (going out), is flowing (coming in)', *es tagt* 'it is dawning', *es dunkelt* 'it is getting dark', *es herbstelt* 'there's a touch of autumn in the air'.

To the above type of traditional impersonal are to be added the large number of occasional impersonals, where the pronoun replaces a definite subject, as *es läutet = die Glocke läutet* 'the bell is ringing', also *= die Türglocke läutet* 'the doorbell is ringing', similarly *es brennt* 'something is burning, there's a fire', also exclamatory 'Fire!', *es duftet* 'there is a fragrant odour', also colloquial 'there's a nice smell', *es gießt* 'it is pouring (with rain)', *es klingelt = die Türglocke klingelt* 'the doorbell is ringing'—an alternative to *es läutet* in this sense—*es klopft* 'someone is knocking, there's a knock', *es raucht* 'something is smoking, there's smoke', *es riecht (nach)* 'it smells, there's a smell (of)', *es stinkt (nach)* 'it stinks, there's a nasty smell (of)', *es zieht* 'there's a draught'. It will not be overlooked, of course, that in all such expressions *es* can equally refer to a subject, so that e.g. *es brennt* may also mean 'it (say, *das Holz* 'the wood') is burning'.

There is a further group of impersonal verbs very different from the preceding in that they are construed with a noun or, in practice far more usually, with a pronoun in the accusative or dative; however, *es* appears regularly only as a sentence-opener, but is otherwise mostly suppressed. Examples with the accusative: *es friert mich* or *mich friert* 'I am cold, starved', the latter alternative being more often met with; similarly *mich fröstelt* 'I feel chilly', *mich dürstet, hungert* 'I thirst, hunger', *mich schläfert* 'I feel drowsy', *mich reut* 'I rue', *mich schmerzt* 'I grieve for', also *mich wundert* beside equally common *es wundert mich* 'I am surprised'. Examples with the dative: *mir graut* or *graust* (*vor* + dat.) 'I have a horror (of)', *mir gruselt* (*bei*) 'my flesh creeps (at)', *mir schwant* 'I have a presentiment', *mir schwindelt* 'I feel dizzy', *mir träumt* 'I dream'. Vacillation between the two cases: *mich* or *mir schaudert* (*vor* + dat.) 'I shudder (at)'.

This last group is not particularly prominent; moreover, most examples are now restricted to elevated literary language: *ihn hungert nach der Gerechtigkeit* 'he hungers after righteousness'. Of those examples which still occur in ordinary style, some can take *es* or *'s* in non-initial position, too. Thus also *mich wundert's*, *mir graut's* or *graust's* (cf. Goethe *"Erlkönig"*: *dem Vater grauset's* 'the father is aghast'), *mir gruselt's*, and such usage has a colloquial ring. It may be added that some of the above concepts are expressed in less formal style by personal verbs, as follows: *ich friere* 'I'm freezing', *ich fröstele* 'I feel chilly', *ich bin durstig, hungrig* 'I'm thirsty, hungry', also equally common *ich habe Durst, Hunger*, further *ich bin schläfrig* 'I'm sleepy', *ich bin schwind(e)lig* 'I feel dizzy', *ich träume* 'I dream'. Remarkably enough, the impersonal *es wundert mich, mich wundert (es)* 'I am surprised', although in everyday use, has in addition an also commonly occurring personal alternative *ich wundere mich*.

Distinct from the above is another group of impersonals which, though likewise construed with a noun or pronoun, nevertheless never omit *es*. Among these are *es juckt mich* or just as commonly *mich juckt es* 'I'm itching', similarly *es kitzelt mich* 'something is tickling me', *es leidet mich nicht* 'I cannot bear', *es lockt, reizt, treibt, zieht mich* 'something entices, tempts, drives, draws me', all regularly used: *es litt unserem Helden nicht mehr in der Heimat, unwiderstehlich zog es ihn in die Fremde* 'our hero could no longer bear being in his own country, he was irresistibly drawn to foreign parts'.

There are many more miscellaneous verbs, the majority retaining *es* in all positions, e.g. *es fehlt* or *mangelt (an)* 'there is a lack (of)', *es hängt davon ab* or *kommt darauf an* 'it depends', *es läuft einem kalt über den Rücken* 'it sends a chill down one's spine', and the ubiquitous *es geht* in numerous idioms, as *es geht mir gut*, or *mir geht es gut* 'I feel well, or I'm doing well (e.g. at my work)', *wie geht's?* 'how are you?', *wie geht's weiter?* 'how does it go from here? what does one do next?', *jetzt geht's los* 'things are starting up, now we're off'. In addition various reflexives, as *es handelt sich um* 'it is a matter of', see further p. 278. However, other commonly occurring examples may omit *es* in non-initial position, notably those based on the verb 'to be': *es ist mir besser*, or *mir ist besser* 'I feel better', *mir ist gut* 'I feel all right', *mir ist nicht gut = mir ist schlecht* 'I don't feel well', *ist Ihnen warm?* 'are you warm?', also *wird Ihnen warm?* 'are you getting warm?', further *er hat seinen Arbeitsplatz verloren, und man kann sich vorstellen, wie ihm zumute ist* 'he has lost his job and one can imagine what he feels like', cf. also *es fällt mir ein*, or *mir fällt ein* 'it occurs to me'.

Lastly, a particularly important example in *es gibt* most often answering to our 'there is, there are' in the sense of existing: *gibt es ihn?* 'is there such a person? does he exist?', *nein, es gibt ihn nicht* 'no, there is no such person, he does not exist', thus substantially the equivalent of *existiert er? nein, er existiert nicht*. Usage is typical in general statements: *es gibt Menschen, die Not leiden* 'there are people who suffer deprivation', *es wird viel Unglück geben* 'there will be much unhappiness', *es hat immer Streit gegeben* 'there has always been quarrelling', or—on another stylistic level—'there have always been differences', (publicity slogan) *zum Glück gibt's Österreich* 'fortunately there's Austria'. Other examples show movement away from the general to the particular: *es gab einen Grund für den Produktionsausfall, nämlich eine schadhafte Maschine* 'there was a reason for the loss of production: a faulty machine', *aber es gab auch Mittel, mit denen wir dem Problem beikommen konnten* 'but there were means by which we could deal with the problem', *also wußten wir, daß es einen Ausweg aus der Schwierigkeit geben würde* 'so we knew there would be a way out of the difficulty'. Colloquial usage may be highly idiomatic, sometimes demanding a range of English equivalents which can only be hinted at here: *was gibt's?* 'what's doing? what's on?', *das gibt's doch nicht* 'you don't say! that's not on'. Notice *was es alles nicht gibt!* 'it takes all kinds!'

The present construction is used in stating a consequence: *so wütete der Sturm gestern in Deutschland. Es gab viele zerstörte Häuser* virtually 'the storm raged so (violently) in Germany yesterday that many houses were destroyed'. By this means German can succinctly express nuances in a way another language cannot: *Überlebende gab es nicht* 'there were no survivors' (as a result of the accident), but *es waren keinerlei Überlebende, die von der Katastrophe hätten berichten können* 'there were no survivors whatever who might have been able to give an account of the catastrophe'.

Given the identity of the basic sense of *es gibt* and *es ist*, it is not surprising that a certain amount of overlapping occurs, and in many contexts either of the two will be applicable: *es gibt*, or *es ist in Indien viel zu bewundern, in Indien gibt es*, or *ist viel zu bewundern* 'there is much to admire in India', *gibt es*, or *sind Fische in diesem Teich?* 'are there any fish in this pond?' In some southern parts of the German-speaking area colloquial *es hat* can replace *es gibt*, e.g. *hat es Fische in diesem Teich?*

Impersonal use also occurs with verbs which are not themselves specifically impersonal, see pp. 249, 278.

Modal Auxiliaries

For inflexions, see p. 102.

It will be convenient to set out, by way of general illustration, the tenses of one of these verbs. We take as our sample *können* 'be able', ignoring the self-evident 3rd sg. subjunctive forms.

Pres. *ich kann das sagen* 'I can say that'
Fut. *ich werde das sagen können* 'I shall be able to say that'
Pret. *ich konnte das sagen* 'I could say that' = 'I was able to say that',

(subj.) *ich könnte das sagen* 'I could say that' = 'I would be able to say that'

Perf. *ich habe das sagen können* 'I have been able to say that'

Fut. perf. *ich werde das gesagt haben können* 'I shall have been able to say that'

Pluperf. *ich hatte das sagen können* 'I had been able to say that', (subj.) *ich hätte das sagen können* 'I could have said that' = 'I would have been able to say that'

Further: *ich kann das gesagt haben* 'I may have said that', *ich konnte das gesagt haben* 'I might (could) have said that' i.e. 'it is perfectly possible that I said it', *ich könnte das gesagt haben* 'I may conceivably have said that'.

The perf. part. *gekonnt* appears in elliptic constructions, e.g. *ich habe es gekonnt* commonly equals *ich habe es tun können* 'I have been able to do it', pp. 257, 291.

The auxiliary may acquire the status of a main verb should the latter be omitted (ellipsis); there may be some semantic change: *ich kann dieses Musikstück auswendig* 'I know this piece of music by heart', i.e. with omission of e.g. *spielen* 'play'.

Notice the word order when a compound tense of a modal verb occurs in a subordinate clause. Instead of coming at the end, the auxiliary precedes the two infinitives; e.g. *ich glaube, daß ich das werde sagen können* 'I believe I shall be able to say that', *ich hatte nicht damit gerechnet, daß ich das hätte sagen können* 'I had not reckoned that I would have been able to say that'.

THE MODALS IN DETAIL

In German as in English, the semantic range of the modal auxiliaries is considerable and usage often highly idiomatic. We now turn to this aspect, the examples which follow being intended to illustrate the main functions with some indication of the subtleties encountered.

dürfen

In the first place this auxiliary denotes permission: *darf ich jetzt gehen? — ja, Sie dürfen* 'am I allowed to go now?—yes, you are' or 'may I go now?—yes, you may', alternatively *dürfte ich jetzt gehen* lit. 'might I go now?' adding a touch of politeness or hesitancy associated with preterite subjunctives, p. 261. Compare further: *möchten Sie Kaffee? — ja gerne, wenn ich bitten darf* 'would you like some coffee?—yes I would, if I may', *man darf sagen, daß unsere Mittel dazu ausreichen* 'one may say that our means are adequate for the purpose', (shop assistant's standard questions) *was darf es sein?* 'what can I get for you?', *darf es etwas mehr sein?* 'does it matter if it's a little over?'

Just as in English 'may' and 'can' are often to all intents and purposes interchangeable, so are *dürfen* and *können*, and with a stylistic difference much as in English. One finds everyday sentences of the type *darf (kann) ich hinausgehen?* 'may (can) I go out?', also 'may (can) I leave the room?', or more formally *er erkundigte sich nach dem Befinden seines Freundes, und wir durften (konnten) das Beste melden* 'he enquired about his friend's health and we could report that he was very well'.

The preterite subjunctive is commonly used to express (a high degree of) probability *das dürfte stimmen* 'that will most likely be right', *es dürfte nicht nötig sein* 'it will hardly be necessary'. Contrast *sie dürften es gesehen haben* 'they will probably have seen it' with *sie hätten es sehen dürfen* 'they would have been allowed to see it'; other examples of the latter construction below. The present subjunctive occurs in written style in subordinate clauses: *er war der Ansicht, man dürfe annehmen, die Angelegenheit sei erledigt* 'he was of the opinion that one could assume the matter was settled', but with a tendency to substitute the more familiar pret. *dürfte*.

In negative use, the corresponding English is very frequently 'must not': *ihr dürft ihn nicht allein lassen* 'you must not leave him by himself' in contrast to *er darf allein gelassen werden* 'he may be left by himself, it is permissible to leave him by himself'. Compare further *er darf nicht rauchen* 'he must not smoke, he is not allowed to smoke', *er durfte nicht rauchen* 'he was not allowed to smoke'—quite different from *er muß (mußte) nicht rauchen* 'he does (did) not have to smoke', but rather close to *er soll (sollte) nicht rauchen* 'he is not to (was not to, should not) smoke'. In fact, in another negative construction, *dürfen* and *sollen* overlap: *das hättet ihr nicht tun dürfen* or *sollen* both 'you shouldn't have done that' in the sense that you had no right to do it, and again different from *das hättet ihr nicht tun müssen*, see this example under *müssen*. Lastly, a nuance of improbability may be present, depending on the context: *das darf (kann) nicht sein* 'that surely cannot be', but on the other hand *das darf und soll nicht sein* where the primary sense is brought out and strengthened 'that m u s t not be'.

können

Primarily expresses capability, and in the nature of the case very often probability: *können Sie mir helfen?* 'are you able to help me? can you help me?', *wir konnten den Redner nicht hören* 'we were unable to (could not) hear the speaker', *ich werde dir noch schreiben können* 'I shall still be able to write to you'.

In contexts expressing possibility English idiom often uses for the present 'may', for the preterite 'might' beside 'could': (present) *es kann sein, daß er den Zug verpaßt hat* 'it may be (it is possible) that he missed the train', *meine Eltern können es gesagt haben* 'my parents may have said so', (preterite) *der Verfasser dieser Ballade ist unbekannt, aber Schiller konnte sie geschrieben haben* 'the author of this ballad is unknown, but S. might (could) have written it' i.e. it is possible that S. was the author, different from *Schiller könnte sie geschrieben haben* with the nuance 'S. may conceivably have written it', also *das neue Gedicht unseres Deutschlehrers ist großartig. Schiller könnte es geschrieben haben* 'our German teacher's new poem is magnificent. S. might (could) have written it'—in view of its style and quality. Finally, in contrast, expressing capability only: *Schiller hätte auch Romane schreiben können, wenn er die Zeit dazu gefunden hätte* 'S. could have written novels, too, if he had found the time'.

Since in English a single word 'could' embraces both indicative and subjunctive functions, one particularly notices the regular differences maintained between indic. *konnte* and subj. *könnte* in German: *damals konnte ich mir nicht vorstellen, daß ich irgendwo besser leben könnte* 'at the time I could not (i.e. was not able to) imagine that I could (i.e. would be able to) live better anywhere else'. At the same time, in another role, the preterite subjunctive can act essentially as an indicative, but adding an element of politeness or caution and the like, hence *könnten* (beside pres. *können*) *Sie sich das vorstellen?* 'could (can) you imagine that?'

The present subjunctive is common in written style in subordinate clauses: *Meldungen aus der Hauptstadt lassen hoffen, die Lage könne sich in den nächsten Tagen beruhigen* 'reports from the capital raise hopes that the situation could calm down in the next few days', the pret. *könnte* being also possible.

The nuance 'know how to' is often present: *können Sie Schach spielen?* 'can you play chess?', *er konnte nicht Auto fahren* 'he couldn't drive (having never learnt)'. From such sentences as *sie kann japanisch sprechen* 'she can speak Japanese' is derived the elliptic *sie kann Japanisch* 'she knows Japanese', by analogy also *sie kann die Sprache* 'she knows the language'.

This auxiliary may sometimes be an alternative to *dürfen, mögen, sollen*, see under these verbs.

The infinitive is regularly substantivized: *sein erstaunliches Können* 'his astonishing ability'. The perfect participle (appearing in elliptic constructions, p. 291) also occurs as an adjective or adverb: *das war wirklich gekonnt* 'that was really masterly', *eine gekonnte Darstellung* 'a masterly interpretation (e.g. of a role)', *gekonnt gemacht* 'expertly done'.

mögen

Cognate with English 'may', this verb likewise expresses probability: *diese Feststellung mag zunächst überraschen* 'this statement may at first cause surprise', *es mögen etwa sechs Monate her sein, daß wir den Plan zuerst besprachen* 'it is probably about six months ago that we first discussed the plan', *er dachte, das Wasser zwischen dem Strand und der Sandbank mochte ziemlich tief sein* 'he thought the water between the beach and the sandbank would be rather deep'. Such sentences have a literary quality. Nevertheless certain colloquialisms do contain *mögen* in the above sense, though more often replaced by *können*, as *es mag (kann) sein* 'it may be', *was mag (kann) es sein?* 'what can it be?', *wo mögen (können) sie es gesehen haben?* 'where can they have seen it?'. Notice *sie mag, mochte (kann, konnte) ihn gut leiden* 'she is, was fond of him'.

The 3rd sg. pres. subj. *möge* occasionally occurs as the main verb in elevated style, also as an alternative to pret. *möchte* (p. 261). It is, however, more usually found in subordinate clauses: *richten Sie ihm bitte aus, er möge die Pferde bereithalten* 'please tell him to (be so good as to) keep the horses in readiness'; it tends to replace *möchte* in this function: (fairy tale, last century) *die Brüder baten den König, er möchte eine neue Bedingung stellen* 'the brothers asked the king if he would make a new condition', contemporary version *möge*. The dominant sense of *möchte* today is 'would like' below, but notice sentences of the type *man möchte verrückt werden* 'it's enough to drive one mad' or a set phrase like *man möchte meinen, daß . . .* 'one would think that . . .' which still have some currency in spoken German, too, though often replaced by *könnte*.

In by far the greatest number of actual occurrences in the living language *mögen* appears as the main verb with the meaning 'like': *wir mögen es* 'we like it', *möchten Sie Tee?* 'would you like tea?', *ich habe ihn nie gemocht* 'I have never liked him', *ich habe ihn nie mögen können* 'I have never been able to like him', further *sie mag (mochte) nicht immer zu Hause sitzen* 'she doesn't (didn't) like to be always sitting at home', *ihr möchtet das auch können, oder?* 'you'd like to be able to do that as well, wouldn't you?', *die Kinder möchten schwimmen lernen* 'the children would like to learn to swim'. As with *wollen* 'want to, wish' the complement may be a *daß*-clause: *er möchte nicht, daß sie zurückkommt* 'he wouldn't like her to come back'.

vermögen

An essentially literary word, more formal than *können*, which can always replace it. Unlike other auxiliaries it is followed by the prepositional infinitive: *in Anbetracht der unvorhergesehenen Schwierig-*

keiten vermag ich nur einen Ausweg vorzuschlagen 'in view of the unforeseen difficulties I am only able to propose one solution', *die Sonne vermochte das finstere Gewölk nicht zu durchdringen* 'the sun was unable to penetrate the dark mass of clouds'.

Substantivized *Vermögen* means 'ability, wealth', whence the participial form *vermögend* 'wealthy'.

müssen

This auxiliary has the meaning 'must, have to': *du mußt Hände und Gesicht waschen* 'you must wash your hands and face', *wieviel müssen wir zahlen?* 'how much have we to pay?', *man mußte zuerst fragen* 'one had to ask first', *sie müssen es getan haben* 'they must have done it', (cliché) *muß das sein?* 'is that necessary?' In written narrative style, German may logically employ a preterite indicative which English is unable to match: *er sah auf die Uhr; der Zug mußte angekommen sein* 'he looked at the clock (deducing) the train must have arrived'.

The commitment expressed by *müssen* differs from the sort of obligation indicated by *sollen*. There can be a difficulty here for the learner in so far as past tenses of both these verbs may correspond to English 'should (have), ought to (have)'. Let us suppose your guests slip surreptitiously into the kitchen and do the washing-up. You eventually find out and remonstrate, good-naturedly, *das hättet ihr nicht tun müssen* 'you shouldn't have done that'. It would have been inappropriate to say *das hättet ihr nicht tun sollen*, since this would have amounted to a reproach, implying that it was not their place to do the washing up. As we have said, English employs the same words to convey both meanings, though we do use distinguishing intonation. Another example: *wo sind die Schlüssel hingekommen? — sie müßten hier hängen* 'where have the keys got to?—they should be hanging here', the alternative *sie sollten hier hängen* again implying a reproach, or complaint: it was somebody's duty to see that the keys were here, they had to be here according to regulation. By the same token *man müßte zuerst fragen* 'one should ask first' is inspired by the speaker's own considerations of tact or politeness, or by some feeling of hesitancy or the like, whereas *man sollte zuerst fragen* implies a strong obligation, as laid down by some rule, coming from the outside and imposed upon the speaker.

The 3rd sg. pres. subj. *müsse* is common in subordinate clauses in written style: *der Hauptmann sagte, man müsse auf eine mögliche Niederlage gefaßt sein* 'the captain said one must be prepared for a possible defeat'.

Notice that *müssen*, unlike 'must', is used with a negative without changing its meaning: *du mußt dich nicht waschen* 'you don't have to get washed', but not of course 'you mustn't get washed' which is *du darfst dich nicht waschen*, see *dürfen*; examples in past tenses: *du mußtest dich nicht waschen, du hast dich nicht waschen müssen* 'you didn't have to get washed, you haven't had to get washed'. In such negative use there is overlapping with *brauchen*, thus *du brauchst dich nicht (zu) waschen* lit. 'you don't need to wash', similarly when challenging a possible deduction: *zwar hat er heute morgen gefehlt, doch deshalb muß er den Kurs nicht aufgegeben haben* 'he was absent this morning, it is true, though that does not necessarily mean that he has given up the course', alternatively *braucht er den Kurs nicht aufgegeben (zu) haben*.

sollen

This auxiliary has a particularly wide range of meaning. It may express, first of all, an obligation placed upon one: *ich soll ihnen mitteilen, daß die Möbel am Nachmittag geliefert werden* 'I am to inform you that the furniture will be delivered in the afternoon'. Further: *man soll* (or, a trifle less forcibly *sollte*) *viel Obst essen* 'one should (ought to) eat plenty of fruit'. In the nature of the case, the present tense of a verb with this meaning frequently expresses a command: *du sollst nicht ehebrechen* 'thou shalt not commit adultery', or an instruction: *er soll sich sofort bei der Polizei melden* 'he is to report to the police at once'.

Distinguish between *Sie hätten es unternehmen sollen* 'you should have undertaken it (instead of ignoring it, or leaving it to others)' and *Sie sollten es unternommen haben* 'you should have undertaken it (you were supposed to, it was your duty so to do)'—the latter could then also correspond to 'you were to have undertaken it'. It is also to be noted that the nature of the obligation expressed by this auxiliary differs significantly from the commitment implied by *müssen*, see contrasting examples under this verb.

In some contexts the degree of obligation may weaken and even wither away: *was sollen wir machen?* has, with the appropriate emphatic intonation, the force of 'what are we to do?' in the strongest meaning of the phrase. But it can also be used in weaker senses, and become in fact no more than a variant of the future tense *was werden wir machen?* 'what shall we do?', p. 234. The same can apply to *was wollen wir machen?*, p. 290.

The preterite *sollte* 'should' is common in conditional sentences: *falls ich zufällig nicht zu Hause sein sollte, werde ich ihnen Bescheid sagen* 'if I should by chance not be at home, I shall let them know', *sollte die andere Seite das Angebot ausschlagen, dann stellen Sie bitte die Verhandlungen ein* 'should the other side reject the offer, then please break off the negotiations'. An apparently related use is seen in the often-heard expression *man sollte glauben* or *meinen*, e.g. *man sollte glauben (meinen), er würde die Lampen reparieren lassen* 'one would think he would have the lamps repaired'. Compare also the use in questions when at the same time the preterite comes so close to the preterite (indic. or subj.) of *können* that the two are virtually interchangeable: *wie sollten (konnten) wir das wissen?* 'how were we to know that?', *sollte (könnte) das der Grund sein?* 'would that be the reason?' Finally, in suitable contexts, a past tense may express what was to be or not to be: *dann verabschiedete ich mich von meinem Bruder — ich sollte ihn niemals wiedersehen* 'then I said goodbye to my brother—I would never (was never to) see him again', also (cliché) *es hat so sein sollen* 'it was meant to be (so)'.

This auxiliary often expresses an intention: *das soll eine Warnung sein* 'that is meant to be a warning', *sollte dies die Reinschrift sein?* 'was this intended to be (also ironically: supposed to be) the fair copy?' The meaning may be dependent on the wider context: *ein neues Wohnviertel sollte hier entstehen, aber die Pläne wurden nicht bewilligt* 'a new residential area was to have been developed here, but the plans were not approved'. Intentions border on wishes: *es soll vergeben und vergessen sein* 'let it be forgiven and forgotten'.

According to context, the meaning 'be said to' is by no means infrequent, usage being practically confined to the present tense: *er soll verunglückt sein* 'he is said to have met with an accident'. Semantically close to the foregoing is the use in such a sentence as *es heißt, sie sollen sich getrennt haben* 'people say they have separated', an everyday alternative to more literary *es heißt, sie hätten sich getrennt.*

Many idiomatic phrases occur, based particularly on the present tense, each with its own peculiar flavour, among them *das soll und muß sein* 'that shall and must be', *er soll nur kommen!* 'just let him come!—and we'll give him a piece of our mind, or such like, *an mir soll es nicht liegen* 'I'll do what I can', more literally 'it won't be my fault (if things go wrong, etc.)', *was soll es denn kosten?* 'what is it going to cost?', *das sollst du noch bereuen* 'you'll live to regret it', *der soll erst noch geboren werden, der das versteht* 'the one who can understand that hasn't been born yet'.

The 3rd sg. pres. subj. *solle* is found in subordinate clauses in written style: (grammar book) *über die Frage, ob man dem Verfall des Konjunktivs entgegenwirken solle, ist die Meinung geteilt* 'opinion is divided on the question of whether one should combat the decline of the subjunctive'.

When used in the negative there is, in one construction, overlapping with *dürfen*, see under this verb.

The present participle *sollend* is met with in phrases like *die selbstverständlich sein sollenden Maßnahmen* 'the measures which ought to be taken as a matter of course'.

wollen

The primary sense of this auxiliary is 'be willing, want to': *willst du Versteck spielen?* 'do you want to play hide-and-seek?', *sie wollten bleiben* 'they wanted to stay', *wollen Sie bitte die Frage wiederholen?* 'will you please repeat the question?', *hättet ihr kommen wollen?* 'would you have wanted to come?', *man muß wollen* 'one must want to'. There may be an object: *wollt ihr es?* 'do you want it?', *ohne es zu wollen* 'without wanting it', *da ist nichts zu wollen* 'there is nothing to be done about it', the same nuances as in English in sentences like *niemand will etwas davon wissen* 'no one wants to know anything about it'. The complement is often a *daß*-clause (child's humorous poem) *und die dummen Lehrer wollen, / daß wir Knollen sammeln sollen* 'and the silly teachers want us to (say) pick potatoes'. Examples with the negative verb: *ich will nicht* 'I won't, don't want to', *die Wunde will nicht heilen* 'the wound won't heal', *die Türen wollten nicht zugehen* 'the doors wouldn't shut'. Naturally enough the meaning is often 'wish', in which sense the auxiliary appears in the preterite (p. 262): *ich wollte, ich hätte eine größere Wohnung* 'I wish I had a bigger flat'.

In given contexts, the sense may be more forceful that English 'want', e.g. *ich will die Zeitung haben* has a somewhat imperious ring, approaching the tone of 'I insist on having the newspaper'; our 'I want the newspaper' may correspond better to *ich brauche* or *möchte die Zeitung*, i.e. 'need, would like'.

By an extension of the sense 'want to', German *wollen* can express an intention: *wir wollen im Sommer nach Italien* 'we plan to go to Italy in the summer'—'we want to go . . .' here answering more to *wir möchten . . . gehen*. Similarly *ich will ihm schreiben* 'I intend to write him', the same nuance again in the cliché *was wollen Sie damit sagen?* 'what do you mean by that?'

Following another line of development 'want' can acquire the sense 'need': (proverb) *gut Ding will Weile haben* 'it takes time to do a thing well'. This sense is well established in a familiar passive construction: *das will überlegt sein* 'that needs to be thought over', *Eulen können fünfhundert Mäuse im Monat fressen — soviel wollen erst einmal gefangen werden* 'owls can eat five hundred mice in a month—all these need to be caught first'. Notice sentences of the type *ich will es nicht bemerkt (gehört, gesehen) haben* 'I'm pretending not to have noticed (heard, seen) it', compare also *ich will nichts gesagt haben* 'never mind what I've been saying'. In constructions like the following the auxiliary expresses a claim to have done something: *sie wollen dich in Athen gesehen haben* 'they claim to have seen you in Athens', *sie will deutsch gesprochen haben* 'she claims to have spoken German'.

As with *sollen*, the modal force of *wollen* may be reduced to a point where it is scarcely perceptible, the verb becoming *de facto* a future auxiliary: *was wollen* (or *sollen*) *wir machen?* can thus have the same meaning as *was werden wir machen?* 'what shall we do?' But another arrangement of words shows unmistakable semantic variation: *wollen wir das machen?* and *sollen wir das machen?* both mean 'shall we do that?', yet with the difference that in the first sentence the speaker registers his own willingness to do it, whereas in the second he leaves the decision to the person or persons spoken to. And both sentences contrast with *was werden wir machen?* again 'what shall we do?', but now with special reference to the alternatives 'shall we?' or 'shall we not?' See also p. 234.

The 3rd sg. pres. subj. *wolle* occasionally occurs in a main clause, as in formal phrases like *man wolle bitte Rücksicht nehmen* 'please show consideration'. It is more usual in subordinate clauses, but again only in written style: *es hieß, er wolle nach Amerika auswandern* 'it was said he wanted to emigrate to America'.

The perfect participle (appearing in elliptic constructions, p. 291) is also used as an adjective and adverb. There is an older sense 'intended, intentional' from which has arisen the more recent sense 'artificial': *es wirkt gewollt und unnatürlich* 'it makes an artificial and unnatural impression'. The present participle *wollend* is met with in the set phrase *nie enden wollender Beifall* 'unending applause' and in the compound *wohlwollend* 'benevolent' from *wohlwollen* 'wish well'.

brauchen

This verb like its English counterpart 'need' has much in common with the modal auxiliaries proper. Especially in colloquial language it is very often heard with the simple infinitive: *man braucht nicht zahlen* 'one needn't pay' beside more or less standard *man braucht nicht zu zahlen*, hence the (well-known) ironical *wer 'brauchen' gebraucht, ohne 'zu' zu gebrauchen, braucht 'brauchen' überhaupt nicht zu gebrauchen*. When compound tenses are used with a simple infinitive, the expected perfect participle is replaced by the infinitive, just as with the modals, hence e.g. *sie hat nicht warten brauchen* 'she hasn't needed to wait', and indeed analogically also with the prepositional infinitive: *sie hat nicht zu warten brauchen* as well as regular *zu warten gebraucht*. Subordinate word order likewise follows the modal practice: *ich bin der Meinung, daß sie nicht so viel wird aus(zu)geben brauchen* 'I am of the opinion that she won't have to spend so much', *sie hat gesagt, daß er es nicht hätte (zu) wissen brauchen* 'she said he needn't have known about it'.

After the pattern of nearly all other weak verbs, the preterite
subjunctive generally fell together with the indicative *brauchte*, which
took over any surviving subjunctive function. But locally, in some
southern districts, a distinct subj. *bräuchte* developed and this form
has recently become very fashionable, both in speaking and writing,
though the more traditional *brauchte* is still common: *wozu bräuchte
(brauchte) man sie auch sonst?* 'what else would one need them for?'
In ordinary conversation, the 1st sg. *brauche* commonly becomes
brauch (p. 14), whence also widespread substandard 3rd sg. *brauch*
after the analogy of the modal auxiliaries proper: *brauch er (zu)
zahlen?* 'need he pay?'—in fact just like English 'need' not 'needs'.

ELLIPTICAL USE

Ellipsis in connection with modal auxiliaries is known from English; in
such cases German follows suit: *ich möchte (ihn besuchen), aber ich
kann nicht* 'I should like to (visit him), but I can't'. In this construction
es, colloquially also *das*, may optionally be used in the second clause,
hence alternatively *aber ich kann es* (or *das*) *nicht*.

Ellipsis of another sort is present in German when verbs of motion
are omitted. This can happen if the verbs in question are used with an
adverb of direction, or equivalent phrase, and also if used with certain
separable prefixes, themselves mostly indicating movement. Omission
is optional, but common, more especially so in the spoken language:
darf ich hinein? or (polite, or with hesitation) *dürfte ich hinein?* 'may
(might) I go in?', *er durfte herüber* 'he was allowed to cross (to this
side)'—*er kann zurück* 'he can return, get back', *wir könnten ohne
weiteres ins Schwimmbad* 'we could easily go to the swimming baths',
hat sie vorbeigekonnt? 'has she been able to get past?'—*sie möchten
ins Theater* 'they would like to go to the theatre'—*muß er mit?* 'must
he come (go, etc.) too?', *ich mußte hinunter* 'I had to go down'—*wir
sollen hinauf* 'we are supposed to go up', *du solltest fort* (or *weg*) *von
hier* 'you should get away from here'—*sie will zu ihrer Mutter* 'she
wants to go to her mother', *er wollte hoch hinaus* 'he had great plans',
wo wollten Sie hin? 'where did you want to go to?'

The verbs *machen* or *tun* 'do' may be left out, again optionally,
when used with *dürfen, können, müssen* or *sollen*, thus *ich darf —
kann, muß, soll — es (machen/tun)* 'I may—can, must, am to—do it',
hence the everyday phrase *ich kann nichts dafür* 'I can't help it' and
the saying *der Mensch kann alles, wenn er will* 'one can do everything
given the will'. Any tense can be involved: *werden wir es dürfen?* 'will
we be allowed to do it?', *allein hätte sie das niemals gekonnt* 'she
would never have been able to do that on her own', *hat er es gemußt* or
gesollt? both 'has he had to do it?' but with the different nuances

described on p. 286. Examples with *wollen* are less general—*ich will es* means rather 'I want it'—but notice such idioms as *es will mir nicht aus dem Kopf* 'I can't get it out of my head', *meine Beine wollen nicht mehr* 'my legs won't carry me any further'.

Suppression of *bedeuten* or *heißen* 'mean' is apparent in constantly occurring idioms of the type *was soll das?* 'what is the point of it?'; in the same way *wozu soll das?* 'what is that for?' is elliptic for *wozu soll das gut sein?* 'what is that good for?' or comparable expression.

19. Prepositions

PREPOSITIONS (and postpositions) govern various oblique cases, falling into two groups: those taking one case only, i.e. accusative, dative, or genitive, and those taking two cases, i.e. accusative and dative, or genitive and dative. With one example (*außer*, p. 302) all three cases are involved. Our aim below is to exemplify characteristic usages.

PREPOSITIONS TAKING THE ACCUSATIVE

These are *bis, durch, für, gegen, ohne, um, wider.*

b i s——*es hat bis nächsten Montag Zeit* 'it can wait until next Monday', *wir brauchen es bis Montag* 'we need it by Monday'—notice the negative *wir brauchen es erst Montag* 'we don't need it until Monday'.

This preposition is not used directly in front of an article or a demonstrative, interrogative, or possessive pronoun; another preposition is interposed and it is this which determines the case: (national anthem) *von der Maas bis an die Memel* 'from the Meuse to the Niemen', *bis zu welchem Zeitpunkt? — bis zu diesem Augenblick* 'until what time?—until this minute', *bis zu unserer Schule* 'as far as our school', *naß bis auf die Haut* 'soaked to the skin'. This last combination can further have two diametrically opposite meanings, namely 'up to and including' or 'up to but not including', depending on context: *er hat das ganze geliehene Geld bis auf den letzten Pfennig zurückgezahlt* understood as meaning 'he has repaid all the money borrowed down to the last penny', but *alle bis auf zwei haben das Examen bestanden* 'all except two have passed the examination'. Ambiguities, however, are not excluded: *das Darlehen wurde bis auf die letzte Rate zurückgezahlt* can equally well mean 'the loan was repaid down to, or except for, the last instalment'. Before the names of towns and countries *bis* corresponds to 'to': *von Genua bis Mailand* 'from Genoa to Milan'; it may be followed by *nach* giving a somewhat emphatic meaning: *Marco Polo reiste bis nach China* 'M.P. travelled as far as China'. See also under *nach*, p. 296.

It may be added that *bis* is commonly used before adverbs or adverbial phrases: *bis jetzt* 'up to now', *bis wann?* 'until when?', *bis hierher* 'up to here', *bis wohin?* 'how far?', *bis nach Pfingsten* 'until after Whitsun', *bis kurz vor Athen* 'until just before Athens', *bis vor einem Jahr* 'until a year ago'.

d u r c h——*durch den Wald* 'through the forest', *durch unsere Freunde* 'through our friends', *durch eigenes Versagen* 'through one's own failure'. The preposition corresponds to English 'by' in sentences like *die Eroberung Englands durch die Normannen* 'the conquest of England by the Normans'. In a passive sentence this use is chiefly restricted to an inanimate agent, in consonance with the usual underlying sense 'by means of, through': *der Soldat wurde durch einen Revolverschuß verletzt* 'the soldier was wounded by a shot from a revolver'. With animates *von* is normally required (p. 297), but if the role of the agent is that of an intermediary, this aspect may be brought out by using *durch*, e.g. *die Auszeichnungen wurden durch den Präsidenten überreicht* 'the awards were presented by the president', alternatively without the special nuance *vom Präsidenten*. Notwithstanding such niceties, the prepositions may interchange merely for stylistic variety: *die Gemeinde in Kolossä ist nicht von Paulus, sondern durch Epaphras, einen Schüler des Apostels, gegründet worden* 'the church at Colossae was founded not by Paul, but by Epaphras, a disciple of the apostle'.

The adverb *hin'durch* is sometimes used to strengthen the preposition: *durch den Wald hindurch* 'right through the forest'.

f ü r——*Geschenke für deinen Bruder und deine Schwester* 'presents for your brother and sister', *groß für sein Alter* 'big for his age', *Datteln esse ich für mein Leben gern* 'I love eating dates', *die Anrede 'Frau' für Unverheiratete setzt sich immer mehr durch* 'as the form of address to unmarried women (the term) *Frau* is more and more gaining acceptance'. Often found with other parts of speech: *für gewöhnlich* 'usually', *für immer* (elevated) 'for ever'.

g e g e n——*gegen die Wand* 'against the wall', *gegen meinen Rat, meine Wünsche* 'against my advice, my wishes', *gegen den Angriff* 'against the attack', *Schalke 04 (null vier) gegen F.C. Köln* 'Schalke 04 versus F. C. Cologne', *gegen den Uhrzeigersinn* 'anticlockwise', *gegen vier Uhr* 'about four o'clock', *gegen Barzahlung* 'cash down', sometimes after adjectives: *grausam gegen das Kind*, 'cruel to the child', *höflich gegen Damen* 'polite to ladies'. See also under *gegenüber, entgegen*, pp. 295, 298.

o h n e——*ohne ein Wort des Dankes* 'without a word of thanks', *gehen Sie immer ohne Hut?* 'do you always go without a hat?' Elliptic use is normal, as in English: *ich kann gut ohne auskommen* 'I can get on well without', *oben ohne* 'topless'. For *mit oder ohne* see under *mit*, p. 296.

u m———*um die Ecke* 'round the corner', *schade um ihn* 'a pity about him', *um die Wette* 'for a bet', *um die Hälfte billiger* 'cheaper by half', *um ein bedeutendes* (*Stück*, usually understood) 'by a great deal'. The adverbs *rings* and especially *herum* may sometimes reinforce the preposition: (*rings*) *um das Grundstück läuft ein Drahtzaun* 'a wire fence surrounds the plot of land', *eine Menge Zuhörer sammelte sich um den Redner* (*herum*) 'a crowd of listeners gathered round the speaker', compare also *um Weihnachten* (*herum*) '(round) about Christmas'. In literary style the adverb *her* often occurs: *die Sonnenstrahlen bildeten einen Lichtring um ihn her* 'the sun's rays formed a ring of light around him'.

w i d e r———synonymous with *gegen*: (Grimm, early editions) *die Prinzessin warf den Frosch wider die Wand* 'the princess threw the frog against the wall', but today confined to a few stereotypes in literary style: *wider Erwarten* 'contrary to expectation', *wider Willen* 'reluctantly'. The word is, however, not unusual in compounds: *der Widerhall* (literary) 'echo', *widersprechen* 'contradict', *widerrechtlich* 'illegal', also *widerwillig* 'reluctant'.

PREPOSITIONS TAKING THE DATIVE

It will be convenient to distinguish between the group of everyday prepositions, generally having a considerable range of meaning and idiomatic application, and those which occur less frequently and are semantically much more restricted. In the former group we place *aus*, *bei*, *gegen'über*, *mit*, *nach*, *seit*, *von*, *zu*.

a u s———*aus dem Fenster* 'out of the window', *aus der Mode* 'out of fashion', *Geschichten aus dem Wiener Wald* 'Tales from the Vienna Woods', *aus dem letzten Jahrhundert* 'from the last century', *aus welchem Grund?* 'for what reason', *aus reinem Gold* 'of pure gold', *was wird aus ihm werden?* 'what will become of him?'

b e i———*beim Busbahnhof* 'by the bus station', *bei uns* (*zu Hause*) 'at our house', *er ist bei meiner Schwester* 'he's at my sister's', *sind Sie beim Arzt gewesen?* 'have you been to the doctor's?', *ich war früher bei der Bahn* 'I used to work on the railway', *bei seiner Ankunft* 'on his arrival', *beim Aussteigen* 'on alighting', *er ist beim Bund* (coll.) 'he's serving in the *Bundeswehr* (Federal Army)', *bei geselligen Tieren gibt es einen Streß durch Vereinsamung* 'in the case of sociable animals stress can be caused by isolation'.

g e g e n 'ü b e r———used before or (more frequently) after the noun: *gegenüber dem Haus* or *dem Haus gegenüber* 'opposite the house', common also in a figurative sense: *gegenüber meinem Bruder* or *meinem Bruder gegenüber war ich klein* 'I was small compared with my brother', but usually before the noun in phrases of time like *gegenüber dem Vorjahr* 'compared with the previous year'. However, it always follows a pronoun: *ihm gegenüber* 'opposite him, compared with him'. The term is further used as a mollified synonym of *gegen*, p. 294: *er wird sich gegenüber anderen Angriffen ebenso verteidigen* 'he will similarly defend himself against other attacks', *höflich Damen gegenüber* 'polite to women'. It may be used redundantly: *ich bin ihm (gegenüber) dankbar* 'I am grateful to him'.

The present word is widely used as an adverb; one will distinguish *das Haus gegenüber* 'the house opposite' from the prepositional use above. At the same time the adverb may be joined to *von* giving a preposition 'opposite', widespread in spoken style: *gegenüber von dem Haus*.

m i t——*mit einer Zange* 'with a pair of tongs', *mit dem Zug* 'by train', *mit anderen Worten* 'in other words', *mit einem Mal* 'all at once', *mit fünf (Jahren)* 'at the age of five', (set phrase) *mit an Sicherheit grenzender Wahrscheinlichkeit* 'with a degree of probability bordering on certainty'. Observe that the dative is used after *mit oder ohne*, e.g. *mit oder ohne den Fußnoten* 'with or without the foot-notes'.

n a c h——*nach zwei Tagen* 'after two days', *nach der Arbeit, nach der Schule* 'after work, after school', *nach langem Hin und Her* 'after much toing and froing', *bitte nach Ihnen!* 'after you!', *nach dem Bundesdorf am Rhein* (humorous) 'to the Federal Village on the Rhine' i.e. Bonn, *von Genua nach Mailand* 'from Genoa to Milan (= bis, p. 293), *nach allen Richtungen* 'in all directions', *die Fenster gehen nach dem Garten* 'the windows look on to the garden'. When meaning 'according to' *nach* is sometimes optionally used after the noun: *dem Gesetz nach* 'according to the law', *meiner Ansicht nach* 'in my opinion', beside *nach dem Gesetz* etc. At other times, it is regularly so used: *allem Anschein nach* 'to all appearances', *(nur) dem Namen nach* '(only) by name'. But always *nach dem Gehör* 'by ear'.

The use of *nach* 'to' is often heard in the north as an alternative to *zu* in cases where the south has only the latter: *ich gehe nach dem* (otherwise *zum*) *Bahnhof* 'I'm going to the station'. Such use is acceptable in writing, too.

s e i t——*seit meinem Besuch* 'since my visit', *wir haben seit langem nichts von Ihnen gehört* 'we haven't heard from you for a long time', *wir warten schon seit einem Jahr* 'we've been waiting for the past year (and still are)'—on the present tense in German, see p. 231.

v o n——*von einer Straßenseite zur anderen* 'from one side of the street to the other', *von Antwerpen nach Vlissingen* 'from Antwerp to

Flushing', *von Kindheit an* 'from childhood (on)', *erwartest du einen Gefallen von ihm?* 'are you expecting a favour from him?', *erzähle mir etwas von deinem Tun und Treiben* 'tell me something of what you've been up to', *abgesehen von allem anderen* 'apart from everything else', *einige von ihnen* 'some of them', *ein Bekannter von mir* 'an acquaintance of mine', *etwas von 'der Sorte* 'something of that sort', *ein Roman vom selben Verfasser* 'a novel by the same author'. Observe that the dative is used after *von . . . bis*, e.g. *von 100 bis 250 Jahren* 'from 100 to 250 years'.

In a passive sentence, *von* is normally used with an animate agent: *England wurde von den Normannen erobert* 'England was conquered by the Normans'. With inanimates the preposition corresponding to English 'by' is more typically *durch* since the underlying sense is so often 'by means of, through' (p. 294), but if the inanimate is the agent proper, then *von* is regular in such cases, too: *die Eiche wurde vom Blitz getroffen* 'the oak was struck by lightning'.

In colloquial German the construction *von* with the noun often corresponds to the more literary genitive, p. 154. It may be noted here that, under the influence of the colloquial, the construction with *von* not infrequently appears in written style as well, cf. *die Einfuhr von spanischer Steinkohle* 'the import of Spanish anthracite', *die Ausfuhr von halbfertigen Waren* 'the export of semi-finished goods', beside stricter literary *die Einfuhr spanischer Steinkohle, die Ausfuhr halbfertiger Waren*.

z u——*geh zu ihm* 'go to him', *setz dich zu ihm* 'sit beside him', *zu beiden Seiten* 'on both sides', *zu Weihnachten* 'at Christmas', *zum Wohl!* 'Cheers!', with the names of towns in a handful of formal contexts: *der Dom zu Mainz* 'the cathedral at M.', redundantly in a colloquial sentence like *er hat zu mir gesagt* 'he said to me'. The preposition may be used with the adverb *hin*, which adds an untranslatable nuance to the meaning. Thus the sentence 'he goes to the window' can be rendered *er geht zum Fenster* or *er geht zum Fenster hin*, the former being the general statement, i.e. 'he goes to the window from any part of the room', the latter implying some distance to the window, requiring a number of steps.

This preposition is often used to mark a consequence, a development, or change: *ein unheilbares Gehörleiden machte Beethoven zum Sonderling* 'an incurable ailment affecting his hearing made B. an eccentric', *mein Bruder ist zum Mann herangewachsen* 'my brother has grown up to be a man', *das Wasser war zu Wein geworden* 'the water had turned into wine'. By the same token: *ich lasse mich nicht zum Narren halten* 'I won't be made a fool of'. The construction is especially common in association with the verb *werden*, when its use may be optional: *sie wurden Bettler* 'they became beggars' beside *sie wurden zu Bettlern* which emphasizes the changed condition. Such use is, however, by no means universal; in particular it is not found in connection with the names of tradesmen, etc.: *er wird Bäcker* 'he is going to be a baker'. Lastly, the preposition expresses purpose: *ich brauche etwas zum Anziehen* 'I need something to wear', hence clichés like *zur Abwechslung* 'for a change', *zum Vergnügen* 'for pleasure', *zum Zeitvertreib* 'to pass the time'.

entgegen, nebst, (mit)'samt; nahe, fern——as stated above, a second group of prepositions governing the dative contains words which occur less often, but are still well known, especially in the following usages: *entgegen meinem Rat, meinen Wünschen*, or *meinem Rat, meinen Wünschen entgegen* 'contrary to my advice, my wishes', to all intents and purposes the same as the more pedestrian *gegen* p. 294, (typically officialese) *zu verkaufen: Haus nebst großem Garten* 'for sale: house with large garden', *samt* or *mit'samt allem Zubehör* '(complete) with all accessories'—simply *mit allem Zubehör* in ordinary speaking, *sie macht es ihrem Mann zuliebe* 'she is doing it for her husband's sake'.

Lastly, two prepositions developing from adjectives used with the dative (p. 158) and which may in part still be regarded as such: *nahe dem Gipfel, dem Gipfel nahe* 'near the summit', *fern der Heimat, der Heimat fern* 'far from home'—the dative is seen unequivocally in e.g. *fern dem Treiben der Welt* 'far from the bustle of the world'—in ordinary style *in der Nähe des Gipfels* or more simply *nahe beim* or *am Gipfel, fern von der Heimat*.

PREPOSITIONS TAKING THE GENITIVE

Given that genitive constructions are essentially a feature of written as opposed to spoken language, the examples that follow belong, in general, to a higher level of style than the simple everyday colloquial.

We refer to representative examples, including the more familiar: *angesichts der Schwierigkeiten* 'in face of the difficulties', *kraft seines Am :* 'by virtue of his office', *ungeachtet seiner Verdienste* 'notwithstanding his merits', (only as a postposition) *neuerer Entwicklungen halber* 'on account of more recent developments' and sometimes forming compounds, as *vorsichtshalber* 'as a precaution'. Compare *seitens der Beteiligten* 'on the part of those involved' with *dies-, jenseits der Alpen* 'on this, that side of the Alps', also *beiderseits* 'on both sides of'.

There is a group of originally adjectival adverbs in *-lich*, e.g. *anläßlich seines Besuches* 'on the occasion of his visit', similarly *bezüglich* 'with reference to', *einschließlich* 'including', *hinsichtlich* 'regarding'. With a further group the present construction is consistently used only when the noun concerned is qualified by an inflecting word, otherwise *von* is commonly required: *anhand der Beispiele* 'with the aid of the examples', but *anhand von Beispielen* 'with the aid of examples', likewise with a pronoun: *anstelle von jemand(em)* 'instead of somebody'; in the case of a singular noun there is a tendency to dispense with a genitive inflexion: *infolge Preisrückgang* 'in consequence of a fall in prices'. Other comparable formations: *aufgrund* 'because of', *inmitten* 'amid', *zugunsten* 'for the benefit of'.

Another group closely follows the above pattern: *außerhalb, innerhalb des Kreises* 'outside, inside the circle', *oberhalb, unterhalb des Ellbogens* 'above, below the elbow', then *außerhalb von Husum* 'outside H.', *der Rhein oberhalb von Bingen* 'the Rhine above B.', further *innerhalb weniger Minuten* 'within a few minutes', but in more popular style *innerhalb von wenigen Minuten*. Compare also (literary) *unweit des Ortes* with (popular) *unweit vom Ort* 'not far from the place'.

Finally, *um . . . willen* with the genitive between the component parts: *um seiner selbst willen* 'for one's own sake'; certain phrases have passed into everyday speech, as *um des lieben Friedens willen* 'for the sake of (a bit of) peace' and of course *um Gottes (Himmels) willen!* 'for God's (heaven's) sake!'

PREPOSITIONS TAKING THE ACCUSATIVE AND DATIVE

The prepositions in question are firstly *an, auf, hinter, in, neben, über, vor, zwischen*. In basic terms, these prepositions are used with the accusative when they denote movement towards a place, with the dative when they denote movement within a place or, as in the vast majority of occurrences, rest at a place. But complications arise when they are used figuratively and to a lesser extent when temporal, each preposition tending to go its own separate way. Somewhat different from the foregoing are *ab, außer, entlang*. These are discussed after the main examples now following.

a n——*sie hängt den Spiegel an die Wand* 'she hangs the mirror on the wall', *der Spiegel hängt an der Wand* 'the mirror hangs on the wall', *die Fliege geht an der Wand spazieren* 'the fly goes for a walk on the wall', further *man klopft an die Tür* 'one knocks on the door', but (impersonal) *es klopft an der Tür* 'there's knocking at the door', *man schreibt es an die Tafel* 'one writes it on the board', but *es steht an der Tafel geschrieben* 'it is written on the board'—the same with *auf*, below. Notice the construction: *er fuhr an dem Haus vorbei* 'he drove past the house'. The basic distinction again in temporal use: *an die siebzig Jahre alt* 'about seventy years old' lit. 'towards' = *gegen* (p. 294), *an einem Sommertag* 'on a summer's day'.

There are great variations in figurative use; the dative is doubtless commoner, but there are also many accusative examples: (dative) *sieben an der Zahl* 'seven in number', *jung an Jahren* 'young in years', *er starb an der Krankheit* 'he died from the disease', *es fehlt an der nötigen Ausrüstung* 'the necessary equipment is lacking', *ich freue mich an dem, was ich habe* 'I take pleasure in what I have', *wir haben ihn an der Stimme erkannt* 'we recognized him by his voice', (accusative) *Erinnerungen an die Kindheit* 'memories of childhood', *Grüße an die Schwester* 'greetings to your sister', *der Bürgermeister appellierte an die Wähler* 'the mayor appealed to the voters', *er glaubt an einen persönlichen Gott* 'he believes in a personal God', *ich denke an die Konsequenzen* 'I'm thinking of the consequences', *man muß sich an die Tatsachen halten* 'one must keep to the facts', *sie hat eine Frage an Sie — haben Sie sich schon an die fleischlose Kost gewöhnt?* 'she has a question for you—have you got used to the meatless diet yet?'

a u f——*sie stellt die Tassen auf den Tisch* 'she puts the cups on the table', *die Tassen stehen auf dem Tisch* 'the cups are on the table', further *man landet auf einem Flugfeld* 'one lands on an airfield', (Upper German) *man schreibt es auf die Tafel* 'one writes it on the board', *es steht auf der Tafel geschrieben* 'it is written on the board'—cf. with *an*, above. In temporal use the accusative is universal: *auf die Minute* 'to the minute', *auf Jahre hinaus* 'for years to come', *auf seine alten Tage* 'in his old age', *ich verschwinde auf einen Augenblick* 'I'm disappearing for a moment'. The accusative is by far the more prevalent in figurative use: *auf jeden Fall* 'in any case', *auf diese Weise* 'in this way', *auf eigene Gefahr* 'at one's own risk', *auf den ersten Blick* 'at first sight', *auf meine Bitte (hin)* 'at my request', *es lag auf eine Entfernung von zwanzig Metern* 'it lay at a distance of twenty metres', *ich freue mich auf Ihren Besuch* 'I look forward to your visit', *er paßt auf die Kinder auf* 'he looks after the children', *wir sind stolz auf Sie und trinken auf Ihr Wohl* 'we are proud of you and drink to your health', *das Konto lautet auf seinen Namen — niemand sonst hat Anspruch auf das Geld* 'the account is in his name—no one else has any claim to the money'. Examples of the less usual dative: *ich halte dich auf dem laufenden* 'I'll keep you informed', *die Verwechslung beruht auf einem Mißverständnis* 'the confusion is due to a misunderstanding'.

h i n t e r——*die Schachtel Streichhölzer ist hinter den Ofen gerutscht — sie befindet sich hinter dem Ofen* 'the box of matches has slipped down behind the stove—it is behind the stove', *du hast eine lange*

Strecke hinter dich gebracht 'you have covered a long distance'. Examples of figurative expressions: *er hält mit seinen Plänen hinterm Berg* 'he keeps his plans to himself', *er beabsichtigt, die Konkurrenz hinters Licht zu führen* 'he intends to hoodwink his competitors', *schreibt euch das hinter die Ohren!* 'take good care to remember that!'

i n——*er geht in die Werkstatt* 'he goes into the workshop', *er bleibt in der Werkstatt* 'he remains in the workshop', *der Schlosser geht in der Wekstatt auf und ab* 'the mechanic walks up and down the workshop'. Notice: *der Zug verschwindet im Tunnel* 'the train disappears into the tunnel', *wir kommen in dem Bahnof an* 'we arrive at the station'. In temporal use: *ins nächste, im nächsten Jahrhundert* 'into the next, in the next century', *heute in acht Tagen* 'today week', *in diesem Alter* 'at this age', *in diesem Zeitalter* 'in this age', *in aller Herrgottsfrühe* 'at the crack of dawn'. In figurative use: (accusative) *wie soll ich solche Gedanken in Worte fassen?* 'how shall I put such thoughts into words?', *könnten Sie ein Treffen in die Wege leiten?* 'could you arrange a meeting?', (dative) *in großer Eile* 'in great haste', *in dieser Weise* 'in this manner'.

n e b e n——*er legt sich neben sie (hin)* 'he lies down beside her', *er liegt neben ihr* 'he lies beside her', *er hat genau neben das Ziel getroffen* 'he succeeded in just missing the target', *neben ihm bin ich ein Stümper* 'compared with him I'm a bungler'.

ü b e r——*sie zieht eine Wolljacke über die Bluse* 'she puts on a cardigan over her blouse', *she trägt eine Wolljacke über der Bluse* 'she wears a cardigan over her blouse', but there are exceptions to this basic difference, e.g. *er ist über die Grenze* 'he is over the border', widely preferred to the logical *über der Grenze*, and reminiscent of the set phrase *er ist über alle Berge* 'he's over the hills and far away', compare also *das alte Rom erstreckte sich über sieben Hügel* 'Ancient Rome extended over seven hills'. Notice idiomatic *ich würde ihn nicht über den Weg trauen* 'I wouldn't trust him an inch'. And in temporal use the accusative is the invariable rule: *übers Wochenende* 'over the weekend', *über fünf Jahre* 'over five years'—but in examples like *nach über fünf Jahren* 'after over five years' it is *nach* which is the true preposition, hence the dative.

As expected in the case of this preposition, the accusative very largely prevails in figurative use: *er errang einen Sieg über den Feind* 'he won a victory over the enemy', *ein König herrscht über sein Volk* 'a king rules over his people', *ich freue mich über die gute Nachricht* 'I am pleased about the good news', *wir denken über die Ereignisse der vergangenen Woche nach* 'we're thinking over the events of the past week', *er liebt die Freiheit über alles* 'he loves freedom more than anything else'—the reader is now invited to translate "*Deutschland über alles*". As implied, the dative is not prominent in figurative examples, but notice *über dem Durchschnitt* 'above average' and such usages as *er ist über dem Werk gestorben* 'he died before he could finish his work' or *über den Erfolgen darf man nicht die Fehler vergessen* freely translated 'success must not blind one to mistakes'.

u n t e r——*er hat es unter das Kopfkissen gesteckt* 'he put it under the pillow', *sie hat es unter dem Kopfkissen entdeckt* 'she discovered it under the pillow'—notice *er versteckte es unter dem Kopfkissen* 'he hid it under the pillow—*sie mischten sich unter die Menge* 'they mingled with the crowd', *wir waren unter den Anwesenden* 'we were among those present'. Observe expressions of the type *er kam unter dem Tisch hervor* 'he came out from under the table'. In temporal use only the dative is applicable: *sie ist unter fünf Jahren* 'she is under five years', *ich bin unter einer Stunde zurück* 'I'll be back in under an hour', (southern) *unter der Woche* 'during the week'. Illustrations of figurative use: (accusative) *wir müssen ihnen unter die Arme greifen* 'we'll have to help them out', *sie wollen die Tochter unter die Haube bringen* 'they want to get the daughter married', (dative, more commonly) *unter diesen Bedingungen* 'under these conditions', *unter dem Befehl* 'under the command', *unter falschem Namen* 'under a false name', *unter aller Kritik* 'beneath contempt'.

v o r——*er tritt vor die Tür* 'he steps up to the door', *er wartet vor der Tür* 'he waits in front of the door'. When temporal the dative is used: *vor seiner Ankunft* 'before his arrival', *heute vor acht Tagen* 'a week ago today'. Other examples: (accusative) *wir wollen ihn nicht vor den Kopf stoßen* 'we don't want him to take umbrage', *was flüsterst du vor dich hin?* 'what are you whispering to yourself?' (dative) *er erschien vor dem Richter* 'he appeared before the judge', *hatte er Angst vor ihm?* 'was he afraid of him?'

z w i s c h e n——*er setzt sich zwischen die Kinder* (*hin*) 'he sits down beside the children', *er sitzt zwischen ihnen* 'he sits between them', figuratively with the dative: *wir vermitteln zwischen den Parteien* 'we are mediating between the parties'.

We now turn to the somewhat different examples referred to above.

a b——differs from the preceding prepositions in that it is found with either case indiscriminately, but with a tendency to prefer the dative; it is essentially officialese: *ab ersten* or *erstem nächsten Monats* 'from the first of next month', *ab vier Jahren* 'from four years on'.

a u ß e r——is remarkable for being in living use with all three oblique cases. It is seen to regularly govern the accusative in a few instances, notably in the idiom *außer allen Zweifel setzen* 'place beyond all doubt', but in one expression it takes the genitive: *außer Landes gehen* 'go abroad, emigrate'. Otherwise, in its various meanings, it is found with the dative: *das steht außer allem Zweifel* 'that is beyond all doubt', *außer dem Gehalt hat er noch Einkünfte aus Investitionen* 'in addition to his salary he has income from investments', *alle außer dir* 'all except you'. Often before an unqualified noun: *außer Dienst* 'retired', *außer Kraft* 'no longer in force', *außer Sicht* 'out of sight'.

e n t l a n g——grammatically ambiguous since it may at one and the same time be seen as an adverb or as a postposition: *der Hund läuft den Weg entlang* 'the dog runs along the path', *Bäume wachsen den Weg entlang* 'trees grow alongside the path', the latter alternatively with a dative preposition: *am Weg entlang*, where the present word is unequivocally adverbial. When, much less usually, in literary style, *entlang* precedes its noun, it governs the dative: *entlang dem Weg*. See also *längs*, p. 304.

PREPOSITIONS TAKING THE GENITIVE AND DATIVE

The variation of cases involved here does not reflect a difference of meaning such as obtains between accusative and dative exemplified in the main examples in the previous section, but purely a difference in style. Apart from exceptions to be mentioned, the prepositions concerned arose in written language when they governed the genitive. Subsequently gaining currency in the spoken language, which had discarded this case (p. 154), they came to be construed colloquially with the dative. Meanwhile the two styles have affected each other with the inevitable complications.

w ä h r e n d——in print regularly with the genitive: *während des Streiks* 'during the strike', *während eines Jahres* 'for (the duration of) a year'. The construction is often imitated in conversation, but a colloquial dative is widespread: *während dem Streik, während einem Jahr*, and not infrequently appears in informal writing, for example, in letters.

w e g e n——in print predominantly with the genitive: *wegen des schlechten Wetters*, less frequently and more stiffly *des schlechten Wetters wegen* 'because of the bad weather', but in ordinary speaking more usually with the dative: *wegen dem schlechten Wetter*, and such forms appear from time to time in print. Use with pronouns, i.e. *wegen mir* 'because of me', etc., is quite common in spoken German, but compounds of the type *meinetwegen*, etc. (p. 73) are regarded as standard. A colloquial *von wegen* is heard locally: *von wegen dem schlechten Wetter.* An otherwise obsolete construction survives in the phrases *von Amts wegen* 'ex officio', *von Rechts wegen* 'by rights'.

a n 's t a t t or abbreviated *s t a t t*——in print predominantly with the genitive: *(an)statt eines neuen Besens* 'instead of a new sweeping brush', but in ordinary speaking commonly with the dative: *(an)statt einem neuen Besen.*

l a u t——less common than the foregoing and found only in formal contexts. It governs a genitive qualified by an inflected word: *laut dieser Berichte* 'according to these reports', otherwise optionally with the dative: *laut Berichte(n)*; in the singular, phrases like *laut Bericht, Gesetz, Vorschrift* 'according to report, law, regulation' are standard.

t r o t z——originally taking the dative—having been first used as a noun, lit. 'defiance (to)'—but under the influence of the examples above coming to predominantly govern the genitive in the written language: *trotz des Regenwetters* 'in spite of the wet weather', but colloquially more often retaining the dative: *trotz dem Regenwetter.* The original dative remains in the standard clichés *trotz allem* or *alledem* 'for all that' and in the conjunction *trotzdem*, p. 266.

d a n k, g e m ä ß, b i n n e n, l ä n g s——an analogical development is observable in some less frequently employed prepositions, traditionally governing the dative, but sometimes found with the genitive due to a feeling that this case will be more appropriate in written style: *dank seinen* or *seiner Bemühungen* 'thanks to his efforts' and (characteristically as a postposition) *Ihren* or *Ihrer Anweisungen gemäß* 'according to your instructions'. Variations again with *binnen* and *längs*, e.g. *binnen eines Monats* or *einem Monat* 'within a month'—but invariably *binnen kurzem* 'shortly'—*Häuser stehen längs des Flusses* or *dem Fluß* 'there are houses along the river', cf. *entlang*, p. 303.

20. Negation

Position of negative adverb

THE negative adverb may appear in various positions in the sentence, in this respect differing from English practice more often than not. Particularly such differences will be exemplified in the following. The adverb *nicht* normally follows the finite verb: *er möchte nicht spielen* 'he doesn't want to play'. If there is an object, the negative follows: *sie wird den Unterschied nicht bemerken* 'she won't notice the difference', but not in cases like *er möchte nicht Karten spielen* 'he doesn't want to play cards', where *Karten spielen* as a single concept remain together. The negative usually precedes the complement in structures like *ich bin nicht der Meinung* 'I'm not of the opinion', while *ich bin der Meinung nicht*, being out of the ordinary, could sound, say, jocular. Generally speaking, *nicht* precedes any word it specially qualifies. Contrast *wir kennen diese Frau nicht* 'we don't know this woman' with *wir kennen nicht diese Frau* 'we don't know her, this woman'—the negative is ordinarily unstressed, its position alone suffices for the sense. Similarly *er hat sich deswegen nicht aufgeregt* 'he wasn't agitated about it', but *er hat sich nicht deswegen aufgeregt* 'he wasn't agitated about t h a t'. Other examples: *ich habe ihm nicht alles erzählt* 'I didn't tell him everything', *er hat es nicht dir versprochen, sondern mir* 'he didn't promise it to you, but to me', *nicht wir haben die Schulden verursacht, sondern andere* 'it wasn't we who caused the debts, but other people'. Exceptionally, in high style, *nicht* can precede the verb: (Menge) *nicht schlummert und nicht schläft der Hüter Israels* 'the guardian of Israel never slumbers, never sleeps'. Also in literary language, the negative may follow the word it specially qualifies in structures like *Himmel und Erde werden vergehen, aber meine Worte nicht* 'heaven and earth shall pass away, but not my words', more ordinary style *aber nicht meine Worte*.

The negative adverb is often used in questions without a negative sense proper, in which case it precedes the object: *haben Sie nicht das neueste gehört?* 'haven't you heard the latest?', different from the genuine negative force of *haben Sie das neueste nicht gehört?* 'have you really not heard the latest?' Or again: *können wir nicht noch eine Flasche kaufen?* 'can't we buy another bottle?', but *können wir noch eine Flasche nicht kaufen?* implying some impediment, such as not having enough money or fearing that stocks may have run out. Also with certain pronouns: *habt ihr nicht etwas* (or *was*) *vergessen?*

'haven't you forgotten something?', but not with personal pronouns: *hast du ihn nicht gesehen?* 'haven't you seen him?' The negative directly follows a subordinating conjunction: *er schaute, ob nicht ein Taxi käme* 'he looked to see if there wasn't a taxi coming', but not if the subject of the clause is an unstressed word: *er schaute, ob es nicht käme* 'if it wasn't coming'.

The ordinary terms for 'never' are *nie* and its common variant *niemals*. Their place in the sentence corresponds in general to that of *nicht*. In emphatic position, however, they regularly precede the finite verb at the head of the sentence: *nie/niemals habe ich im entferntesten darüber nachgedacht* 'never have I even remotely thought about it', otherwise *ich habe nie/niemals . . .* 'I have never . . .' Synonymous *nimmer* is, in the standard language, an obsolescent literary word, except in emphatic combination with *nie*, e.g. *nie und nimmer werde ich jenen Tag vergessen* 'never, never shall I forget that day'. It survives independently, however, in South German colloquial, keeping the basic sense 'not any more': *den siehst du nimmer* 'you'll never see him again', *da wohnt er nimmer* 'he doesn't live here any longer', elsewhere *den siehst du nie wieder, hier wohnt er nicht mehr*.

Redundant negative

If the main clause contains a negative, a second, redundant negative is common, though optional, in subordinate clauses introduced by *bevor* or its synonym *ehe*, thus *ich möchte mich nicht festlegen, bevor/ehe ich ihn (nicht) gesehen habe* 'I wouldn't like to commit myself before I've spoken to him'. Clauses introduced by *bis* may follow the same pattern: *bis du (nicht) dein Brot aufgegessen hast, darfst du keinen Kuchen haben* 'until you've eaten up your bread you can't have any cake'. The redundant negative is usual in the language as ordinarily spoken.

Double negative

The double negative is traditional: (folksong) *nichts brennet so heiß, / wie heimliche Liebe, / von der niemand nichts weiß* 'nothing burns so hot as secret love that no one knows anything about'. It survives unimpaired in the unaffected speech of certain districts: *ich habe kein Kleingeld nicht* 'I have no small change' and may be regarded as a tolerable regionalism. More generally, it may have an emphatic function: (ordinary colloquial) *ich habe keine Zeit für niemand und nichts* 'I have no time for anybody or anything'; it can appear in literary style: (after Henzen) *Rankes Ausspruch, gewaltiger als Luther sei wohl nie ein Schriftsteller in keiner Nation aufgetreten, ist nicht übertrieben* 'R.'s statement that never in any nation did a writer arise wielding greater power than L., is not exaggerated'. A repeated negative is required in structures like *ich will keinen Laut hören von keinem von euch* 'I don't want to hear a sound from any of you', (Goethe) *keine Luft von keiner Seite! / Todesstille, fürchterlich* 'not a breeze from any side! / (a) dead calm, awesome'.

21. Agreement

GENDER

General use of the masculine

DISCREPANCIES between natural and grammatical gender are, of course, legion. Inanimate objects are frequently masculine or feminine: *der Korb* 'the basket', *die Wolke* 'the cloud'. Conversely, animate beings are sometimes neuter: *das Kind* 'the child', *das Weib* (most often pejorative) 'the woman', *das Mitglied* 'the member (of a club, etc.)', likewise diminutives: *das Mädchen* or *Mädel* 'the girl', (poetic) *das Knäblein* 'the (small) boy'.

Further discrepancies occur as between masculine and feminine. The statement *die Katze ist ein Haustier* 'the cat is a domestic animal' includes *der Kater* 'the tom', the statement *der Hund ist ein Haustier* includes *die Hündin* 'the bitch'. This latter, the so-called general use of the masculine, is of practical concern. To begin with, it is common in the predicative position: contrast *die Närrin lachte nur* 'the foolish woman simply laughed' with *Hilde, du bist ein Narr* 'H., you are a fool' rather than *Närrin*, which would sound stilted in this context. But usage varies and each case must be taken on its own merits. Thus one could say *Gerda ist eine gute Schülerin* 'G. is a good pupil' (often idiomatically 'G. is good at school'), but not *ein guter Schüler*, which would refer to a boy. On the other hand, one finds both *sie ist Architekt* and *Archtektin* 'she is an architect', where the former sounds rather stiff and not at all personal as does the latter, for the masculine is preferred in formal contexts. Thus, in announcement of a lecture: *Referent — Frau Dr. (Doktor) Schulz*, but in a discussion on the lecture afterwards one would hear, e.g. *die Referentin sagte . . .* 'the speaker said . . .'. Appropriately one finds on the back of an envelope only the formal masculine: *Absender — Erika Schwarz*. The masculine is also general in certain set expressions: *sie ist Herr der Lage* 'she is master of the situation', *meine Mutter war kein Freund von Pillen* 'my mother was not keen on pills'.

Discrepancies can also arise when a noun has no feminine form: *sie ist unser Gast, ein starker (schwacher) Esser* 'she is our guest, a good (poor) eater'. Similarly *der Bote* 'the messenger' could be male or female, likewise its compound *Dienstbote* '(domestic) servant'. The up-to-date term for the sentry is *der Wachposten*, but not long ago it was *die Schildwache*, so the sentry was then grammatically feminine.

It didn't take long for a wit to put two and two together: (after A. von Villiers) *ich hatte damals einen Dienstboten — dieser wurde schwanger von einer Schildwache, mit der er ein Liebesverhältnis angeknüpft hatte. Er wurde entbunden, und sie weigerte sich, ihre Vaterschaft anzuerkennen* 'I had a servant at the time—"he" became pregnant by a sentry with whom "he" had had a love affair. "He" was delivered of a child, and "she" refused to acknowledge "her" paternity'.

The use of the adjective *weiblich* 'feminine' with purely masculine forms is also a possibility; it occurs typically in the plural: *weibliche Studenten* 'women students' as an alternative to *Studentinnen*, only relatively rarely in the singular: *Frau Thatcher wurde 1979 Britanniens erster weiblicher Premier* 'in 1979 Mrs Th. became Britain's first woman prime minister'.

See further under 'Pronouns' below.

Pronouns

Where there is a discrepancy between natural and grammatical gender, a pronoun ordinarily appears in the natural gender, except in the case of the relative: *so ein reizendes Mädchen! Von ihr waren alle entzückt* 'such a charming girl! All were enchanted by her', but with grammatical gender: *das Mädchen, das wir gestern kennenlernten, wird morgen wiederkommen* 'the girl that we got to know yesterday will be coming again tomorrow'. The possessive, too, ordinarily takes the natural gender: *Schwesterchen hat ihr neues Kleid an* 'sister has her new dress on'. Strict grammatical concord in these matters is associated with special styles, e.g. technical: (biology text-book) *das befruchtete Weibchen der Waldameise wirft nach dem Hochzeitsflug seine vier locker sitzenden Flügel ab* 'after the nuptial flight the fertilized female of the red ant sheds her four loosely attached wings', often too in the fairy tale: (Grimm) *da wollten die Zwerge Schneewittchen begraben, aber es sah noch so frisch aus wie ein lebender Mensch und hatte noch seine schönen roten Backen* 'then the dwarfs wished to bury Snow White, but she still looked as fresh as a living person and still had her lovely red cheeks'. In practice the masculine is rarely involved, but compare (Grimm) *das Schneiderlein stellte sich, als ob es schliefe* 'the tailor pretended to be asleep'.

The general use of the masculine (above) also applies to the pronoun: *das kann ein jeder sagen* 'anyone can say that', *aus den Männern klug werden? wenn einem der eigene Ehemann dauernd Rätsel aufgibt?* 'understand men? when your own husband keeps you guessing?', *kannst du dich noch an seine Eltern erinnern? — nein, an keinen von beiden* 'can you still remember his parents?—no, neither of them'. With inanimates, however, the neuter may be expected:

mɾ̈chtest du einen Apfel oder eine Birne? — danke, keines von beiden 'would you like an apple or a pear?—no, thanks, neither'.

Personal names

Diminutive-style personal names ordinarily keep their natural gender: *Lieber Paulchen, Liebe Gretel.* But in certain literary styles the grammatical gender is appropriate, e.g. (theatre critic on a production of *Käthchen von Heilbronn*) *das Käthchen, das seinen Ritter mit piepsiger Stimme anzirpt, ist eher eine Verwandte von Rotkäppchen als von Penthesilea* 'K. who addresses (lit. chirps to) her knight in a squeaky voice is more like a relation of Red Ridinghood's than P.'s'.

NUMBER

Collective use of the singular

The outstanding examples, paralleled in English, are *Korn* 'corn' and *Haar* 'hair', also with the meanings 'grain (of corn)', and '(single) hair', though for the former *Körnchen* is the more usual term, while the latter can, in local use, be rendered *Härchen*—on such use of the diminutive, see p. 128. It may be added that, in spoken German, pl. *Haare* is very widely used, e.g. *wie sehen deine Haare aus! du mußt sie schneiden lassen!* 'look at your hair! you must have it cut!', sg. *Haar*, the normal form in print, being stylistically somewhat elevated.

Singular for plural

A proposition like 'they all took off their hats' is most commonly expressed *sie nahmen alle den Hut ab*, since they have only one hat apiece; however, pl. *die Hüte* may be used as well. In certain cases only the (traditional) singular is possible: *die Matrosen verloren das Leben* or *kamen ums Leben* 'the sailors lost their lives'. (The articles may be replaced by possessives: *ihren Hut, ihre Hüte, ihr Leben.*)

Except in the case of feminines, nouns denoting weights and measures remain in the singular even when qualified by a numeral or other word indicating plurality: *hundert Gramm Quark* 'a hundred grammes of curds', *einige Pfund Mehl* 'a few pounds of flour', *zehn Zentimeter lang* 'ten centimetres long', *fünf Grad Kälte* 'five degrees below freezing'. The practice has spread to such terms as *Faß, Glas, Sack, Schritt*, though without entirely replacing the logical plural, so *zwei Faß Bier* 'two barrels of beer' beside *zwei Fässer Bier*. In the former, *Faß* sounds like a measure, in the latter the barrels are tangible as separate objects. Occasionally usage is stabilized one way or another: *auf zwanzig Schritt Entfernung* 'at a distance of twenty paces', but *zehn Schritte entfernt* 'ten steps away'.

Comparable to the above are expressions relating to money: *vier Pfund* 'four pounds', but *vier englische Pfunde* 'four English pounds', *sechs Mark* 'six marks', *fünfzig Pfennig* 'fifty pfennigs', though *fünfzig Pfennige* is also quite commonly heard, the plural otherwise indicating separate pfennig pieces; *Mark* is invariable, the coins being *Markstücke*. Notice idioms like *(die) fünfzehn Mann* '(the) fifteen men', *zwei Stück Kuchen* 'two pieces of cake', *von diesen nahm sie zehn Stück* 'she took ten of these', *drei Paar Socken* 'three pairs of socks'. The numerals *hundert, tausend,* and *Dutzend* 'dozen' are also treated in this way, pp. 76 f.

The terms *Liter* and *Meter* (p. 51) have, of course, dative plural in *-n*, and this inflexion is usually found in print: *mit fünf Litern* 'with five litres', *in einer Tiefe von zehn Metern* 'at a depth of ten metres', but not when preceding a noun, as in the synonymous *in zehn meter Tiefe*. The ordinary colloquial largely disregards the inflexion: *mit fünf Liter*, etc.

In contrast to the above, feminines are always used in the logical plural: *zwei Tonnen Müll* 'two tons of refuse', similarly *drei Flaschen Sekt* 'three bottles of champagne', *vier Portionen Eis* 'four helpings of ice cream' or 'four ices', *fünf Tassen Tee* 'five cups of tea'. At the same time, a shorthand singular is common when ordering, as in a restaurant: *zwei Limonade* 'two lemonades', *drei Kaffee* 'three coffees', *vier Eis* 'four ices', also *zweimal Limonade*, etc.

Subject and verb

The festival names *Ostern* 'Easter', *Pfingsten* 'Whitsun', *Weihnachten* 'Christmas' are plural forms, witness (proverb) *weiße Weihnachten, grüne Ostern* 'a white Christmas, a green Easter'. They are, however, followed by a singular verb: *Pfingsten steht vor der Tür* 'Whitsun is almost upon us'.

A double subject formed by allied concepts may be felt as a unity and take a singular verb: (on a holiday postcard) *Laune und Stimmung ist gut* something like 'we're feeling fine', (idiomatic) *an ihm ist Hopfen und Malz verloren* 'he's a dead loss', and the proverb *gleich und gleich gesellt sich gern* 'birds of a feather flock together'.

We have seen that *es* occurs as the subject of a construction with the verb 'to be' and a noun predicate, when it will be followed by the plural verb if required: *es sind Türken* 'they are Turks', p. 193. The neut. sg. demonstratives may also be so used: *dies (das) sind Türken* 'these (those) are Turks', and the interrogatives *welches? was?* are found in the same construction, p. 212. In addition, *es* as a sentence-opener (p. 194) often appears with a plural verb: *es kamen viele Menschen* 'many people came'.

When two nouns of different number are joined by the verb 'to be' as subject and predicate, the verb will be in the plural: *die Hälfte waren Versager* 'half were duds', *der Termin, den man ihm setzt, sind acht Tage* 'the time he is given is eight days', i.e. a week. When a noun denoting a quantity is followed by a plural noun the verb may be indifferently singular or plural: *eine Anzahl Fehlanzeigen liegt* or *liegen vor* 'a number of nil returns are to hand', *die Hälfte der Muster ist* or *sind beschädigt* 'half the samples are damaged', but with a tendency to prefer the plural in everyday use: *eine Menge Ausländer waren anwesend* 'a lot of foreigners were present'.

22. Clause Combination

Co-ordination

Co-ordinate clauses may be placed together with or without a connecting word: *er setzte sich an den Tisch, nahm einen Bogen Papier und fing an zu zeichen* 'he sat down at the table, took a sheet of paper and began to draw'. Clauses are sometimes connected by demonstrative pronouns and very often by adverbs, many of which are demonstrative in origin. Coming first in the clause, they are regularly followed in second position by the finite verb. In view of their function as words connecting clauses we speak of pronominal and adverbial conjunctions in addition to the co-ordinating conjunctions proper.

PRONOMINAL CONJUNCTIONS

Demonstrative pronouns are common in simple, everyday speech: *Käsekuchen, den habe ich gern* 'I like cheese cake'. They are often preferred to relative pronouns: instead of (relative) *es gibt Leute, die nie zufrieden sind*, the spoken language will commonly have *es gibt Leute, die sind nie zufrieden*. Both sentences correspond idiomatically to our 'there are people who are never satisfied', English being in this instance unable to express in so many words the stylistic difference implicit in the German.

ADVERBIAL CONJUNCTIONS

We mention first a number of conjunctions whose demonstrative origin is still evident: *da* 'then' and the compounds *dagegen* 'on the contrary', *daher* and *darum* with their synonyms *deshalb*, *deswegen* 'on this (that) account, so', further *des'gleichen* 'likewise', *demnach* or *demzufolge* 'accordingly', *dessen'ungeachtet* 'nevertheless', also *außerdem* and in educated style *über'dies* 'besides, moreover' and *unter'dessen* 'meanwhile'. Ultimately demonstrative are also *dann* 'then' and the compound *dennoch* 'and still'. Other frequently occurring adverbial conjunctions include *also* 'so', *auch* 'also', *ferner* or *weiter* 'further', *folglich* 'consequently, so', *jetzt* or *nun* 'now', *kaum* 'hardly', *so* 'so, thus', *sonst* 'or else', *vielmehr* 'rather'; alternative word order is possible after *doch* or *jedoch* 'however', p. 331.

Specimen sentence: *er war ohnehin überlastet, also* (or *daher, darum, deshalb, deswegen, folglich) konnte er diese zusätzliche Arbeit nicht übernehmen* 'he was overworked as it was, so he couldn't take on this additional job'.

CO-ORDINATING CONJUNCTIONS

Co-ordinating conjunctions are *und, auch, sowie (auch), sowohl . . . als* or *wie¯ (auch), oder, entweder . . . oder, weder . . . noch, aber, sondern, außer, denn,* discussed here in this order. Co-ordinating conjunctions do not affect word order, except as mentioned below.

u n d——'and' requires no special comment except to note that it occasionally affects the word order, p. 330.

a u c h——'also' functions both as an adverb and as a conjunction. It often strengthens *und,* e.g. *wir arbeiten mit ihm und auch mit seinem Bruder* or *und mit seinem Bruder auch* 'we work with him and also with his brother' or 'and with his brother, too'. In the spoken language in particular *auch* commonly stands alone: *wir arbeiten mit ihm, auch mit seinem Bruder.* Similarly *in jenem Haus ist weder Heizung noch Licht, (und) auch kein Wasser* 'in that house is neither heating nor light, and no water (either)'. Out of this emphasizing function arose the use of *auch* in a way which adds nothing to the preceding clause, but instead draws attention to part of it or to something implied in it: *niemand hier hat Geld, auch er nicht* 'nobody here has any money, and he hasn't either'.

s o 'w i e——the literal sense 'just as, the moment' is often lost, leaving a residual sense 'and, also, as well as'; it may be strengthened by *auch,* e.g. *das Land exportiert Getreide und Gemüse sowie (auch) Obst* 'the country exports grain, vegetables and (also) fruit'. This conjunction requires subordinate order: *wir stellen orthopädische Schuhe her sowie diese (auch) reparieren* 'we manufacture orthopaedic shoes as well as repairing them', a reflexion of its original meaning as a subordinating conjunction: *man wird dem Kleinen helfen, sowie man jedem Kind (auch) hilft* 'one will help the little fellow just as one helps any child', cf. *(genauso) wie,* p. 321.

s o 'w o h l . . . a l s or *w i e*——'both . . . and'; the choice *als* or *wie* may be locally conditioned, *auch* is added optionally: *in Cottbus und Bautzen sprechen viele Menschen sowohl sorbisch als* or *wie (auch) deutsch* 'in C. and B. many people speak both Lusatian and German'.

o d e r——'or': *Geld oder Leben!* 'your money or your life!', often as an interrogative in elliptic use, i.e. *oder?* for *oder (etwa) nicht?* 'or (perhaps) not?': *das wollen Sie doch 'sicher nicht, oder?* 'you surely don't want that, or do you?' The alternative proposition need not be so stark; in fact it may be weakened to the extent that it approaches the value of *nicht wahr? gelt?* (p. 141), the slight remaining difference being scarcely expressible in English: *du kommst wohl mit, oder?* 'I suppose you will be coming, won't you?'

e n t w e d e r . . . o d e r——'either . . . or'; *entweder* can optionally affect the word order, as illustrated on p. 331.

w e d e r . . . n o c h——'neither . . . nor': *weder fest noch flüssig, sondern gasförmig* 'neither solid nor liquid, but gaseous'. Inversion of subject and verb after both words: (a literary style) *weder hatte er sich gewaschen, noch hatte er sich gekämmt* 'neither had he washed himself, nor had he combed his hair', ordinarily *er hatte sich weder gewaschen noch gekämmt.*

a b e r——'but': (saying) *klein, aber mein* '(only) small, but mine'; often takes second place in the sentence: *wie aber* (higher style than *aber wie*) *ist es überhaupt zur Mumifizierung im alten Ägypten gekommen?* 'but how did mummification in ancient Egypt actually come about?' Second place is usual when the two verbs share the same subject: *das verletzte Tier versuchte auf die Beine zu kommen, fiel aber wieder* 'the injured animal tried to get on to its feet, but fell down again'. In somewhat elevated diction, a pronoun precedes the conjunction: *er suchte überall nach dem Schlüssel, fand ihn aber nicht* 'he looked for the key everywhere, but didn't find it', ordinary style: *aber er fand ihn nicht.* When in second position, the translation 'however' is often appropriate: *die Kinder aber mußten neue Schuhe bekommen* 'the children, however, had to get new shoes'. See further under *sondern.*

s o n d e r n——'but', expressing an incompatible contrast between some word in its own clause and a word in the preceding (negative) clause: *führe uns nicht in Versuchung, sondern erlöse uns von dem Übel* 'lead us not into temptation, but deliver us from evil', *sie ging nicht direkt zum Warenhaus, sondern zuerst zur Bank* 'she didn't go straight to the store, but went to the bank first'. It may be optionally replaced by *im Gegenteil* or be used with it redundantly: *wir sind nicht glücklich darüber, (sondern) im Gegenteil höchst unglücklich* 'we are not happy about it, (but) on the contrary extremely unhappy'. If the contrast is compatible, *aber* is required: *er ist zwar nicht jung, aber doch sehr gesund* 'he's not young of course, but very fit all the same'; on the other hand incompatibly: *nicht jung, sondern alt* 'not young, but old', *kein Glück, sondern nur Unglück* 'no luck, but only misfortune'. Finally, *nicht nur . . . sondern auch*, invariable regardless of compatibility or otherwise, and with inversion of subject and verb in the first part: *nicht nur ist er jung, sondern er ist auch gesund* 'not only is he young, but he is healthy too'.

a u ß e r——'unless, except': *diese Arbeit ist nicht zu schaffen, außer du packst mit an* 'this job can't be done unless you lend a hand as well', *er fand nichts außer Trümmer* 'he found nothing but rubble'. This word is also a preposition, pp. 302 f.

d e n n——has the meaning and syntactic function of English 'for': *das Kind konnte nicht gut laufen, denn es war noch keine achtzehn Monate alt* 'the child couldn't walk very well, for (because) it was not yet eighteen months old'. In modern style one tends to substitute 'because', either optionally, as above, or usually: *er bleibt zu Hause, denn er ist stark erkältet* 'he's staying at home because he's got a heavy cold'. German *weil* may likewise be substituted for *denn*, but then with subordinate order, e.g. *weil er stark erkältet ist*, p. 320. Unlike 'for', however, *denn* remains a very common word, and the unidiomatic use of 'for' instead of 'because' sometimes heard when Germans speak English, is a direct reflection of the native *denn*.

Subordination

Subordinate clauses may be joined to a main clause either with or without a connecting word. Connecting words are the subordinating conjunctions. The placing together of clauses without a connecting word is termed asyndeton.

ASYNDETON

Dependent assertions can be linked to the main clause without a conjunction: *die Schwierigkeit ist, sie hat noch kein Reifezeugnis* 'the difficulty is, she hasn't got her A-levels yet', *es ist besser, sie bleibt noch ein Jahr in der Schule* 'it will be better if she stays another year at school', *ich bin überzeugt, sie schafft die Prüfung schon* 'I'm certain she'll get through the exam all right', *sie muß doch einsehen, sie hätte sonst keine Chance, eine passende Stelle zu bekommen* 'she must surely understand that, if she doesn't, she stands no chance of getting a suitable job'. Such constructions are especially favoured in the spoken language.

On conditional sentences construed without a conjunction, see p. 263, likewise in indirect statement, pp. 273 f.

SUBORDINATING CONJUNCTIONS

Subordinating conjunctions are a very numerous category and like their co-ordinating counterparts may consist of more than one word. As the overall rule, the finite verb stands at the end of the clause introduced by the subordinating conjunction, p. 332. Such conjunctions occur in conditional and concessive clauses, in indirect statement, etc., and in final and consecutive clauses, see pp. 263 ff. *passim*. In the following we illustrate the use of the more common conjunctions not dealt with in the constructions just referred to, plus a selection of those occurring less frequently.

a l s——'when' in reference to a definite time in the past: *als er voriges Jahr in Prag war, versuchte er, etwas Tschechisch zu sprechen* 'when he was in Prague last year, he tried to speak a little Czech'; *als* thus contrasts with the indefinite *wenn*, p. 321. Optionally, the second clause may open with *da*, i.e. *da versuchte er, etwas Tschechisch zu sprechen*, and such use is quite common, particularly in the language as spoken. In colloquial style *als* in this function may be replaced by *wie*, p. 321.

The conjunction is further found in comparison clauses after a comparative: *er ist viel jünger als ich bin* or a trifle pedantically *als ich es bin*; such clauses are, of course, often curtailed: *er ist viel jünger als ich*. The colloquial may again substitute *wie*.

The present conjunction is used in a statement of manner: *der Fremde entpuppte sich als Hochstapler* 'the stranger turned out to be a confidence trickster', *der Professor hat sich eher als Forscher profiliert denn als Lehrer* 'the professor distinguished himself as a researcher rather than as a teacher' (where *denn* in an old meaning 'than' is retained to avoid having *als* twice, colloquially *wie als*). Contrast the somewhat different use of *wie* in such statements.

The conjunction occurs to some extent in structures of the type *das sind so viel Kohlen als du tragen kannst* 'that is as much coal as you can carry' and *ich komme so schnell als möglich* 'I'll come as quickly as possible', but in all cases *wie* is the more generally used alternative.

Finally, the conjunction is met with in the co-ordinating combination *sowohl . . . als (auch)*, p. 314.

b e v o r or *e h e*——'before': *bevor (ehe) er zum Film ging, hatte er in verschiedenen Theaterstücken mitgewirkt* 'before going into films he had acted in various plays on the stage'. The two terms are interchangeable, but in the spoken language *bevor* is heard more than *ehe*.

b i s——'till, until, by the time': *es kann noch eine ganze Weile dauern, bis er mit dieser Arbeit fertig ist* 'it may take a bit of time yet till he's finished with this job', *bis er mit dieser Arbeit fertig ist, sind wir wohl längst Rentner* 'by the time he's finished with this job we'll have long been pensioners'.

d a——'since, as': *da sie eine Deutsche ist, die in England lebt, versucht sie alles von zwei Seiten zu betrachten* 'since she is a German living in England, she tries to look at everything from two sides'. Sometimes, though not very often, the main clause optionally opens with redundant *so*, i.e. *so versucht sie alles*, etc.

In literary style, the conjunction is occasionally seen in a temporal function: *in dem Augenblick, da sie sich zum Gehen wandte* 'at that moment, when she turned to leave', otherwise *wo, als.* Compare further *jetzt da wir Zeit haben, können wir ein bißchen spazierengehen* 'now that we have time, we can go for a little walk'. The conjunction may also introduce a contrasting statement: *warum mußt du das tun, da du (doch) weißt, daß ich's nicht mag?* 'why do you have to do that when you know I don't like it?', cf. *wo*, p. 322.

e h e, see *bevor.*

i n 'd e m——'while, as' and 'in that, by'. The former sense is the primary one, when the action of the two clauses is always simultaneous: *indem er dies sagte, öffnete er seinen Zauberkasten* 'while (as) he was speaking these words, he opened his box of tricks', *ich entfernte mich, indem ich versprach, ihn in Wien zu besuchen* 'I left him, promising to visit him in Vienna'.

Now another sentence, e.g. *indem ich wieder einmal über das Rätsel nachdachte, fiel mir plötzlich die Lösung ein* 'while I was thinking again about the riddle, the answer suddenly occurred to me', could easily lend itself to the interpretation 'in that I was thinking', i.e. by thinking, about the riddle, etc. This secondary sense is well established; it is in fact by far the commoner: *er gewann den Rechtsstreit, indem er nachwies, daß die fragliche Unterschrift gefälscht worden war* 'he won the legal action by proving that the signature in question had been forged', *wir können die Wähler nicht belügen, indem wir von Steuersenkungen sprechen und gleichzeitig die Sozialabgaben anheben* 'we cannot lie to the electors by talking about lowering taxation and at the same time raising the social security contributions'.

This conjunction is proper to rather formal written language. In more pedestrian style and in conversation, the former sense is expressed by *während* or *wie*, the latter by *dadurch, daß.*

j e n a c h 'd e m (o b)——'according to whether': *man verdient gut oder schlecht, je nachdem (ob) man tüchtig ist oder nicht* 'you earn well

or badly, according to whether you're good at your job or not'—optional
ob is often added in simpler style, a bit like our 'according as to
whether'. Elliptic use is common: *machst du Überstunden?* — *je
nachdem* 'do you work overtime?—it (all) depends' for, say, *je
nachdem wie die Aufträge einlaufen* 'depending on how the orders
come in'.

k a u m   d a ß——'hardly', in literary diction only: *kaum daß wir uns
von dem Schock erholt hatten, als ein zweiter Sprengsatz explodierte*
'hardly had we recovered from the shock when a second device
exploded', in ordinary style: *kaum hatten wir uns von dem Schock
erholt*, etc.

n a c h 'd e m——'after': *erst nachdem die Trümmer beseitigt
worden waren, konnte mit dem Wiederaufbau begonnen werden* 'only
after the rubble had been removed was it possible to start rebuilding'.
Now it is tempting to see in a temporal sequence a causal connection,
in which case the above sentence can be interpreted as 'only since, i.e.
only because, the rubble had been removed, etc.' Such practice is
common in the south: *nachdem* (otherwise *da*, *weil*) *das so ist* 'since
that is so', to be regarded as a tolerable regionalism. Also substandard
nachdem wie.

n u n——'now that', in literary style only: *nun er wohlhabend ist,
kennt er uns nicht mehr* 'now that he is well-to-do, he doesn't want to
know us any more', ordinarily *jetzt da* (southern also *jetzt wo*) *er
wohlhabend ist*, etc.

s e i t ,   s e i t 'd e m——'since'; *seitdem* is common in print, but *seit* is
the more usual form in speaking: *wir kenne ihn, seitdem* (*seit*) *wir hier
wohnen* 'we've known him since we've been living here', *seitdem* (*seit*)
er seine Arbeitsstelle verloren hat, ist er sehr deprimiert 'since he lost
his job he has been very depressed'.

s o——occurs in concessive clauses, pp. 265 f.; it preserves an archaic
sense 'if' in the phrase *so* (also *wenn*) *Gott will* 'God willing'; it
introduces consecutive clauses in the combination *so daß*, p. 277, and
combines with other adverbs to form the following conjunctions.

s o 'b a l d or *s o 'w i e*——'as soon as': *sobald* (especially
conversational *sowie*) *ich von dir höre, werde ich meiner Mutter
Bescheid sagen* 'as soon as I hear from you, I shall let my mother
know'. Also widespread substandard *sobald wie*; this redundant *wie*
may be heard with the comparable formations below, too.

s o 'f e r n——'so long as, provided that': *Sie arbeiten in diesem*

Raum, sofern Sie nicht nebenan gebraucht werden 'you work in this room so long as you are not needed next door'.

s o 'l a n g e——'as long as': *er hat sich immer so benommen, solange ich ihn kenne* 'he has always behaved like that as long as I have known him'.

s o 'o f t——'as often as': *kommen Sie nur, sooft Sie wollen* 'just come as often as you wish'.

s o 'v i e l, s o 'w e i t——'as far as': *soviel* or *soweit wir wissen* 'as far as we know'; in most contexts, however, only *soweit* is current: *soweit man den Markt einschätzen kann* 'as far as one can judge the market'.

Further: *s o . . . w i e*——'as . . . as', in familiar style: *er läuft so schnell wie er kann* 'he runs as quick as he can'; less familiar: *er läuft so schnell er kann.*

w ä h r e n d——'while': *während ich die Eier koche, kannst du den Tisch decken* 'while I'm boiling the eggs, you can lay the table', *er hockt über seinen Büchern, während sie meistens vorm Fernseher sitzt* 'he pores over his books, while she mostly sits in front of the TV set'.

w a n n——'when'; the conjunctive function arose from the interrogative *wann?* in reported speech: *ich erkundigte mich, wann er die Arbeit anfangen würde* 'I asked him when he would begin the work', then by analogy in comparable sentences: *sagt uns, wann ihr geht* 'tell us when you're going', *ich weiß nicht, wann ich zurück bin* 'I don't know when I'll be back'. In such sentences *wenn* would only mean 'if', p. 263.

w e i l——'because': *ich fahre auf zwei Wochen ans Meer, weil ich dringend Erholung brauche* 'I am going to the seaside for two weeks because I urgently need a rest'. The causal clause may be optionally anticipated by *deshalb* or *deswegen*, e.g. *ich konnte (deshalb, deswegen) so schnell hier sein, weil ich ein Taxi genommen habe* 'I could only get here so quickly because I took a taxi'; if *nur* or *bloß* 'only' appears in the main clause, the adverbs mentioned will be normally used: *ich konnte nur deshalb*, etc.

w e n n——'when', in clauses referring to the present or future: *ich höre gern zu, wenn er Klavier spielt* 'I like to listen when he plays the piano', *er wird es ihr sagen, wenn sie anruft* 'he'll tell her when she rings up'. A past tense can have future reference: *er mußte im Büro sein, wenn der Anruf kam* 'he had to be in the office when the telephone call came'. In all these sentences, however, *wenn* can equally mean 'if'; German tolerates this ambiguity, since the wider context normally indicates which sense is implied.

Except as above, *wenn* with a past tense has the indefinite meaning 'whenever': *wenn er in Prag war, versuchte er etwas Tschechisch zu sprechen* 'whenever he was in Prague, he tried to speak a little Czech', thus contrasting with *als*, which refers to a single occasion, p. 317. In practice, however, one usually strengthens *wenn* by adding *immer*, i.e. *wenn immer* (or less formally *immer wenn*) *er in Prag war*, etc. Optionally, the second clause may open with *da*, especially in the spoken language, i.e. *da versuchte er, etwas Tschechisch zu sprechen*. See also *wann*, above.

w i e——'how, as, when'. Of these meanings, the first is the earliest developing from the interrogative *wie?* in reported speech: *ich fragte, wie es ihm ging* 'I asked how he was getting on', then analogically e.g. *wir sahen zu, wie der Schmied dem Pony die Hufeisen auflegte* 'we watched how the blacksmith shod the pony', with but a short step from 'how' to 'as', hence also 'we watched as the blacksmith shod the pony'. In other sentences the conjunction acquires a temporal meaning: *wie ich vorbeiging, hörte ich jemanden rufen* 'as (virtually the same as 'when') I was passing, I heard someone call'. As a result, particularly in the spoken language, *wie* can replace *als*, p. 317: *wie ich ein kleiner Junge war* 'when I was a little boy'. In the sense 'as', *wie* can be supported by *so*, e.g. *es traf sich, wie* or *so wie er vorausgesagt hatte* 'it came about as he had prophesied'.

The present conjunction is also used in comparison clauses after a positive: *er ist genauso alt wie ich bin* or a trifle pedantically *wie ich es bin* 'he is exactly as old as I am'. Such clauses are, of course, often curtailed: *er ist genauso alt wie ich*, hence sentences like *er sieht aus wie sein Vater* 'he looks like his father'. In spoken German, *wie* is widely used after a comparative, too (instead of *als*): *er ist viel jünger wie ich*; locally, a conflation of both conjunctions may occur: *viel jünger als wie ich*.

This conjunction is further used in a statement of manner, when the meaning is 'like': *er ist davongelaufen wie ein geölter Blitz* 'he ran off like greased lightning'; the same meaning is also expressed by 'as': *ich wanderte einsam, wie eine Wolke* 'I wandered lonely, as a cloud', but is nevertheless different from the use of *als* in such statements.

Finally, *wie* is usual in structures of the type *das sind so viel Kohlen wie du tragen kannst* 'that is as much coal as you can carry' and *ich komme so schnell wie möglich* 'I'll come as quickly as possible'; all the same, the alternative *als* is occasionally found.

w o——'where', this principle meaning naturally developing from the interrogative *wo?* in reported speech: *ich wünschte, er wäre (dort), wo der Pfeffer wächst* 'I wish he was there where the pepper grows', i.e.

an unpleasant place a long way off. Similarly the compound forms: *ich merke, woher der Wind bläst* 'I see the way things are going'.

In the regional idiom of the south a number of secondary usages can be met with: (causal) *du hast doch so viel Zeit für dich, wo du nicht mehr arbeitst!* 'but you've plenty of time since you're not working any more!', (temporal) *wo ich noch jung war, bin ich oft in den Bergen gekraxelt* 'when I was young, I often went climbing in the mountains'. Compare further *jetzt wo wir Zeit haben, können wir ein bissel spazierengehen* 'now that we have time, we can go for a little walk'. The conjunction may also introduce a contrasting statement: *wie'so* (common alternative to *warum*) *mußt du das tun, wo du (doch) weißt, daß ich's nicht mag?* 'why do you have to do that when you know I don't like it?' It is noticeable that the meanings of these colloquial examples correspond to the meanings evolved by the standard conjunction *da* above, in origin an adverb also.

Just occasionally, *wo* may have a temporal sense in the standard language, e.g. *zu einer Zeit, wo* to all intents and purposes 'at a time when', see under 'Relative *wo*', p. 324.

z u 'm a l——'especially since', in educated style: *man erwog die Einführung eines Schutzzolls, zumal neunzig prozent dieser Produkte aus dem Ausland kamen* 'the introduction of a protective tariff was being considered, especially since ninety per cent of these products came from abroad'.

RELATIVE CLAUSES

Inflecting relative pronouns

Relative clauses are most commonly linked to the main clause by the relative pronoun *der, die, das* (p. 71); it takes its gender and number from its antecedent in the main clause, its case is determined by the function it performs in its own clause. The finite verb in the relative clause stands at the end: *dies ist der Wagen, der gestern repariert wurde* or *den man gestern reparierte* 'this is the car which (or, that) was repaired yesterday', *wo sind die Menschen, mit denen wir reden müssen?* 'where are the people we have to speak to?' lit. 'to whom we must speak' and we note that, though the relative may be frequently omitted in English, this is but rarely the case in German, see 'Unlinked relative clauses' below. The genitive precedes the word governing it: *ein Baum, dessen Blätter gefallen sind* 'a tree whose leaves (or, the leaves of which) have fallen', pl. *die Bäume, deren Blätter . . . , Alfred Nobel stiftete einen Fonds, aus dessen Zinsen jährlich sechs Preise erstellt werden* 'A.N. set up a fund, from the interest on which six prizes are provided annually'.

The forms compounded with *-wegen, um . . . willen* (p. 73) are confined to literary style: *der Hof, dessentwegen* (more ordinarily *wegen dem*) *wir dorthin gereist waren, war bereits verkauft* 'the farm, on account of which we had made the journey there, was already sold', *die Gesundheit seiner kranken Frau, um derentwillen er nach Italien gezogen war, wurde völlig wiederhergestellt* 'the health of his ailing wife, for whose sake he had moved to Italy, was fully restored'.

In the written language, *welcher, -e, -es* is an occasional stylistic alternative to *der, die, das*; it has, however, no genitive (p. 72), only *dessen, deren* being possible. This literary pronoun, which in the last century was so very common and regarded as elegant, has now a somewhat stilted ring, but its use is prescribed to avoid an accumulation of homophones: *die, welche die Verbrecher festnahmen* 'those who apprehended the criminals', although in the language as spoken, accentuation and intonation make such mechanical substitution unnecessary: *die* (stressed, rising tone), *die die* (unstressed); another possibility would be *diejenigen, die die*. The present pronoun is neverthless commonly heard in the jocular *ich bin derjenige, welcher* (fem. *diejenige, welche*, etc.) 'I'm the person in question'. This pronoun is as one with the relative adjective: *es heißt, man lernt nie aus, welcher Feststellung ich mit ganzem Herzen beipflichten kann* 'it is said that one lives and learns, which statement I can wholeheartedly endorse'.

In a few contexts, the relative pronoun can appropriately be followed by *da*, e.g. *Philosophen, die da behaupten* 'philosophers who maintain', where *da* adds a certain emphasis to the predicate, at the same time hinting at some emotional engagement on the speaker's part, naturally absent from the matter-of-fact *Philosophen, die behaupten*. An example in context: *ich hasse es, sagte die Siebzigjährige, immer dieselbe Frage zu beantworten, die da lautet: Was ist das Geheimnis Ihrer Jugend?* 'the seventy-year-old lady said, I hate always answering the same question, which goes: what is the secret of your youth (i.e. youthful appearance)?' Also after *was, wer*, pp. 324, 327.

The relative clause is of much more frequent occurrence in the written language, the spoken style commonly using paratax instead. The first sample sentences above would, in casual speech, as like as not be replaced by *dies ist der Wagen, man hat ihn gestern repariert*. Or again: *ich kenne eine Frau, die von ihrem Mann getrennt ist* 'I know a woman who is separated from her husband', but more casually: *ich kenne eine Frau, die ist von ihrem Mann getrennt* lit. 'I know a woman, she is separated from her husband', similarly *das ist eine Sache, aus der keiner klug wird* 'that is something no one can fathom', in familiar style *das ist eine Sache, da wird keiner klug draus*.

Relative adjective

The relative adjective is *welcher* (p. 61): *wir wollen lieber nicht sagen, in welchem Zustand wir ihn gefunden haben* 'we would rather not say in what condition we found him', *es ist auffallend, mit welcher Zurückhaltung er deutsch spricht* 'it is noticeable how reluctant he is to speak (lit. with what reluctance he speaks) German', also in concessive clauses: *unsere Kirche heißt alle willkommen, ganz gleich welcher Glaubensrichtung sie angehören* 'our church welcomes all regardless of whatever denomination they belong to'.

Uninflected *welch* occurs in the phrases *welch ersterer, welch letzterer* 'the former of which, the latter of which'.

Relative *wo*

In given cases, a relative pronoun in the dative may be replaced, optionally, by the relative adverb *wo* 'where', as in the often heard *die, wo* (or *denen*) *das Herz noch jung ist* 'those who are still young in heart'. It may also replace a relative pronoun governed by a preposition. Practice in German and English may correspond: *es ist ein Land, wo* (or *in dem*) *das Volk unfrei ist* 'it is a country where (in which) the people are not free', but not necessarily so: *das war zu einer Zeit, wo* (or *in der*) *alle Dichtung mündlich überliefert wurde* 'that was at a time in which all poetry was transmitted orally', although here the conjunction *als* 'when' could be substituted in both languages. In certain expressions, however, only *wo* is possible: *der Ort, wo Fuchs und Hase sich 'Gute Nacht' sagen* lit. 'the place where fox and hare bid each other good night' i.e. 'the back of beyond'.

Relative *was*

If the main clause is itself the antecedent, the relative is *was*, e.g. *Iwan spricht akzentfrei englisch, was bei Russen recht selten ist* 'Ivan speaks English without an accent, which is quite unusual for Russians', *sie ging im Regen spazieren, was ich sehr merkwürdig fand* 'she went for a walk in the rain, which I found very strange'. The same applies if the antecedent is a neuter indefinite pronoun: *alles, was da kreucht und fleucht* lit. 'all that creeps and flies' i.e. 'every living thing', often quoted from Schiller (*kreucht, fleucht* = modern standard *kriecht, fliegt*; on *da*, see p. 323), *einiges von dem, was er gebracht hat, ist für uns unbrauchbar* 'some of the things he has brought are useless to us'. The genitive is *dessen* (p. 71): *nichts, dessen ich mich entsinne* 'nothing (which) I recall'. The indefinite may be adjectival: *manches Haarsträubende, was er zum besten gab, wird kaum der Wahrheit entsprochen haben* 'many of the hair-raising things he described will hardly have been true'. Similarly after neuter adjectives when substantivized: *das Beste, was wir finden können* 'the best we can find', also *das erste, was sie tut, wenn sie nach Hause kommt* 'the first thing she does when she gets home', *das letzte, was ich mir wünsche* 'the last thing I want'. Occasionally, *das* as well as *was* occurs, the former being more specific: *etwas, das ich nicht begreifen kann* 'a matter I cannot comprehend', *(irgend) etwas, was ihn zu stören scheint* 'something (or other) which appears to disturb him'. But by no means all speakers make this fine distinction, and it is noticeable that in the spoken language of many districts *was* has completely ousted the relative *das*, e.g. *das Dings, was du in der Hand hast* 'the thingummy you've got in your hand'; this use has crept into the speech of the educated, too, and may be seen in print.

Relative pronoun replaced by adverbial form

Provided that its antecedent is a thing, not a person, a relative pronoun preceded by one of several common prepositions (p. 211) may—in appropriate circumstances—be replaced, optionally, by the adverbial *wo(r)-*. The tone is then more formal; compare the following openings of a business and a private letter: *wir bestätigen den Erhalt Ihres Schreibens, worin Sie uns über den gegenwärtigen Stand der Verhandlungen mit der Firma Müller GmbH unterrichten* 'we acknowledge receipt of your letter in which you inform us as to the present state of negotiations with Messrs Müller Ltd.', *herzlichen Dank für Deinen lieben Brief, in dem Du so viel Spannendes aus Deinen Ferien erzählst* 'thank you so much for your kind letter in which you tell (me) of the many exciting things that happened during your holiday'. It may, however, be stressed that the latter construction would be equally acceptable in the first example; the reverse in the second example, on the other hand, would seem unduly stilted. It must also be said that, except as below, the adverbial construction is now relatively little used, the language by and large preferring the independent preposition with the relative pronoun, felt to be more precise. But if the antecedent is the main clause itself, the use of the adverbial relative remains standard practice: *die Hersteller mußten zu unerwartet niedrigen Preisen verkaufen, wodurch erhebliche Verluste entstanden* 'the producers had to sell at unexpectedly low prices, through which considerable losses arose'.

It remains to be said that, in purely literary style, conventional relatives not referring to persons may be replaced by archaizing *da(r)-*, e.g. *jenseits des Don liegt ein weites Gebiet, darüber* (= *worüber, über das*) *im vierten Jahrhundert die Goten herrschten* 'beyond the Don lies a wide area, over which the Goths ruled in the fourth century'.

Relative with 1st and 2nd person pronouns

If the antecedent is *ich, wir, du, ihr*, also *Sie*, the pronoun is repeated after the relative: *ich, der ich ein armer Sünder bin* 'I who am a poor sinner', *ihr, die ihr mich retten könnt* 'you who can save me', the reason for such repetition being that the unqualified relative, which is itself a 3rd person pronoun, would require the 3rd person verb. The above is, in the nature of the case, a bookish construction and is avoided in the commonly occurring use with the pronoun *es* and the verb *sein*, e.g. *du bist es also, der so viel Theater gemacht hat* 'so it's you who made all the fuss', where the verb in the relative clause is regularly in the 3rd person.

Relative in regional usage

There are various local divergencies from standard use. Especially in Swabian German, *wo* functions as the ordinary relative word: *Leute, wo kein Geld haben* 'people who have no money'; in parts of Central Germany, *was* has been similarly generalized: *Leute, was kein Geld haben* comparable to our own substandard 'people what have no money'. In other places, these words are used after the regular relative pronoun, thus also locally in the central area *Leute, die wo kein Geld haben*, in Upper German often *Leute, die was kein Geld haben*.

Unlinked relative clauses

The verbs *heißen* and *sich nennen* are associated with an exceptional construction in which the relative clause is not linked to the main clause by any relative word. Examples: *wir kennen einen hübschen Ort, heißt Zorge* 'we know a pretty place (which is) called Z.', *es gibt einen Schlangenfraß, nennt sich Schulessen* 'there's some awful muck called school dinner'.

There are certain expressions in which the demonstrative pronoun *der, die, das* effectively means 'the one who', etc.: *die mir gefällt, hält nichts von mir* 'the one (feminine) I like thinks nothing of me', *der dort steht, ist ihr Freund* 'the one standing over there is her boyfriend', *die so denken, machen einen großen Fehler* 'those who think like that are making a big mistake'. The same sense may be expressed by the more literary *derjenige, der*, etc., p. 206. It may be of interest to note that the saying *Ehre dem Ehre gebührt* 'honour to whom honour is due' is, historically speaking, an example of the present construction. Although today *dem* is felt to be a relative 'to whom', the original meaning was 'honour to him, honour is due'.

Close to the above is a construction employing the pronouns *wer, was*, etc.: *wer zuletzt lacht, lacht am besten* 'he who laughs last, laughs best'. The conventional translation 'he who' with its rather formal flavour must not disguise the fact that this construction is very common and occurs in contexts calling for a more colloquial rendering: (political slogan) *wer sich von Kohl einseifen läßt, wird von Strauß rasiert* 'if you let yourself be lathered (additional figurative meaning 'be taken in') by K., you'll be shaved by S.'. The pronoun may be followed by affective *da*, p. 323: (magazine) *wer da glaubt, Moskau lasse sich besänftigen, irrt sich gewaltig* 'anybody who believes that Moscow will be appeased is making a big mistake'. Further: *was noch übrig bleibt, könnt ihr unter euch teilen* 'what's left over you can divide among yourselves', also *worauf es ankommt, werden wir bald erfahren* 'we shall soon learn what is at stake'. Notice the proverbial *wen die Götter lieben, der stirbt jung* 'whom the gods love, die young' and popular expressions of the type *was ein rechter Bauer ist, der geht bei Wind und Wetter aufs Feld* which we can only paraphrase 'a good farmer is out and about in all weathers'. From this construction arose the general use of *wer* as an indefinite pronoun, p. 215.

23. Word Order

IT is not difficult to see that word order in German is to a large extent a matter of the position of the finite verb, which can come first, second, or at the end of its clause.

FINITE VERB FIRST

First position is natural in questions when there is no interrogative word: *hast du genug Geld?* 'have you enough money?' and in the syntactical development of such sentences seen in conditional clauses: *hast du genug Geld, dann können wir zwei Kilo kaufen* 'if you have enough money, we can buy two kilos', *wäre der Wechselkurs gefallen, so hätten die Banken einiges gewonnen* 'if the rate of exchange had fallen, the banks would have made some gains'. Further in wishes: *könnten wir es nur vergessen!* 'could we but forget it!' and in concessive clauses of the type *sei die Lage jetzt noch so schwierig, in einem Jahr wird sie sich gebessert haben* 'difficult though the position may now be, it will have improved in a year's time', *mag es noch so stark regnen, die Arbeit muß weitergehen* 'however hard it may rain, the work must go on'. The verb is likewise placed first in the hortative and imperative: *gehen wir! laßt uns gehen!* 'let us go!', *geh (du)!* '(you) go!', also *gehen Sie!* though this form is historically a present subjunctive (p. 260)—the same construction also in *Grüß (dich*, etc.) *Gott!* 'God greet (you)!', a greeting widely used in the far south, but otherwise in such use the subject comes first: *Gott behüte!* 'God forbid!', p. 261.

Initial position is not unknown in statements. In literature it has an archaic or poetic flavour: (bible) *spricht der Herr* 'the Lord sayeth', (folksong) *kommt ein Vogel geflogen* 'a bird comes a-flying'. In colloquial style, this order may be heard in dramatic narrative: *geht da plötzlich die Tür auf, stürzt ein wildfremder Mann ins Zimmer* 'suddenly the door opened and a man, a total stranger, rushed into the room'—on the present tense in German, see p. 231. Initial position is also found in a type of exclamatory statement: *'ist sie nicht klug!* 'my word, she i s clever!'. In origin, such a sentence is simply a modification of the interrogative *ist sie nicht klug?* 'isn't she clever?' which, of course, expects the answer 'yes'. As soon as this (negative) exclamatory pattern was established, corresponding positive exclamations became possible, hence synonymous *'ist sie klug!* Other examples:

'hast du Glück! 'you a r e lucky!', *'war das eine Hetze!* 'that w a s a rush!', *'hat er ausgesehen!* 'what a sight he looked!' In another colloquial use, initial position with an emphatic nuance occurs as follows: *dort sind die Äpfel aus unserem Obstgarten — können Sie welche mitnehmen* 'the apples from our orchard are over there—you can take some with you'.

First position is also seen in emphatic commands using the indicative: *geht ihr raus!* 'out with you!', *wirst du Ruhe geben!* 'be quiet, I say!'. Exceptionally, substandard *bist du so gut!*, etc. 'be so kind' (p. 247) is not necessarily emphatic. This position is normal in connection with (unstressed) *doch*, e.g. *hatte ich doch 'Glück!* 'how fortunate I was!'. It further occurs in the traditional phrase *weiß Gott!* 'God knows!', whence analogically *weiß der Kuckuck!* 'heaven (lit. 'the cuckoo') knows!', etc.—such phrases are, however, purely interjections, otherwise regular *Gott weiß*. Finally, first position again in sentences with *mögen*, as *mag kommen, was will* 'come what may'; other examples, p. 261.

FINITE VERB SECOND

The finite verb takes second place in statements which form a main clause, the first element in normal order being the subject: *wir sind gestern angekommen* 'we arrived yesterday'. Theoretically, however, any part of the sentence can come first, which generally implies at least a slight emphasis on the part so placed (see further below): *gestern sind wir angekommen, angekommen sind wir gestern*. The first place is very often taken by the object: *ihr Hochzeitskleid hättet ihr sehen müssen!* 'you should have seen her wedding dress!', *fette Speisen mag ich nicht* 'I don't like fatty foods', and just as often by a prepositional phrase: *für jede Antwort gibt es Punkte* 'there are marks (points) for every answer', *in der Innenstadt kam der Verkehr zum Erliegen* 'in the city centre the traffic came to a halt'. For particular emphasis an infinitive may precede, as very commonly in spoken style: *hinübergehen darfst du nicht* 'you mustn't go across'. Not infrequently, in more cultivated language, an inseparable word-group comes first: *auf einen gemeinsamen Nenner bringen läßt sich das nicht* 'those things cannot be reduced to a common denominator', *in einen derartigen Beruf einsteigen möchte ich schon* 'I should indeed like to enter such a profession'.

The finite verb may be preceded by an 'if' clause: *ist der Mangel auf Material- oder Fertigungsfehler zurückzuführen, leisten wir selbstverständlich kostenlos Ersatz* 'if the fault is due to defects in the material or in the manufacturing process, we shall of course replace the article free of charge'. It may likewise be preceded by a subordinate clause: *nachdem er sich ausgezogen hatte, legte er sich ins Bett* 'after he had undressed, he got into bed', *ohne ein Wort zu sagen, wandte sie sich um und ging davon* 'without saying a word, she turned round and walked away', but a *was* clause commenting on the main clause is regarded as paratactical and does not therefore affect word order: *was noch schlimmer war, sein Gehalt wurde gekürzt* 'what was worse still, his salary was reduced'. Several types of concessive clause are similarly treated as paratactical, and the same is occasionally true of a conditional clause, see examples *passim* pp. 263 ff. It may happen that two main clauses share the same logical subject; for purposes of word order, they are treated as separate clauses: *die einzelnen Wörter einer Sprache dürfen nicht isoliert, sie müssen vielmehr im Zusammenhang des Satzes betrachtet und gelernt werden* 'the individual words of a language are not to be seen and learnt in isolation, but rather in the context of the sentence'.

The finite verb may come second after a conjunction: *er tat, als hätte er nichts gesehen* 'he acted as though he had seen nothing'. The verb further comes second in dependent clauses which have no conjunction: *ich meine, er müßte bald hier sein* 'I think he should be here soon', although historically speaking this is a case of two main clauses in juxtaposition, the regular word of such clauses remaining unchanged. Inversion of subject and object is found with verbs of saying, thinking, etc. after a quotation or its equivalent: *"gut", sagte sie, "wir fahren sofort"* ' "good", she said, "we'll go at once"', *großartig! habe ich gedacht* 'great! I thought'.

After conjunctions, etc.

The conjunctions *aber* and *sondern* 'but', *denn* 'because', *oder* 'or' are not regarded as forming part of a clause and therefore do not modify the word order: *aber er antwortete* 'but he replied', and similarly (literary) *es 'sei denn* 'unless': *die Polizei darf nicht eingreifen, es sei denn, ein Hausfriedensbruch liegt vor* 'the police may not interfere unless there is a violation of the privacy of a person's house'. The conjunction *und* is regularly so treated; exceptionally, however, for stylistic variety in the written language, it may cause inversion of subject and verb: (private letter) *unlängst machten wir einen Ausflug nach Villach, und hatten wir sehr schönes Wetter* 'we recently took a trip to V., and had lovely weather', (business communication) *wir wollen Sie davon benachrichtigen, daß Ihr Sparkassenzertifikat am 25. September 1985 fällig wird, und machen wir Ihnen zur Wiederanlage folgende Angebote* 'we wish to inform you that your Savings Bank Certificate matures on 25th September 1985, and make you the following offers for reinvestment'.

Other conjunctions may be optionally regarded as part of the clause, in which case they affect the word order. These are *entweder* 'either' and the adverbial *doch* or *jedoch* 'however': *entweder er kommt* or *kommt er morgen oder wartet bis übermorgen* 'he will either come tomorrow or wait until the day after tomorrow', *doch (jedoch) sein Geld ging aus* or *ging sein Geld aus* 'however his money ran out'.

The particles or adverbs *auch* 'too', *bereits* and *schon* 'already', and *kaum* 'hardly' refer either to the whole clause, in which case they are treated as independent elements affecting the word order, or else they qualify a certain word with which they then form a single syntactic unit having no influence on the order of words: *auch trank er übermäßig* 'he drank immoderately, too', *auch er trank übermäßig* 'he, too, drank immoderately', *bereits* or *schon hatte mein Bruder die nötigen Schritte unternommen* 'my brother had already taken the necessary steps', *bereits* or *schon mein Bruder hatte die nötigen Schritte unternommen*, stressing *mein Bruder*, something like 'even my brother, etc.', *kaum blieb ein Platz frei* 'hardly a seat remained vacant', *kaum ein Platz blieb frei*, stressing *ein Platz*, something like 'not a single seat, etc.' Notice also a use of the negative particle: *nicht er ist dafür verantwortlich* 'it is not he who is responsible'.

FINITE VERB AT THE END

It is convenient to distinguish usage in main and subordinate clauses.

Main clauses

Final position in a main clause occurs chiefly in exclamations, though such use is optional, second position being equally a possibility: *wie wir gelacht haben!* 'how we laughed!', *wie warm das Wetter ist!* 'how warm the weather is!', *was er uns alles erzählt hat!* 'the things he told us!', alternatively, and in these examples stylistically somewhat more elevated: *wie haben wir gelacht! wie ist das Wetter warm! was hat er uns alles erzählt!* In simpler style *was* may be substituted for *wie*, e.g. *was wir gelacht haben!* also *was haben wir gelacht!*, the word order again optional, but this time without any tangible stylistic difference, and the same applies to alternatives of the type *was du für ein dummer Kerl bist! was bist du für ein dummer Kerl!* 'what a silly chap you are!'

Final position is also seen in clauses introduced by *je*, e.g. *je tiefer man in die deutsche Sprache eindringt, desto mehr Gefühl bekommt man für deren Feinheiten* 'the better one gets to know the German language, the more feeling one acquires for its finer points'. Note the parallelism in the proverbial *wes Brot ich esse, des Lob ich singe* 'I sing the praise of him whose bread I eat'.

It goes without saying that the second position becomes final position also in sentences like *die Glocke läutet*; for the purpose of classification such examples are referred to the second position, as in *die Glocke läutet hell* 'the bell rings clear'.

Subordinate clauses

It is, of course, in subordinate clauses introduced by a subordinating word (conjunction, relative pronoun) that the finite verb characteristically takes the final position: *er erkundigte sich, ob sie Zeit hätte* 'he enquired if she had time', *sie sagte, daß sie ihn sehen würde* 'she said that she would see him', *dort liegt das Haus, in dem sie früher gewohnt haben* 'there is the house they used to live in', *die Eltern, hieß es, wüßten am besten, was gut für die Kinder sei* 'the parents, it was said, would know best what was good for the children'.

Variations of the general rule are seen in the construction where the infinitive replaces the perfect participle (p. 257), as in the sentence *er hat nicht helfen wollen* 'he didn't want to help'; in a subordinate clause, both infinitives follow the finite verb: *sie weiß, daß er nicht hat helfen wollen* 'she knows that he didn't want to help'. Also with three infinitives: *man stellt sich vor, daß er hat betteln gehen müssen* 'one imagines that he had to go begging', where *betteln gehen* is naturally felt as a unit. By the same token, a phrase attached to an infinitive will not be separated from it: *ich frage mich, wie die Menschen in diesen Unruheherden jemals werden zur Ruhe kommen können* 'I wonder how the people in these troubled places will ever be able to settle down peacefully'. When the finite verb is *werden*, however, practice often varies, thus *wir wissen nicht, ob er sich in der neuen Stellung wird behaupten können* or *behaupten können wird* 'we don't know if he will be able to hold his own in his new post'. The former alternative is reminiscent of certain spoken styles and there is some consensus that the finite verb should preferably come at the end, unless that would upset the rhythm of the sentence. This precept is illustrated in the last example but one above—the alternative *zur Ruhe kommen können werden* hardly being elegant. Less usually, the stylistic problem may be resolved by placing the finite verb between the infinitives: (magazine) *"ich glaube, daß Österreich seine Neutralität gar nicht verteidigen wird müssen", sagte der Außenminister* ' "I believe that Austria will not be called upon to defend her neutrality at all", the foreign minister said', an arrangement sometimes heard in the spoken language with other auxiliaries, too: *sie weiß, daß er nicht helfen hat wollen*.

As a further variation, an infinitive with *zu* follows the finite verb in more popular style: *da es aufgehört hatte zu regnen, haben wir unseren Spaziergang fortgesetzt* 'since it had stopped raining, we continued our walk', in a literary style: *da es zu regnen aufgehört hatte, setzten wir unseren Spaziergang fort*. On the other hand, expressions of the type *ich habe zu tun* may not be so modified, e.g. only *ich will nichts mehr mit ihr zu tun haben* 'I won't have anything more to do with her'. Compare the position of a *wie* clause: in everyday language e.g. *er wird kämpfen wie ein Löwe* 'he will fight like a lion', more formally *er wird wie ein Löwe kämpfen*, and similarly an *als* clause: *er wird auftreten als Bauer* 'he will appear (say, in a play) as a farmer', alternatively *er wird als Bauer auftreten*.

In the spoken language, though not normally in writing, other deviations from the general rule can be heard locally, as when the finite verb is followed by an infinitive: *Gott behüte, daß ich blind soll werden!* 'God forbid that I should go blind!', *das ist der Mann, von dem du wirst gehört haben* 'that is the man you will have heard about'. A perfect participle may, again in local use, follow its finite part: *ich weiß, wie das gemacht ist worden* 'I know how it has been done'.

It will have been noticed that in certain of the examples above, the verbal elements in the subordinate clause occur in the same order as they would in a main clause, in spite of the subordinating conjunction. This tendency, most evident in the unaffected colloquial, can also appear after other conjunctions, e.g. *ich habe mein Geld bei der Postsparkasse angelegt, weil dort ist der Zinssatz höher* 'I've put my money into the post office savings bank, because the rate of interest is higher there', *obwohl er erzählt die tollsten Geschichten, ist doch überall ein Quentchen Wahrheit dran* 'although he tells the most fantastic tales, there's a grain of truth in all of them'. It goes without saying that such usage is substandard.

FINITE VERB NOT IN FINAL POSITION IN SUBORDINATE ORDER

Despite the overall rule that the finite verb comes last in a subordinate clause (as above), it is nothing unusual today to find a prepositional phrase taking precedence over the verb and appearing in final position itself. This order will often be preferred to keep sense groups together, notably when a relative clause has to be accommodated: *er versicherte, daß er nicht verbittert sei über das, was in Deutschland vorgehe* 'he gave an assurance that he was not embittered by what was going on in Germany'. Final position may be chosen for emphasis, following the principle that an important concept may come last, p. 346; feeling for rhythm and sentence balance can also play a part here, as elsewhere these days, the freer practice of the spoken language being more and more reflected in writing: *ihr Mutterherz blutete bei dem Gedanken, daß ihr Sohn hinausgeschickt werden könnte in das Inferno der Schlachtfelder* 'her mother's heart bled at the thought that her son could be sent out into the inferno of the battlefields', *ich war froh, daß ich noch zu jung gewesen war für diesen Krieg* 'I was glad that I had been too young for this war', *hier werden die Voraussetzungen geschaffen, damit die Menschen freundlich sein können zu einander* 'here the conditions are being created for people to be kind to each other', *das sind gewaltige Investitionen, die uns unabhängig machen können von Importen* 'these are huge investments which can make us independent of imports', *ich sage dir, was ich gesehen habe beim Nachbarn* 'I'll tell you what I saw next door'. A prepositional adverb may likewise occupy the final position: *er sagt, daß nicht viel übrig bleibt davon* 'he says that not much of it remains'. Whereas, in given cases, such word order may be the more spontaneous, it can nevertheless be regarded as optional, hence alternatively e.g. *die uns von Importen unabhängig machen können*, or *was ich beim Nachbarn gesehen habe*.

POSITION OF INFINITIVE

The infinitive normally takes the final position both in a main clause and in its own clause: *die Schauspielerin beschloß, ein Ausreisevisum zu beantragen, weil sie es satt hatte, sich systemkonform zu verhalten* 'the actress resolved to apply for an exit visa because she was fed up with conforming to the system', *neun Monate später durfte sie ausreisen* 'nine months later she was allowed to leave', the same construed with the perfect: *neun Monate später hat sie ausreisen dürfen*. The infinitive takes precedence over a perfect participle: *solche Fehler wollen erklärt werden* 'such errors call for explanation'.

At the same time, in principle as described in the preceding section, a prepositional phrase will often be found after the infinitive: *der erste Freund entschuldigte sich, er könne ihn nicht begleiten wegen anderer Geschäfte* 'the first friend excused himself (saying, p. 270) he could not accompany him on account of other business', *die Absicht der Regierung war klar: die Bevölkerung sollte sich abfinden mit Teilung und Trennung* 'the intention of the government was clear: the population was to resign itself to division and separation'. Such order is very common in spoken language: *du sollst nicht laut reden über diese Dinge!* 'you shouldn't talk about these things aloud!', *wieviel wollen Sie ausgeben für einen neuen Wagen?* 'how much do you want to give for a new car?' In this style adverbs, too, especially prepositional adverbs, frequently take precedence over the infinitive: *man kann ihm nicht helfen dabei* 'one can't help him (in the matter), *wie viel können wir wegschmeißen davon?* 'how much of it can we chuck out?', but also e.g. *das kann eingeplant werden noch* 'that can still be allowed for (in the planning)'.

For emphasis, the infinitive may take the first position in the sentence, see pp. 247, 346.

POSITION OF PERFECT PARTICIPLE

Like the infinitive, the perfect participle is normally placed at the end of the main clause: *Simmel hat einen neuen Roman geschrieben, und endlich wird er vom Fernsehen ernst genommen* 'S. has written a new novel and, at last, he is being taken seriously by television'. The infinitive, however, takes precedence over this participle, see previous section. In subordinate clauses the finite verb has the prior claim to final position, p. 331.

As with the infinitive and for the same reasons, a prepositional group often follows the participle: *das Lichtgott wird symbolisiert durch das Feuer* 'the god of light is symbolized by fire', *er war hell begeistert von diesem Land und seinen Leuten* 'he was thrilled by this country and its people', *jahrelang machte er als Schauspieler von sich reden, jetzt ist es still geworden um ihn* 'as an actor, he was for years in the news, but now he is forgotten'. This is sometimes the idiomatically usual order: *was habt ihr Schönes mitgebracht aus Wien?* 'what nice things have you brought back from Vienna?', *ich habe mich sehr geärgert über den Fehler* 'I was very annoyed about the mistake', *du hast dich da ein bißchen vergaloppiert mit deiner Kritik* 'you've made a bit of a mistake there with your criticism'.

The above word order is also commonly used to prevent a participle getting too far adrift from its auxiliary: (after Cicero) *sie haben gehandelt mit dem Mut von Männern und der Einsicht von Schulknaben* 'they have acted with the courage of men and the wisdom of schoolboys', at the same time conveniently keeping sense groups together: *vor zwei Monaten hat sie Schluß gemacht mit dieser Beziehung, die keine mehr war* 'two months ago she put an end to this relation which really no longer existed'. At the same time, the spontaneous colloquial may break up a sense-group, keeping the more significant element in its regular place: *sein Vater hat schon einiges zurückgezahlt von dem Darlehen* 'his father has already repaid a certain amount of the loan', (letter) *dein Onkel hat dieses Buch nicht gekannt, aber andere Bücher hat er gern gelesen von Agnon* 'your uncle didn't know this book, but he enjoyed reading other books by A.'.

Adverbs, too, may take precedence over the participle, especially in casual speech: *habt ihr viel gehört davon?* 'have you heard much about it?', *ich habe ihn gar nicht gesehen heute* 'I haven't seen him today at all', more or less equivalent to *habt ihr viel davon gehört?* or *heute habe ich ihn gar nicht gesehen*, cf. p. 345.

The perfect participle is often used without a finite form, when it commonly comes last in its clause: (caption) *die barocke Klosterkirche Grauhof, 1711 von Augustiner Chorherren erbaut* 'the baroque monastic church "Grey Court", built in 1711 by Augustinian canons'; it may be followed by a prepositional phrase: *Gebühr bezahlt beim Postamt* 'postage paid (at the post office)'. It is, however, frequently moved forward to the first place in its clause: (caption) *ein Selbstporträt Picassos aus seiner Blauen Periode, datiert aus dem Jahre 1901* 'a self-portrait by Picasso from his Blue Period, dated 1901'. For stylistic variation, initial and final position can occur side by side: (encyclopedia) *Barock: Kunstrichtung von zirka 1680 bis 1850, gekennzeichnet durch verschnörkelte, dekorative, üppige Formen, in Italien zur höchsten Blüte entfaltet* 'Baroque: artistic school from c.1680 to 1850, characterized by ornate, decorative, luxuriant forms, developed to the peak of perfection in Italy'. Initial position is usual in such examples as *der Koran, übersetzt und erläutert von . . .* 'the Koran, translated and commented on by . . .', the participles being placed next to the word they refer to.

POSITION OF PRESENT PARTICIPLE

The present participle, like the perfect, may be used without a finite form, when it usually comes last in its clause: *der alte Mann stand am offenen Fenster, die geschäftige Menge unten auf der Straße wehmütig beobachtend* 'the old man stood by the open window, wistfully contemplating the bustling crowd in the street below', *nichts Böses ahnend ging ich die Straße entlang, da sah ich dich, mein Freund!* 'I was walking down the street anticipating no ill, then suddenly I saw you, my friend!'. In some instances the participle may, optionally, stand first: *ausgehend von den Ergebnissen der letzten Meinungsumfrage, rechnen wir mit einem Regierungswechsel nach den Wahlen* 'judging by the results of the last opinion poll we are expecting a change of government after the elections'.

POSITION OF PHRASES INTRODUCED BY *ALS* OR *WIE*

These will either be enclosed within the sentence or clause, or else placed at the end; where alternatives are possible, the latter will be the less formal: *ein schöneres Haus als dieses haben wir nie gehabt*, alternatively e.g. *nie haben wir ein schöneres Haus gehabt als dieses* 'never have we had a nicer house than this one', *man sah, daß sie genauso verblüfft waren wie wir selber* 'one saw that they were just as amazed as we were ourselves', similarly *er hat wie ein Narr gehandelt* or *er hat gehandelt wie ein Narr* 'he acted like a fool'. In non-comparative use, however, the phrase will ordinarily be enclosed: *er*

wird als Freund zu Ihnen kommen 'he will come to you as a friend',
but in emphatic order *er wird zu Ihnen kommen als Freund.*

VERBS WITH SEPARABLE PREFIX

According to the basic canon the separated prefix is to be placed at the
end of the main clause: *sie klagten ihn wegen Diebstahls an* 'they
accused him of theft', and similarly at the end of any clause with direct
word order: *es hieß, sie klagten ihn wegen Diebstahls an* 'it was said
they accused him of theft'. In subordinate order, however, the prefix
gives way to the verb: *es wurde berichtet, daß sie ihn wegen Diebstahls
anklagten* 'it was reported that they accused him of theft'.

Nevertheless, in contemporary usage, there is a tendency to move
the separated prefix closer to the verb by allowing an otherwise
intervening prepositional phrase to take the final position. Thus
instead of *nächsten Montag findet eine Tagung über den Mißbrauch
von Alkohol statt* 'a conference on the abuse of alcohol is taking place
next Monday', many will nowadays prefer the alternative *nächsten
Montag findet eine Tagung statt über den Mißbrauch von Alkohol.*
Other examples: *die Wahlversammlung klang aus mit dem Deutsch-
landlied* 'the election meeting closed with the (German) national
anthem', *unser aller Leben hängt ab von Energie* 'the lives of us all
depend on energy'. This order is quite common in everyday style:
(slogan) *machen Sie mit bei der Staatslotterie!* 'have a go in the state
lottery!', just like conversational *wir kommen nicht durch mit dem
Auto* 'we can't get through with the car'.

Clauses of various sorts can come between the verb and its prefix:
*die Krankheit klingt dann, wenn nicht eine zusätzliche Ansteckung
erfolgt, die den Patienten belastet, in Kürze wieder ab* 'the illness then
soon subsides provided that no additional infection takes place which
adversely affects the patient'. In line with the trend nowadays towards
keeping verb and prefix closer to each other, the above sentence could
well appear as *die Krankheit klingt dann in Kürze wieder ab, wenn
nicht eine zusätzliche Ansteckung erfolgt, die den Patienten belastet.*
This more direct order has, in any case, always been the rule in the
spoken language.

In popular style an infinitive with *zu* follows the prefix: *es hört auf
zu regnen* 'the rain's stopping', more formally *es hört zu regnen auf.*
Popular style is obviously required in the following: *eine Katze trifft im
Dunkeln auf eine Fledermaus. "Verdammt noch mal", schimpft sie,
"jetzt fangen die Biester auch noch an zu fliegen"* 'a cat came across a
bat (lit. 'flittermouse') in the dark. "Damn it", she cursed, "now the
beggars are starting to fly as well"'. A long infinitive phrase will
normally follow the prefix in any register: *darauf hoben die Geigen an,*

träumerisch eine längst vergessene Melodie zu spielen 'thereupon the violins began dreamily to play a long forgotten melody' (*anheben* 'begin' only in high style).

INCAPSULATION

As in English, an attributive adjective is often preceded by an adverb or other complement: *diese etwas merkwürdige Geschichte* 'this rather curious story', *die drei Mann starke Abordnung* 'the three-man-strong delegation'. In German, such complements exceed anything possible in English: *eine bis zu zwei Tonnen schwere Ladung* 'a load of up to two tonnes'. This is typically the case before participles in formal written style: (pres. part.) *der am Wegrand stehende Baum* 'the tree standing by the wayside', *eine die ganze Familie angehende, aufregende Nachricht* 'an exciting piece of news concerning the whole family', (perf. part.) *in buntes Papier schön eingewickelte Geschenke* 'presents nicely wrapped up in brightly coloured paper', *auf eine im einzelnen nicht mehr ganz aufgeklärte Weise* 'in a manner never fully elucidated in detail'. Quite involved complements are not unusual: *Träger des europäischen Realismus war ein seiner selbst bewußtes, aus den Quellen der Aufklärung und der Französischen Revolution schöpfendes, an modernen liberalen und demokratischen Ideen orientiertes Bürgertum* 'the exponent of European realism was a middle class, conscious of itself, drawing from the springs of the Enlightenment and the French Revolution, (and) guided by modern liberal and democratic ideas'.

In less formal style, alternative constructions will be employed, generally a relative clause: *der Baum, der am Weg steht*, etc.

DATIVE AND ACCUSATIVE

As the general rule the indirect (dative) object precedes the direct (accusative) object in so far as these are both nouns: *ich gebe dem Gepäckträger den Koffer* 'I give the porter the suitcase'. The same applies when the indirect object is a pronoun: *ich gebe ihm den Koffer* 'I give him the suitcase'. A pronoun as the direct object, however, precedes the indirect: *ich gebe ihn dem Gepäckträger* 'I give it (the suitcase) to the porter', *ich gebe ihn ihm* 'I give him it'.

Modifications of the general rule

The normal dative–accusative order may be reversed: *ich gebe den Koffer dem Gepäckträger*. Taking this sentence in isolation, the indirect object is now emphasized, hence e.g. *ich gebe den Koffer dem Gepäckträger, nicht dem Schaffner* 'not to the ticket collector'. Such order can be syntactically convenient: *ich gebe den Koffer dem*

Gepäckträger, der ihn zum Zoll bringt 'who takes it to the customs'. The accusative may also be placed first to bring it into closer contact with some previous mention: *was sollen wir mit den vielen Koffern machen? — gib den großen dem Gepäckträger, die kleinen tragen wir selber* 'what shall we do with all the suitcases?—give the big one to the porter, and we'll carry the little ones ourselves'. Or sentence balance may require this order: *ich gebe den Koffer dem Gepäckträger mit dem großen Schubkarren* 'I give the suitcase to the porter with the large barrow'.

If the direct object is an animate, but the indirect an institution or the like, the former precedes regardless of any emphasis: *man lieferte den Terroristen seinem Heimatland aus* 'the terrorist was extradited to his country of origin', similarly *er überließ den Freund seinem Schicksal* 'he left his friend to his fate'—by contrast e.g. *ich kann Ihrem Freund die Ware billig überlassen* 'I can let your friend have the goods cheap'.

When both objects are pronouns, the normal accusative–dative order can in certain cases be reversed, so emphasizing the direct object. Contrast (usual order) *er stellte sie mir vor* 'he introduced her to me', *er stellte mich ihr vor* 'he introduced her to me', but (emphatic order) *er stellte mir 'sie (ihr 'mich) vor.*

In the colloquial of some areas the pronoun *es* in the reduced form *'s* may ordinarily follow *mir, dir,* thus *er zeigt mir's* 'he shows it to me', *sie hat dir's erzählt* 'she told you it', otherwise *er zeigt es* (or *'s) mir, sie hat es* (or *'s) dir erzählt.* The form *'s* is admissible in written work, too.

When, in a neutrally couched statement, the indirect object only is a personal pronoun, it is placed between an inverted subject and verb unless the former is itself a personal pronoun or *man* 'one': *nachher hat mir meine Mutter alles erzählt* 'afterwards my mother told me everything', but *nachher hat sie (man) mir alles erzählt.* Should the direct as well as the indirect object be a personal pronoun, then both are usually moved forward: *nachher hat es mir meine Mutter erzählt,* but *nachher hat sie (man) es mir erzählt.* By contrast the order *nachher hat meine Mutter mir alles (es mir) erzählt* places some emphasis on the subject. Such order is, however, occasionally obligatory to avoid ambiguity: *die Nachbarin ist wieder da; gestern hat meine Tochter sie besucht* 'our neighbour is back again; my daughter visited her yesterday', the order *hat sie meine Tochter besucht* making *sie* the subject.

Word order as above is also found in questions: *hat dir meine Mutter alles erzählt? hat es dir meine Mutter erzählt?* beside (with some emphasis on the subject) *hat meine Mutter dir alles (es dir) erzählt?,* substituting the personal pronoun as subject: *hat sie dir alles (es dir) erzählt?* Notice with emphatic order *hat sie alles 'dir erzählt?* In given cases, as here, emphasis may be realized in speaking simply by stressing, regardless of word order, hence also *hat sie 'alles dir erzählt?*

In subordinate clauses, the indirect pronoun can optionally precede the noun subject: *die Bardame hatte gesehen, wie ihm der Schankwirt* (or *wie der Schankwirt ihm*) *das Diebsgut abkaufte* 'the barmaid had seen the licensee buying the stolen goods from him'; the direct object can equally well be a pronoun: *wie ihm der Schankwirt es* (or *wie der Schankwirt es ihm*) *abkaufte.*

Adverbs and adverbial phrases are regularly placed between the two objects provided that the direct object is not a personal pronoun: *der Pfarrer überbrachte deinem Vater heute morgen die traurige Nachricht* 'the vicar passed on the sad news to your father this morning', *mein Mann hat mir gestern zu unserem Hochzeitstag einen Pelzmantel geschenkt* 'yesterday my husband made me a present of a fur coat for our wedding anniversary'. But such complements follow when the direct object is a personal pronoun: *der Pfarrer überbrachte sie deinem Vater heute morgen, mein Mann hat ihn mir gestern zu unserem Hochzeitstag geschenkt.*

PERSONAL PRONOUN OBJECT

Like any other object, a personal pronoun in this function follows the finite verb in direct order: *unser Sohn hat ihn mehrmals getroffen* 'our son has met him several times'. In the case of the pronoun, the same commonly applies when subject and verb are inverted, except when the subject itself is a personal pronoun or *man* 'one', hence commonly *heute morgen hat ihn unser Sohn getroffen* 'our son met him this morning', but always *heute morgen hat er ihn getroffen*. The pronoun object may similarly precede the noun subject in subordinate order: *da ihn Marianne nicht kannte* 'since M. didn't know him', but substituting a pronoun: *da sie ihn nicht kannte.*

The order object–subject, however, causes ambiguity when the animate object is *sie* 'her, them' and the subject a feminine or plural, p. 339. In such cases the order must always be subject–object: *sie ist nicht zu Hause? — wo hat meine Schwester sie denn gesehen?* 'she's not at home?—so where did my sister see her?', *wo hat sie meine Schwester denn gesehen?* meaning of course 'so where did she see my sister?'. Similarly *dann haben meine Eltern sie bemerkt* 'then my parents noticed them'. By analogy, this order may be found in other cases as well, particularly when the finite verb is an auxiliary, e.g. alternative *heute morgen hat unser Sohn ihn getroffen*, likewise *da Marianne ihn nicht kannte*. The same again in questions: *hat ihn unser Sohn getroffen?* or *hat unser Sohn ihn getroffen?* Further in this connection emphasis may be involved, the subject or object coming first depending on which is the more significant: *kann der Arzt mich schon heute sehen? — nein, erst morgen kann Sie der Arzt sehen* 'can the doctor see me today?—no, the doctor can only see you tomorrow'.

It goes without saying that here, as elsewhere in related matters of word order, pronouns other than personal pronouns or *man* are treated as nouns, hence e.g. *gestern hat mich jemand* (or *jemand mich*) *gefragt* 'yesterday someone asked me', *da uns niemand* (or *niemand uns*) *kennt* 'since no one knows us'.

REFLEXIVE PRONOUN

Where relevant, the rules given in the preceding two sections in so far as they relate to personal pronouns are in principle also valid for the reflexive pronoun. It, too, basically follows the finite verb: *etwas regt sich* 'something's stirring', *sein Sohn hat sich verletzt* 'his son injured himself'.

Compare further: *er muß sich die Hände waschen* 'he must wash his hands', *er muß sie sich waschen* 'he must wash them'. The pronoun again commonly follows the inverted verb, and always so when the subject is a personal pronoun or *man* 'one': *dann sieht sich der Gast um*, possible also *dann sieht der Gast sich um* 'then the guest looks around', but always *dann sieht er sich um*. Likewise in questions: *regt sich etwas?* or (but in this particular example rather unusual) *regt etwas sich?* 'is something stirring?', *hat sich sein Sohn verletzt?* or *hat sein Sohn sich verletzt?* 'did his son injure himself?' The object may similarly precede the noun subject in subordinate order: *da sich seine Freundin eine Wohnung einrichtet, kann sie jede Mark gebrauchen* 'since his girlfriend is furnishing a flat, she can use every mark', on the other hand with a pronoun subject *da sie sich eine Wohnung einrichtet*, etc., further *es ist nicht nötig, daß sich Schwiegermutter und Schwiegertochter furchtbar lieben, sie heiraten sich ja nicht* 'it is not necessary for mother-in-law and daughter-in-law to be frightfully in love with each other, after all they don't marry each other', but substituting a pronoun subject only *daß sie sich furchtbar lieben*. Observe that, as a rule of thumb, *sich* will immediately follow a relative pronoun: *oft sind es die Lehrer, die sich über das Benehmen der Jugend am meisten beklagen* 'it is often the teachers who complain most about the behaviour of young people'.

Notwithstanding the general tendency outlined above, the reflexive pronoun is sometimes preferably used not before, but after the subject noun: *wenn ein Volk sich von einem Tyrannen verleiten läßt* 'if a nation allows itself to be misled by a tyrant' may be felt as more formal or more elegant than the banal-sounding *wenn sich ein Volk von einem Tyrannen verleiten läßt*. Out of similar considerations the reflexive may be moved away from an interrogative pronoun: *der Kulturattaché hat gewiß den Überblick, wer in der DDR sich mit Russistik befaßt* 'the cultural attaché will have an overall picture of those (scholars) in the GDR who are concerned with Russian language and literature'. The pronoun is thus somewhat mobile, a quality often taken advantage of by the poets: (Goethe) *in der ungeheuren Weite / reget keine Welle sich* 'on the vast expanse not a wave is stirring'.

Finally, the reflexive pronoun heads an infinitive phrase: *jetzt haben sie die Gelegenheit, sich von dieser Verpflichtung zu befreien* 'now they have the opportunity to free themselves from this commitment'.

Other personal pronouns used reflexively follow the above practices, e.g. *ich muß mir die Hände waschen* 'I must wash my hands', *ich muß sie mir waschen* 'I must wash them', or *jetzt hast du die Gelegenheit, dich von dieser Verpflichtung zu befreien* 'now you have the opportunity to free yourself from this commitment'.

ADVERBS

Two or more adverbs together

Adverbs or adverbial phrases, occurring adjacently, will in general follow the sequence time–manner–place: *sie fliegen morgen mit der Concorde nach New York* 'they are flying to N.Y. tomorrow by Concorde'. Where adverbial elements are of the same kind, the general precedes the specific: *gestern um sieben Uhr* 'yesterday at seven o'clock'. Despite the overall rule, the order manner–place is reversed in sentences like *man kann dort gut essen* 'one can eat well there', where *gut* is felt to be the word most emphatically qualifying *essen* and therefore placed next to it. The order is also reversed if the place rather than the time is to be more emphasized: *warum ist in Buxtehude nach sechs Uhr abends nie etwas los?* 'why is there never anything doing in B. after six o'clock in the evening?'

Adverb and noun object

A direct object, other than a personal pronoun, commonly follows an adverb or adverbial phrase: *ich schreibe selten lange Briefe* 'I rarely write long letters', *wir haben hier das Gemüsefeld, dort den Rasen* 'we have the vegetable patch here, (and) the lawn there', *Frau Becker kocht immer in der Früh einen Haferbrei* 'Mrs B. always makes porridge in the morning'. In the written language the object may appear at some distance from the verb: *Fritz Haber erhielt für die Entwicklung der Ammoniaksynthese, Grundlage für die Massenerzeugung von*

Kunstdünger, 1918 den Nobelpreis 'F.H. received the Nobel prize in 1918 for the development of the synthetic ammonia process, the basis for the mass production of artificial fertilizer'. In certain instances this order adds a touch of emphasis to the adverbial element: *im Deutschen gibt es in der Wortfolge mehr Möglichkeiten als im Englischen* (alternatively *mehr Möglichkeiten in der Wortfolge*) 'in German there are more possibilities in word order than in English'. Final position may be associated with special emphasis, p. 346.

SUBJECT MOVED BACK

In basic order in a statement the finite verb follows directly after its subject: *die Menschen haben immer Sorgen* 'people always have worries'. In case of inversion the opposite naturally applies *gewiß haben die Menschen immer Sorgen* 'certainly people always have worries'. Given inversion, however, the subject (except when a personal pronoun or *man* 'one') may become separated from the verb, notably by personal pronouns, p. 340).Such a subject may also be moved back to or towards the end of the sentence if considerations of sentence rhythm or emphasis are felt to require it; final position may be associated with special emphasis, p. 346. Examples from a magazine: *am 9. Okt. 1955 wurde in der Bundesrepublik das Lottospiel eingeführt* 'on the 9th of Oct. 1955 *Lotto* (a lottery using sets of figure combinations) was introduced in the Federal Republic', *den höchsten Gewinn machte im Juli eine 38jährige Hausfrau aus Niedersachsen: fast 7 Millionen Mark* 'a 38-year-old housewife from Lower Saxony had the highest win: nearly 7 million marks', *es spielen pro Woche rund 25 Millionen Menschen Lotto* 'about 25 million persons per week take part in the lottery'. Since practice in such matters depends on feeling rather than stringent rules, alternatives are often possible. For instance, the first sentence above could equally well have appeared in normal order: *am 9. Okt. 1955 wurde das Lottospiel in der Bundesrepublik eingeführt*.

POSITION OF RELATIVE CLAUSE

The relative clause normally follows its antecedent: *man traut einem Menschen, der ehrlich ist* 'one trusts a person who is honest'. But this order may be stylistically inappropriate. According to the general rule one would have e.g. *man kann einem Menschen, der ehrlich ist, trauen* 'one can trust a man who is honest'. But such a sentence is rather lop-sided, and one will normally substitute *man kann einem Menschen trauen, der ehrlich ist*. On the other hand the sentence *man kann einem Menschen, der ehrlich ist, voll und ganz* ('whole-heartedly') *trauen* is well balanced and stylistically acceptable, the relative retaining its usual position. But one could hardly place the relative clause directly after its antecedent in this sentence: *heute haben wir eine Rundfahrt in München gemacht, die wirklich interessant war* 'today we made a tour through Munich, which was really interesting'. In certain structures, however, alternatives may be equally possible: *ist das wasserbeständig, was du drauf gibst* or less informally *ist das, was du drauf gibst, wasserbeständig?* 'is what you are putting on it waterproof?'

INFLEXIONS AND WORD ORDER

The freedom enjoyed by German in point of word order is, to no small extent, the due to the varying forms of the articles, giving the language a great advantage over English in this respect. To take the simplest of examples, the sentence 'the father sees the daughter' can be given in German as either *der Vater sieht die Tochter* or *die Tochter sieht der Vater*, ambiguity being excluded since *der Vater* can only be the subject. When the normal order is reversed, the position of the object at the head of the sentence serves to emphasize or otherwise highlight it, depending on the wider context—for details of such matters, see *passim* in the next section. In the same way German makes great use of the personal pronouns. Thus 'he sees the daughter' is either *er sieht die Tochter* or *die Tochter sieht er*, the latter again an everyday arrangement also unmatched in English.

But there are limitations to the German, too. If one is to express 'the mother sees the daughter' only *die Mutter sieht die Tochter* is possible, *die* as much as 'the' being invariable for nominative and accusative and unable to distinguish between subject and object. Similarly with a pronoun, thus 'she sees the daughter' is only *sie sieht die Tochter*, the sense being again fixed by the basic rule of sequence subject–verb–object. Nevertheless free order is still possible if the sense remains unambiguous: *seine Frau malt die Tür* 'his wife is painting the door' can therefore be changed to *die Tür malt seine Frau*. The same is possible when subject and object differ in number: *die ostgermanischen Sprachen vertritt das Gotische* 'Gothic represents the East Germanic languages'. Indeed, German can go further, for even in otherwise ambiguous statements the basic order may occasionally be reversed, especially in the spoken language, the wider context and the accentuation precluding any misunderstanding: *hat die Mutter die Schwester auf dem Jahrmarkt getroffen? — nein, vielmehr die 'Tochter hat sie getroffen* 'did mother meet her sister at the fair?—no, to be more precise, she met her daughter'.

EMPHATIC WORD ORDER

Particular cases of emphatic word order have, from time to time, already been mentioned. The following is intended as a more general statement.

Emphasized part first

Where variation of the basic sequence subject–verb–object is allowable, as it most often is, emphatic word order becomes possible, emphasis being most characteristically obtained by placing the object at the head of the sentence: *dich wollten wir sehen* '(it was) you we wanted to see', the emphasized word carrying an appreciable stress. The emphasis is often relatively slight and in many cases will not be expressed, and sometimes scarcely expressible, in idiomatic English, e.g. *Kuchen esse ich gern* 'I like (eating) cake', but with a nuance approaching 'cake is what, or one of the things, I like eating', further *Fehler machen die meisten von uns* 'most of us make mistakes', *leid tun mir alle, die ein solches Lehrbuch durchackern müssen* 'I'm pretty sorry for all those who have to plough through a textbook like that'. The indirect object or other dative may also stand first: *deinem Vater sagst du das?* 'are you telling that to your 'father?', *nicht mir hat er das versprochen, sondern dir* 'it wasn't me he promised it to, but you', *einem geschenkten Gaul schaut man nicht ins Maul* 'one doesn't look a gift horse in the mouth'.

An object is often placed first to bring it into closer relation to some previous mention, so adding an element of emphasis: *ich habe meinen braunen Mantel reinigen lassen, und den ziehe ich jetzt an* 'I've had my brown coat cleaned and I'm going to put it on now'. This order is normal in such contexts as *haben Sie alte Kämme? — alte Kämme werfe ich weg* 'have you any old combs?—I throw old combs away'.

Complements of the verbs 'to be' and 'to become' may likewise be emphasized by being placed first: *Medizin war der Tee zuerst, Getränk wurde er danach* 'tea was first a medicine, it became a beverage later'.

Nouns may be separated from their adjectives, especially when these denote quantities; this practice has the effect of emphasizing both noun and adjective. Thus *er gibt keine Ruhe* 'he gives (one) no rest' often becomes *Ruhe gibt er keine*, similarly *Kriegsschiffe ankerten nur wenige im Hafen von Peiraieus*, say, 'as for warships, only a few anchored in Piraeus harbour'.

Other parts of the sentence may come first. Adverbs and adverbial (prepositional) phrases commonly occur initially: *nur selten schreibe ich lange Briefe* 'only rarely do I write long letters', *schneller geht's nicht* 'it can't be done quicker', *vier Tage arbeitete er so* 'for four days he worked like that', *auf lumpige zehn Mark kommt es mir nicht an* 'I'm not bothered about a measly ten marks', *länger als eine Woche trägt man einen Pyjama nicht* 'one doesn't wear a pair of pyjamas for longer than a week'. In the same way an infinitive, often together with a complement, can stand first: *spazierengehen darf sie schon, nur arbeiten darf sie noch nicht* 'she is allowed to go for walks, but she mustn't work yet', *klar sehen kann man das in seinem späteren Werk* 'that can clearly be seen in his later work', compare also *leuchtende Beispiele, denen nachzueifern ich nicht gewillt bin* 'shining examples I am not prepared to emulate'. Perfect participles, too, often open the sentence: *geschehen ist nichts* 'nothing has happened'; they may be qualified: *sehr gefreut hat es mich zu hören, wie unverdrossen Sie weiterarbeiten* 'I was very pleased, too, to hear that you are steadily working on'. As in English, but in practice more frequently, whole clauses can be moved to the front: *ob er kommen wird, bleibt unsicher* 'whether he will come remains uncertain', *daß die Firma in Schwierigkeiten war, wußte man schon lange* 'that the firm was in difficulties had been known for a long time'.

Emphasized part last

Emphasis may be obtained by moving words to the end of the sentence. Particularly prepositional phrases are often so treated: (overheard on a most unseasonable summer's day) *die Ostsee wird noch zufrieren im Sommer* 'the Baltic will be freezing over in summer as well'. Compare further *merkwürdig, daß er es so weit gebracht hat mit seinem Handicap* 'remarkable that he has got on so well considering his handicap'. These examples can be taken together with those on pp. 333 f., where some prepositional phrases come at the end without necessarily implying emphasis, though they could do so and this would be brought out in the spoken language by the stress.

The object may be placed at the end, thus highlighting it: *von der Astronomie weiß heutzutage fast jeder wenigstens etwas* 'almost everybody nowadays knows at least something about astronomy'. Occasionally the subject, too, is moved back to final position: *zu diesen Zeiten unterrichten die Kinder die Studenten* 'at these times the students (as opposed to the regular teachers) teach the children', see also under 'Inflexions and Word Order', p. 344.

It sometimes happens that this sort of emphatic order in German corresponds to non-emphatic order in English—we ignore here the possibilities of emphatic stress on a given word, which are in principle the same in both languages. Thus *jetzt* is emphatic by position in *wir trinken Kaffee jetzt*, but 'we'll take coffee now' is non-emphatic, the corresponding non-emphatic German being *wir trinken jetzt Kaffee*. By the same token, *in England* is emphatic by position in *Lebensmittel sind teurer in England*; non-emphatic order would be *Lebensmittel sind in England teurer*, idiomatically equivalent to 'food is dearer in England'.

Initial and final position interchangeable

In numerous examples, especially prepositional phrases in initial and final position are more or less interchangeable: *bei Franz muß alles schnell gehen* beside *alles muß schnell'gehen bei Franz* 'with F. (you know) everything has to be done quickly', *über Schottland habe ich leider wenig gelesen* and *ich habe leider wenig gelesen über Schottland* 'unfortunately I have read little about Scotland', *von ihr lasse ich mich nicht aus dem Konzept bringen* or *ich lasse mich nicht aus dem Konzept bringen von ihr* 'I'm not going to let 'her put me off'.

Adverbs, too, are sometimes involved: *damals hat er viel getrunken*, also *er hat viel getrunken damals* 'at the time he was drinking a lot', non-emphatic *er hat damals viel getrunken* 'he was drinking a lot at the time'. We may add that in this, as in so many sentences, the flexibility of German word order enables other words—here the object and the perfect participle—to be placed in emphatic positions in a way unparalleled in English, hence commonly *viel hat er damals getrunken, viel hat er getrunken damals*, and *getrunken hat er damals viel, getrunken hat er viel damals*.